T0293079

Mastering
OpenTelemetry™ and Observability

Enhancing Application and Infrastructure Performance and Avoiding Outages

Steve Flanders

WILEY

Copyright © 2025 by John Wiley & Sons, Inc. All rights, including for text and data mining, AI training, and similar technologies, are reserved.

Published by John Wiley & Sons, Inc., Hoboken, New Jersey.
Published simultaneously in Canada and the United Kingdom.

ISBNs: 9781394253128 (paperback), 9781394253142 (ePDF), 9781394253135 (ePub)

No part of this publication may be reproduced, stored in a retrieval system, or transmitted in any form or by any means, electronic, mechanical, photocopying, recording, scanning, or otherwise, except as permitted under Section 107 or 108 of the 1976 United States Copyright Act, without either the prior written permission of the Publisher, or authorization through payment of the appropriate per-copy fee to the Copyright Clearance Center, Inc., 222 Rosewood Drive, Danvers, MA 01923, (978) 750-8400, fax (978) 750-4470, or on the web at www.copyright.com. Requests to the Publisher for permission should be addressed to the Permissions Department, John Wiley & Sons, Inc., 111 River Street, Hoboken, NJ 07030, (201) 748-6011, fax (201) 748-6008, or online at www.wiley.com/go/permission.

Trademarks: WILEY and the Wiley logo are trademarks or registered trademarks of John Wiley & Sons, Inc. and/or its affiliates, in the United States and other countries, and may not be used without written permission. OpenTelemetry is a trademark of The Linux Foundation. All other trademarks are the property of their respective owners. John Wiley & Sons, Inc. is not associated with any product or vendor mentioned in this book.

Limit of Liability/Disclaimer of Warranty: While the publisher and author have used their best efforts in preparing this book, they make no representations or warranties with respect to the accuracy or completeness of the contents of this book and specifically disclaim any implied warranties of merchantability or fitness for a particular purpose. No warranty may be created or extended by sales representatives or written sales materials. The advice and strategies contained herein may not be suitable for your situation. You should consult with a professional where appropriate. Further, readers should be aware that websites listed in this work may have changed or disappeared between when this work was written and when it is read. Neither the publisher nor author shall be liable for any loss of profit or any other commercial damages, including but not limited to special, incidental, consequential, or other damages.

For general information on our other products and services, please contact our Customer Care Department within the United States at (800) 762-2974, outside the United States at (317) 572-3993. For product technical support, you can find answers to frequently asked questions or reach us via live chat at https://support.wiley.com.

If you believe you've found a mistake in this book, please bring it to our attention by emailing our Reader Support team at wileysupport@wiley.com with the subject line "Possible Book Errata Submission."

Wiley also publishes its books in a variety of electronic formats. Some content that appears in print may not be available in electronic formats. For more information about Wiley products, visit our web site at www.wiley.com.

Library of Congress Control Number: 2024944897

Cover image: © CSA Images/Getty Images
Cover design: Wiley

SKY10087415_100924

To my kids, Haven and Addison Flanders—May you always have the courage to chase your dreams with unwavering determination. Never let anyone dim the light of your aspirations or tell you what you can or cannot achieve. Believe in yourself, follow your heart, and remember that your potential is limitless. Your dreams are your own; only you can bring them to life.

About the Author

Steve Flanders is a founding member of the OpenCensus and OpenTelemetry projects and has over a decade of hands-on experience in the monitoring and observability space. As a Senior Director of Engineering at Splunk, a Cisco company, he oversees the Splunk Observability Cloud Platform, including the metrics engine and analytics capabilities. Steve also spearheads Splunk's OpenTelemetry contributions. He was previously instrumental in building what is now the Splunk APM product at Omnition and the Log Insight product at VMware. A sought-after speaker and blogger, Steve frequently shares his insights at prominent conferences like KubeCon and on his blog at `https://sflanders.net`. He holds an MBA from MIT, underscoring his blend of technical acumen, strategic vision, and entrepreneurial spirit.

Acknowledgments

Writing this book has been a labor of love, a journey marked by both immense challenges and profound rewards. The countless hours spent researching, writing, and revising have culminated in a work that I hope will provide valuable insights and guidance to everyone, regardless of background or experience. It was not easy to distill a complex topic like observability, but it was worth the effort. This book would not have been possible without the support and encouragement of many remarkable individuals and teams.

First and foremost, I would like to express my deepest gratitude to my partner, Lily Wang, for her unwavering support and understanding during the long hours and late nights dedicated to this project. Your patience and encouragement kept me going even when the task seemed daunting.

I am profoundly thankful to my colleagues, collaborators, and friends whose expertise and insights have greatly enriched this book. Your willingness to share your knowledge and feedback while engaging in stimulating discussions has been invaluable. Thank you, Fabrizio Ferri-Benedetti, for always providing timely feedback and suggestions. It is because of you the idea of Riley was created! Thank you, Jason Plumb, Pablo Collins, and Antoine Toulme, for reading early drafts and providing valuable initial feedback. Thank you, Alpesh Sheth, for supporting me in writing this book.

I also want to express my sincere gratitude to the technical reviewers who provided meticulous and constructive feedback on short notice. Your attention to detail and commitment to accuracy have been instrumental in shaping the contents of this book. Thank you, Tigran Najaryan and Morgan McLean, for providing an extensive review of the material on short notice. Thank you, Tyler Yahn, for providing a thorough review both technically and grammatically across multiple chapters, especially Chapters 1, 2, and 4. Thank you, Dmitrii Anoshin and Siim Kallas, for your thorough technical review of Chapters 5 and 6, respectively.

To the illustrator, publishers, and editorial team, thank you for your guidance and support throughout the publication process. Your professionalism and dedication ensured that this book reached its highest potential. Special thanks to Kenyon Brown for the opportunity to write this book, Tom Dinse for all the editing and formatting suggestions, and Navin Vijayakumar for keeping me on track. Also, a special thanks to Emily Griffin for bringing Riley, Jupiterian, and Watchwhale to life through relatable illustrations.

To the OpenTelemetry community, thank you for your innovative work and commitment to excellence, which continues to inspire and push the boundaries of what is possible. Being the second-most active project in the Cloud Native Computing Foundation is an amazing accomplishment and speaks to the need for an open standard and framework for telemetry data. To all the previous, current, and future authors, bloggers, and speakers on the topic of OpenTelemetry and observability, thank you for creating relevant information and sharing your knowledge. For anyone considering contributing to the project or sharing your experience, please do! The OpenTelemetry community is friendly and welcoming. We need your help to make the project even better. In the spirit of giving back, you will find a list of issues and pull requests (PRs) I submitted when writing this book in the appendix of this book.

Finally, I want to acknowledge all the readers and practitioners in the field of observability. Your passion for continuous improvement and innovation drives the evolution of this domain. It is my hope that this book serves as a valuable resource in your ongoing journey to master OpenTelemetry and achieve excellence in observability.

Thank you all for being part of this rewarding journey.

Contents

Foreword

To build and operate any complex system, whether it be inventory in warehouses, money in bank accounts, or large computer systems, you need to be able to understand what you have built and how it is currently operating. The observability tools that we rely on today have a long history; in one way or another, they have existed since the beginning of the computing industry. As relatively high-scale (for their era) computing services started to come about in the 1980s and early 1990s, commercial tools that analyzed their performance also became available. As the dot-com boom of the late 1990s and then the proliferation of easily accessible cloud infrastructure drove more and more firms to build high-scale web services, the market and capabilities of what we now call observability tools increased dramatically.

Throughout this period, one of the biggest challenges that these tools faced was how to get the right data into them. This is harder than it seems, as early solutions would capture some combination of logs and metrics, requiring integrations with a handful of operating systems and known technologies like databases and message queues. Getting visibility into a modern microservices environment requires distributed traces, application metrics, profiles, and other types of data that must be captured from every web framework, RPC system, database client, and so forth, each of which are different for each programming language. Each of these integrations must be maintained to ensure that it does not break when the data source gets updated; this is extremely expensive for vendors to build and for customers to set up, leading to poor coverage and for customers to be semipermanently locked in to their vendors.

We created OpenTelemetry to break this logjam. By providing a single set of APIs, agents, and a protocol, we allowed software developers to both emit and capture distributed traces, metrics, profiles, and logs easily and with the strong semantic conventions needed to gain valuable insights from analyzing it. This has fundamentally changed people's relationships with observability tools. Thanks to OpenTelemetry, they are more accessible and widely used than ever before—and of higher quality, as vendors and open source solutions have redirected the effort that they used to spend on data collection to providing better solutions. Both end users and those who want to emit data from shared code are no longer locked in to vendor-specific interfaces, and anyone can take control of creating custom telemetry, filtering their data, and sending it wherever they would like. OpenTelemetry now has over 1,200 developers contributing to it every month, making it one of the largest open source projects in the world—a testament to its utility and how much it has changed things.

That being said, tools are only as good as one's ability to properly use them, and OpenTelemetry is no exception. OpenTelemetry is now an essential part of building and operating services of any scale, and this book will guide you through the problems that it can be used to solve (and those that it should not), OpenTelemetry's various components, best practices and examples of using OpenTelemetry successfully, and how to apply it to your codebase and organization to achieve your goals.

—Morgan McLean, Senior Director of Product Management, Splunk

Introduction

Welcome to *Mastering OpenTelemetry and Observability*, a comprehensive guide designed to help you navigate the complex and ever-evolving landscape of observability. As organizations increasingly rely on distributed systems and microservices architectures, the need for robust observability solutions has never been greater. OpenTelemetry, or OTel as it is called, is an open source and vendor-agnostic observability framework. It has emerged as a critical technology in this field, providing standardized tools for collecting and analyzing telemetry data across various platforms and technologies. In addition, OTel is extensible, with the ability to handle the telemetry needs and observability platforms of today and the observability landscape of the future.

This book aims to equip you with the knowledge and skills necessary to harness the full potential of OTel and build a solid observability foundation. Whether you are a developer, DevOps engineer, site reliability engineer (SRE), sales engineer, support engineer, information technology (IT) manager, engineering manager (EM), product manager (PM), C-level executive, or really any role that involves software or infrastructure, the insights and practical guidance offered in this book will empower you to observe, diagnose, and optimize your systems effectively.

You will begin by exploring the fundamental concepts of observability, tracing its evolution from traditional monitoring practices to modern, holistic approaches. You will gain a deep understanding of the three pillars of observability—metrics, logs, and traces—and how they interrelate to provide a comprehensive view of system health and performance. The core of this book delves into OpenTelemetry, starting with its architecture and components, including the specification, instrumentation, and the Collector. Next, the OTel demo environment, known as the Astronomy Shop, is explored so you can experience the power of OTel firsthand. Deep dives on all the major components, including step-by-step instructions, are provided on how to instrument your applications and collect, process, and send your telemetry data using OTel. You will also learn about important topics such as context propagation, distributions, and integrating OTel with popular observability platforms like Prometheus and Jaeger.

With a solid foundation in observability and OTel, you will move on to adopting and scaling observability in large and complex environments. From obtaining stakeholder buy-in to handling high volumes of telemetry data to ensuring performance and reliability, you will discover practical solutions to common challenges faced by organizations today. This is followed by considerations for observability platforms, whether existing or new.

Beyond technical guidance, this book also addresses the human and organizational aspects of observability. This is because building a culture of observability within your team and organization is crucial for success. This book discusses strategies for fostering collaboration, continuous improvement, and proactive incident response, ensuring that observability becomes an integral part of your operational practices. Finally, this book explores emerging trends and innovations in observability, including the role of artificial intelligence (AI) and machine learning (ML) in predictive analytics, the evolution of observability standards, and the potential impact of new technologies on the industry.

Mastering OpenTelemetry and Observability is more than just a technical manual; it is a journey into the heart of modern system monitoring and optimization. By the end of this book, you will have the knowledge and confidence to implement robust observability solutions that enhance your system's reliability, performance, and overall user experience.

Before you begin reading, there are a few things to know:

- This book has been written in a way that tries to make it approachable to the largest audience possible. Examples of this include:
  - The book does not use contractions to make it easier for non-native English speakers.
  - Every abbreviation used in every chapter is defined first.
  - Relatable examples and metaphors will be found throughout the book.
  - Hyperlinks to additional information are provided throughout the book so you can learn more about the topics being discussed.
- A fictitious but likely relatable story is embedded into every chapter. Through it, you will learn how an enterprise company migrating to the cloud was struggling to achieve observability. With each challenge experienced, you will see how a determined site reliability engineer (SRE) helps her company embrace OTel and improve observability.
- Some terminology is used throughout this book that you should be aware of, including:
  - **Back end:** The data access layer of an application, which often includes processing and persistence of data.
  - **Framework:** A structure on which other things are built. For example, OTel is a telemetry framework that can be extended to support various use cases.
  - **Front end:** The presentation layer of an application, which is often a user interface (UI) or user-facing way to interact with an application.
  - **Instrumentation:** Software added to an application to generate telemetry data. Various forms of instrumentation are available, including automatic, which is injected at runtime, manual, which is added with the existing code, and programmatic, which is a particular form of manual instrumentation where specific libraries or frameworks have already been instrumented (also called *instrumentation libraries*).
  - **Platform:** An environment in which software is executed. An observability or monitoring platform typically consists of one or more back end and front end components.

- **Telemetry:** Data used to determine the health, performance, and usage of applications. Examples of telemetry include metrics, logs, and traces. This data is typically sent to a platform or back end.

- The OTel project is constantly evolving, and changes are frequently released. The examples provided in this book were tested against specific versions of OTel. Where possible, they were created in a generic way that should work as the project advances. With that said, it is possible that changes have been made that will result in differences from what is documented. If this occurs, checking the GitHub repository associated with this book (covered next) and reading the latest OTel documentation and release notes is recommended. The minimal recommended and maximum tested versions of OTel components for this book are as follows:
  - OTel Demo, also known as the Astronomy Shop, version 1.11 is the minimum supported version. This is to get OpenSearch support. Up to version 1.11.1 has been tested.
  - Collector (core and contrib) version 0.95.0 is the minimum supported version. This is to get JSON encoding for the OTLP receiver and exporter. Up to version 0.109.0 has been tested.
  - Python instrumentation version 1.23.0/0.44b0 is the minimum supported version. This is to get support for Flask and Werkzeug 3.0 or higher. Up to version 1.27.0/0.48b0 has been tested.
- This book is accompanied by a GitHub repository, which can be found at `https://github.com/flands/mastering-otel-book` and will be updated at least annually. If you notice any issues with the information presented in this book, please open a GitHub issue. The contents of this repository include:
  - All code examples provided in the book
  - Status information about OTel components
  - Post-production modifications
  - Changes to support the latest OTel advancements

The Mastering Series

The *Mastering* series from Sybex provides outstanding instruction for readers with intermediate and advanced skills, in the form of top-notch training and development for those already working in their field and clear, serious education for those aspiring to become pros. Every *Mastering* book includes:

- Real-World Scenarios, ranging from case studies to interviews, that show how the tool, technique, or knowledge presented is applied in actual practice
- Skill-based instruction, with chapters organized around real tasks rather than abstract concepts or subjects
- Self-review test questions, so you can be certain you're equipped to do the job right

Chapter 1

What Is Observability?

In modern software development and operations, observability has emerged as a fundamental concept essential for maintaining and improving the performance, reliability, and scalability of complex systems. But what exactly is observability? At its core, observability is the practice of gaining insights into the internal states and behaviors of systems through the collection, analysis, and visualization of telemetry data. Unlike traditional monitoring, which primarily focuses on predefined metrics and thresholds, observability offers a more comprehensive and dynamic approach, enabling teams to proactively detect, diagnose, and resolve issues.

This chapter will explore the principles and components of observability, highlighting its significance in today's distributed and microservices-based architectures. Through a deep dive into the three pillars of observability—metrics, logs, and traces—you will understand the groundwork for how observability can transform the way resilient systems are built and managed.

IN THIS CHAPTER, YOU WILL LEARN TO:

- Differentiate between monitoring and observability
- Explain the importance of metadata
- Identify the differences between telemetry signals
- Distinguish between instrumentation and data collection
- Analyze the requirements for choosing an observability platform

Definition

So, what is observability in the realm of modern software development and operations? While many definitions exist, they all generally refer to observability providing the ability to quickly identify availability and performance problems, regardless of whether they have been experienced before, and help perform problem isolation, root cause analysis, and remediation. Because observability is about making it easier to understand complex systems and address unperceived issues, often referred to in the software industry as *unknown unknowns*,[1] the data collected must be correlated across different telemetry types and be rich enough and immediately accessible to answer questions during a live incident.

The Cloud Native Computing Foundation (CNCF), described more fully later in this chapter, provides a definition for the term *observability*:[2]

> *Observability is a system property that defines the degree to which the system can generate actionable insights. It allows users to understand a system's state from these external outputs and take (corrective) action.*
>
> *Computer systems are measured by observing low-level signals such as CPU time, memory, disk space, and higher-level and business signals, including API response times, errors, transactions per second, etc. These observable systems are observed (or monitored) through specialized tools, so-called observability tools. A list of these tools can be viewed in the Cloud Native Landscape's observability section.*[3]
>
> *Observable systems yield meaningful, actionable data to their operators, allowing them to achieve favorable outcomes (faster incident response, increased developer productivity) and less toil and downtime.*
>
> *Consequently, the observability of a system will significantly impact its operating and development costs.*

While the CNCF's definition is good, it is missing a few critical aspects:

- The goal of observability should be where a system's state can be *fully understood* from its external output *without the need to ship code*. This means you should be able to ask *novel questions* about your observability data, especially questions you had *not* thought of beforehand.
- Observability is not just about collecting data but about collecting *meaningful data*, such as data with context and correlated across different sources, and storing it on a platform that offers rich analytics and query capabilities *across signals*.
- A system is truly observable when you can troubleshoot *without prior knowledge of the system*.

The OpenTelemetry project, which will be introduced in Chapter 2, "Introducing OpenTelemetry!," provides a definition of observability that is worth highlighting:

> *Observability lets you understand a system from the outside, by letting us ask questions about that system without knowing its inner workings. Furthermore, it allows you to easily troubleshoot and handle novel problems—that is, "unknown unknowns." It also helps you answer the question, "Why is this happening?"*
>
> *To ask those questions about your system, your application must be properly instrumented. That is, the application code must emit signals such as traces, metrics, and logs. An application is properly instrumented when developers don't need to add more instrumentation to troubleshoot an issue, because they have all of the information they need.*[4]

In short, observability is about collecting critical telemetry data with relevant context and using that data to quickly determine your systems' behavior and health. Observability goes beyond mere monitoring by enabling a proactive and comprehensive understanding of system behavior, facilitating quicker detection, diagnosis, and resolution of issues. This capability is crucial in today's fast-paced, microservices-driven, distributed environments, where the complexity and dynamic nature of systems demand robust and flexible observability solutions. Through the lens of the CNCF and OpenTelemetry, you can see observability is not just defined as a set of tools and practices but as a fundamental shift toward more resilient, reliable, and efficient system management.

Real World Scenario

RILEY JOINS JUPITERIAN

Riley (she/her) is an experienced site reliability engineer (SRE) with deep observability and operations experience. She recently joined Jupiterian to address their observability problems and work with a new vendor. Riley joined Jupiterian from a large private equity (PE) advertising company, where she was the technical lead of the SRE team and was responsible for a large-scale, globally distributed, cloud native architecture. Before that, she was the founding member of a growth startup where she developed observability practices and culture while helping scale the business to over three million dollars in annual recurring revenue (ARR). Riley was excited about the challenge and opportunity of building observability practices from the ground up at a public enterprise company transitioning to the cloud.

Jupiterian is an e-commerce company that has been around for more than two decades. Over the last five years, the company has seen a massive influx of customers and has been on a journey to modernize its tech stack to keep up with demand and the competition. As part of these changes, it has been migrating from its on-premises monolithic application to a microservices-based architecture running on Kubernetes (K8s) and deployed in the cloud. Recently, outages have been plaguing the new architecture—a problem threatening the company and one that needed to be resolved before the annual peak traffic expected during the upcoming holiday season.

For the original architecture, the company had been using Zabbix, an open source monitoring solution to monitor the environment. The IT team was beginning to learn about DevOps practices and had set up Prometheus for the new architecture. Given organizational constraints and priorities, they did not have the time to develop the skill set to manage it and the ever-increasing number of collected metrics. In short, a critical piece of the new architecture was without ownership. On top of this, engineering teams continued to add data, dashboards, and alerts without defined standards or processes. Not surprisingly, this resulted in the company having difficulty proactively identifying availability and performance issues. It also resulted in various observability issues, including Prometheus availability, blind spots, and alert storms. In terms of observability, the company frequently experienced infrastructure issues and could not tell if it was because of an architecture limitation or an improper use of the new infrastructure. As a result, engineers feared going on-call, and innovation velocity was significantly below average.

The Jupiterian engineering team had been pushing management to invest more in observability and SRE. Instead, head count remained flat, and the product roadmaps, driven primarily by the sales team, continued to take priority. With the service missing its service-level agreement (SLA) target for the last three months, leadership demanded a focus on resiliency. To address the problem, the Chief Technology Officer (CTO) signed a three-year deal with Watchwhale, an observability vendor, so the company could focus on its core intellectual property (IP) instead of managing third-party software. An architect in the office of the CTO vetted the vendor and its technology. Given other organizational priorities, the engineering team was largely uninvolved in the proof of concept (PoC). The Vice President (VP) of Engineering was tasked with ensuring the service's SLA was consistently hit ahead of the holiday period as well as the adoption and success of the Watchwhale product. He allocated one of his budget IDs (BIDs) for a senior SRE position, which led to Riley being hired.

Background

The term *observability* has been around since at least the mid-20th century and is mainly credited to Rudolf E. Kálmán, a Hungarian American engineer who used it in a paper about control theory.[5] Since then, the term has been used in various fields, including quantum mechanics, physics, statistics, and perhaps most recently, software development. Kálmán's definition of observability can be summarized as a measure of how well the internal states of a system can be inferred from knowledge of its external outputs.[6]

OBSERVABILITY ABBREVIATION

Observability is often abbreviated as O11y (the letter *O*, the number *11*, and the letter *y*), as there are 11 characters between the letter *O* and the letter *y*. While it is the number 11, the ones are pronounced as the letter *l*—thus, the abbreviation is pronounced *Ollie*. This abbreviation standard is common for longer words in software. For example, Kubernetes, a popular cloud native open source project, is often referred to as K8s and pronounced *kay-ates* for the same reason.

Cloud Native Era

In software, the term *observability* has become popular due to the rise of cloud native workloads. Since the turn of the century, the software industry has seen a progression that has included moving from bare metal machines to virtual machines (VMs) to containers. In addition, there has been a shift from owning, deploying, and managing hardware to leasing data center equipment to deploying in the cloud. But what does *cloud native* mean? One way to answer this question is to look to the CNCF. The foundation is part of the Linux Foundation and defines itself as:

> *The open source, vendor-neutral hub of cloud native computing, hosting projects like Kubernetes and Prometheus to make cloud native universal and sustainable.*[7]

Perhaps not surprisingly, the CNCF has created a definition for the term *cloud native*:

> *Cloud native practices empower organizations to develop, build, and deploy workloads in computing environments (public, private, hybrid cloud) to meet their organizational needs at scale in a programmatic and repeatable manner.* They are characterized by loosely coupled systems that interoperate in a manner that is secure, resilient, manageable, sustainable, and observable.
>
> *Cloud native technologies and architectures typically consist of some combination of containers, service meshes, multi-tenancy, microservices, immutable infrastructure, serverless, and declarative APIs—this list is non-exhaustive.*

Monitoring Compared to Observability

Before the cloud native era, it was common to see patterns including on-premises software, monoliths, separate development and operations teams, and waterfall software development with long release cycles. In this prior generation, the term *observability* had not been adopted yet, and instead, the term *monitoring* was used. Sometimes, these terms are used interchangeably, but their meanings are not identical. The Merriam-Webster dictionary defines monitoring as the ability "to watch, keep track of, or check usually for a special purpose."[8] It defines observability as the ability "to come to realize or know especially through consideration of noted facts."[9] The distinction between monitoring and observability is important. With monitoring, you track items but must infer why something occurred or how it is related to another event. With observability, you use information to prove facts and use that knowledge to determine how or why something behaves the way it does. Observability allows for first principle thinking, or the ability to validate assumptions not deduced from another assumption.[10]

In software, both observability and monitoring rely on specific data types—primarily metrics and logs with some tracing—but the usage of the data differs. Before the cloud native era, most software ran on-premises and was often developed and deployed as a monolith or single code base or application. As a result, problem isolation, or where the problem originated, was easy to identify when issues occurred, and scaling typically consisted of adding more resources to the monolith, known as *scaling up* or *scaling vertically*. When issues arose, the problem was either the monolith, the infrastructure the monolith was running on top of, or whatever application was calling into or called by the monolith (see Figure 1.1). To monitor the monolith, operational teams needed the ability to be alerted about specific, known symptoms, sometimes referred to as *known knowns*. Monitoring systems did exactly that.

To provide monitoring, either your application needs to be instrumented to emit health data or you are required to infer the health of the application by watching its external behavior. In either case, the data collected needs to be able to track and answer questions about availability, performance, and security. This data collection needs to be added before issues happen; otherwise, you cannot proactively determine nor quickly resolve the problems as they arise.

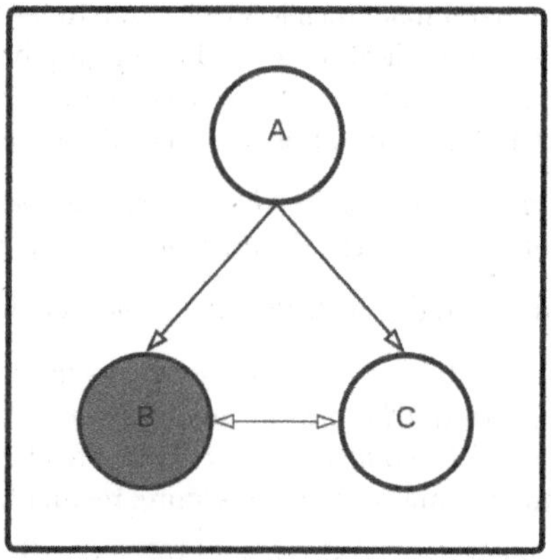

Figure 1.1
An example of a monolithic application experiencing an issue. The square represents the monolith, while the circles represent different functions or features within the monolith. In this example, the B function is experiencing problems, denoted by the service's gray shading. This may or may not result in issues with the A and C functions.

Types of Monitoring

There are two different types of monitoring. First, there is monitoring based on data exposed from the internals of the system. This means the application makes specific data available for external systems to gather. This type of monitoring is sometimes called *white box monitoring* because you can see into the system,[11] though a better name would be *internally provided monitoring*. Second, there is monitoring based on external behavior. This means the application does not make any data available beyond what is required for the application to function. As such, an external system must infer what an application is doing. This type of monitoring is sometimes called *black box monitoring* because you cannot see into the system,[12] though a better name would be *externally provided monitoring*.[13]

In many cases, application developers add instrumentation as necessary, including to measure performance and investigate issues during development and operations. Engineers responsible for monitoring the health and performance of these applications would typically send telemetry data to a monitoring platform. Based on this telemetry data, the engineer would then define alerts with static thresholds. To determine these thresholds, an engineer would need to know what problems to expect beforehand, thus enabling *proactive monitoring*; otherwise, new thresholds would have to be defined after an issue is identified, which is known as *reactive monitoring*. One way to think about monitoring is like a doctor who collects certain pieces of information from a person and compares that data against known baselines to understand the symptoms being experienced and to determine the health of the person. The monitoring of heart rate, blood pressure, and temperature in humans is like the monitoring of CPU (central processing unit), memory, and disk usage in applications.

While monitoring with static thresholds provides some awareness of potential system issues, it is not without its limitations. Take, for example, CPU utilization, which represents the rate at which an application is operating expressed as a percentage. If CPU utilization is very high, this could be a symptom of a system issue and, as such, something you want to be notified about. For example, you could define an alert when the CPU utilization exceeds 95 percent for some period of time. In fact, such a definition is common in traditional monitoring applications. The problem is, such an alert may not indicate a problem but instead indicate that the application is using its resources efficiently. What is missing from this symptom is context, including how other related components are behaving, and correlation, including changes within the environment. Another limitation of traditional monitoring tools is the difficulty in alerting on issues that do not manifest as high resource consumption or latency.

The introduction of cloud native workloads made traditional monitoring even less effective. In this new world, workloads are run in the cloud and often consist of many small applications, called *microservices*, that are isolated to individual functionality. For example, an authentication service or a notification service. Microservices make it easier to deploy more instances, known as *scaling out* or *scaling horizontally*, and allow for specific components to be scaled as needed. These microservices typically run on immutable infrastructure using declarative APIs (application programming interfaces). In addition, they are run with DevOps practices and with the help of site reliability engineers (SREs).[14] Software release cycles are also more frequent and leverage continuous integration and continuous deployment or CI/CD pipelines. The decoupling and elasticity of applications enable developers to reduce duplicated efforts and scale to meet demand, but often at the cost of being able to troubleshoot the system and keep it available. In this era, it is the "unknown unknowns" that need to be addressed.

Due to the difficulty in troubleshooting microservice-based architectures, a popular meme was shared throughout the community:

> *"We replaced our monolith with micro services so that every outage could be more like a murder mystery."* @honest_update[15]

With cloud native workloads, problem isolation became a problem. This is because when one microservice has an issue, it could impact upstream or downstream services, causing them to have problems as well (see Figure 1.2). Using traditional monitoring, the net result is alert storms and the need to investigate every issue on every service in order to get to the root cause and remediation. Of course, there are other issues with cloud native workloads as well. For example, there is an inability to have complete visibility into the infrastructure as it is being managed by a third party and prone to dynamic changes.

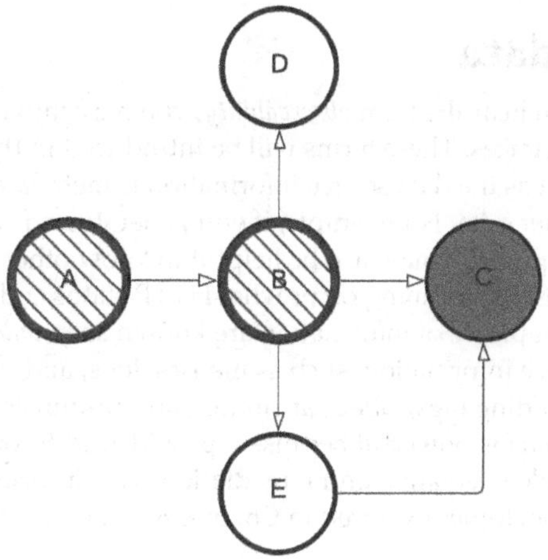

FIGURE 1.2 An example of a microservice-based architecture experiencing an issue. Each circle represents a different microservice. In this example, multiple microservices are experiencing an issue, denoted with gray lines, though one service is the root cause of the problem, denoted with gray shading. Note not all services called by the root cause service are impacted.

Going back to the doctor analogy, assume you have a large group of people who are all part of the same community, and multiple people become sick around the same time. While you may want to help everyone experiencing symptoms concurrently, it requires many doctors and resources. In addition, focusing on the symptoms of the patients does not address the root cause issue, which is that people are getting sick from something, and it is spreading instead of being contained. The sickness may cause other problems to arise as well. For example, doctors may become sick and thus become unable to care for patients, or businesses might need to shut down because they do not have enough employees to work. Without containment, an infectious disease can spread uncontrollably. This analogy is similar to the changes necessary due to the shift to cloud native workloads. For example, instead of paging all service owners during an outage and burning out engineers, the more sustainable approach is to contain the problem and page the root cause service. Observability helps with containment.

When dealing with complex systems, it is ideal when you can address things you are aware of and understand, referred to as *known knowns*, as well as things you are not aware of and do not understand, referred to as *unknown unknowns*, using the same solution. See Table 1.1 for different states of awareness and understanding. A goal of observability is to provide the ability to answer the "unknown unknowns." At the same time, it contains the building blocks necessary to address the "known knowns." As a result, observability may be considered a superset of monitoring.

TABLE 1.1: A 2×2 matrix showing states of awareness and understanding. Monitoring systems are optimized to address "known knowns" where observability systems can address all aspects but especially "unknown unknowns."

		AWARENESS **KNOWN**	**UNKNOWN**
Understanding	**Known**	Aware of and understand	Aware of but do not understand
	Unknown	Understand but not aware of	Neither aware of nor understand

Metadata

When you hear the term *observability*, you may initially think about data sources such as metrics, logs, and traces. These terms will be introduced in the next section, but something just as important as the data source information is metadata. While a fancy word, metadata is just data about other data. For example, if you generate and collect a metric, such as the total number of HTTP requests, it may also be helpful to know other information about that metric, such as which host it is running on or what HTTP status code was returned for that request. These additional pieces of information are known as *metadata* and are typically attached to traditional data source information, such as metrics, logs, and traces. Metadata may go by other names as well, including tags, labels, attributes, and resources.

Metadata is powerful because it provides additional information to data sources, which helps with problem isolation and remediation. This information may even contain context and correlation, topics explored in Chapter 8, "The Power of Context and Correlation." Without metadata, observability is harder to achieve. Metadata is typically represented as a key-value pair, such as `foo="bar"`. The *key* is the name for the piece of metadata and is often referred to as a *dimension*. The *value* can be of various forms, including numbers or strings and the uniqueness of the values is referred to as *cardinality*. Other ways to represent metadata also exist. For example, in unstructured log records, metadata is sometimes presented as just a value where the name is inferred—an example is provided in the "Logs" section later in this chapter.

Dimensionality

In observability, *Dimensionality* refers to the number of unique *keys* (sometimes called *names*) within a set. It is represented by attributes or labels associated with telemetry data, allowing for more granular and detailed analysis. Each piece of telemetry data can have multiple dimensions that provide context about the data. These dimensions enable the grouping, filtering, and slicing of data along various axes, which is crucial for deep analysis and troubleshooting. Examples of dimensions include:

- Time
- Application, such as `service.name` and `service.version`
- Host, such as `host.name` and `host.arch`
- User, such as `enduser.id` and `enduser.role`
- HTTP, such as `http.route` and `http.response.status_code`

These dimensions would allow you to ask your telemetry to show you data such as:

- All `502` errors in the last half hour for host `foo`
- All `403` requests against the `/export` endpoint made by user `bar`

Dimensionality, which may also be referred to as the width of telemetry data, is a foundational concept in observability that greatly enhances the depth and utility of telemetry data. It matters because it enables more detailed, contextualized, and actionable insights, which are essential for maintaining and improving the performance and reliability of modern distributed systems. In practice, dimensions are indexed by observability platforms to support capabilities, including auto-complete and real-time analysis of key-value pairs, that assist with troubleshooting.

Cardinality

In observability, *Cardinality* refers to the number of unique values for a given key within a set. *High cardinality* refers to a large number of unique values, whereas *low cardinality* indicates fewer unique values. For example, a dimension like HTTP status code, which includes values such as `404` or `500`, is bounded and has low cardinality, whereas a dimension like a user, session, or transaction ID is unbounded and is likely to have high cardinality. Monitoring and observability platforms care about cardinality. For example, if a platform supports indexing of keys, it likely needs to return values for those indexed keys quickly. For high cardinality metadata, this can prove challenging to visualize and very expensive to compute. In short, cardinality affects the storage, performance, and usability of telemetry data. High cardinality presents both opportunities for detailed insights and challenges in terms of resource consumption and data management. Effectively managing cardinality is essential for maintaining scalable, efficient, and actionable observability systems.

Semantic Conventions

Another concept you should be aware of is *semantic conventions*, or semconvs for short. These are standardized dimensions, or keys, for metadata and ensure consistency in how data is recorded, labeled, and interpreted across different systems and services. It may also contain standardized cardinality, or values for these dimensions. For example, it is common to have semconvs for HTTP-related data. An example of this may include the key for the HTTP route, such as `http.route`, or the response status code, such as `http.response.status_code`. Semconvs can be grouped into multiple different categories, such as the aforementioned HTTP. Other categories would include databases, exceptions, host metrics, function as a service, and messaging, to name a few. Each category would have multiple semconvs defined. Semconvs may be signal specific or apply to more than one signal type. Semconvs matter because they enable context and correlation and provide data portability. For example, if the same key is used to represent the same data, then it is easy to see its behavior across systems and environments. In addition, if keys are consistently named, they can be leveraged identically across different platforms.

Data Sensitivity

Metadata can contain sensitive information. For example, names or email addresses may be attached to data sources and leak personally identifiable information (PII). In addition, internal business logic, such as Internet protocol (IP) addresses or hostnames, may be considered sensitive information. This information would generally only be sent to the configured observability platforms, but that configuration can change over time. In addition, while only restricted users may have access to the platform data, for example, employees of a company authenticated via Security Assertion Markup Language (SAML), without proper data permissions, such as role-based access control (RBAC), it is possible that sensitive information is exposed to employees who should not have access to such information. Given that metadata can contain virtually anything, care must be taken to ensure proper data configuration, scrubbing, and access control.

Signals

The *three pillars of observability* is an industry phrase that you have likely encountered. The three pillars refer to metrics, logs, and traces. While these pillars are just data sources and do not inherently provide observability, they are recognized as fundamental types of telemetry data needed to understand the behavior and performance of systems. Another comparable term or acronym in the observability space is *MELT*, which stands for metrics, events, logs, and traces. These are the most common data sources, but they are far from exhaustive. Other examples include profiling and sessions. Data sources have a variety of names in the industry, including diagnostics, telemetry, signals, or data sources. For the purposes of this book, and in alignment with OpenTelemetry, the term *signals* will be used going forward. It is important to note that signals do not inherently provide observability, though they are necessary to enable it.

Metrics

A *metric*, sometimes referred to as a *metric record*, *measurement*, or *metric time series* (MTS), is a set of data points represented as a time series with metadata. A *time series* is a set of data points over some period of time. To generate a time series, an instrument takes one or more measurements. For example, a speedometer measures speed, and a measurement could be taken every tenth of a second but recorded every minute. Metrics also have signal-specific metadata terms. For example, *attributes*, *dimensions*, *labels*, and *resources* are all terms used with metrics that refer to some kind of metadata.

A metric contains a name, value, timestamp, and optionally additional metadata. Note that multiple types of metric values exist. For example, it may be a single value, such as a counter, or a multi-value, such as a histogram. Here is an example of a metric from Prometheus, an open source metric solution that will be described in more detail later:

```
http_requests_total{method="post",code="200"}     1027     | 1395066363000
```

The example Prometheus metric is made up of various components, including:

- Name—`http_requests_total`
- Metadata—`{method="post",code="200"}`
- Value—`1027`
- Timestamp—`1395066363000`

Metrics are one of the primary data sources used to engage on-call engineers as well as troubleshoot availability and performance issues. It is pervasive for alerts and dashboards to be configured based on metric data. Generally, aggregated metrics, like those shown in Figure 1.3, provide the most value because they identify behaviors over time and can be used to determine anomalies. Some popular methods for analyzing aggregated metrics include:

- RED, which stands for requests, error, and duration and was popularized by Tom Wilkie.[16] The idea is for every object to monitor the number of requests, the number of those requests that result in an error, and the amount of time those requests take. In general, this information can be used to determine user experience.
- USE, which stands for utilization, saturation, and errors and was popularized by Brendan Gregg.[17] The idea is for every object to monitor the percentage of time the object was busy, the amount of work (queue size) for the object, and the number of errors. In general, this information can be used to determine object experience.
- Four golden signals, which include latency, traffic, errors, and saturation and was popularized by the Google SRE Handbook.[18] The idea is for every object to monitor the time it takes to service a request, the amount of demand placed on the object, the rate of requests that fail, and the fullness of the object. This is like RED but includes saturation.

In addition, metrics are used to define service-level indicators (SLIs) that measure the performance of applications. These SLIs are used to define and measure service-level objectives (SLOs) which determine whether applications are operating within acceptable bounds. Service-level agreements (SLAs) are also defined and calculated based on metrics to determine whether applications are meeting specified customer expectations.

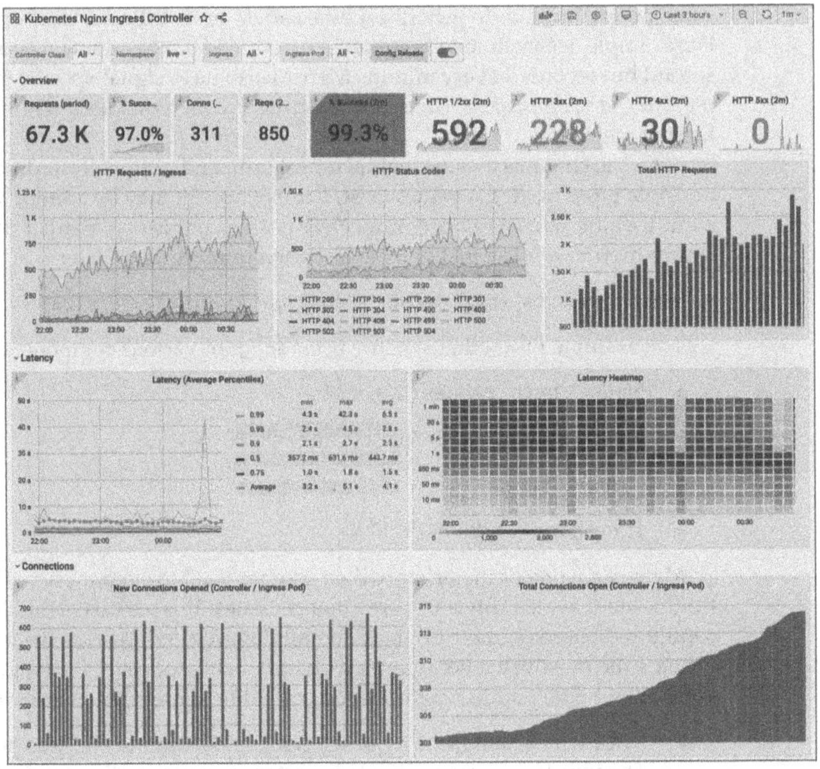

FIGURE 1.3 A Grafana dashboard displaying aggregate metric information.

LEARNING MORE ABOUT SLIs, SLOs, AND SLAs

SLIs, SLOs, and SLAs are critical topics that are outside the scope of this book. If you are looking to learn more about these concepts, be sure to read the *Google Site Reliability Engineering (SRE)* book, which is freely available online.[19]

Given the ever increasing number of objects in an environment and the need to collect more and more data, metric platforms need to be able to process and store a large number of metrics quickly. Various techniques are used to control the amount of data generated, processed, and stored. For example, the interval at which metrics are generated within the application or stored within an observability platform can be different from the resolution displayed in charts. Aggregation techniques are used to achieve these different granularities, including aggregation policies and rollups. In short, these strategies provide a summarized view of granular data over specific time intervals. Regardless of the techniques used, end users consume charts or alerts from this collected, analyzed, and queried data.

Several open source metric instrumentation frameworks and standards have become popular over the years. For example, the following solutions were popular in the monitoring era:

- StatsD (`https://github.com/statsd/statsd`)
- Graphite (`https://graphite.readthedocs.io/en/stable/overview.html`)

- Nagios (`https://www.nagios.org`)
- Telegraf (`https://www.influxdata.com/time-series-platform/telegraf`)
- Zabbix (`https://www.zabbix.com`)

In the observability era, the following projects have gained popularity:

- Grafana (`https://grafana.com/grafana`)
- OpenTelemetry (`https://opentelemetry.io`)
- Prometheus (`https://prometheus.io`)
- M3 (`https://m3db.io`)

Programming languages also have their own frameworks that can be leveraged to generate metric data. For example:

- Java Management Extensions (JMX) (`https://en.wikipedia.org/wiki/Java_Management_Extensions`) for Java
- `System.Diagnostics.Metrics` for .NET

There are also a variety of open source third-party frameworks, such as Micrometer (`https://micrometer.io`) for Java.

Logs

A *log*, sometimes called a *log record*, is a time-based event with metadata. A log typically contains a timestamp, severity, message, and optionally additional metadata. Logs have signal-specific metadata terms. For example, *attributes*, *fields*, and *resources* are all terms used with logs that refer to some kind of metadata.

A log can be either:

- Structured, meaning the message and other components are stated in a known regular syntax, making them easily recognizable and parsable. Structured logs are becoming the standard in cloud native workloads. Here is an example of a structured log in JavaScript Object Notation (JSON) format:

```
"@timestamp":"2024-07-01T10:07:13.425Z", "log.level": "INFO", "message":
  "Tomcat started on port(s): 8080 (http) with context path ''" "service.name":
  "springpetclinic","process.thread.name":"restartedMain","log.logger":
  "org.springframework.boot.web.embedded.tomcat.TomcatWebServer"}
```

or

- Unstructured, meaning the message is a string that could contain almost anything and whose metadata may be irregular and inconsistent requiring the parsed format to be dynamically inferred and often incomplete. Unstructured logs were more common before cloud native workloads, but they are still present given the broad adoption of unstructured syslog from legacy systems. Here is an example of an unstructured syslog message:

```
212.87.37.154 - - [01/Jul/2024:10:07:13 +0000] "GET /favicon.ico HTTP/1.1" 200
  3638 "-" "Mozilla/5.0 (Macintosh; Intel Mac OS X 10_11_6) AppleWebKit/537.36
  (KHTML, like Gecko) Chrome/52.0.2743.116 Safari/537.36"
```

In the preceding example, the `200` is an example of metadata where the name is missing and must be inferred. The value represents the HTTP response status code.

In addition to the format, logs can also be of different types. For example, events may be thought of as a unique signal but could also be thought of as a specific kind of log. Events contain the same information as a log record and could be structured or unstructured. What makes events unique is that they indicate that something happened. For example, a deployment to production could be denoted as an event and used to determine whether key performance indicators (KPIs) changed because of the deployment. Aligned with OpenTelemetry, events will be treated as a subtype of log records throughout this book.

Individual logs can be helpful in determining the root cause of issues as well as for security use cases, including providing an audit log of changes. Logs can also contain metric data. If properly parsed, aggregate data extracted from logs can be helpful to determine the health and behavior of a system. In either case, log payloads are significantly larger than metrics, and as such, more data needs to be processed and stored.

It is common for log data required for security purposes to have requirements about collecting all the data for a minimal period of time and even guaranteeing the data is not lost through, for example, a disk-based queue. In addition, keeping logs that identify root causes is also essential. As a result, collecting all logs or at least all logs at a certain severity level is common. *Severity* is a term used in logging to determine the type of logs to collect. The general severity levels are `TRACE`, `DEBUG`, `INFO`, `WARN`, `ERROR`, and `FATAL`. Care should be taken when deciding which severity level to collect, as improper log collection can impact observability.

Logs have developed open standards over time thanks in part to syslog. Multiple Requests for Comments (RFCs)[20] have been created for syslog, including:

- RFC 3164 (`https://datatracker.ietf.org/doc/html/rfc3164`)
- RFC 5424 (`https://datatracker.ietf.org/doc/html/rfc5424`)
- RFC 5425 (`https://datatracker.ietf.org/doc/html/rfc5425`)
- RFC 5426 (`https://datatracker.ietf.org/doc/html/rfc5426`)
- RFC 6587 (`https://datatracker.ietf.org/doc/html/rfc6587`)

While these open standards helped define protocol and data model support, they were created in response to proprietary and commercial solutions. In turn, several open source solutions emerged, and commercial solutions were forced to support these open standards. Of course, other open standards exist beyond the aforementioned standards. Most notable are the OpenTelemetry Logs Data Model[21] and the Elastic Common Schema.[22] Additional open standards and their importance will be covered in Chapter 2.

Traces

A *trace* is a recording of a time-based transaction or end-to-end request with metadata. A trace contains a unique identifier (ID), a start and end time, one or more spans, and optionally additional metadata. A *span* is a single step in a transaction and typically captures service or function calls, making it easy to follow the progression of a transaction. It contains similar information to a trace, including a unique ID, two timestamps (start and end), and optionally additional metadata. In addition, spans contain a parent ID, which is null for the first span, known as the *root span*. Spans have signal-specific metadata terms. For example, *attributes*, *tags*, and *resources* are all terms used with spans that refer to some kind of metadata.

Next, an example of a simplified trace (some metadata has been removed) is shown in JSON format. This example was produced using the OpenTelemetry protocol exporter. You will learn more about the OpenTelemetry protocol exporter and use the payload shown next in Chapter 5, "Managing the OpenTelemetry Collector." You can either create a file named `otlphttp-trace.json` and save the content now or access it from the book's GitHub repository when you reach Chapter 5.


```
{
  "resourceSpans": [
    {
      "resource": {
        "attributes": [
          {
            "key": "host.name",
            "value": { "stringValue": "web01.sflanders.net" }
          },
          {
            "key": "service.name",
            "value": { "stringValue": "frontend" }
          }
        ]
      },
      "scopeSpans": [
        {
          "scope": {
            "name": "io.opentelemetry.armeria-1.3",
            "version": "2.3.0-alpha"
          },
          "spans": [
            {
              "traceId": "80dcfdf0f3fe1a032e53facf9ae2ceca",
              "spanId": "f041a77c36ad23ae",
              "parentSpanId": "f4426a2e1f99e8a0",
              "flags": 1,
              "name": "GET /",
              "kind": 2,
              "startTimeUnixNano": "1718649061103266000",
              "endTimeUnixNano": "1718649061105462875",
              "attributes": [
                {
                  "key": "http.response.status_code",
                  "value": { "intValue": "200" }
                },
                {
                  "key": "http.request.method",
                  "value": { "stringValue": "GET" }
                },
```

(continued)

```
                {
                  "key": "http.route",
                  "value": { "stringValue": "/" }
                }
              ],
              "status": {}
            },
            {
              "traceId": "80dcfdf0f3fe1a032e53facf9ae2ceca",
              "spanId": "f4426a2e1f99e8a0",
              "parentSpanId": "",
              "flags": 1,
              "name": "GET",
              "kind": 3,
              "startTimeUnixNano": "1718649061098436000",
              "endTimeUnixNano": "1718649061105925208",
              "attributes": [
                {
                  "key": "http.response.status_code",
                  "value": { "intValue": "200" }
                },
                {
                  "key": "http.request.method",
                  "value": { "stringValue": "GET" }
                }
              ],
              "status": {}
            }
          ]
        }
      ],
      "schemaUrl": "https://opentelemetry.io/schemas/1.24.0"
    }
  ]
}
```

Looking at an example of a trace, you may notice that it looks like a structured log. Traces are like multiple structured logs that have been stitched together. The significant difference between a trace and a log is that a trace natively provides context and correlation. Context and correlation are possible by creating and passing an ID through a transaction. In fact, traces require that consistent context propagation be used end-to-end. This means all services in a transaction need to be instrumented and configured to use the same context propagation mechanism, and context must be allowed to flow between all services. Passing context, especially between disparate systems across various protocols, is difficult. As a result, trace instrumentation is not as prevalent as metrics and logs today.

While context passing is generally done via HTTP headers, the creation process is defined by the standard implemented. Several standards exist, with W_3C Trace Context[23] being the standard for cloud native workloads. Other standards also exist, including B3 from the open source Zipkin project[24] and Amazon's trace ID for its proprietary X-Ray service[25]. The same trace ID standard must be used in order for tracing to work properly, and HTTP headers must be allowed to pass between all services. As a result, the decision on the context format is important.

CONTEXT PROPAGATION FORMAT RECOMMENDATION

In order for tracing to work properly, all services in a transaction must use the same context propagation format. If different context propagation formats are used across services then traces will be broken or disconnected. While continuing to use an existing context propagation format is acceptable, using W_3C Trace Context in greenfield environments, or those without existing tracing, is highly recommended. If a proprietary context propagation format is used, it is recommended to consider switching to an open standard, such as W_3C Trace Context, to future-proof the architecture and ensure data portability.

Trace data can be more easily consumed visually. Each trace can be represented as a waterfall, as shown in Figure 1.4.

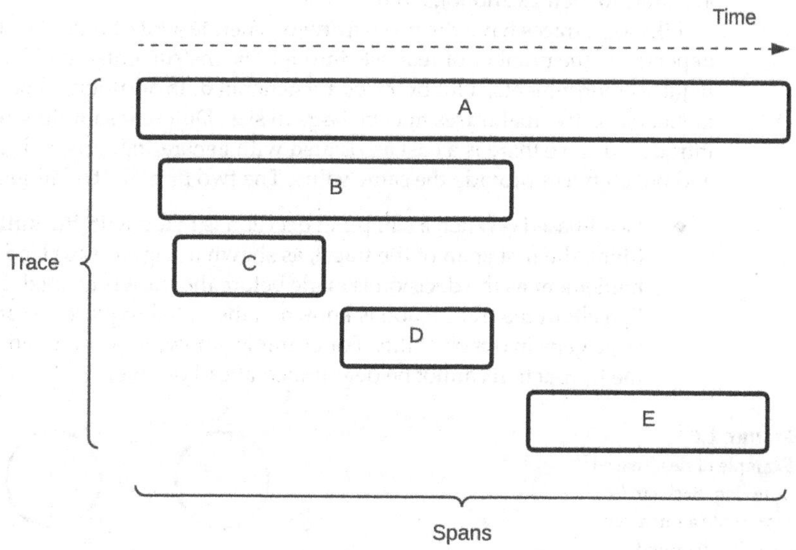

FIGURE 1.4 An example of a generic trace represented as a waterfall. This waterfall example could be further enhanced by denoting if an error occurred at any step in the transaction.

While example traces, often referred to as *exemplars*, can be useful, especially after problem isolation has occurred, aggregate trace information is helpful in determining system health and performance. In addition, aggregate data can be used to construct service graphs of an environment, as shown in Figure 1.5. Traces also contain other signals. At the very least, traces contain RED metrics. Metadata within a trace may also contain metric information, and spans can contain events. Events are essentially a specific type of log, as described in the "Logs" section earlier in this chapter. In addition, spans with errors can also contain logs.

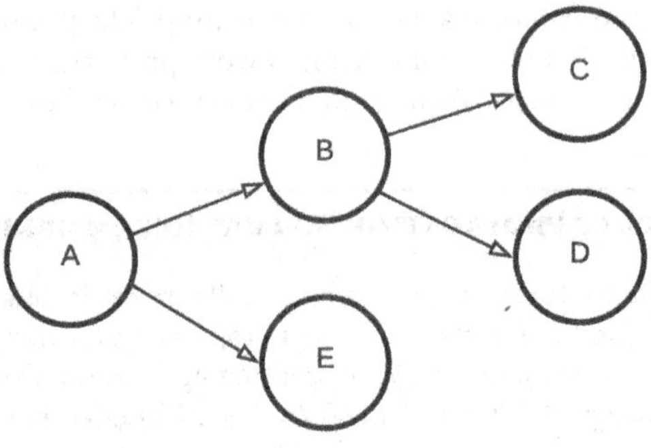

FIGURE 1.5
An example of a generic trace represented as a service map. As you may have noticed, this service map was constructed from the waterfall example shown previously. This service map example could be further enhanced to include RED metric data.

The concept of tracing has been around for a long time[26] and has been implemented in various ways. For example, logs customized to include and pass an ID have been used to provide tracing capabilities. Before the cloud native era, most tracing was proprietary, either developed in-house or provided by commercial vendors. Now, open source and open standards have changed this—a topic that will be explored in Chapter 2. In summary, OpenTelemetry has emerged as the tracing (metrics and logs too) standard, with W_3C Trace Context as the context format (made available to metrics and logs too).

Like logs, traces have the propensity to generate a lot of data. The number of traces generated depends on the number of requests through the instrumented paths of the architecture. For high request environments, a lot of traces are generated. In addition, depending on the amount of metadata, individual traces may be large in size. Different sampling techniques have been introduced since there is a cost associated with generating, processing, and storing trace data, and not all traces provide the same value. The two primary techniques are:

- Head-based—When a sampling decision is made with the initial request in a transaction (think the first span of the trace), as shown in Figure 1.6. Head-based sampling is easy to implement as the decision is made before the trace is created. However, not all information about the transaction is known in the initial request, so sampling here can result in large gaps in observability. For example, knowing whether an error will happen later in the transaction cannot be determined ahead of time.

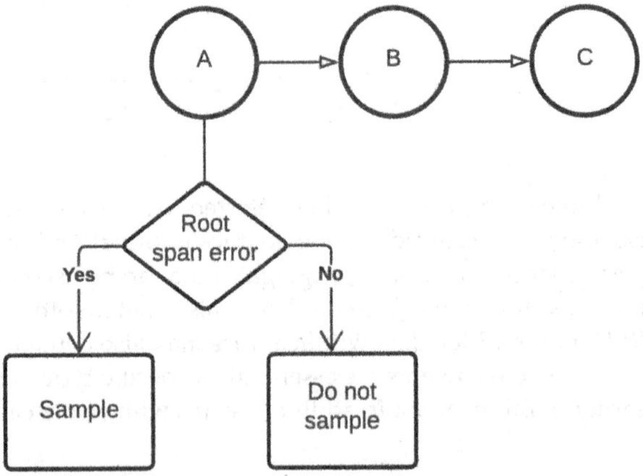

FIGURE 1.6
Example of head-based sampling. Each circle represents a microservice. The diamond represents a decision made within the service and the rectangles represent the action taken.

- Tail-based—When a sampling decision is made at the end of the transaction (think after the last span of a trace), as shown in Figure 1.7. Tail-based sampling requires generating and storing (typically in-memory) all information about the trace until the transaction is complete (typically done by waiting some period of time) and then making a sample decision. As such, tail-based sampling is significantly more complicated to implement and can consume substantially more resources, especially at a large scale. With that said, it has all the data, so it can make better sampling decisions than head-based sampling.

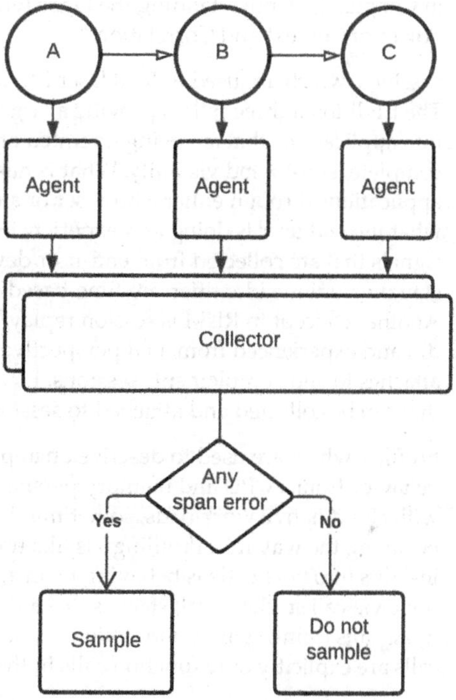

FIGURE 1.7 Example of tail-based sampling. Each circle represents a microservice. All microservices send data to a local agent, which sends data to the same node in a gateway cluster. The diamond represents a decision made by the gateway nodes, and the rectangles represent the action taken.

It is worth noting that sampling and filtering are similar concepts but not the same. For example, configuring tail-based sampling to collect all traces for which at least one span has an error is an example of filtering. Alternatively, collecting 10 percent of traces for which at least one span has an error is an example of sampling. While sampling can be used to reduce the amount of data stored, analyzing all trace data is critical to achieving observability. For instance, regardless of whether a trace is sampled, the aggregate RED metrics provided by the spans in the trace are necessary to achieve observability. To collect these metrics, processing of all spans is required. In addition, sampling can impact your ability to achieve observability if not properly configured. In short, trace sampling requires careful consideration and is not a magic solution.

Other Signals

While understanding and collecting the traditional three pillars is critical to achieving observability, other data sources are also important and should be considered. Some to be aware of include:

- Baggage, which is metadata passed between spans that must be explicitly added to signals. An example use case for this signal is adding metadata from further up the stack to telemetry that happens much later. While this concept is common in tracing, it may not be familiar to all readers. It is also a different type of signal in that it must exist in the presence of another signal, such as metadata on a different signal. Baggage will be covered in Chapter 4, "Understanding the OpenTelemetry Specification," and Chapter 8, "The Power of Context and Correlation."
- Sessions, which are used in Real User Monitoring (RUM) to analyze user experience (UX). The traditional three pillars provide a large amount of the data required to get visibility into applications that are being operated or depended on. Still, they do not provide complete, end-to-end visibility. What is missing is the user side. The end user connects to applications through either a browser or a mobile device. It is essential to understand what the end user is doing and experiencing, and that is where RUM helps. Sessions are signals that are collected from end-user devices, and they are similar to traces. They contain a unique identifier, are time-based, and optionally have additional metadata. Another concept in RUM is session replay,[27] which captures a snapshot of what the user did and experienced from a UI perspective. Session replay captures different data but attaches to and complements sessions. Finally, crash analytics is important and something that can be collected and attached to session data.
- Profiles, which are used to describe an application's execution and to understand code behavior from a CPU and memory perspective. Even if you can get to problem isolation with cloud native workloads, sometimes it can be hard to know why an application is behaving the way it is. Profiling[28] is like tracing within an application and provides deeper insights into how code is behaving in an application. The collection of profiling data is done via call stacks. A call stack is like a trace in that it contains a unique identifier, one or more calls (think spans), and optionally additional metadata. The difference is that the calls are explicitly only function calls in the application code.

Collecting Signals

As you can see, the three pillar signals are similar in terms of the general structure containing time-based information that can be analyzed. Traces provide a documented path of a transaction, similar to contact tracing in the medical field. They help identify where an issue occurred (problem isolation) as well as its impact. Traces are useful in answering at least the *where* question. Metrics typically collect symptoms, like a doctor checking vitals, and help identify what happened and/or changed. Metrics are useful in answering at least the *what* question. Logs can provide security information as well as the specific reasons behind a system's behavior, and they are like a medical record containing an audit of what has been done and who did it. Logs are useful in answering at least the *why* and *who* questions. While each of these signals is powerful, they are all necessary to have full observability.

Given that all three signals are similar, why were three signals created instead of one? To answer this question, consider some of the differences:

- Metrics emit small payloads at very frequent intervals. As a result, performance is critical. Metrics are usually not collected nor sent anywhere by default. While it is easy to add metrics and many frameworks exist, most metrics do not contain context or correlation information.
- Logs can contain richer information than metrics but, as a result, have larger payloads, and parsing requires proper formatting. Logs are usually written to a destination like a disk or a remote solution. While frameworks exist to add logs to applications, developers add most logging manually. Like metrics, most logs do not contain context or correlation.
- Traces are similar to logs. While they are easier to parse, it requires assembling an entire trace to realize the full potential. Traces require passing a context (typically a header) between requests. In addition, adding trace instrumentation is often significantly more challenging than metrics or logs. Trace payloads are as big, if not bigger, than logs and are frequently sampled.

Instrumentation

Adding something to an application to generate, process, and emit signals is known as *instrumentation*. Instrumentation, which will be covered extensively in Chapter 6, "Leveraging OpenTelemetry Instrumentation," may be signal specific or support more than one signal type. Applications can be instrumented in the following ways:

- Manual, sometimes called *code-based*, meaning a developer needs to add it directly into the code. Manual instrumentation offers a lot of flexibility but comes at the cost of developer cycles to add and maintain.
- Automatic, sometimes called *zero-code*, meaning it can be injected into the application, most commonly at runtime. Automatic instrumentation is convenient and is often easier to use when getting started. Still, it can only truly instrument known frameworks, may not provide as much detail as desired, and is not as customizable as manual instrumentation.
- Via an instrumentation library, sometimes called *programmatic*, meaning a library or framework comes with built-in instrumentation. While still a form of manual instrumentation, this approach requires less instrumentation knowledge and code changes. In addition, it handles aspects such as context propagation by default. With that said, an instrumentation library only instruments a known library.
- A combination of approaches, meaning more than one way. For example, manual and automatic or manual and programmatic can be used together.

Hopefully, it does not come as a surprise that adding instrumentation to applications in order to generate, process, and emit signals is not "free." While instrumentation is optimized to minimize the resources required, it will still consume some amount of CPU time and memory. How much overhead do they introduce? Like many things in life, it really depends. It depends on factors including:

- Where instrumentation is added—For example, in a frequently called or latency-sensitive path, sometimes called a *hot path*

- What is required to generate it—For example, blocking or asynchronous calls
- What processing is done—For example, regular expression matching
- If the data requires transformation—For example, aggregations or renaming
- How and where the data is exported—For example, buffer and retry logic

While tests can be performed and results published, they depend on various factors that may or may not be applicable to your environment. In general, automatic instrumentation may have more overhead than properly implemented manual instrumentation. In addition, automatic instrumentation may impact the startup time of applications, including Java-based applications. It is strongly recommended that you test the overhead of any instrumentation you add to your applications before deploying it to production. If you experience performance problems, check the documentation and configuration for potential issues, upgrade to the latest version to see if the issue has been resolved, and review release notes or known issues to see if others have reported it. If you are unable to find anything, then be sure to clearly document everything necessary to reproduce the issue and file an issue.

Real World Scenario

WATCHWHALE PUSHES APM

One of Riley's first tasks was to meet with the Watchwhale vendor and determine the adoption plan. The vendor account team was encouraging Riley and Jupiterian to manually instrument their microservices with Watchwhale instrumentation so that engineers could start taking advantage of application performance monitoring (APM) capabilities. They believed that introducing APM, a technology Jupiterian was not currently leveraging, would provide better visibility into the environment and allow the on-call team to be more proactive. The instrumentation was open source but developed and managed by Watchwhale.

Riley understood the importance of instrumenting applications to generate, process, and export telemetry data, but she was concerned about using proprietary instrumentation. For example, if the leadership team at Jupiterian changed and decided to bring in a different observability vendor in the future, then this instrumentation would need to be ripped out and replaced. While Watchwhale did offer some automatic instrumentation, Riley knew that she would eventually need to work with developers to add manual instrumentation for custom code and enrich the telemetry with metadata. Instead, she proposed ingesting the current observability data, namely Prometheus metrics, into Watchwhale and later dealing with instrumentation and APM.

Push Versus Pull Collection

In general, signals can be collected via push or pull mechanisms. Push means that the application sends the signal to a configured destination. The push mechanism is ubiquitous for logs and traces. Examples include a log being written to a log file or spans being sent to an agent or directly to an observability platform. The alternative is pull, where applications make their signal data available, and some other system collects this data. For cloud native workloads, the pull mechanism is most common for metrics. Examples include a collector configured to gather data from an endpoint such as the Kubernetes (K8s) API or scraping a Prometheus endpoint for metrics. Of course, metrics can also be pushed and at least logs could be pulled.

While either mechanism is acceptable to use, it is important to note the differences. One of the biggest issues is that pull-based mechanisms require the data to be exposed to a different system. As a result, proper security measures must be in place. Beyond this, whichever mechanism is used needs to be able to account for issues in collecting/sending data, including buffering and retry logic, and introduces the potential for overhead that must be accounted for.

Data Collection

You can collect signal data in a variety of ways. In addition, several data collection architectural topologies can be adopted. Each architecture depends on a multitude of factors, including security, cost, and configuration. Perhaps the most straightforward architecture is to have applications emit their signal data directly to an observability platform for processing and storing, as shown in Figure 1.8. There are a variety of reasons why you might consider this model, including:

- Simplicity—This architecture may be chosen when getting started or for small or noncomplex environments. It reduces the number of hops between telemetry generation and persistence.
- Efficiency—For some environments, an agent may consume too many resources or provide capabilities that are not required for the use case. Examples of such environments may include serverless functions or Internet of Things (IoT) devices.

Some of the drawbacks include the potential overhead to applications to handle buffer and retry logic as well as concerns around token management, processing configuration, and data loss risk (due to small retry buffers).

FIGURE 1.8 An application emitting telemetry data directly to a vendor-based observability platform. Everything to the left of the dashed line is within the customer's environment, while the vendor provides everything to the right.

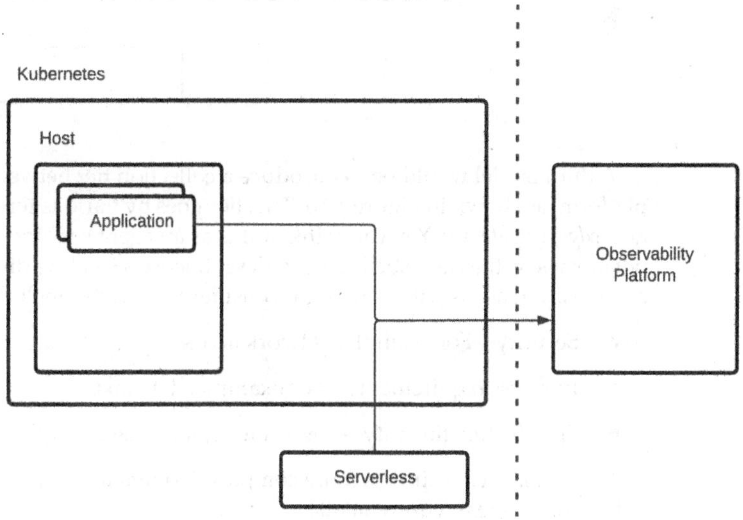

Another common model is to deploy an agent close to the application, as shown in Figure 1.9. "Close" may mean directly in the application as a separate binary, as a sidecar to the application, or on the host the application is running on. There are a variety of reasons why you might consider this model, including:

- Middle ground—Host-level agents are common as they offer a reasonable trade-off between the deciding factors. They also separate the responsibility of telemetry generation from processing and transmission.
- Consistency—Agents make it easier to handle security concerns and centralize configuration. This is especially important in polyglot environments.

On the flip side, agents need to be appropriately sized to support the amount of data received, processed, and exported, which can be challenging. In addition, agents introduce another hop and configuration point between the telemetry data and the observability platform.

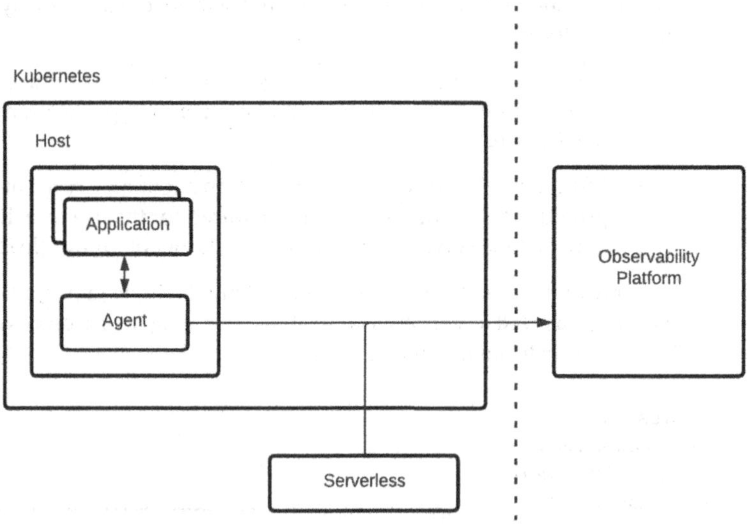

FIGURE 1.9 An application that emits its telemetry data to an agent running nearby, and the agent sends the data to a vendor-based observability platform. Everything to the left of the dashed line is within the customer's environment, while the vendor provides everything to the right.

A third model would be to introduce a collection tier between the agent and the observability platform, as shown in Figure 1.10. This tier goes by various terms, including *aggregation, collection, edge,* or *gateway*. You can think of this as an agent sending to another agent, though that may not always be the case, such as serverless functions sending directly to a collection tier. There are a variety of reasons why you might consider this model, including:

- Security—For example, network access
- Business requirements—For example, data lake
- Specific functionality—For example, tail-based sampling

While this architecture is more complex, it offers the greatest flexibility and can handle a variety of business requirements.

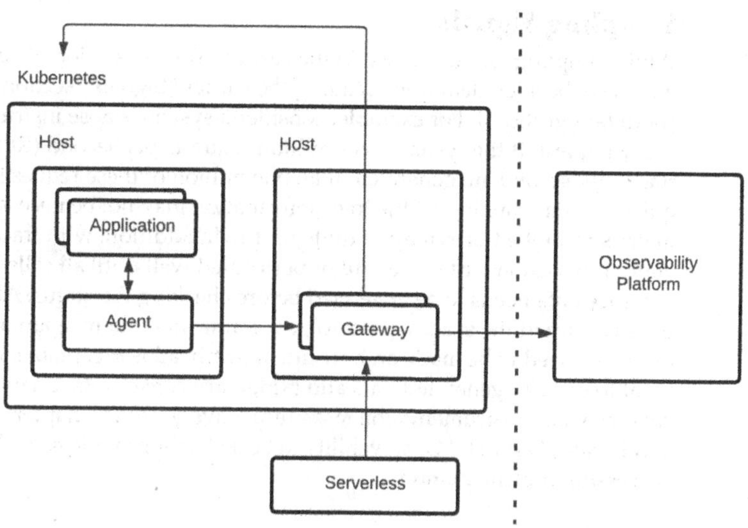

FIGURE 1.10 An application that emits its telemetry data to an agent running nearby, the agent sends the data to an edge cluster (gateway), and the edge cluster sends the data to a vendor-based observability platform. Everything to the left of the dashed line is within the customer's environment, while the vendor provides everything to the right.

As discussed previously in the "Signals" section, one consideration is the amount of signal data generated. One technique to reduce the amount of signal data sent to an observability platform is to filter it at the collection level. Of course, filtering is also useful for other reasons, including security, such as filtering out PII data. Filtering at the collection level reduces additional overhead on the application and makes centralized configuration easier. Data collection and processing will be covered extensively in Chapter 5.

Real World Scenario

RILEY AVOIDS VENDOR LOCK-IN AGAIN

With the focus on consuming Prometheus metrics, the vendor suggested deploying the Watchwhale agent between the applications and the Prometheus platform. They stated their agent supported sending data to their platform and Prometheus concurrently. They also noted the Watchwhale agent collected critical information about the infrastructure and used it to add metadata to the telemetry data being collected beyond what Prometheus provided. They claimed this metadata was essential to achieving observability and being able to ask any question of the data.

Riley asked if the Watchwhale agent supported federated Prometheus server scraping, as this would allow her to easily tap into the existing architecture and try out the Watchwhale solution. Alternatively, she would need to deploy another agent, which would require a design document, architecture review, security review, and a migration plan, not to mention ongoing maintenance. The vendor stated that the Watchwhale agent was not designed to scrape a Prometheus cluster as large as the one run at Jupiterian. Riley told the vendor she would run some tests and get back to them regarding the data collection architecture.

Sampling Signals

While sampling was discussed in the earlier "Traces" section, its use extends beyond tracing. As may have been evident upon reading the earlier "Signals" section, the amount of data generated could be significant. For example, consider a system whose instrumentation generates a trace for every request. If the system has a million requests per second (RPS), then that means a million traces per second are generated. If all one million of these requests are successful and completed quickly, then retaining all the trace information may not be necessary. However, at least the RED metrics from the traces may be quite useful. In addition, with traces, you will not know if the entire transaction was successful or performed well until all calls have completed. This means the trace data needs to be generated before checking the status. Alternatively, if all one million traces returned the exact same error, collecting all of them again may not make sense. Ultimately, decisions need to be made on how much overhead is acceptable, how much data to generate, what to do with generated data and budgetary constraints. Chapters 5 and 6 will cover data collection and instrumentation tasks respectively, while Chapters 10, "Observability Antipatterns and Pitfalls," and 11, "Observability at Scale," will provide considerations guidance to ensure successful implementation.

FILTERING AND SAMPLING

Two terms you will hear regarding processing signal data are *filtering* and *sampling*. Filtering allows you to remove a subset of data from a dataset. For example, maybe you only want to collect data that has or does not have a particular piece of metadata. You can think of filters as a gate allowing only specific data to pass through based on predefined rules. Sampling can offer the same capability. For example, you can sample traces where at least one span has an error denoted through metadata semantic conventions. Sampling can also be configured to perform additional operations. For example, you could configure sampling only to collect 5 percent of traces for a given transaction, known as *probabilistic sampling*. In short, sampling can be thought of as a superset of filtering.

The concept of sampling exists to provide data flexibility. Sampling allows a subset of data to be generated or collected based on defined rules. For example, with tracing, you could choose to sample only initial requests for a specific operation or only if any span in a trace contains an error. Sampling decisions made at the initial request can be made via head-based sampling, whereas decisions after the initial request can be made via tail-based sampling. Similar scenarios exist for other signals as well. For example, collection interval, chart resolution, and exemplars, described earlier in the "Metrics" section, are all forms of sampling. Another example is profiling, which has the notion of temporal collection sampling or collection for a fixed period of time. Sampling rules are flexible and often involve metadata, further highlighting the need for proper metadata enrichment of signal data. What is important to remember is that sampling is a trade-off decision between observability, price, and complexity.

Real World Scenario

RILEY STAYS FOCUSED ON METRICS

The vendor also mentioned that Jupiterian would want to deploy the Watchwhale reducer when APM instrumentation is configured. This component offered tail-based sampling, which they stated helped reduce the amount of non-important telemetry data collected to minimize noise and cost. They noted that a single instance could easily be scaled up and was enough for most environments.

They also mentioned that multiple instances could be clustered and used with Redis. Riley understood the value proposition of tail-sampling but was worried about the availability issues of a single instance and the complexity of managing a distributed system of reducers. Luckily, she did not need to worry about this piece, as the focus was on consuming Prometheus metrics.

Observability

Once you generate, collect, and process telemetry data, you need to decide where to store the data and how to analyze it in a way that provides observability. There are many solutions in the market today that offer various capabilities. You need to determine what your requirements are. Considerations may include:

- Scalability—Is the solution able to scale to your needs? Ingesting the data is only one part of the story, the time-to-alert, ability to index, and query response time all also matter.
- Reliability—Is the solution able to meet your availability requirements? What happens if it goes down?
- User experience—Can you easily navigate across signals and how easily can you programmatically configure or access your data?
- Ease of use—How difficult is it to ask questions about your observability data?
- Performance—How quickly are results returned for queries?
- Security—What about compliance requirements such as SOC 2 Type II, PCI, and HIPAA?
- Cost—How much does the product cost and what options does the solution provide to manage expenses?
- Lock-in—Are you able to leverage open standards or proprietary solutions?

Platforms

While signals are critical to achieving observability, so is the platform to store, analyze, query, chart, and alert on the signal data. While observability platforms will be covered in Chapter 9, "Choosing an Observability Platform," it is important to know that the market has a wide range of open source and commercial solutions available. Here are some of the most popular open source observability platforms:

- Prometheus (`https://prometheus.io`) is a CNCF project that provides a platform to store, alert, and query metric data. Grafana (`https://grafana.com/oss/grafana`) can be configured to display Prometheus data in the form of charts and dashboards. Note that Grafana is open source but not part of the CNCF. It is primarily maintained by Grafana Labs, a for-profit company. In addition, there is Thanos (`https://thanos.io`), another CNCF project that can be used to make Prometheus highly available with long-term storage capabilities.
- Jaeger (`https://jaegertracing.io`) is a CNCF project that provides a platform to store, query, and visualize trace data.

- OpenSearch (`https://opensearch.org`) provides a platform to store, alert, and query log data, as well as a frontend called OpenSearch Dashboards. Fluentd (`https://www.fluentd.org`) and Fluent Bit (`https://fluentbit.io`) are CNCF projects that provide a log agent that can send data to platforms, such as OpenSearch. Note that Elasticsearch (`https://github.com/elastic/elasticsearch`) and Kibana (`https://github.com/elastic/kibana`) are also popular, though were not considered open source for a period of time after Elastic, a for-profit company, moved the projects to the Server Side Public License (SSPL).[29] Elastic has since changed its license again adding AGPL and allowing it to be called open source again.[30]

Application Performance Monitoring

In the cloud native world, application performance monitoring, or APM,[31] has become more mainstream. It existed in the previous generation, but given that problem isolation was usually easier, profiling was more commonly used when needed. APM relies on the traces signal, and one of its most significant benefits is that it provides native context and correlation—something not typically found in the other major signals. Observability is sometimes conflated to be the same as APM. Given that one of the major pain points around cloud native monitoring is problem isolation, this may not be surprising. With that said, APM adoption is not nearly as prolific as metrics and logs in part because instrumentation is a challenging problem, and most people have become comfortable troubleshooting applications using primarily metrics and logs. In addition, just adding APM does not inherently give you observability. Beyond the signals, it is the correlation of the data and the ability to ask and answer unknown questions about your environment with that data that gives you true observability. In 2022, Gartner renamed the APM Magic Quadrant to the APM and Observability Magic Quadrant to help eliminate this confusion.[32] In 2024, Gartner renamed it again to the Magic Quadrant for Observability Platforms.[33] Speaking of the Magic Quadrant, feel free to check it out for commercially available observability platforms. The CNCF Landscape[34] is another good resource for commercial and open source observability solutions. This book will focus primarily on open source solutions.

The Bottom Line

Differentiate between monitoring and observability. Monitoring and observability, while often used interchangeably, serve distinct purposes in the realm of system management. Monitoring involves the regular collection and analysis of predefined metrics and logs to ensure that systems are operating within expected parameters. It is a reactive approach, focusing on known issues and performance thresholds. Observability, on the other hand, is a proactive and comprehensive practice that goes beyond monitoring. It involves instrumenting systems to provide deep insights into their internal states, enabling teams to uncover and diagnose previously unknown issues and anomalies. While monitoring tells you when something is wrong, observability helps you understand why.

Master It What is the difference between a "known known" and an "unknown unknown"?

Explain the importance of metadata. Raw telemetry data is not sufficient to achieve observability; it must be enriched. Metadata is a crucial piece of enrichment because it provides context to the raw telemetry data collected from various systems. Metadata can include information about the environment, version, location, and other attributes that help in identifying and contextualizing the data points. This enriched context allows for more accurate analysis, correlation, and troubleshooting, making it easier to pinpoint the root causes of issues and understand the behavior of the system under different conditions.

Master It What are the differences between dimensionality, cardinality, and semantic conventions?

Identify the differences between telemetry signals. Telemetry signals, the data components that power observability, typically include at least metrics, logs, and traces. Metrics are measured data, most commonly numerical representations, collected over intervals, such as CPU usage or request latency, providing a quantifiable view of system performance. Logs are timestamped records of discrete events that have occurred within the system, offering a detailed and chronological narrative of actions and states. Traces represent the flow of requests through various services in a distributed system, helping to visualize and understand the interactions and dependencies between components. Each signal type provides a unique perspective, and together, they offer a holistic view of the system's health and performance.

Master It Why are there at least three separate ways to collect telemetry data from applications?

Distinguish between instrumentation and data collection. Instrumentation and data collection are foundational activities in achieving observability. Instrumentation involves integrating code within applications to generate telemetry data, including metrics, logs, and traces, that reflect the internal state and activities of the system. This can be done through manual coding or using libraries and frameworks like OpenTelemetry. On the other hand, data collection involves gathering this telemetry data from various sources, processing it, and transporting it to observability platforms for storage, analysis, and visualization. Effective instrumentation ensures that the correct data is generated, while robust data collection ensures that this data is reliably transmitted and available for analysis.

Master It Given instrumentation, why is data collection necessary?

Analyze the requirements for choosing an observability platform. Selecting the right observability platform requires careful consideration of several factors. Scalability is crucial to handle the growing volume and velocity of telemetry data in modern systems. Integration capabilities are important to ensure the platform can seamlessly work with existing tools and technologies. The platform should support comprehensive data ingestion and processing capabilities for metrics, logs, and traces. It should offer advanced analytics and visualization tools to make sense of the data. Security and compliance features are also essential to protect sensitive data and meet regulatory requirements. Cost-effectiveness and ease of use are also critical factors, ensuring that the platform delivers value without excessive complexity or expense. By carefully evaluating these requirements, organizations can choose an observability platform that effectively supports their operational needs and strategic goals.

Master It How are observability platforms different from APM?

Notes

1 https://en.wikipedia.org/wiki/There_are_unknown_unknowns
2 https://glossary.cncf.io/observability
3 https://landscape.cncf.io
4 https://opentelemetry.io/docs/concepts/observability-primer
5 https://www.sciencedirect.com/science/article/pii/S1474667017700948
6 https://en.wikipedia.org/wiki/Observability
7 https://www.cncf.io
8 https://www.merriam-webster.com/dictionary/monitor
9 https://www.merriam-webster.com/dictionary/observe
10 https://en.wikipedia.org/wiki/First_principle
11 https://en.wikipedia.org/wiki/White_box_(software_engineering)
12 https://en.wikipedia.org/wiki/Black_box
13 https://sre.google/sre-book/monitoring-distributed-systems
14 https://sre.google/workbook/how-sre-relates
15 https://twitter.com/honest_update/status/651897353889259520
16 https://grafana.com/files/grafanacon_eu_2018/Tom_Wilkie_GrafanaCon_EU_2018.pdf
17 https://www.brendangregg.com/usemethod.html
18 https://sre.google/sre-book/monitoring-distributed-systems
19 https://sre.google.com/sre-book/service-level-objectives
20 https://en.wikipedia.org/wiki/Request_for_Comments
21 https://opentelemetry.io/docs/specs/otel/logs/data-model
22 https://www.elastic.co/guide/en/ecs/current/ecs-reference.html
23 https://www.w3.org/TR/trace-context
24 https://github.com/openzipkin/b3-propagation/tree/master
25 https://docs.aws.amazon.com/xray/latest/devguide/xray-concepts.html
26 https://netman.aiops.org/~peidan/ANM2019/7.TraceAnomalyDetection/ReadingList/2010Google_Dapper.pdf
27 https://en.wikipedia.org/wiki/Session_replay
28 https://en.wikipedia.org/wiki/Profiling_(computer_programming)
29 https://www.elastic.co/blog/elasticsearch-is-open-source-again. Open source license changes are becoming more common, especially for popular projects (https://www.infoworld.com/article/3486307/the-open-source-community-strikes-back.html)
30 https://blog.opensource.org/the-sspl-is-not-an-open source-license
31 https://en.wikipedia.org/wiki/Application_performance_management
32 https://www.gartner.com/reviews/market/application-performance-monitoring-and-observability
33 https://www.gartner.com/reviews/market/observability-platforms
34 https://cncf.landscape2.io

Chapter 2

Introducing OpenTelemetry!

Given that the complexity of modern software systems continues to grow, the need for a unified and robust observability framework becomes increasingly critical. OpenTelemetry has emerged as a comprehensive solution designed to standardize the generation, collection, and analysis of telemetry data across diverse environments. Chapter 1, "What Is Observability?," introduced you to the term observability in the context of software. In addition, it defined key concepts, including signals, metadata, and sampling. By now, it should be clear that while observability is powerful, it takes work to achieve, and considerations around vendor neutrality need to be made. This chapter will introduce you to OpenTelemetry, exploring its origins, architecture, and core components. It will also set the stage for a deep dive into the open standard and reference implementations in future chapters.

IN THIS CHAPTER, YOU WILL LEARN TO:

- Recognize observability problems and the need for open standards
- Explain the history and goals of the OpenTelemetry project
- Identify the OpenTelemetry components and project status

Background

Now that you understand a bit more about what observability is and why it matters, it is time to explore some challenges experienced in this space and the solutions that were developed as a result.

Observability Pain Points

As already mentioned, in order for systems to be observable, you need to instrument applications such that they can generate, process, and emit telemetry data. In addition, you need to collect this data through push and pull mechanisms. These requirements result in the need to install something within applications and the environment regardless of the observability platforms the data feeds into. There is a wide range of platforms, languages, frameworks, and integrations from which telemetry must be generated and collected in order to provide observability.

Back in the monitoring days, commercial vendors would introduce proprietary solutions to provide the required instrumentation and data collection. Given that each vendor wanted to offer the same amount of monitoring, they had to invest in a solution that would work with their platform. As a result, each vendor created their own unique solution, which resulted in different features, semantics, supported integrations, user experiences, and performance. It became clear that standards were necessary for instrumentation and data collection, so at least basic correlation could be provided, and platforms could rely on specific data being available to ensure consistent functionality. Examples of these standards included defining data formats and protocols. Some early examples of these standards were discussed in Chapter 1.

Existing commercial companies, often referred to as *vendors*, were forced to adopt these standards. As a result, new startups were able to enter the market and take advantage of these new standards. Even with open standard support, vendors still provided proprietary collection mechanisms to send to their proprietary platforms. The proprietary nature allowed these companies to offer features above and beyond the open standards but also continued to lock end users into proprietary solutions. *Vendor lock-in* occurs when the switching cost to another vendor becomes too great. Instrumentation and data collection is one way to lock in end users.

Timeline of application performance monitoring (APM) instrumentation and platforms (a similar timeline could be constructed for metrics and logs):

- Late 1980s to late 1990s (pre-APM): Proprietary instrumentation and platforms to monitor and manage the performance of applications. Examples include HP OpenView, IBM Tivoli Monitoring, and BMC Patrol.
- Late 1990s to early 2000s (first-generation APM): Proprietary APM instrumentation and platforms primarily for monolithic, on-premises applications. Examples include Wily Technology and Precise Software Solutions.
- Mid to late 2000s (second-generation APM): Proprietary APM instrumentation and platforms primarily for distributed, on-premises applications. Examples include Dynatrace and AppDynamics.
- Late 2000s to mid 2010s (third-generation APM): Proprietary APM instrumentation and platforms with the emergence of open source solutions primarily for distributed, cloud-based applications. Examples include New Relic (proprietary) and Zipkin (open source).
- Mid to late 2010s (cloud native and open source revolutions): Open source APM instrumentation and platforms enter the market. Examples include Jaeger, OpenTelemetry, and Loki (all open source). Commercial startups including Lightstep, Honeycomb, and Omnition enter the market offering a proprietary APM platform that leverages open source instrumentation and data collection. Datadog, a proprietary metrics vendor, enters the APM market offering an open source platform but proprietary instrumentation leveraging these open standards. In addition, cloud providers provide APM services and begin to adopt these open standards.
- Late 2010s to now (first-generation observability): The Jaeger project deprecates its instrumentation and collector in favor of OpenTelemetry. In addition, New Relic open sources its instrumentation libraries. Beyond this, every major vendor announces support for OpenTelemetry. Vendors now offer an observability suite of which APM is only one part. Beyond collecting metrics, logs, and traces, the focus is on context and correlation to reduce downtime and address performance issues.

Over time, instrumentation and data collectors became more and more powerful and proprietary. Consumers of these proprietary solutions began to take on vendor dependencies, such as manually editing code or integrating collectors into their configuration management tooling, making it harder to switch observability platforms. Vendor neutrality is powerful for end users because it gives them more data choice and freedom. In addition, it allows them to take advantage of new solutions as they become available more quickly. Unfortunately, high switching costs introduce friction that locks in end users. For example, replacing manual instrumentation is no small task, nor is learning how to properly maintain, scale, and configure a new collection architecture. Beyond this, the time put in to create alerts, charts, and dashboards that are not reusable across products because of data differences also hampers data sovereignty and innovation.

Taking a step back, while it is possible that platforms may have unique functionality, most of the functionality is the same even if the data consumed is slightly different. For example, every vendor solution must offer a minimum set of expected features, including dashboards and alerts. If proprietary instrumentation or collection mechanisms are needed, then perhaps the open standards are not extensible enough to meet end-user needs. Initially, proprietary instrumentation and collection was intellectual property (IP) and a competitive advantage. As open source commoditized the space, the question was, why would every vendor want to make the same foundational investment around instrumentation and collection before they could even think about offering unique platform functionality? This is especially true for startups attempting to penetrate the market.

On the consumer side, requirements were vast and ever-changing. For example, a large company may comprise multiple business units (BUs), each consisting of multiple scrum teams. These teams may have come in from an acquisition, an internal re-org, or new hiring. Unless there is a top-down mandate, it is possible these teams are using different software to achieve observability. If so, it is highly likely that different instrumentation and data collection mechanisms will be used. Beyond supportability and security, the choices made may make it difficult to provide observability in the future. For example, if different context propagation mechanisms are being used and later end-to-end visibility is required across the applications, then changes would be necessary.

As you can see, there are several problems in this space, including:

- Inconsistent features
- Vendor lock-in
- Supportability and security concerns
- Duplication among vendors
- Lack of standardization, including context and correlation across signals and semantic conventions (semconvs)

Real World Scenario

VENDOR ESCALATION AT JUPITERIAN

Riley received a meeting invite from the VP of Engineering at Jupiterian. The vendor reached out to him, raising concerns about the progress made on the adoption of Watchwhale. The VP wanted to know why Riley was not following the vendor's recommendations. Riley explained the importance of proving out the solution while not ending up in a vendor lock-in situation. She said the plan was to start by consuming Prometheus metrics and then expand into other use cases. She also let the VP know she was looking into the OpenTelemetry (OTel) project and would make a formal proposal regarding the next steps.

The Rise of Open Source Software

Before observability became mainstream, one major disruption in software was the popularization of open source software, or OSS. OSS sought to provide functionality to the masses, provide standardization, and eliminate commercial advantage and lock-in. The Open Source Initiative[1] (OSI) exists with a mission to define and defend the open source definition. Relevant examples of popular OSS solutions include those found in the:

- Linux Foundation,[2] which includes the projects in the Cloud Native Computing Foundation (CNCF).
- Apache Software Foundation,[3] including projects such as Cassandra, Druid, Flink, Hadoop, Kafka, and Spark.

These projects provide a general way to perform a particular type of operation. Over time, they became so popular that vendors, especially cloud providers, began to rely on them and even offer them as managed services for a fee. Examples include Amazon EMR,[4] which is managed Apache Hadoop and Spark, and Google Dataproc,[5] which is managed Apache Flink, Hadoop, Spark, and others.

Beyond open source implementations, open standards were also created and gained popularity, as discussed in Chapter 1. For the tracing signal, OpenTracing,[6] or OT, emerged as an open standard in 2015 out of Lightstep (acquired by ServiceNow) and joined the CNCF in 2016. It sought to define a tracing specification from which vendor-neutral instrumentation could be created. OT offered the flexibility to work with any tracing solution, whether open source or commercial. The advantage was simple: open standards stopped vendor lock-in and future-proofed engineering investments into observability. This was especially important for APM and the tracing signal, which at the time predominately required adding complex manual instrumentation to applications. With OT joining the CNCF, open source observability platforms were quick to get on board, with Jaeger and Zipkin offering full OT support.

Another popular project in the open source observability space is Prometheus. First made available in 2012 and joining the CNCF in 2016, it offered a robust and scalable metric platform. The project also provided open source metric instrumentation more than a year before OT was created. This approach was like an open source version of what commercial vendors offered. Given the broad adoption of the Prometheus platform, it was reasonable to assume that the instrumentation would also gain momentum. Over time, perhaps the instrumentation could also be the basis for an open standard. As it turned out, OpenMetrics[7] was formed in 2018 and joined the CNCF in 2022. OpenMetrics sought to create and extend a specification for the Prometheus exposition format,[8] and in November of 2022, the first version was released. Since that time, there has not been much said or done with OpenMetrics outside of the Prometheus project. In March of 2024, Prometheus announced its commitment to OpenTelemetry and use of OpenMetrics purely for Prometheus[9] and in August OpenMetrics was archived.[10]

CLOSED SOURCE TO OPEN SOURCE TO VENDOR-NEUTRAL

Initially, signal instrumentation and data collection were proprietary and closed source. Given the pain points described earlier in this chapter, some vendors began to open source some aspects. An example is Datadog, a commercial vendor that open sourced its Datadog Agent. Even though it was open sourced, it was still proprietary as it only supported sending data to the Datadog platform. These days, vendor-neutral solutions are mainstream, with projects such as OpenTelemetry leading the way. Not only are these projects open source, but they support a variety of platforms, giving users control of their data.

While OT gained momentum, it only solved a part of the observability problem, namely around the APM space and specifically for instrumentation. Given that APM alone does not provide observability, there was room to expand the scope. As a result, in 2017, Google and Microsoft announced the OpenCensus (OC) project.[11] This project looked to create an open standard and implementation for traces, metrics, and logs. Its goal was to do so in a single instrumentation to reduce end-user friction and offer context and correlation across signals as well as the infrastructure. It also desired to provide a single collector capable of handling all three signals—a component developed by Omnition (acquired by Splunk, then Cisco), who joined the project shortly after the initial announcement. OC quickly gained momentum, but having both OT and OC resulted in a lot of confusion in the community. With two standards offering a Venn diagram of capabilities, all at different levels of maturity, end users were left wondering which project to invest in and rely on. It was clear something needed to be done.

Introducing OpenTelemetry

Luckily, the two project groups collaborated well and agreed to merge, forming the OpenTelemetry (OTel) project in early 2019 and immediately joining the CNCF (see Table 2.1). To ease migration to OTel, the project offered compatibility shims from OT and OC. In addition, they agreed that once OTel was mature enough to be relied on, they would archive the prior two projects.

OpenTelemetry ABBREVIATION

The project is called OpenTelemetry (no space between "Open" and "Telemetry"), and it is abbreviated as OTel (first two letters capitalized). Note, that it is not OT, as OT is the abbreviation for OpenTracing.[12]

OTel's mission is "to enable effective observability by making high-quality, portable telemetry ubiquitous." (`https://opentelemetry.io/community/mission`)

OpenTelemetry SCOPE

The word "enable" is important in OTel's mission. OTel enables observability by providing an open standard and reference implementation to generate, collect, process, and export telemetry data for any environment. OTel does not inherently offer observability and, as a result, does not provide an observability platform or back end. Instead, it supports a wide range of open source and commercial platforms.

The project's vision is that telemetry should be easy, universal, vendor-neutral, loosely coupled, and built-in. What you may have already noticed is that OTel is a standards body that provides a reference architecture that others can adopt and extend. Why is this needed? In part because end users are demanding a vendor-neutral solution to instrument and collect telemetry data—something that can be proved with data. OTel is the second most active project in CNCF behind only Kubernetes (K8s) per DevStats (`https://all.devstats.cncf.io/d/1/activity-repository-groups?orgId=1`), which is a CNCF-provided report on project activity. In addition, all major observability vendors and cloud providers contribute to and have adopted OTel (`https://opentelemetry.io/ecosystem/vendors`). Finally, end users, including individuals and companies, are contributing to and adopting OTel (`https://opentelemetry.io/ecosystem/adopters`). It is clear that OTel is solving a real pain point that needs to be addressed—the goal of observability for everyone in a vendor-agnostic way. Of course, the project also introduces its own pain points, including maturity (quickly being resolved) and ease of use. To understand the project, it is important to understand the components, which will be covered in the next section.

TABLE 2.1: Timeline of major open source observability projects through 2023

YEAR	PROJECT RELEASED (CONTRIBUTOR)	JOINED CNCF
2010	Elasticsearch (Elastic)	
2011	Fluentd (Treasure Data)	
2012	Prometheus (SoundCloud), Zipkin (Twitter)	
2014	Fluent Bit (Treasure Data), Grafana (Grafana Labs), Kubernetes (Google)	
2015	Jaeger (Uber), OpenTracing (Lightstep acquired by ServiceNow)	
2016	Envoy (Lyft), Linkerd (Buoyant)	Fluent Bit, Fluentd, Kubernetes, OpenTracing, Prometheus
2017	Istio (Google), OpenCensus (Google, Microsoft, and Omnition acquired by Splunk acquired by Cisco)	Envoy, Jaeger, Linkerd
2018	OpenMetrics (Grafana Labs and Prometheus)	
2019	OpenTelemetry (OpenCensus and OpenTracing)	OpenTelemetry
2021	OpenSearch (Amazon)	
2022		Istio, OpenMetrics, (OpenTracing archived)
2023		(OpenCensus archived)
2024		(OpenMetrics archived)

OpenTelemetry Components

The OTel project is large and made up of multiple components. While the OTel GitHub organization comprises over 60 active repositories (`https://github.com/orgs/open-telemetry/repositories`), many repositories are related and can be grouped together. These repositories can broadly be grouped into four categories, as shown in Figure 2.1. There are also some repositories, such as OpAMP and Weaver, outside of these four general categories.

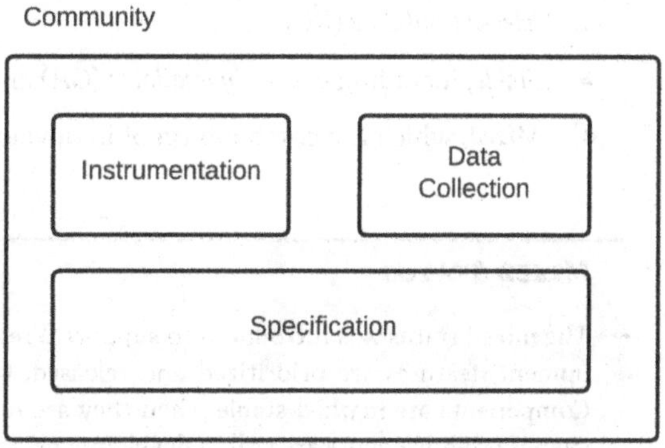

FIGURE 2.1 High-level grouping of OTel components. The specification is an open standard and foundational to the project. The instrumentation and data collection components are reference implementations that adhere to the specification. Nothing is possible in the OTel project without its community.

Each category can further be broken down:

- Specification: Contains data, API, and SDK components, which will be explored in Chapter 4, "Understanding the OpenTelemetry Specification."
- Data Collection: Contains receivers, processors, exporters, connectors, and extensions components, which will be explored in Chapter 5, "Managing the OpenTelemetry Collector."
- Instrumentation: Contains signal-specific API and SDK components as well as signal-agnostic SDK components, which will be explored in Chapter 6, "Leveraging OpenTelemetry Instrumentation." It also typically includes instrumentation libraries for popular libraries and frameworks.

Project Status

For most open source projects, stabilizing and reaching maturity takes a long time. OTel is no exception to this. OTel has a large number of contributors and stakeholders, and the project scope is large. One way to measure the status and maturity of the project is through the status donated by the CNCF project maturity levels (`https://www.cncf.io/project-metrics`), which include:

- Graduated
- Incubating
- Sandbox

As of mid 2024, OTel is in the *incubating* status. As described in Chapter 1, the three pillars of observability, known as signals in OTel, are critical to demonstrating the project's maturity. Given that all three pillars are stable in OTel, it is reasonable to assume it will reach graduated within the next year or so. The formal request has already been submitted: `https://github.com/cncf/toc/pull/1271`. In addition to the overall project, a status is donated for each component and subcomponent within OTel (`https://opentelemetry.io/status`), as shown in Table 2.2. The common statuses are:

- *Design*, including proposal and not implemented
- *In Development* (formerly known as *experimental*), including *not implemented*, *alpha*, *beta*, and *release candidate* (RC)
- *Stable*, including *generally available* (GA) and *deprecated*
- *Mixed*, which is a combination of in development and stable states

MIXED STATUS

The mixed status was introduced to support OTel's continued evolution. Like most software development, features are prioritized and released, but not everything can be done simultaneously. Components are marked stable when they are ready to ensure supportability and grow maturity, even if other elements are still in development. What you should be aware of is that stable components have backward compatibility guarantees, whereas in development components do not. As a result, using in-development components in production is not recommended unless you fully understand the implications of a breaking change and are willing to accept the risk.

In-development components *should not* be used in production because they may experience breaking changes. The likelihood of breaking changes reduces as the component gets closer to a stable status. In general, beta components are ready for initial testing and feedback, while RC provides a final opportunity to provide feedback. Deprecated components will only see fixes for critical security issues and will be removed in a future release. *Do not* depend on deprecated components and migrate away as soon as possible.

TABLE 2.2: OTel component status and maturity

LIFECYCLE PROGRESSION FROM EARLY TO LATE							
Proposal	Not Implemented	In Development	Alpha	Beta	RC	GA	Deprecated
Design		In development				Stable	
Mixed (two or more of the above statuses)							

At KubeCon North America 2023, the OTel project hit a critical milestone, with the logs signal being announced as stable. This announcement meant that all three pillars of observability were marked stable in the specification. While this was a critical milestone, it is important to note that the stability of the signals does not mean the stability of all the components that rely on it. For example, semconvs are separate from the stability of the signal, with only HTTP being declared stable at the same conference—more on this below. While the component documentation lists the OTel status, it is difficult to see it per component. As such, each component section that follows, the component status will be listed.

> **DETERMINING THE LATEST STATUS**
>
> The OTel project is rapidly evolving, with some components marked stable and some components marked in development (previously experimental). While the information provided in this book was current at the time of publication, statuses may have changed. Please refer to the GitHub repository that complements this book (`https://github.com/flands/mastering-otel-book`) or the OTel documentation for the latest status information.

SPECIFICATION

The specification is the open standard and is foundational to all reference implementations, namely data collection and instrumentation. It is made up of four primary subcomponents:

- Data Specification: Used to define implementation guidance, data models, semconvs, and protocols
- API Specification: Used to define the instrumentation interface standard for applications
- SDK Specification: Used to define the standard for processing and exporting signals provided by the API specification
- Versioning and Stability: Used to define versioning scheme and support guarantees

Each subcomponent's stability is provided per signal, as shown in Table 2.3. The details of the specification will be explored in Chapter 4, but the quick takeaways are:

- It is an open standard designed to support other existing open standards and extensible to future use cases.
- It defines the core concepts of the project, including resources.
- In general, you do not need to read or understand the specification to get started with the project (though still recommended).

TABLE 2.3: Specification signal and component status as of 2024. In short, the three pillars of observability and baggage are all stable. Metrics and logs are being extended and profiling has been introduced[13] but is not implemented yet.

	COMPONENT		
SIGNAL	**API**	**SDK**	**PROTOCOL**
Baggage	Stable	Stable	N/A
Tracing	Stable	Stable	Stable
Metrics	Mixed[1]	Mixed[2]	Stable
Logs	Mixed[3]	Stable	Stable
Profiling	Not Implemented	Not Implemented	In Development

Source: Adapted from [13].

[1] *New capabilities (gauge and advisory parameters) are in development.*

[2] *New capabilities (cardinality limits and exemplars) are in development.*

[3] *Bridge is stable, and events are in development.*

DATA COLLECTION

The OTel Collector is a significant component and primary data collection mechanism in the project. We will explore the details of the Collector in Chapter 5, but the quick takeaways are that it supports:

- A robust and extensible architecture to receive, process, and export traces, metrics, and logs
- A variety of form factors, including agent and edge processing as well as push and pull collection mechanisms
- A variety of integrations, including Prometheus, Fluent Bit, Apache Arrow, and eBPF, to name a few

The Collector consists of two separate repositories known collectively as *core* (`https://github.com/open-telemetry/opentelemetry-collector`) and *contrib* (`https://github.com/open-telemetry/opentelemetry-collector-contrib`). The core repository contains the required components to use OTel end-to-end. The contrib repository contains additional components that either provide niche capabilities or are helpful to leverage other open source or commercial products. For most environments, at least some components will be needed from the contrib repository, though rarely all of them. The stability of components in the core repository is shown in Table 2.4. All components in the contrib repository are in development as of 2024.

TABLE 2.4: Collector core components and signal status as of mid 2024. Note that OTLP is the default data format used by the OTel project and will be explored more in Chapter 4.

COMPONENT	NAME	TRACES	METRICS	LOGS
Receiver	OTLP (gRPC + HTTP)	Stable	Stable	Stable
Processor	Batch[1]	Beta	Beta	Beta
	Memory Limiter[2]	Beta	Beta	Beta
Exporter	OTLP (gRPC)	Stable	Stable	Beta
	OTLPHTTP	Stable	Stable	Beta

[1] *The batch processor will be moved to receiver and exporter helpers in the future.*
[2] *The memory limiter processor will be moved to receiver and exporter helpers in the future.*

There are several additional repositories related to the Collector. Other repositories include:

- Packaging
  - Helm (`https://github.com/open-telemetry/opentelemetry-helm-charts`)
  - Operator (`https://github.com/open-telemetry/opentelemetry-operator`)
  - Releases (`https://github.com/open-telemetry/opentelemetry-collector-releases`)
- Integrations
  - Apache Arrow (`https://github.com/open-telemetry/otel-arrow`)
  - Network (eBPF) Collector (`https://github.com/open-telemetry/opentelemetry-network`)
  - OpAMP (agent management) (`https://github.com/open-telemetry/opamp-go`)

Of course, for the Collector, OTel publishes binaries for all major CPU architectures (`https://github.com/open-telemetry/opentelemetry-collector-releases/releases`) as well as Docker images (`https://hub.docker.com/u/otel`).

INSTRUMENTATION

Instrumentation is provided to generate telemetry data in your application with OTel. We will explore the details of instrumentation in Chapter 6, but the quick takeaways are that it supports:

- A robust and extensible architecture to generate, process, and export signals

- A single instrumentation solution for more than ten languages that supports traces, metrics, and logs
- Manual and automatic instrumentation

OTel provides instrumentation for the following languages:

- .NET (`https://github.com/open-telemetry/opentelemetry-dotnet`)
- Android (`https://github.com/open-telemetry/opentelemetry-android`)
- C++ (`https://github.com/open-telemetry/opentelemetry-cpp`)
- Erlang/Elixir (`https://github.com/open-telemetry/opentelemetry-erlang`)
- Java (`https://github.com/open-telemetry/opentelemetry-java`)
- JavaScript, including server and browser (`https://github.com/open-telemetry/opentelemetry-js`)
- Go (`https://github.com/open-telemetry/opentelemetry-go`)
- PHP (`https://github.com/open-telemetry/opentelemetry-php`)
- Python (`https://github.com/open-telemetry/opentelemetry-python`)
- Ruby (`https://github.com/open-telemetry/opentelemetry-ruby`)
- Rust (`https://github.com/open-telemetry/opentelemetry-rust`)
- Swift (`https://github.com/open-telemetry/opentelemetry-swift`)

INSTRUMENTATION

OTel provides instrumentation, but so do other projects. For example, .NET offers `System.Diagnostic.DiagnosticSource`. This class has native OTel API support, meaning you can use it directly instead of using the .NET instrumentation provided by OTel. Of course, you will still need to add the OTel SDK and the appropriate exporter to collect the telemetry data.[14] It is also possible that a library or framework could be enhanced to produce telemetry in addition to its current capability. This is known as an *instrumentation library*. The long-term vision of the OTel project is for all framework and library owners to add native OTel capabilities. Some have, while others have been created and hosted within the OTel community. For example, OTel Java provides many stand-alone library instrumentations (`https://github.com/open-telemetry/opentelemetry-java-instrumentation/blob/main/docs/supported-libraries.md#libraries--frameworks`).

Repository structures for OTel instrumentation vary. Some languages, like Python, opt for a core (`https://github.com/open-telemetry/opentelemetry-python`) and contrib (`https://github.com/open-telemetry/opentelemetry-python-contrib`) structure like the Collector. Others, like Java, separate manual instrumentation (`https://github.com/open-telemetry/opentelemetry-java`) from automatic instrumentation (`https://github.com/open-telemetry/opentelemetry-java-instrumentation`) and offer additional capabilities in a contrib repository (`https://github.com/open-telemetry/opentelemetry-java-contrib`). Finally, some languages, like C++ or Swift, leverage a single repository for everything.

Support for instrumentation is primarily denoted by two aspects: signals and supported versions, as shown in Table 2.5. In the case of signals, there are also differences between manual and automatic instrumentation. Note that OTel instrumentation provides compatibility and support for a minimum version or runtime and most only support active or maintenance long-term support (LTS) versions and runtimes. For example, the OTel Java instrumentation supports Java 8 and higher (`https://github.com/open-telemetry/opentelemetry-java/blob/main/VERSIONING.md#language-version-compatibility`), while the OTel Node.js instrumentation only supports active or maintenance LTS versions of Node.js (`https://github.com/open-telemetry/opentelemetry-js?tab=readme-ov-file#supported-runtimes`).

TABLE 2.5: OTel instrumentation and signal status as of mid 2024. Information in this table will change over time, so check the OTel documentation for the latest information. OTel instrumentation typically supports active versions of the language. In addition, each signal provides manual instrumentation at a minimum. The profiling signal was added in March of 2024 and will eventually be added to all languages.

			MANUAL			**AUTOMATIC**	
LANGUAGE	**SUPPORTED VERSIONS**	**TRACES (T)**	**METRICS (M)**	**LOGS (L)**	**T**	**M**	**L**
Android	21+	In development	In development	In development			
C++	Active versions (14, 17, and 20)	Stable	Stable	Stable			
DotNet	.NET Framework >3.5 and .NET	Stable	Stable	Stable	X	X	
Erlang/Elixir	23+/1.13+	Stable	In development	In development			
Go	Active versions	Stable	Stable	In development	X		
Java	8+	Stable	Stable	Stable	X	X	X
JavaScript (server)	Active versions (8.12.0+)	Stable	Stable	In development	X		
JavaScript (client)	Active versions	Stable	Stable	In development			

TABLE 2.5: OTel instrumentation and signal status as of mid 2024. Information in this table will change over time, so check the OTel documentation for the latest information. OTel instrumentation typically supports active versions of the language. In addition, each signal provides manual instrumentation at a minimum. The profiling signal was added in March of 2024 and will eventually be added to all languages. *(CONTINUED)*

		Manual			Automatic		
Language	**Supported Versions**	**Traces (T)**	**Metrics (M)**	**Logs (L)**	**T**	**M**	**L**
Kotlin	1.6+	Stable	Stable	Stable	X	X	X
PHP	Active versions (8+)	Stable	Stable	Stable	X		
Python	Active versions (3+)	Stable	Stable	In development	X	X	X
Ruby	Active versions	Stable	Not Implemented	Not Implemented			
Rust	Active versions (1.64+)	In development	In development	In development			
Swift	Active versions (5+)	Stable	In development	In development			

Looking at Table 2.5, you will notice a lot of functionalities in development or not implemented. OTel prioritized the tracing signal first, metrics second, logs third, and everything else afterward. In addition, each language varies in terms of its general use or number of OTel maintainers. As an example, Java is significantly more active than Ruby, and, as it turns out, Java is used significantly more in production than Ruby. Beyond this, you will notice that automatic instrumentation is in development for all languages. The primary reason for this is that semconvs are not fully stable. With unstable semconvs, it is impossible to have stable automatic instrumentation as stability around breaking changes cannot be guaranteed.

Automatic Instrumentation Status

While manual instrumentation is stable for most languages and signals, automatic instrumentation remains in development. This is because automatic instrumentation relies on OTel semantic conventions and the majority of conventions are in development. Using automatic instrumentation in production is fine as long as you are aware that changes to semantic conventions may impact configured charts and alerts in your observability platform.

Speaking of semconvs, it is also important to understand their status, as shown in Table 2.6. As it turns out, most semconvs are still in development, meaning they could change. The biggest impact is on the platforms receiving this data and the content built from the data, such as charts, dashboards, and alerts. The status of the semconv should not prevent you from adopting OTel, but you should be aware that changes may result in unexpected behavior. Ways to deal with changing semantic conventions are covered in the "Dashboards and Alerts" section of Chapter 7.

TABLE 2.6: OTel instrumentation language and semconv category status as of mid 2024. Note that semconv categories vary by signal and each category contains multiple defined names.

	CATEGORY			
LANGUAGE	**HTTP**	**DATABASE (DB)**	**MESSAGING**	**OTHER**
Android	In development	In development	In development	In development
C++	In development	In development	In development	In development
DotNet	In development	In development	In development	In development
Erlang/Elixir	In development	In development	In development	In development
Java	Stable	In development	In development	In development
JavaScript	Stable	In development	In development	In development
Go	Stable	In development	In development	In development
PHP	In development	In development	In development	In development
Python	In development	In development	In development	In development
Ruby	In development	In development	In development	In development
Rust	In development	In development	In development	In development
Swift	In development	In development	In development	In development

The categories for semantic conventions vary per signal:

- Traces: General, compatibility, cloud events, cloud providers, databases, exceptions, function-as-a-service (FaaS), feature flags, HTTP, object stores, messaging, and remote procedure calls (RPCs)[15]
- Metrics: General, cloud providers, database, FaaS, HTTP, RPC, and system metrics[16]
- Logs: General, exceptions, and feature flags[17]

In addition, each category contains multiple semconvs. For example, the HTTP category defines over 20 semconvs. You may be wondering how future breaking semconv changes will be handled even after semconvs become stable. To address this, OTel has the notion of a schema and a schema version number that follows semver 2.0. For semconv changes post-stability, a schema version number will be passed. For observability platforms with OTel schema support, handling different schema versions without impacting observability will be possible. More information about OTel schemas will be provided in Chapter 4.

COMMUNITY

Finally, there is the community, which is critical to the project's continued success. To ensure structure, OTel has a defined process for governing, managing, communicating, and recognizing community members. For example, OTel has an elected *governance board* (GB) and a *technical committee* (TC). These two bodies oversee the project and work with the CNCF. Contributors to the project can become members by hitting annual contribution requirements. Any GitHub contribution, whether code, issue, or comment, counts toward the contribution requirements. It is easy to see all the community events as well as get involved by visiting the community page (`https://opentelemetry.io/community`).

Beyond this, the project is made up of multiple *special interest groups* (SIGs) and *working groups* (WGs). A SIG is permanent and has at least approvers and maintainers responsible for that specific part of the project. SIGs are often responsible for one or more GitHub repositories, though that is not a requirement. Multiple SIGs exist for the specification as well as for implementation. Examples include the semantic convention specification SIG and the language-specific instrumentation library SIGs. WGs are temporary and formed to address issues that cross SIG boundaries. Examples of WGs include agent management and profiling. Both SIGs and WGs have regularly scheduled meetings that are open to the public and recorded. Contributors and users alike are encouraged to participate!

Following are the primary ways to contribute to or participate in OTel. While the project is large and the participation options may sound overwhelming, you can choose which areas of the project to follow. In addition, you will find the OTel community is welcoming and always willing to help.

- GitHub (`https://github.com/open-telemetry`): Where code, documentation, and issues exist. In addition, discussions and decisions often take place here.
- SIG or WG (`https://github.com/open-telemetry/community#special-interest-groups`): Listen, present, and provide feedback in person or the included Google Doc. This is where topics and milestones are discussed.
- CNCF Slack workspace (`https://cloud-native.slack.com/archives/CJFCJHG4Q`): Watch, comment, and post in relevant channels and threads. This is where asynchronous communication takes place. It can be a good place to ask questions, though issues should be reported on GitHub.
- Conferences: KubeCon + Cloud Native Con + Observability Day (`https://www.cncf.io/kubecon-cloudnativecon-events`) are significant events for the OTel project. In addition, there is OTel Community Day (`https://events.linuxfoundation.org/open-telemetry-community-day`) and other events that focus on observability such as DevOps Days and Monitorama.
- Social media: The OTel community can be found on platforms such as Hacker News, Mastodon, Stack Overflow, and X (formerly Twitter).

A few other important parts of the community to be aware of include:

- OTEPs, or OpenTelemetry Enhancement Proposals (`https://github.com/open-telemetry/oteps`). This is where proposed cross-cutting additions or changes are made to the project for any of its various components. Examples of OTEPs include adding new components, such as new tracer configuration options, or changing behavior, such as modifying extensibility requirements. Many OTEPs end up resulting in specification additions or changes.
- The OTel website (`https://github.com/open-telemetry/opentelemetry.io`) hosts documentation and information, including the blog, community, ecosystem, and status.

Real World Scenario

Riley Asks a Trusted Source

Riley remembered seeing a LinkedIn post from her former colleague Niko (they/them) talking about OTel, and decided to reach out. They were fans of the project, having deployed it successfully at scale in production. Niko recommended looking into the OTel Collector as an easy way to start adopting the project in her brownfield environment. They also suggested joining the CNCF Slack workspace to stay updated on the latest OTel information.

Niko shared that they got a speaker submission accepted and would be presenting at Observability Day. They asked whether Riley would be attending KubeCon this year, so hopefully, they could catch up. Riley stated that while her company did not have a travel budget this year, she had negotiated the ability to attend KubeCon North America every year as part of accepting her position. Niko and Riley agreed to meet up for lunch after the presentation.

OpenTelemetry Concepts

Beyond the core components, there are several important concepts in the OTel project that provide value and are important to understand. Some of these concepts are unique to OTel, while others are borrowed from other projects.

Distributions

Distributions (`https://opentelemetry.io/docs/concepts/distributions`) are different packaging formats of OTel components, sometimes with minor modifications. A classic example of this can be seen in the Collector releases repository (`https://github.com/open-telemetry/opentelemetry-collector-releases`), which includes core, contrib, and K8s Collector distributions. Third parties may also offer distributions outside of OTel. For example, many vendors offer distributions. A vendor distribution may be desired because it provides a minimal set of components, is easier to configure for a particular vendor, or includes additional features beyond what OTel provides. The concept of distribution is not unique to OTel. K8s also has the notion of distributions for similar reasons.[18] Easily relatable examples of K8s distributions include cloud providers like Azure Kubernetes Service (AKS).

You may be wondering if you should ever use a non-OTel distribution. Like most things, it depends. Leveraging a vendor distribution, for example, may provide support guarantees, including security and bug fixes, faster than the OTel community does. Generally, vendor distributions focus on support concerns and ease of use. You should be cautious with any vendor distribution that offers capabilities outside of OTel that will not be contributed upstream, as it may result in vendor lock-in.

You should consider using distributions when:

- The distribution provides the components you need.
- The distribution makes it easier to use OTel components.

You should avoid using distributions when:

- The distribution contains proprietary components.
- The distribution has no plans to upstream changes.

Distributions are most common for data collection components, such as the OTel Collector. Collector distributions will be covered in Chapter 5. For instrumentation, you could consider automatic instrumentation as a type of distribution separate from manual instrumentation. In addition, some languages, such as Java, include extensibility mechanisms that can be used to customize the instrumentation. Instrumentation distributions will be covered in Chapter 6.

Pipelines

Pipelines are used by OTel instrumentation and the Collector. You should think of pipelines as the configured way signals flow through a system. While this concept will be covered in depth in Chapter 5 and Chapter 6, it is worth noting that both the instrumentation and the Collector leverage the concept of a pipeline, though in slightly different ways—instrumentation needs to generate data, while Collectors need to receive data. Otherwise, the flow is the same with some amount of processing and one or more export destinations, as shown in Table 2.7.

TABLE 2.7: OTel component and pipeline flow

COMPONENT	PIPELINE FLOW
Instrumentation	Providers, Generators, Processors, Exporters
Collector	Receivers or Connectors, Processors, Exporters or Connectors

While the OTel protocol, referred to as OTLP, will be covered in Chapter 4, it is important to note that it is used to power the OTel project and the concept of pipelines. *All data generated or consumed by OTel components gets converted to OTLP*. This is what allows OTel to receive data in one format but export it in a different format. It is also what allows a single set of processors to work regardless of format. As a result, OTLP and the specification are a superset of open standards and capabilities, allowing the project to offer an extensible and vendor-neutral solution.

RESOURCES

At a high level, *resources* are a specific form of metadata applied to signals. More specifically, they are used to provide information about the origin of a signal. Resource information includes data such as the `service.name` and `service.version` as well as the `host.name`. Resource information is immutable, which means it does not change through the lifecycle of the application. In general, it is generated at service start and attached to any or all signal data generated. Resource information is a primary source of context and correlation for signals in OTel. Given that resource information is a top-level construct, it can be leveraged to batch data to reduce payload sizes. The net result is that resource information assists with problem isolation by providing the data necessary to understand where a problem is occurring. It also guarantees it is consistently applied to all signal data. The notion of and use of resources is one of the primary differences between OTel and other instrumentation or data collection forms.

Resources are defined in the SDK portion of the specification and added to signals via detectors defined in instrumentation or the Collector.[19] Semconvs for resources also exist, as shown in Table 2.8.[20]

TABLE 2.8: Resource and semconv status as of mid 2024

RESOURCE TYPE	STATUS
Cloud Provider	In development
Compute Unit	In development
Compute Instance	In development
Environment	In development
Service	Mixed (`service.name` and `service.version` stable)
Telemetry	Mixed (`telemetry.sdk.*` stable)

Resources are just one type of metadata in OTel. Another type of metadata seen across signals in OTel is *attributes*. Attributes may also have signal-specific names like labels for metrics, or tags for spans. Unlike resources, attributes are mutable, which means it can change through the lifecycle of the application. For example, a trace can have unique event attributes, static resource attributes, and dynamic operation attributes.

Registry

Given that the OTel project is large and interacts with many aspects of software development and infrastructure, the long tail of libraries, plug-ins, integrations, and other useful tools is more than the community can undertake on its own. While OTel wants to keep all core capabilities within the project, it also wants to integrate with as many frameworks, environments, and other projects as possible. As a result, OTel has a *registry* that lists first-party and third-party solutions that work with or extend OTel (`https://opentelemetry.io/ecosystem/registry`). The notion of a registry comes from the OpenTracing project.[21]

While OTel does not support third-party solutions, other end users, companies, and/or vendors may. Here are some examples of what the registry provides:

- Automatic instrumentation for specific frameworks and languages.
- Instrumentation and Collector components, including generators, receivers, processors, exporters, and extensions. Vendor components are listed here as well as components for other open source projects.
- OTel components for instrumentation languages not hosted by OTel, including Crystal, Dart, Haskell, Kotlin, OCaml, Perl, and Scala.

Roadmap

OTel is a constantly evolving project. Initially, it focused on delivering the API, SDK, and data specification for 1) traces, 2) metrics, and 3) logs. At this point, that work is mostly done, though some aspects, such as exemplars for metrics and events for logs, remain a work in progress (WIP). The specification will continue to evolve over time, though there are no plans to introduce any breaking changes to stable parts. The OTel specification even states, "Note that we currently have no plans for creating a major version of OpenTelemetry (API) past v1.0."[22] The biggest area of investment for the initial specification will be semconvs, as their stability is required to see broad adoption of OTel into other open source projects—a major goal for the project.

Information about the roadmap at the time this book was published can be found in the Appendix. For the latest information, see the OTel roadmap at: `https://opentelemetry.io/community/roadmap`. More information about the future of OTel will be provided in Chapter 12, "The Future of Observability."

The Bottom Line

Recognize observability problems and the need for open standards. Understanding the nuances of observability is essential for maintaining the health and performance of modern distributed systems. One of the primary challenges in achieving effective observability is recognizing the problems associated with disparate monitoring tools and proprietary solutions. These fragmented approaches can lead to inconsistent data, lack of interoperability, and significant gaps in visibility. The need for open standards becomes evident as organizations strive for comprehensive, coherent, and scalable observability solutions. Open standards facilitate the seamless integration of telemetry data across various systems and platforms, ensuring that teams can obtain a unified view of their operational environments.

Master It What is an open standard and why does it matter?

Explain the history and goals of the OpenTelemetry project. The OTel project represents the convergence of two significant open source projects, OpenTracing and OpenCensus, with the goal of creating a single, unified framework for generating, collecting, and analyzing telemetry data. OTel's primary objectives include providing a vendor-neutral, open standard for observability, enhancing interoperability, and simplifying the implementation of observability practices. By standardizing telemetry data, OTel allows organizations to achieve better insights into their systems, regardless of the underlying technologies or vendors they use.

Master It What does the OTel project provide, and what does it intentionally not provide?

Identify the OpenTelemetry components and project status. At its core, OTel comprises several key components: APIs, SDKs, and the Collector. The APIs and SDKs provide the means for instrumenting applications, enabling the collection of traces, metrics, and logs. The Collector serves as a pipeline that can receive, process, and export telemetry data to various observability platforms, providing flexibility and scalability. The OTel project is actively developed and widely adopted, with support for numerous programming languages and integrations with major observability platforms. Its robust community and continuous development ensure that it remains at the forefront of observability solutions, evolving to meet the demands of increasingly complex system architectures.

Master It Is OTel generally available (GA) and production-ready?

Notes

1 `https://opensource.org/osd`
2 `https://www.linuxfoundation.org`
3 `https://www.apache.org`
4 `https://aws.amazon.com/emr`
5 `https://cloud.google.com/dataproc`
6 `https://opentracing.io`
7 `https://openmetrics.io`
8 `https://prometheus.io/docs/instrumenting/exposition_formats`
9 `https://prometheus.io/blog/2024/03/14/commitment-to-opentelemetry`
10 `horovits.medium.com/openmetrics-is-archived-merged-into-prometheus-d555598d2d04`
11 `https://opencensus.io`
12 `https://opentelemetry.io/docs/specs/otel/#project-naming`
13 `https://opentelemetry.io/blog/2024/profiling`
14 `https://learn.microsoft.com/en-us/dotnet/core/diagnostics/distributed-tracing-instrumentation-walkthroughs`

15 https://opentelemetry.io/docs/specs/semconv/general/trace
16 https://opentelemetry.io/docs/specs/semconv/general/metrics
17 https://opentelemetry.io/docs/specs/semconv/general/logs
18 https://kubernetes.io/partners
19 https://opentelemetry.io/docs/concepts/resources/#resource-detectors
20 https://opentelemetry.io/docs/specs/semconv/resource
21 https://opentracing.io/registry
22 https://opentelemetry.io/docs/specs/otel/versioning-and-stability/#a-note-on-replacing-signals

Chapter 3

Getting Started with the Astronomy Shop

You can read about all the value OpenTelemetry provides and why observability matters, but they are just words until you see it in action. Now that you have a better understanding of what observability is and how OpenTelemetry helps power it, it is time to take OpenTelemetry and open source observability for a spin. In this chapter, you will embark on a practical journey to apply OpenTelemetry to a fictional e-commerce application called the Astronomy Shop. The hands-on examples in this chapter will guide you through the initial steps of integrating OpenTelemetry into a real-world project, demonstrating how to instrument applications for comprehensive observability. By working through this scenario, you will gain a concrete understanding of how to collect, analyze, and leverage telemetry data to monitor and optimize system performance. Whether you are new to OpenTelemetry or looking to deepen your expertise, the Astronomy Shop will serve as a tangible, relatable context to illustrate the powerful capabilities of observability in action.

IN THIS CHAPTER, YOU WILL LEARN TO:

- Get started with the Astronomy Shop
- Customize the Astronomy Shop
- Walk through troubleshooting scenarios

Background

The demonstration application used to show the power of OpenTelemetry (OTel) and observability is called the Astronomy Shop and is available in the OTel Demo repository (`https://github.com/open-telemetry/opentelemetry-demo`). It offers the ability to set up a polyglot, or multiple programming languages, microservices-based e-commerce application leveraging stable OTel components and sending data to popular open source observability platforms, including Jaeger, Prometheus, and OpenSearch. Docker and Kubernetes (K8s) deployments are supported. The demo application is based on the Google Online Boutique,[1] which was used as the OpenCensus Hipster Shop Demo.[2] It has been customized for OTel, including supporting additional languages and offering advanced capabilities.

Architecture

The Astronomy Shop showcases OTel's stable capabilities. It includes instrumentation for 12 languages with trace support for all languages (`https://opentelemetry.io/docs/demo/trace-features`), metric support for more than half of them (`https://opentelemetry.io/docs/demo/metric-features`), and basic log support for almost half of them (`https://opentelemetry.io/docs/demo/logging-features`). Be sure to check out the links for supported signal features, as each signal has different capabilities that may or may not be leveraged depending on the service.

While OTel provides an architecture diagram for the Astronomy Shop (`https://opentelemetry.io/docs/demo/architecture`), it may be difficult to understand. Figure 3.1 provides a simplified version of the architecture. Each service in the diagram is written in a different language and may support either HTTP or gRPC communication. These services are instrumented via automatic, manual, and/or library mechanisms and support some combination of traces, metrics, and logs. Given that OTel is a rapidly evolving project, the Astronomy Shop is updated regularly. The supported languages, instrumentation, and signals for version 1.11 are provided in the Appendix. For the latest information, see `https://opentelemetry.io/docs/demo/services`.

FIGURE 3.1 A simplified (not all services are listed) service map of the Astronomy Shop environment. The shown service map comes from the GCP microservices demo, which is the foundation of the Astronomy Shop demo.[3]

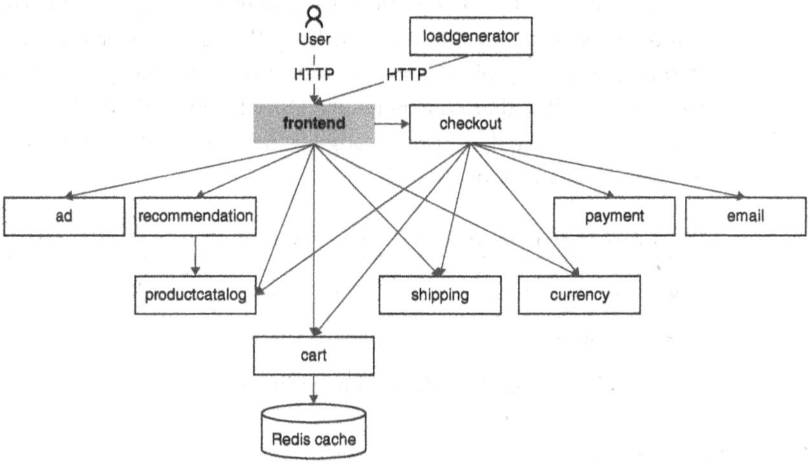

Prerequisites

First, decide whether you want to run the Astronomy Shop using Docker or K8s. Docker is typically more accessible, especially when running the application locally, but K8s may better represent your production environment—and if you are comfortable using K8s, it may be the better option. All the information in this chapter will be based on version 1.11 of the Astronomy Shop (`https://github.com/open-telemetry/opentelemetry-demo/releases/tag/1.11`) and based on a Docker deployment. For new versions of the Astronomy Shop, be sure to check the documentation in case of any changes.

The prerequisites for Docker are documented at `https://opentelemetry.io/docs/demo/docker-deployment` and include:

- Docker.
- Compose version 2.0.0 or higher.
- 6 GB of free RAM. (Verify at the preceding link in case of changes.)
- Make is an optional prerequisite to get started more easily.

The prerequisites for K8s are documented at `https://opentelemetry.io/docs/demo/kubernetes-deployment` and include:

- K8s version 1.24 or higher.
    - *Important*: Some OTel components require a minimum or maximum version of K8s. If using new versions of OTel components, verify the required K8s version.
- 6 GB of free RAM (Verify at the preceding link in case of changes).
- Helm is recommended, and Helm version 3.9 or higher is required if used. In addition, the OTel Helm chart version must be 1.11 or higher.
- You may run K8s on top of Docker when running the demo locally. In this case, Docker is also required.

The OTel demo application functionality is identical across environments. Running the Astronomy Shop with Docker will be the primary focus of this chapter.

Getting Started

Getting started is straightforward once the prerequisites are met. First, download or clone the GitHub repository located at `https://github.com/open-telemetry/opentelemetry-demo`. Next, from within the top-level repository folder, you can start the demo application in one of the ways shown next. Starting the minimal services is sufficient for most examples in this chapter. Run either the Docker or Make command shown next.

- Docker:

```
# Full demo environment with all services and tests
#docker compose up --force-recreate --remove-orphans -detach

# Minimal demo environment with a subset of services and no tests
# Removes accounting, fraud detection, and kafka services
# Removed frontend and trace-based tests
docker compose -f docker-compose.minimal.yml up \
  --force-recreate --remove-orphans -detach


# Full demo environments with tests and Observability-Driven Development (ODD)
# Leverages Tracetest (https://tracetest.io/) to build/run tests against traces
#docker compose --profile odd up --force-recreate --remove-orphans -detach
```

- Make:

```
#make start
make start-minimal
#make odd
```

The Astronomy Shop will take a while to start the first time. This is because all the Docker container images need to be pulled down. On subsequent starts, the process should be significantly faster. Updated layers must be pulled down when new releases are published and used. This means starting new releases the first time will take more time than subsequent starts.

If you want to make local changes to individual services while the Astronomy Shop is running, the following Make commands are available:

- To restart a specific service:

```
make restart service=<service_name>
```

- To rebuild a specific service:

```
make redeploy service=<service_name>
```

If you check the Makefile,[4] you will see these shortcuts issue Docker Compose commands:

```
# Run with redeploy command only
docker compose build <service_name>

# Run with restart or redeploy command
docker compose stop <service_name>
docker compose rm -force <service_name>
docker compose create <service_name>
docker compose start <service_name>
```

When you are done with the demo, be sure to stop it to save resources by running one of the following commands. Do not run these now; you will use the Astronomy Shop in subsequent sections.

- Docker:

```
docker compose down --remove-orphans --volumes
```

- Make:

```
make stop
```

Note that the state is not saved when you stop the Astronomy Shop using the preceding commands. In short, you will start from a clean state on each start. This is because of the flags or options passed to the Docker command. More information about these options can be found here: `https://docs.docker.com/reference/cli/docker/compose/down/#options`.

Accessing the Astronomy Shop

Once everything is running, you can access the Astronomy Shop from your browser by navigating to `http://localhost:8080`. From here, you will be greeted by the web store frontend, as shown in Figure 3.2.

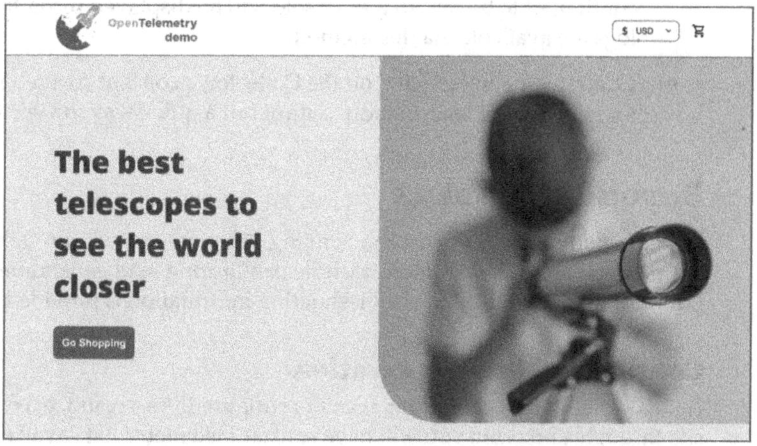

FIGURE 3.2 The OTel Astronomy Shop demo application home page.

Now, you should try out the web store! For example, you can click the Go Shopping button and select items to put in your cart. Once you are satisfied with your order, you can check out. Upon checking out, you will notice that the billing information has already been entered, but you can change the details if desired. Finally, you can place your order. As you can see, the Astronomy Shop feels like a typical e-commerce website.

Accessing Telemetry Data

Because the Astronomy Shop is the OTel demo application, everything has already been configured to demonstrate the power of stable OTel components through popular open source observability platforms. The following platforms are used:

- Metrics are stored in Prometheus.
- Logs are stored in OpenSearch.
- Traces are stored in Jaeger.

Telemetry data can be accessed as follows:

- Metrics and logs via Grafana are located at `http://localhost:8080/grafana`.
- Traces via Jaeger are located at `http://localhost:8080/jaeger/ui`.

As of version 1.11 of the Astronomy Shop, only a subset of services has been instrumented with OTel logs. The easiest way to see these logs in Grafana is by going to the Dashboards > Demo > Demo Dashboard and scrolling down to the Application Logs section. You can change the service for which logs are shown at the top of the dashboard. By default, the `adservice` is selected. At some point, you may want or need to see logs, including non-OTel logs, outside of Grafana—for example, if you make changes and want to check for errors. While not officially documented, there are various ways to access logs, including:

- Run `docker compose logs` or `docker compose logs <service>`. Note that only logs configured to be sent to the console will be displayed using this method. In short, not all logs are available via this method.
- Configure debug logging on the Collector, a concept covered in the next section. Debug logging is not a user-friendly output but a quick way to view the logs before indexing.

Beyond the Basics

With the Astronomy Shop up and running, it is time to walk through the different configuration options available. These options include configuring load generation, feature flags, tests, and the OTel Collector. In addition, troubleshooting information is provided.

Configuring Load Generation

A load generation tool is automatically configured. As a result, even without interacting with the site through a browser, you will have constant telemetry data available. To see the state of the load generation, visit the UI shown in Figure 3.3 at `http://localhost:8080/loadgen`.

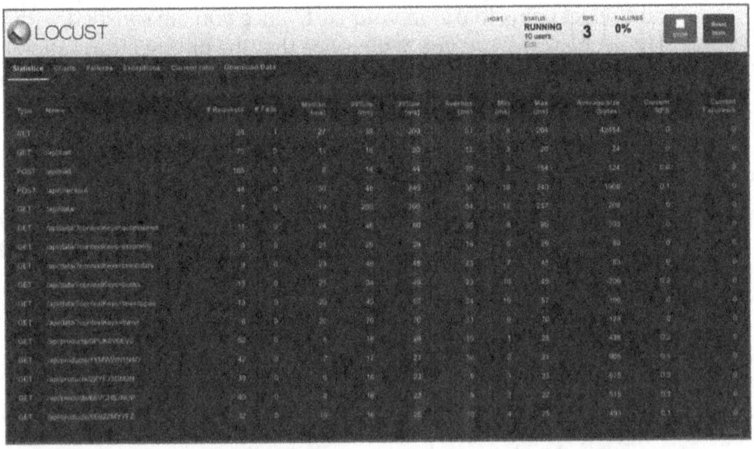

FIGURE 3.3 Load generation tool powered by Locust available as part of the Astronomy Shop.

In the upper-right corner, you can increase or decrease as well as start and stop the load generation, as shown in Figure 3.4. You will also see the number of requests per second (RPS) and failure percentage for the requests.

If you select the Edit link, you can specify the number of users and how quickly to spawn them, as shown in Figure 3.5. Be careful when setting these values, as too many users or too quick of a spawn rate may result in issues, including slow demo performance and service restarts due to high resource utilization.

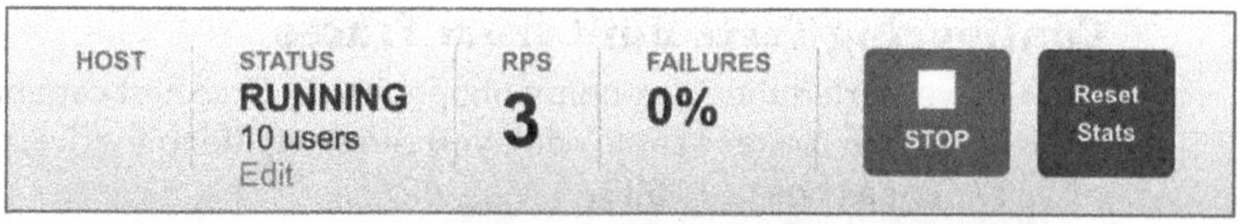

FIGURE 3.4
Load generation settings and statistics.

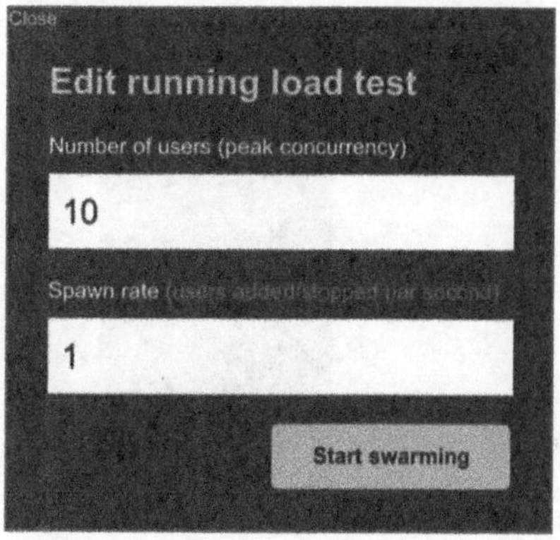

FIGURE 3.5
Load generator settings to control the number of concurrent users as well as the spawn rate. The higher the number of users, the more resources that are required to run the Astronomy Shop.

Configuring Feature Flags

As of version 1.11, the ad service generated errors by default. In the future, it is likely the OTel demo application will not have any configured errors by default. Be advised that you may see a few errors in the telemetry data, but this is typically due to the initial start of the Astronomy Shop or a restart due to resource utilization. The Astronomy Shop supports enabling different error scenarios to test OTel capabilities and your ability to achieve observability. For example, you can add errors to certain services or introduce a memory leak issue. You need to edit the feature flag service (flagd) configuration to enable scenarios. As of version 1.11, the only option is to edit the JSON configuration file located at `src/flagd/demo.flagd.json`. (If you are using a new version, check the documentation for a possible UI.) For example, if you want to enable the recommendation service cache failure scenario, you should change the default variant to `"on"`:

```
"recommendationServiceCacheFailure": {
  "description": "Fail recommendation service cache",
  "state": "ENABLED",
  "variants": {
    "on": true,
    "off": false
  },
  "defaultVariant": "on"
},
```

If the JSON file is updated while the Astronomy Shop is not running, it will take effect when it starts. If the JSON file is updated while the Astronomy Shop is running, then changes may or may not take effect. If they do not take effect, then see `https://github.com/open-telemetry/opentelemetry-demo/issues/1625` and either restart the flagd service by running `make restart service=flagd` or restart the Astronomy Shop with something like `make stop && make start-minimal`.

Configuring Tests Built from Traces

If you have started the Astronomy Shop with the Tracetest capability outlined in the "Getting Started" section (`make start odd`), you can navigate to the Tracetest UI (shown in Figure 3.6) at `http://localhost:11633`.

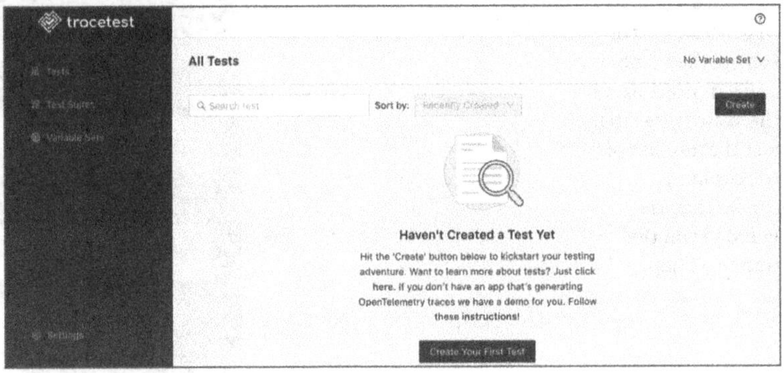

FIGURE 3.6 The home page for the Tracetest UI that is available as part of the Astronomy Shop.

From here, you can create tests based on traces. To do so, follow a procedure like the following:

1. Select Create.
2. For Trigger, keep the default of HTTP Request and select Next.
3. Select the Choose Example drop-down and the Otel – Get Product option. Select Next.
4. Select Create & Run.

The test will now run in the background. While the test will take several seconds to complete, you can review the test configuration in the left panel and the response data in the right panel. Soon, you should see a "Trace has been fetched successfully" notification. Switch to the Trace tab at the top to see the analysis of the test.

Configuring the OTel Collector

While it is great that the OTel demo application comes with open source observability platforms to see the value of OTel end-to-end, you may wish to see data in a different platform or try out other capabilities of OTel. To do this, you can update the OTel configuration. Given that all data flows through the Collector, editing the Collector configuration is the best way to start. While Collector configuration will be covered in Chapter 5, "Managing the OpenTelemetry Collector," in short, you need to edit a YAML file to change the configuration. The OTel demo application supports leveraging an extra YAML, which is just a secondary configuration file that is located at `src/otelcollector/otelcol-config-extras.yml`. The extra YAML file gets merged with the default YAML configuration, located at `src/otelcollector/otelcol-config.yml`. There are a couple of important things to note when editing the extra YAML file:

- Objects are merged and arrays are replaced.
- If overridden, the `spanmetrics` exporter must be included in the array of exporters for the `traces` pipeline. Not including this exporter will result in an error.

Suppose you wanted to change the location where trace data was sent. In that case, you should edit the extra YAML file, add the exporter you want to leverage, create an override of the `traces` service pipeline, and restart the Collector service or the entire Astronomy Shop. For example, if you wanted to add another OTLP destination for traces, you would add the following, then either restart the Collector service or the Astronomy Shop, as outlined in the "Getting Started" section, for the configuration to take effect:

```
exporters:
  otlphttp/example:
    endpoint: <your-endpoint-url>

service:
  pipelines:
    traces:
      exporters: [otlp, debug, spanmetrics, otlphttp/example]
```

If you look in the exporter section of the default Collector configuration file, you will notice one of the exporters enabled is the `debug` exporter. The `debug` exporter is configured to use the default settings. As a result, it provides only statistical information. To see the raw data being exported, you must increase the verbosity in the `debug` exporter. You can either override the `debug` exporter in the extra YAML file or create a new named `debug` exporter like the following:

```
exporters:
  debug/detailed:
    verbosity: detailed

service:
  pipelines:
    logs:
      exporters: [otlp/logs, debug/detailed]
```

Once this has been added to the extra YAML and the Collector is restarted, you can review the logs by running `docker compose logs otelcol`. You can see all the logs generated and sent to the Collector with the preceding changes. Note that verbose debugging should be used only for *non-production* and *low-volume* traffic. Also, note that verbose debugging can consume *significant resources* and *may result in Collector restarts* if the Collector is not sized and configured properly.

Real World Scenario

WATCHWHALE OTel SUPPORT

After researching the OTel Collector's capabilities, Riley was convinced OTel was the right solution to adopt. She asked the Watchwhale account team if they supported using the OTel Collector. While they recommended using their Watchwhale Agent, they said the Collector could send data to the Watchwhale platform. They did warn that support for the upstream Collector was "best effort." Given the broad community support for OTel and the amount of money Jupiterian was paying for Watchwhale, Riley acknowledged the risk and decided to move forward.

She requested a link to documentation on how to configure the Collector to send data to Watchwhale. She learned that she needed to specify a specific destination URL, generate Watchwhale API tokens via the UI or API, and add Watchwhale API tokens securely to the Collector configuration per signal. With the appropriate information, she configured the OTel's Astronomy Shop Demo on her laptop. She configured it to send data to her Watchwhale account in addition to the open source observability platforms running locally. Given this was a non-production environment, she opted to add the API token in plain text to the YAML file. She made a note to use AWS Secrets Manager support in the Collector over environment variables when moving to production.

With everything configured, she could now compare the functionality of Prometheus and Watchwhale without changing the production environment!

Configuring OTel Instrumentation

While the OTel demo application comes with OTel instrumentation fully configured, it is possible to change the instrumentation to meet your needs or help you gain comfort with OTel instrumentation. While instrumentation configuration will be covered in Chapter 6, "Leveraging OpenTelemetry Instrumentation," in short, you edit the application code to add or change aspects, including attributes, span events, and span status. After saving the changes, you need to redeploy the changed service (`make redeploy service=<service>`). After running this command, you will receive feedback on the build status and, assuming it is successful, you will be able to see your instrumentation changes in the configured observability platform.

The Astronomy Shop contains a polyglot microservices architecture enabling you to test any stable OTel instrumentation. Check the demo services documentation (`https://opentelemetry.io/docs/demo/services`) for possible instrumentation changes.

Troubleshooting Astronomy Shop

While the OTel demo application is tested extensively, you may encounter unexpected situations. In general, stopping and starting the Astronomy Shop should get you back online. If this does address the issue, then the problem is likely related to resource utilization. For example, one or more containers may consume more resources than the configuration allows. Alternatively, the entire application may be consuming more than Docker, K8s, or the local system has available. One reason why this might happen is due to user configuration, such as increasing load generation. If local changes were made at the repository level and a restart does not fix the issue, then reverting the changes or checking the logs is recommended. When the Astronomy Shop is running, live logs for all services can be reviewed by running `docker compose logs -f` (remove the `-f` flag to see all logs as of the time the command was run). Alternatively, logs for individual services can be reviewed by running `docker compose logs -f <service_name>`.

Another helpful thing to check is how long the containers have been running. Unless containers are manually restarted, the uptime should be roughly the same time, as all containers are started together. If one or more containers show shorter uptimes than the rest, this may indicate an issue being experienced, such as resource limits being hit. To check the uptime of containers, you can run `docker ps`.

Astronomy Shop Scenarios

Now that you understand how to get the Astronomy Shop running and configured, it is time to get some hands-on experience navigating different scenarios demonstrating the power of OTel. Please note that these examples were created and verified using the OTel demo version 1.11. If you are using a newer version of the demo, you may be unable to reproduce these scenarios. If you do experience issues with a newer version, your options include:

- Checking the GitHub repository associated with this book
- Checking the OTel documentation for the latest documented scenarios
- Reverting to version 1.11 to simulate the scenarios documented in the following sections

Troubleshooting Errors

An easy way to demonstrate the power of OTel is by generating and searching for errors. Here is a way to simulate this situation:

1. Enable the `defaultVariant` for the `productCatalogFailure` feature flag in `src/flagd/demo.flagd.json` and save the file. See the "Configuring Feature Flags" section earlier for more details.
2. If the Astronomy Shop is running when you make this change, you may need to restart the flagd service by running `make restart service=flagd`, as described in the "Configuring Feature Flags" section, for the changes to take effect. Otherwise, start the Astronomy Shop.
3. In the browser, navigate to the Jaeger UI located at `http://localhost:8080/jaeger/ui`.
4. From the Service drop-down, select the `checkoutservice`. (Note that you could search for the `productcatalogservice`, but for this scenario, a specific trace is being used to demonstrate error propagation.)
5. In the Tags input box, enter `error=true`.

6. Click the Find Traces button.
7. If you do not get any results, wait a few minutes, and then click the Find Traces button again. You can also try increasing the Limit Results to a higher number.
8. When you get results, select a trace by clicking on a circle in the graph that, on hovering, says, `loadgenerator: POST` or by clicking a row in the table below the graph, as shown in Figure 3.7.

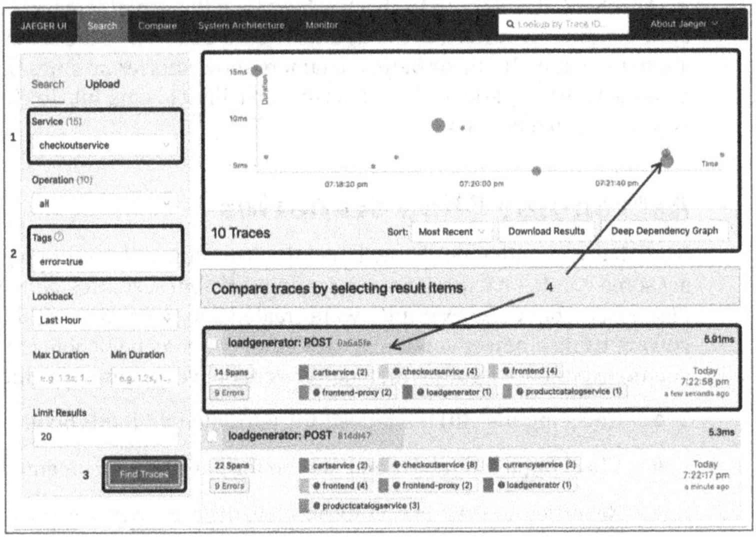

FIGURE 3.7 Jaeger UI searching for traces from the product catalog service (1) where at least one span has an error tag (2). Examples of such traces (3) can be viewed by selecting a circle in the graph or a row in the table below the graph (4).

9. You will notice that several spans contain errors, as denoted by an exclamation point, as shown in Figure 3.8.

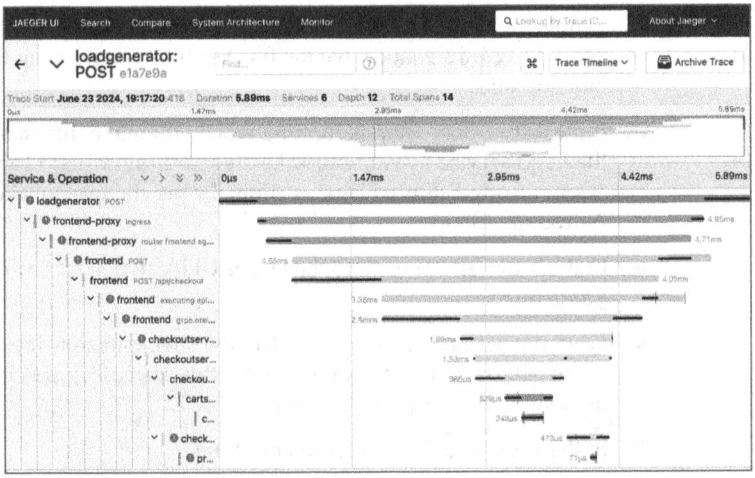

FIGURE 3.8 Example trace containing the product catalog service and at least one span with an error tag. All spans with an error have an exclamation point to the left of the service name.

10. Click the `productcatalogservice` span to expand it, and then the Tags header to expand the cell, as shown in Figure 3.9.

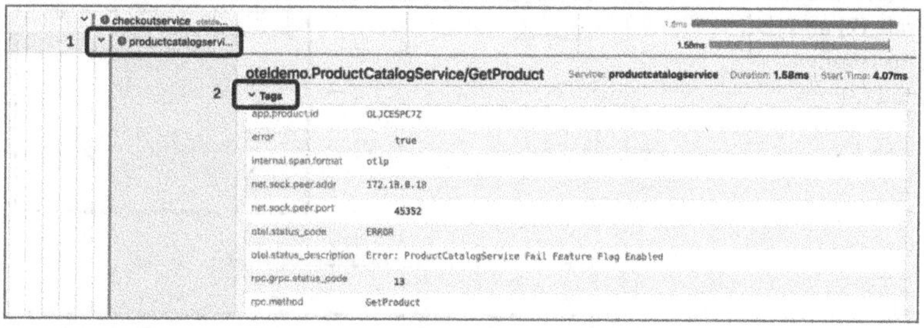

FIGURE 3.9 Tags from a product catalog service span accessed by selecting the span name (1) and then the Tags header (2).

11. Check the tags to determine the reason for the error.
12. Click the `checkoutservice` span directly above the `productcatalogservice` span, and then the `Tags` header to expand the cell within the `checkoutservice`.
13. Check the `checkoutservice` tags to determine the reason for the error (see Figure 3.10).

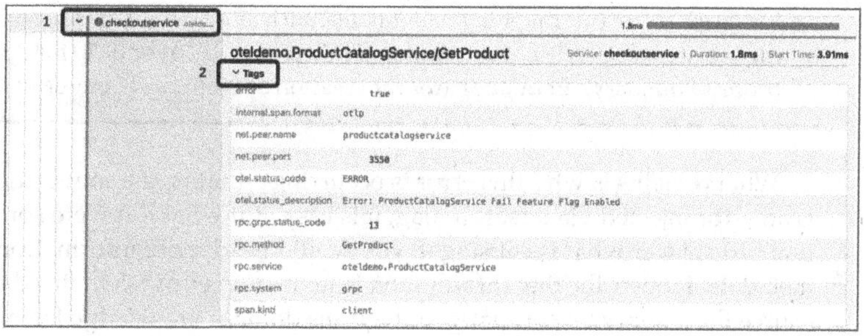

FIGURE 3.10 Tags from a checkout service span accessed by selecting the span name (1) and then the Tags header (2).

You used traces and the Jaeger UI to investigate the issue in this scenario. Upon investigation, you learned that the most nested span error, the `productcatalogservice`, was where the problem originated. You also noted that the error propagated to all upstream services, including the `checkoutservice` and the `frontend`.

While you identified a service generating an error, also known as *problem isolation*, you do not know how much traffic is experiencing that problem yet. To determine that from Jaeger, select the Monitor tab at the top of the page (see Figure 3.11) and then change the Service to `productcatalogservice`. Now you can see that around 10 percent of the traffic is failing, and the call failing is `/GetProduct`.

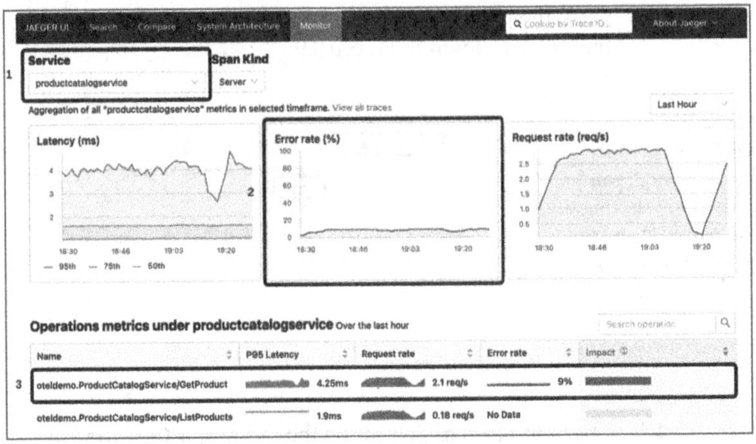

FIGURE 3.11 Jaeger UI Monitor tab for the product catalog service (1). Notice the error rate (2) and the operation name impacted (3).

SPAN KIND

Spans should contain a piece of metadata known as a *span kind*, as shown in Figure 3.12. The span kind provides a hint to the tracing platform on how the trace should be assembled. Span kind values include `Client` (for outgoing remote calls, such as an outgoing HTTP request), `Server` (for incoming remote calls, such as an incoming HTTP request), `Internal` (for operations that do not cross a process boundary), `Producer` (for the creation of a job), and `Consumer` (for the processing of a job).

What remains is why this error is occurring—that is, the root cause. Given that you know this is an error injected via a feature flag, it is easy. But what if it were some random error in production? To answer what is causing it, you would need more information, typically in the form of metadata. Hopefully, that information is tagged on your telemetry data and not in some data source that cannot be correlated or requires domain knowledge from a subject matter expert (SME). Assuming the additional information is available, you would need the ability to analyze the metadata and look for what could be causing the errors. Analysis of the metadata on spans generating errors may show they are coming from a variety of sources, including:

- A certain build number (application)
- A particular customer (user)
- A specific container, host, region, or location (infrastructure)

Unfortunately, Jaeger does not provide an easy or scalable way to do tag analysis on spans. This means manual searching needs to be done, an SME is needed, or work must be put in to provide this functionality. Of course, this is on top of ensuring that sufficient metadata is added to all signal data. For this scenario, if you could do a tag analysis, you would find that all errors come from a particular product ID. You will find that all `productcatalogservice` spans that contain errors have a tag of `app.product.id=OLJCESPC7Z`. You can replace the search condition `error=true` with `app.product.id=OLJCESPC7Z` to manually confirm that all error spans from `productcatalogservice` contain this product ID.

As you can see, this is a simple example of a synthetic error. This scenario demonstrates how easy it is to search for errors from traces and isolate the issue. With that said, you needed to know what service to look at; otherwise, you would have needed to search each to determine where errors are located. In addition, you needed to manually search, as Jaeger does not provide a built-in way to alert about certain scenarios. In production environments, manually searching for problems is not scalable.

Ideally, configured alerts are used before a significant issue arises, but regardless, alerts are typically the starting place to investigate production issues. In the worst case, end users report issues, which triggers an investigation. From the onset, people typically start with metrics to check the health of the environment. Here are the steps you can take to start with metrics in this scenario:

1. In the browser, navigate to the Grafana UI located at `http://localhost:8080/grafana`.
2. Click into the Search or jump to. . . box.
3. Select Dashboards > Demo > Demo Dashboard.
4. From the Service drop-down, select `productcatalogservice`.
5. If you do not see results for any of the Spanmetrics panels, then you may need to change the min step for the widgets to `30s`. To do this, select the three dots in the upper right of a widget in the panel and select Edit. For each letter (A, B, C . . .) in the Query (at the bottom of the page), select Options to expand, and enter the min step value. After completing for all letters in the query, select Apply at the top of the screen. Repeat for each impacted widget.
6. Notice that the Error Rate for `productcatalogservice` by span name returns results and that these errors started recently, as shown in Figure 3.12.

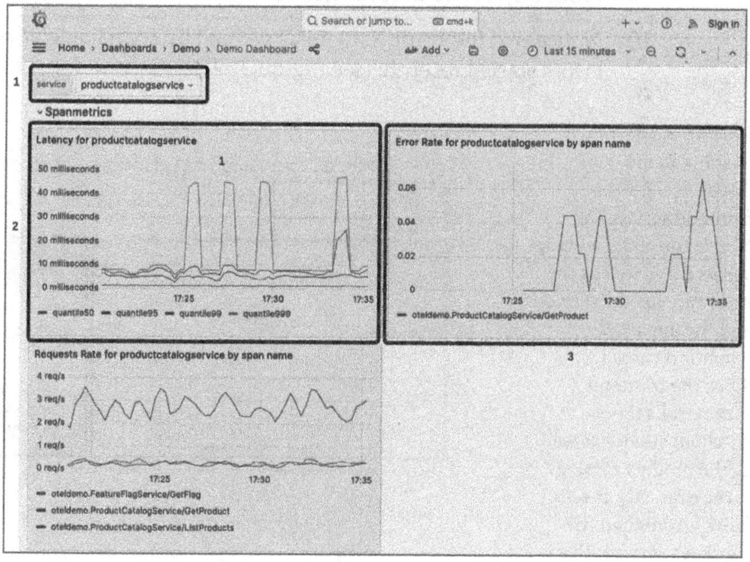

FIGURE 3.12 Grafana Demo Dashboard for the product catalog service (1). Notice the p99.9 latency spikes (2) as well as the error rate for the service and the impacted operation name (3).

7. From the Service drop-down, select `frontendservice`.
8. Notice that the Error Rate for `checkoutservice` by span name (see Figure 3.13) also returns results and that these errors started recently.

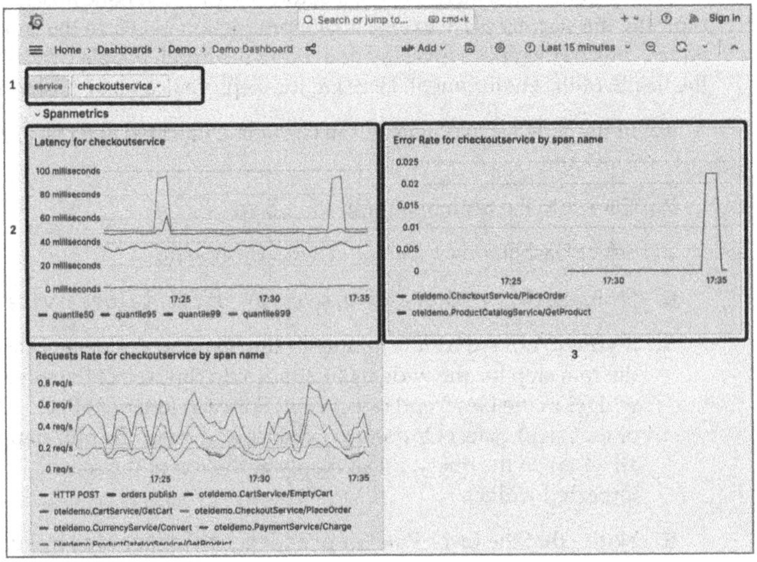

FIGURE 3.13 Grafana Demo Dashboard for the checkout service (1). Notice the p99.9 latency spikes (2) as well as the error rate for the service and the impacted operation name (3).

9. From the Service drop-down, select `frontend`.
10. Notice that the Error Rate for `frontend` by span name also returns results and that these errors started recently (see Figure 3.14).

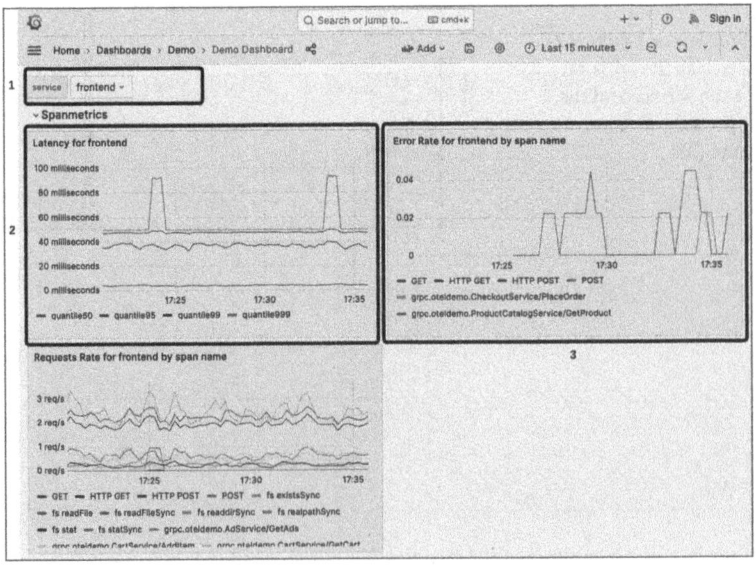

FIGURE 3.14 Grafana Demo Dashboard for the frontend service (1). Notice the p99.9 latency spikes (2) as well as the error rate for the service and the impacted operation name (3). Since the frontend service calls the checkout service as well as the product catalog service directly, it sees more errors than the checkout service. This is because the frontend service is reporting transitive errors.

For Grafana, you can see that the Demo Dashboard required knowing which service to look at. While you could select each option in the drop-down, it is more likely that you either configured and received an alert or had information from another source that helped isolate the issue. For example, you may have configured an alert when errors on a span were outside of normal bounds, resulting in your checking the Demo Dashboard. If you did configure such an alert, you might have been alerted about multiple services, including the `checkoutservice` and the `frontendservice`, even though the issue started from the `productcatalogservice`. If different teams own these services, each team may have been paged to investigate the issue. As you can see, while alerts are important to be notified about issues, care must be taken to ensure alerts are isolated and actionable.

Alternatively, the Spanmetrics Demo Dashboard configured within Grafana makes it possible to review information across all services. Select Demo from the breadcrumbs near the top of the page, and then select the Spanmetrics Demo Dashboard. This dashboard provides latency and error information. If you scroll down to the Top 7 span_names and Errors (APM Table) widget (Figure 3.15), you will see that the `oteldemo.ProductCatalogService/GetProduct` call is generating many errors. This call is one of many services reporting errors, so it may not be apparent if there is an actual issue and where it is coming from.

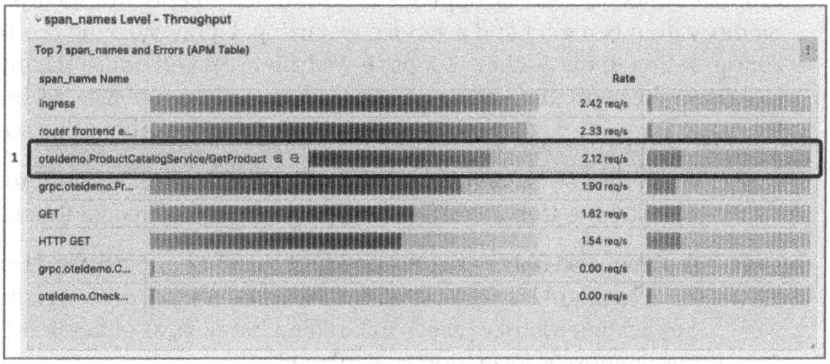

FIGURE 3.15 Grafana Spanmetrics Demo Dashboard. Notice the error rate for the product catalog service (1).

As you can see, multiple ways to investigate errors based on telemetry data exist. All the examples to date have focused on manual and reactive troubleshooting to show the value of OTel and observability solutions quickly.

Troubleshooting Availability

On the one hand, while errors are a potential scenario to be concerned with, intermittent errors may occur within an environment and may not represent an issue worth investigating. On the other hand, the availability of services is typically something to be concerned about. Next, you will simulate an availability issue and troubleshoot it. To get started:

1. Start the Astronomy Shop.
2. Open a browser and navigate to Grafana located at `http://localhost:8080/grafana`.
3. Search for and select the Demo Dashboard. On the dashboard, select the `productcatalog` service, change the time range on the upper-right side to Last 15 minutes, and select the drop-down next to the refresh dashboard icon to the right of the time picker and select 5s.

4. In the browser, go to the load generation site located at `http://localhost:8080/loadgen`.
5. Select Edit in the upper-right corner to configure the number of concurrent users.
6. Change the users to 3,000 and spawn to 50, and then select Save.
7. In the browser, go back to the Grafana dashboard and watch it over the next few minutes. You will notice the latency and request rate spike and, shortly thereafter, dip.
8. While the spikes should be expected, the dip is likely not. Why do you think this happened?
9. From the CLI, run `docker ps`. You should notice that the `loadgenerator` service restarted. (It may not be the only service that restarted.)
10. On the same Grafana dashboard, scroll down to review the Application Metrics. What do you notice?

While you might have been able to guess why the spike subsided, hopefully, the telemetry data provides enough evidence to confirm. In short, the `loadgenerator` service's memory utilization steeply increased, plateaued, and then steeply dropped. This is a good indication of a memory limit being hit and a service restarting. Upon checking the `loadgenerator` container configuration in the `docker-compose.yml` file, you will notice the limit is set to `120M`. If you want to sustain the configured concurrency, then you must increase this limit to prevent the availability issue. There are a couple of important things to note about this scenario:

- When the load generator service restarts, the settings revert to the default. If you want to simulate the scenario after the restart, you must change the settings again.
- You may also notice that the `productcatalog` or even the `frontend` restarted. These services might have restarted for the same reason. Still, it cannot be confirmed from the Application Metrics panels in Grafana because, as of version 1.11, only Python-based CPU and memory information is displayed.

Try this scenario again, but this time change the spawn rate to 150 instead of 50. While the same situation occurs, the memory spike is not shown in the memory widget. Why not? The reason is that the metric collection interval is set at 10 seconds, and since the spike and dip occur within the 10-second window, the data is not properly captured. This is one of the trade-offs of sampling. Collecting data less frequently reduces costs but also reduces visibility.

Troubleshooting Performance

Another important and more complex example that demonstrates the power of OTel is generating and searching for latency or performance issues. Here is a way to simulate this situation:

1. Enable the `defaultVariant` for the `recommendationServiceCacheFailure` feature flag in `src/flagd/demo.flagd.json` and save the file. See the "Configuring Feature Flags" section earlier in this chapter for more details.
2. If the Astronomy Shop is running when you make this change, you may need to restart the flagd service by running `make restart service=flagd`, as described in the "Configuring Feature Flags" section, for the changes to take effect. Otherwise, start the Astronomy Shop.

3. Open a browser and navigate to the load generation site located at `http://localhost:8080/loadgen`.
4. Select Edit in the upper-right corner to configure the number of concurrent users.
5. Change the users to `50` and spawn to `1`, and then select Save.
6. In the browser, navigate to the Grafana UI located at `http://localhost:8080/grafana`.
7. Search for and select the Demo Dashboard. On the dashboard, select the `recommendation service`, change the time range on the upper-right side to Last 15 minutes, select the drop-down next to the refresh dashboard icon to the right of the time picker, and select 5s.
8. Wait 10 minutes and then check the dashboard. What do you notice?
9. If you do not see results for any of the Spanmetrics panels, you may need to change the min step for the widgets to `30s`. To do this, select the three dots in the upper right of a widget in the panel and select Edit. For each letter (A, B, C, D) in the Query (at the bottom of the page), select Options to expand, and enter the min step value. After completing for all letters in the query, select Apply at the top of the screen. Repeat for each impacted widget.

You should see a spike in latency and memory, as shown in Figure 3.16.

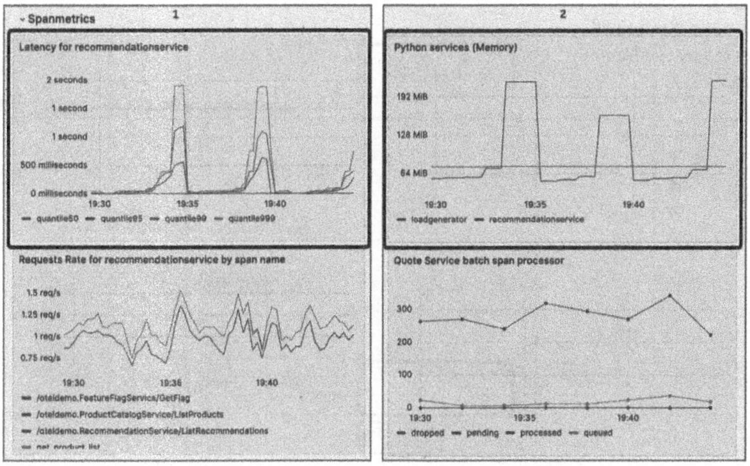

FIGURE 3.16 Example of the demo dashboard for the recommendation after running the latency scenario. Be sure to check out the graphs for latency (1) and memory (2).

Real World Scenario

WATCHWHALE'S METRIC SUPPORT

Riley decided to enable the recommendation service cache failure feature flag in the Astronomy Shop Demo. Since she deployed the demo application locally and configured it to send data to both her existing Prometheus instance as well as Watchwhale using the OTel Collector, she could determine what it would take to configure the Watchwhale platform. Riley started by looking at

Watchwhale's built-in dashboards and alerts. Next, she attempted to create her own dashboards and alerts. She recorded her findings to discuss with the account team and determine whether she was missing anything.

After review, the account team strongly recommended using the Watchwhale Agent, as they noticed several pieces of data were missing from the Collector. They identified missing container statistics from kubelet as well as important pod labels. Riley was surprised and concerned by this finding. She returned to the OTel demo application and noticed that it restricted the pod labels applied and did not configure the Kubelet stats receiver. Relieved, she confidently assured the account team that the issues found were easily addressable.

Why are these spikes occurring? This may initially look like the troubleshooting availability scenario, but the behavior is not quite the same. The `recommendationservice` appears to be restarting, but it does so under consistent load. If you look closely at the memory graph, you will notice that memory usage is gradually increasing over time. Perhaps this is a memory leak. Use Jaeger to see what else is going on:

1. In the browser, navigate to the Jaeger UI (see Figure 3.17) located at `http://localhost:8080/jaeger/ui`.

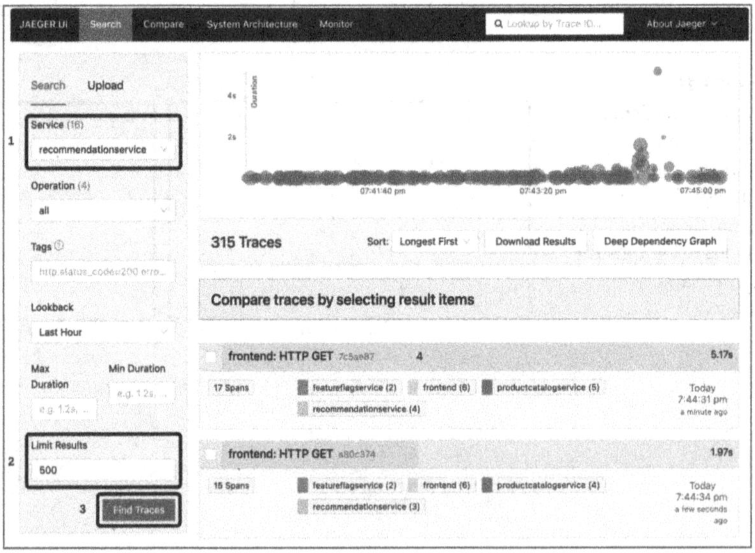

FIGURE 3.17 A Jaeger search (3) for traces that contain the recommendation service (1) sorted by the longest duration (2).

2. Select the `recommendationservice`, increase the Limit Results to 500, select Find Traces, and then change the Sort to Longest First.
3. Select the trace with the largest duration.
4. Notice that the `recommendationservice` spans have the largest duration. Expand the `get_product_list` operation and then its Tags (see Figure 3.18).
5. You should notice this span has some application-specific metadata. Two values from the application metadata are suspicious: `app.cache_hit` is `false`, and `app.product.count` is large.

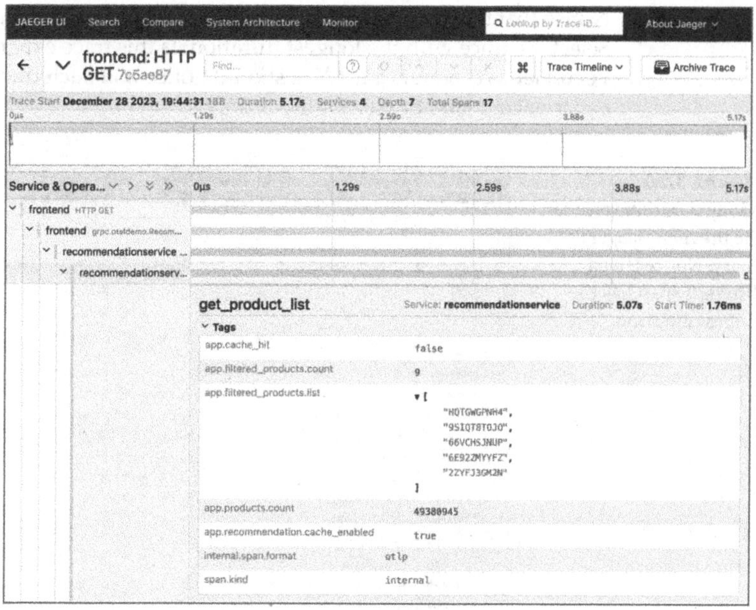

FIGURE 3.18 A long duration trace for the previous Jaeger query. Notice that the recommendation service span has the longest duration.

6. Select Search in the Jaeger top navigation bar to validate whether slow `recommendationservice` spans have similar attributes.

7. Select the `recommendationservice`, enter a tag of `app.cache_hit=true`, increase the Limit Results to 500, select Find Traces, and then change the Sort to Longest First (see Figure 3.19).

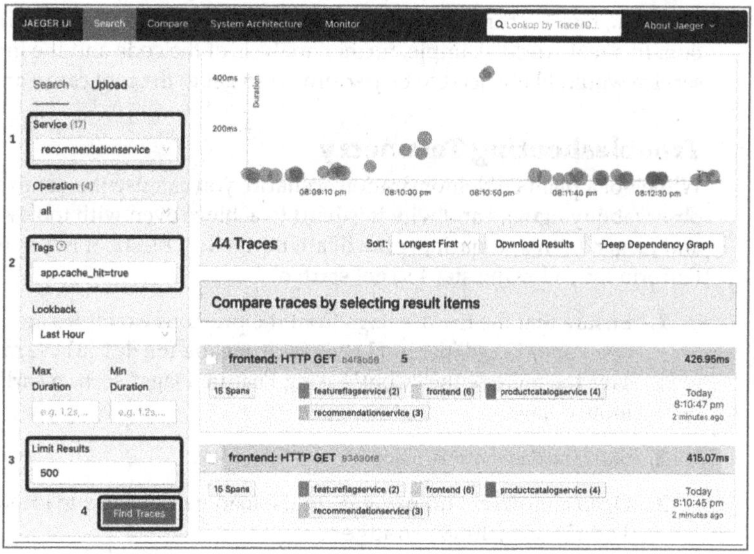

FIGURE 3.19 A Jaeger search (4) for traces that contain the recommendation service (1) with a specific tag (2) and sorted by the longest duration (3).

8. Notice that most, if not all, of the results are under 100 milliseconds in duration. Select the trace with the longest duration. Is this trace experiencing latency with the `recommendationservice`? You should notice that such traces have a different span experiencing latency (see Figure 3.20).

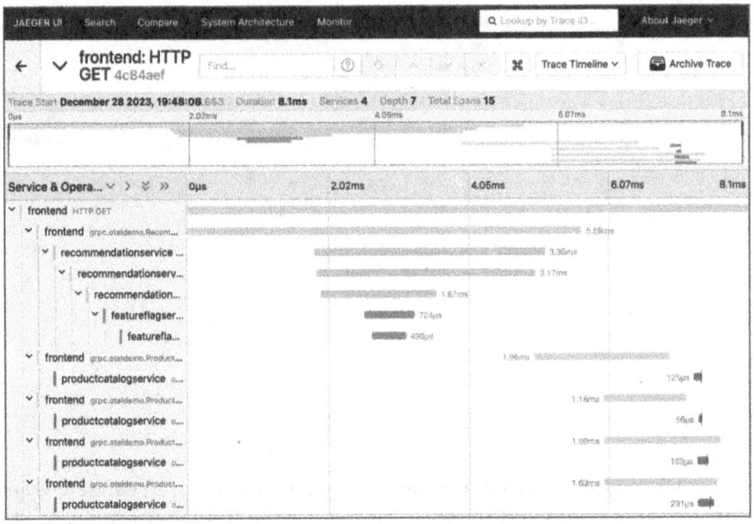

FIGURE 3.20 A long duration trace for the previous Jaeger query. Notice that a different span has the longest duration.

9. Change the tag in the search to `app.cache_hit=false`, rerun the search, and change the Sort to Longest First.

10. Notice that the results have a longer duration with this query.

Again, this is a contrived scenario, so it is easy to perform root cause and implement remediation. In a real-world example, further analysis of the code and the interactions with the impacted service would likely need to be performed to get to the root cause and remediation.

Troubleshooting Telemetry

While not a planned demonstration scenario, you can use the demo application to see why observability matters and why it is hard to achieve even with tools such as OTel, Prometheus, and Jaeger. In this scenario, you will attempt to troubleshoot issues with the telemetry data. Perform the following steps to get started:

1. Ensure that the feature flags from the previous examples are disabled. To confirm this, open `src/flagd/demo.flagd.json`, ensure the `defaultVariant` is off for each flag, and save the file. See the "Configuring Feature Flags" section earlier in this chapter for more details.

2. Start the Astronomy Shop.

3. Open a browser and navigate to the load generation site located at `http://localhost:8080/loadgen`.

4. Select Edit in the upper-right corner to configure the number of concurrent users.
5. Change the users to `1600` and spawn to `50`, then select Save.
6. Switch to the Charts tab and watch as the load increases. Wait about a minute until Total Requests per Second stabilizes around 400 and Response Times begins to increase.
7. Switch to the Failures tab, and you will likely see a couple of HTTP 503 failures.
8. Search for these failures in Jaeger by selecting the `frontend-proxy` service and entering a tag of `http.status_code=503`. Did you find any errors? Did you find all the errors from the Failures tab on the load generation UI?
9. Go back to the Charts tabs in the load generator UI. Notice how the latency fluctuates quite a bit over time.
10. Within 10 minutes after increasing the load, you should start seeing a large spike in latency, even higher than the initial spike when the load was being increased, and RPS will decrease.
11. Search for high latency traces in Jaeger by selecting the `loadgenerator` service, selecting Find Traces, and sorting by Longest first. If you do not see traces around one second in length, increase the Limit Results and try again. You can increase the Limit Results to `1500`, though the larger the number, the longer it will take to return results.
12. Click one of the high latency traces and see what request is taking long. You should find that `GET` or `POST` requests from the frontend service are slow. Using just the telemetry solutions, determine why these requests are slow.
13. Using just the telemetry solutions, determine if containers are restarting. If so, determine why they are restarting.

The point of this scenario is to demonstrate that observability—even with telemetry data and powerful observability platform capabilities—is hard. Achieving observability and being able to use it during live production issues to get services back online requires an investment. In order to answer the questions in this scenario, several things need to be added, including:

- Additional telemetry data or changes to the sampling strategy should be made so that errors in the load generation UI are also included in the observability data.
- Alerts should be created for situations including container restarts, anonymous latency or RPS behavior, and specific errors.
- More dashboards should be created to show the health of services, including resource utilization and limits as well as changes in behavior.

The Bottom Line

Get started with the Astronomy Shop. The Astronomy Shop provides a hands-on introduction to integrating OpenTelemetry into a real-world application with open source observability platforms. This fictional e-commerce platform serves as an excellent sandbox for experimenting with telemetry collection and instrumentation. Through the prescriptive guidance in this chapter, you learned the foundational steps of implementing OpenTelemetry, including adding instrumentation to track critical metrics, logs, and traces.

Master It Which components of the OTel project does the demo application showcase?

Customize the Astronomy Shop. The Astronomy Shop is batteries-included, meaning it showcases all the stable functionality OTel has to offer out of the box. Customizing the Astronomy Shop allows you to tailor the observability setup to meet your specific needs and requirements. By modifying the default configurations and adding custom instrumentation, you can learn about OTel and observability platforms while focusing on the most relevant aspects of the application for your use case. Customization ensures that you can derive maximum value from the telemetry data collected, making your observability efforts more meaningful and actionable.

Master It In order to send telemetry data to a different observability platform, which OTel component would you change and how would you change it?

Walk through troubleshooting scenarios. The Astronomy Shop supports enabling troubleshooting scenarios to highlight the power of OTel and observability solutions. Walking through troubleshooting scenarios with the Astronomy Shop demonstrates the practical utility of OTel and observability platforms in diagnosing and resolving issues. Through real-world examples, you learned how to utilize the collected telemetry data to identify performance bottlenecks and trace errors, and to understand system behavior under various conditions. These scenarios highlight the importance of comprehensive observability in maintaining application reliability and performance.

Master It How do you enable troubleshooting scenarios in the Astronomy Shop?

Notes

1 `https://github.com/GoogleCloudPlatform/microservices-demo`

2 `https://github.com/census-ecosystem/opencensus-microservices-demo`

3 `https://github.com/GoogleCloudPlatform/microservices-demo/blob/main/docs/img/architecture-diagram.png`

4 `https://github.com/open-telemetry/opentelemetry-demo/blob/main/Makefile`

Chapter 4

Understanding the OpenTelemetry Specification

Now that you have experienced the value OpenTelemetry provides, it is time to deep dive into the project's various components. As mentioned, the foundational framework underpinning the entire OpenTelemetry project is its open standard, known as the *specification*. The specification defines the standards and protocols for generating, collecting, and exporting telemetry data, ensuring consistency and interoperability across diverse systems and platforms. By understanding the OpenTelemetry specification, you will gain insight into how different components of OpenTelemetry work together seamlessly to provide comprehensive observability.

While you do not need to review the specification to start taking advantage of OpenTelemetry, it does cover important concepts that explain how OpenTelemetry behaves and what to expect. In addition, the specification is used to define the instrumentation and the Collector covered in the subsequent chapters. This chapter will cover the key elements of the specification, including the data model, the APIs and SDKs, and the OpenTelemetry Protocol (OTLP).

Note that this chapter is quite technical and meant primarily for software developers. It also uses signal-specific terminology that you may not be familiar with. When possible, alternative definitions and explanations will be provided for clarity. All code examples are available in the book's GitHub repository (`https://github.com/flands/mastering-otel-book`).

IN THIS CHAPTER, YOU WILL LEARN TO:

- Distinguish between OpenTelemetry versioning and stability, including support guarantees.
- Understand the OpenTelemetry data model, including protocol support and OTLP.
- Differentiate between the OpenTelemetry API and SDK.

Background

The OpenTelemetry (OTel) specification (`https://opentelemetry.io/docs/specs/otel`) is critical to ensure consistency across implementations. For example, while there are programming language–specific nuances, you do not want differences in behavior or output. The specification promotes software best practices. It is designed to separate responsibilities (API versus SDK), maintain backward compatibility, and ensure that OTel users with different operational roles—which product managers often refer to as *personas*—can perform their roles with minimal interference. It is organized into the following four major categories (which will be broken down in the subsequent sections):

- API, which includes signal and context
- SDK, which includes signal, configuration, and resource
- Data, which includes semantic conventions (in a separate repository), communication protocols (in a separate repository) and management (in a separate repository), and compatibility with other standards
- General, which includes versioning, stability, and guidelines

One question that you might immediately raise is what the difference is between the API and the SDK, especially given that both provide definitions for signals. As shown in Figure 4.1, the API provides an interface to generate but not emit telemetry data. At the same time, the SDK contains and implements the API and provides the functionality necessary to configure, process, and export telemetry data. The separation between the API and SDK is an intentional design decision in the OTel project for multiple reasons:

- Separation of concerns: Library authors, application owners, and operators have different responsibilities and goals. Combining concerns results in each of these users having to perform the duties of the other roles to achieve their goals.
- Dependencies: If the API and SDK were coupled, depending on the API would mean depending on the SDK and its numerous dependencies. In addition, libraries and frameworks must be able to use instrumentation without causing a transitive dependency conflict. The SDK is likely to contain transitive dependencies that would result in conflicts.
- Extensibility and optimization: While the SDK is designed to be extensible and performant, there is always a trade-off when attempting to optimize between these two aspects. A single SDK may not be ideal for all use cases. Separation of the API from the SDK provides necessary flexibility.
- Long-term stability: Adding manual instrumentation may result in a large number of API calls being added to an application. As such, manual instrumentation may result in a significant dependency on the API. If breaking changes are introduced, then a lot of work would be required to update these calls. As a result, long-term support of the API is critical. This is not the case for the SDK.

Decoupling the API and SDK Example

An example of the power of separating the OTel API and SDK can be seen in the Microsoft .NET `System.Diagnostic.DiagnosticSource`, as described in Chapter 2, "Introducing OpenTelemetry!." Microsoft had `Activity` interfaces that could be used to generate trace and metric data before OTel existed. In short, they already had a tracing and metrics API. With a few changes (version 5.0.0 or newer), they aligned closely with the OTel specification. In addition, they offer an OTel API shim (`https://github.com/open-telemetry/opentelemetry-dotnet/blob/main/src/OpenTelemetry.`

Api/README.md#instrumenting-using-opentelemetryapi-shim) that can be used if you want to leverage OTel terminology, such as *Tracer* and *Span*. They also support using the Microsoft API with the OTel SDK (https://learn.microsoft.com/en-us/dotnet/core/diagnostics/distributed-tracing-instrumentation-walkthroughs). For more information, see the OTel documentation (https://opentelemetry.io/docs/languages/net/instrumentation/#a-note-on-terminology). If the OTel API and SDK had not been decoupled, then Microsoft would have needed to create a new API and migrate users, which would have been very disruptive.

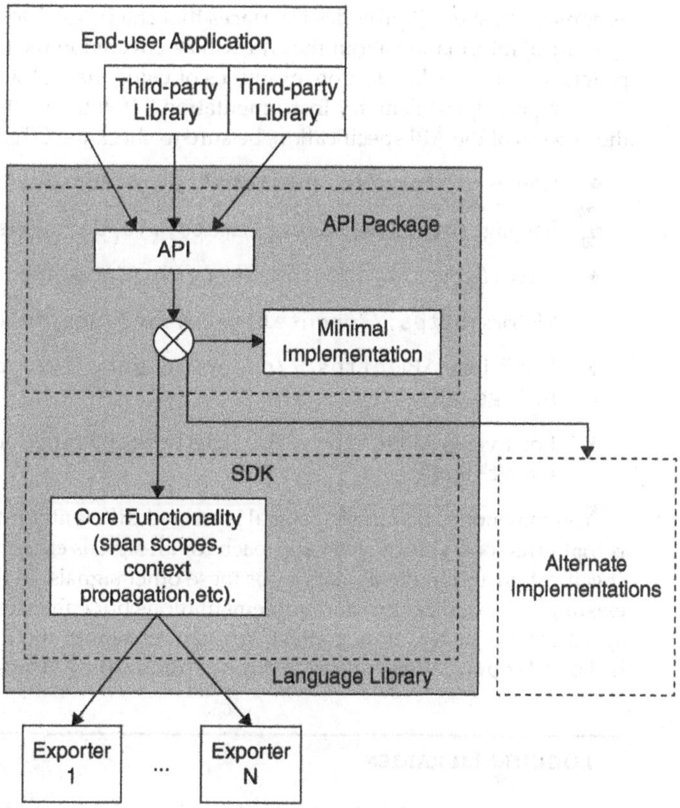

FIGURE 4.1 Visualization of the generic design for OTel instrumentation.[1]
Source: [1] / OpenTelemetry Authors/ CC BY 4.0.

API Specification

As mentioned, the OTel API provides an interface to generate but not emit telemetry data. It is required to implement instrumentation. The goals of the API include minimizing transitive dependencies and maximizing supportability. The API specification contains definitions of the following components:

- Signals, including baggage, traces, metrics, and logs
- Context, including propagators
- Attributes

API Definition

Application programming interfaces (or APIs[2]) are common in software and used to provide programmatic access to software. In short, they provide a contract on how to interact with an object. As the name implies, the OTel API specification is a definition or contract for an API. It "consists of the cross-cutting[3] public interfaces[4] used for instrumentation. Any portion of an OpenTelemetry client which is imported into third-party libraries and application code is considered part of the API."[5] In software, interfaces are ways to interact with software and can be public or private. Public interfaces are meant to be interacted with outside of a library, including by third parties or nonproviders of the code. The OTel API specification covers all signals as well as context. In short, it provides interfaces that can be used to instrument applications with OTel.

Critical information about the API will be covered in the following sections, but not for every provided interface. In addition, examples of using the API will be covered in Chapter 6, "Leveraging OpenTelemetry Instrumentation." If you are interested in learning more about all the aspects of the API specification, be sure to check the OTel documentation:

- Context (`https://opentelemetry.io/docs/specs/otel/context`)
- Baggage (`https://opentelemetry.io/docs/specs/otel/baggage/api`)
- Traces (`https://opentelemetry.io/docs/specs/otel/trace/api`)
- Metrics (`https://opentelemetry.io/docs/specs/otel/metrics/api`)
- Log Bridge API (`https://opentelemetry.io/docs/specs/otel/logs/bridge-api`)
- Log Events API (`https://opentelemetry.io/docs/specs/otel/logs/event-api`)

You may notice that the log signal is treated differently from other signals. The reason for this is that OTel took a clean-sheet approach for all signals except logs and provided a complete specification and implementation for these other signals. In the case of logs, OTel leverages existing log specifications and implementations but enhances them with additional OTel-based specifications such as trace context. You can read more about how logs are handled in OTel here: `https://opentelemetry.io/docs/specs/otel/logs`.

Logging Libraries

OTel does not provide logging libraries. Instead, OTel relies on existing implementations and enhances them with capabilities including trace context and OTLP exporting. An example of OTel logging can be found in .NET logging. .NET offers `Microsoft.Extensions.Logging`, which can be used in conjunction with `OpenTelemetry.Logs`. For more information, see `https://learn.microsoft.com/en-us/dotnet/core/extensions/logging`.

API Context

While context has been mentioned several times throughout this book, it is not a concept that has been explored deeply. This is because up until this point, you have not been exposed to manual instrumentation, and context has been provided automatically. OTel defines context as "a propagation mechanism which carries execution-scoped values across API boundaries and between logically associated execution units."[6] Propagation as a concept should be familiar from Chapter 3, "Getting Started with the Astronomy Shop," where an error propagation example using traces was explored. The execution-scoped values are values contained within the context. The context itself may hold many of these values. It itself is not a value. The context itself is immutable. To propagate a context with different values, a new context is created from the original with updated values. In short, context is a state that can be accessed through the lifecycle of a transaction. This state is usually represented as key-value pairs and is passed between different APIs and services, most commonly through HTTP headers.

The notion of context is not unique to OTel, and where language-specific non-OTel context mechanisms exist, OTel specifies that they should be used. OTel mandates that context be supported, so if such a mechanism does not exist in a language, then the OTel implementation must provide it.

Another important concept related to context is propagators. Propagators are "objects used to read and write context data to and from messages exchanged by the applications."[7] Examples of propagators were covered in the "Traces" section of Chapter 1, "What is Observability?". Within the tracing signal, context propagation is a concept that has been around for a while and has various open standards available. OTel officially supports W_3C, B3, and Jaeger propagators for all languages.[8]

Finally, while baggage is technically a signal, it behaves just like context. In fact, baggage interacts with context and propagators. Baggage is a set of application-defined properties.[9] It can be inserted or extracted from context and passed between arbitrary boundaries. Of course, given that context is immutable, baggage is also immutable.[10]

API Signals

A variety of API interfaces are supported for every signal. In general, the interface structure is *Signal Provider*, *Signal Recorder*, and, if applicable, a *Subcomponent of the Signal Recorder*. For example:

- Traces support `TracerProvider`, `Tracer`, and `Span`.
- Metrics support `MeterProvider`, `Meter`, and `Instrument`.
- Logs support `LoggerProvider` and `Logger`.

These interfaces will become important in Chapter 6 when you will manually instrument an application. Until then, here is what you should know about these interfaces:

- A Signal Provider is a stateful object that holds all the Signal Recorders.
- An application should use a single Signal Provider and may have one or more Signal Recorders.
- A Signal Provider must provide a way to get its respective Signal Recorder.
- A Signal Provider must be the only way to create a Signal Recorder.
- The interfaces supported by signals are vast and signal specific.

API Implementation

While the API is built as a self-sufficient dependency, by itself, no telemetry data will be delivered to an observability platform, as shown in Figure 4.2. As a result, most end users will not use the stand-alone API independently. They will install the SDK.

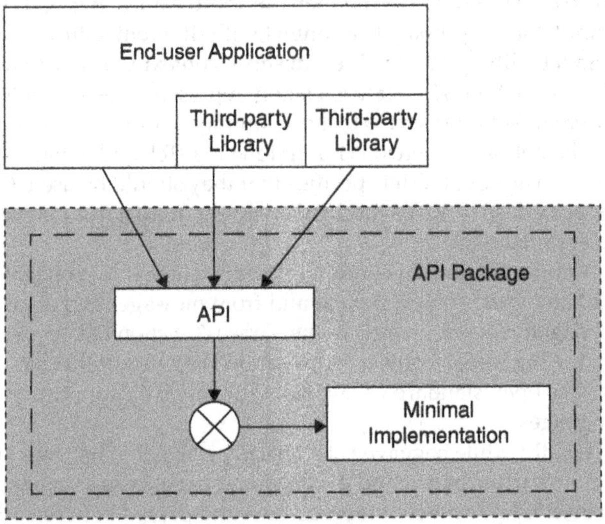

FIGURE 4.2 Visualization of how the OTel API would be implemented in an application.[11] In short, an application or third-party library would call the OTel API. The OTel API only contains the constructs to add instrumentation. By itself, it does not support exporting data other than to the console.

Source: [11] / OpenTelemetry Authors/ CC BY 4.0.

> **TIMESTAMP RESOLUTION**
>
> As mentioned in Chapter 1, all signal data should include a timestamp. OTel supports up to nanosecond resolution for traces (`https://opentelemetry.io/docs/specs/otel/trace/api/#time`), metrics (`https://opentelemetry.io/docs/specs/otel/metrics/data-model/#sums`), and logs (`https://opentelemetry.io/docs/specs/otel/logs/data-model/#field-timestamp`), whereas traces only require a minimum of millisecond resolution (`https://opentelemetry.io/docs/specs/otel/trace/api/#timestamp`). The reason for this is that some popular tracing instrumentation and platforms only support millisecond resolution, and OTel wanted to ensure compatibility.

SDK Specification

As mentioned, the OTel SDK implements the API and provides the interfaces necessary to configure, process, and export telemetry data. It is required to implement instrumentation. The primary goal of the SDK is to export data. In addition, it makes it easy to leverage the API and provides the tools necessary to get value out of the telemetry data generated. The SDK specification includes definitions of the following components:

- Signal-specific processors, exporters, and samplers

- Configuration
- Resources

SDK Definition

Software development kits, or SDKs, are common in the software space and are used to provide a collection of tools that software developers can use to build or leverage software quickly and in a standardized way. SDKs often include one or more APIs. Examples of SDKs include the Java Development Kit (JDK)[12] and the Cloud SDK for Google's Cloud Platform.[13] Per the OTel specification, "the SDK is the implementation of the API provided by the OpenTelemetry project. Within an application, the SDK is installed and managed by the application owner."[14] As you may recall from the API definition, the API specifies all cross-cutting concerns. The SDK provides public interfaces for non-cross-cutting concerns. The SDK separates these public interfaces into the following two categories:

- Constructors are used by application owners and include configuration objects, environment variables, and SDK builders.
- Plug-in interfaces are used by plug-in authors and include processors, exporters, and samplers.

The OTel SDK specification covers these interfaces for all signals as well as:

- Configuration: OTel requires that SDK configuration be possible programmatically and via a file, while environment variables (envvars) are optional.
- Resources: OTel requires that the SDK provide access to a resource with at least semantic attributes with a default value. A resource is an "immutable representation of the entity producing telemetry."[15] Beyond the options to create and merge resources, resource detectors may be implemented to add metadata automatically.

In short, the OTel SDK implements interfaces that can be used to instrument applications with OTel. Critical information about the SDK will be covered in the following sections, but not for every interface. In addition, examples of using the SDK will be covered in Chapter 6. If you are interested in learning more about all the aspects of the SDK specification, be sure to check the OTel documentation:

- Configuration (`https://opentelemetry.io/docs/specs/otel/configuration/sdk-configuration`)
- Resources (`https://opentelemetry.io/docs/specs/otel/resource/sdk`)
- Traces (`https://opentelemetry.io/docs/specs/otel/trace/sdk`)
- Metrics (`https://opentelemetry.io/docs/specs/otel/metrics/sdk`)
- Logs (`https://opentelemetry.io/docs/specs/otel/logs/sdk`)

SDK Signals

For every signal, common functionality for a Signal Provider is supported, including shutdown (what to do when the application is asked to stop) and force flush (how to ensure all in-memory data is exported to avoid data loss—especially useful during a shutdown) as well as integrating with signal-specific processors and exporters. Other signal-specific functionality is also provided. While the API provides the functionality necessary to generate telemetry data, the SDK provides functionality for concerns beyond telemetry generation. The Signal Provider implementation stores this configuration information.

Two terms mentioned multiple times in this book but not defined deeply are processors and exporters. As the names imply, processors do something with the data, whereas exporters send the data to some destination. These concepts will be explored further in Chapter 5, "Managing the OpenTelemetry Collector," and Chapter 6. For now, you should know that the SDK defines interfaces to configure processors and exporters. These interfaces are used by the Signal Provider when telemetry is emitted as well as during shutdown and force flush. In terms of processors, all telemetry data signals except metrics (so traces and logs) require a simple (passthrough) and a batch (wait a period of time or until a specific size is reached) processor. In terms of exporters, requirements are signal-specific:

- Traces: OTLP, standard out (stdout), Jaeger, and Zipkin
- Metrics: OTLP, standard out (stdout), in-memory, and Prometheus
- Logs: OTLP and standard out

Finally, the SDK defines defaults and limits, compatibility and concurrency requirements, and signal-specific requirements.

METRICS AND PROCESSORS

The metric signal does not currently define a processor interface. While the default metric SDK behavior can be thought of as batching, it is distinct in that it does not preserve the original measurements. It will aggregate all these values into a single value. In addition, a metric filter is in development,[16] but it is also not a processor. Most metric processing is done in the Collector today. It is possible that instrumentation-based metric processors will be introduced in the future.

SDK Implementation

The SDK replaces the minimal implementation in the API with functionality that translates OTel API calls into data that is ready to be exported, as shown in Figure 4.3. Most end users will leverage the OTel SDK when running instrumented applications.

Data Specification

The OTel data specification covers the requirements for data models, communication protocols, semantic conventions, and compatibility guidelines with other standards. Critical information about the data specification will be covered in the following sections, but not for every option. In addition, examples of using the data specification will be covered in Chapter 5 and Chapter 6. If you are interested in learning more about all the aspects of the data specification, be sure to check the OTel documentation:

- Data models, including for metrics (`https://opentelemetry.io/docs/specs/otel/metrics/data-model`) and logs (`https://opentelemetry.io/docs/specs/otel/logs/data-model`)

- Protocols, including the OTel Protocol, known as OTLP (`https://opentelemetry.io/docs/specs/otel/protocol`), and the Open Agent Management Protocol, known as OpAMP (`https://opentelemetry.io/docs/specs/opamp`)
- Semantic conventions (semconvs) (`https://opentelemetry.io/docs/specs/otel/semantic-conventions`) and telemetry schemas (`https://opentelemetry.io/docs/specs/otel/schemas`)
- Compatibility (`https://opentelemetry.io/docs/specs/otel/compatibility`)

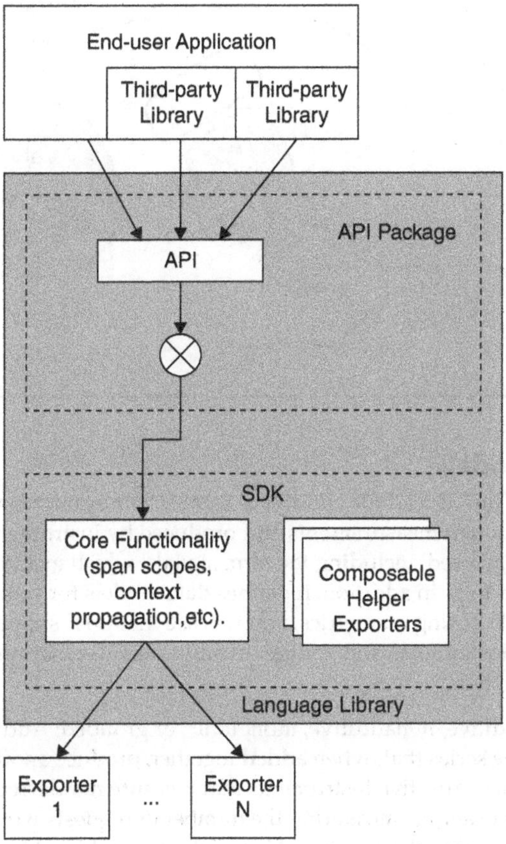

FIGURE 4.3 Visualization of how the OTel SDK would be implemented in an application.[17] The SDK contains the API and allows for configuration, processing, and exporting capabilities. Source: [17] / OpenTelemetry Authors/ CC BY 4.0.

Real World Scenario

WATCHWHALE'S OTel COMMITMENT

Riley knew that adopting Watchwhale would require client-side changes, such as configuring the Whalewatch endpoint and API token, and server-side changes, such as creating new dashboards and alerts. She knew that while a proof of concept (PoC) can easily prove capabilities, the long-term investment required to realize the complete value would be significant. Riley was interested in adopting the OTel specification to future-proof any investment the company made. She asked the Watchwhale account team about their support for OTel standards, including the OTel Protocol (OTLP), telemetry schemas, and semantic conventions. The account team reinforced their support for OTel and ensured her that full OTel compatibilities were planned. They provided a link to a blog post demonstrating this commitment. She made a note to follow up with the account team and test these capabilities once available.

Data Models

Chapter 1 introduced the concept of signals. For example, metrics were defined as time series created through measurements and produced by instruments. The OTel specification defines the terminology used, including the term signals, which includes data sources such as metrics, traces, and logs. In addition, it defines data models for signals, including metrics, as shown in Table 4.1. Focusing on metrics, you will see that OTel supports various instruments, including counters, histograms, and gauges. In addition, OTel instruments have multiple properties, including being:

- Additive, nonadditive, monotonic, or grouped: Additive instruments produce summable time series that, when added together, produce another meaningful and accurate time series. Additive instruments that measure nondecreasing numbers are called *monotonic*. For example, measuring the number of requests would be additive and monotonic, while measuring the number of connections would just be additive. Nonadditive instruments produce time series that should not be summed together, such as the data used for gauges. Grouped time series are represented as a histogram.
- Synchronous or asynchronous: Synchronous instruments are invoked by what they measure, while asynchronous instruments periodically collect measurements. For example, measuring the number of requests would typically be synchronous, while measuring the CPU time would be asynchronous.

Metrics are aggregated, which involves combining multiple measurements into a single data point. How aggregation occurs depends on the instrument's properties. OTel comes with default aggregations for each instrument. Additive instruments such as counters use a sum aggregation;

histograms are both an instrument and aggregation type; and nonadditive instruments such as gauges use the last available measurement. Default aggregations can be changed by creating a view. In short, a view is used to customize the output of the metric data generated. The time span over which the data is exported, known as *temporality*, also matters. For example, an exported sum can be either *cumulative*, indicating that measurements are accumulated for the life of the instrument, or *delta*, indicating that measurements are reset each collection period. This distinction can be significant based on what the observability platform supports. Histograms can be either *explicit buckets*, meaning they are defined during initialization, or *exponential*, meaning the buckets are dynamically computed based on an exponential scale. Temporality is not applicable to the Last Value aggregation. Temporality is configured when creating instrumentation. Beyond temporality, metrics can also be reaggregated in the following ways:

- Spatial: Used to reduce the number of attributes on a metric
- Transformative: Used to change the temporality of metrics that are sum aggregated (cumulative to delta or vice versa)

TABLE 4.1: The metric instruments available in OTel, along with their associated properties, type, and default aggregation

INSTRUMENT	PROPERTIES	TYPE	DEFAULT AGGREGATION
`Counter`	Monotonic	Synchronous	Sum
`UpDownCounter`	Additive	Synchronous	Sum
`ObservableCounter`	Monotonic	Asynchronous	Sum
`ObservableUpDownCounter`	Additive	Asynchronous	Sum
`Gauge`	Nonadditive	Synchronous	Last Value
`Observable Gauge`	Nonadditive	Asynchronous	Last Value
`Histogram`	Grouped	Synchronous	Histogram

Like metrics, OTel also provides a log data model. In short, a log record is made up of one or more fields. In addition, a field can be either a named top-level field or a map containing arbitrary values of different types. Table 4.2 shows the list of possible fields in a log record.

TABLE 4.2: Field names available to log records and what they mean

FIELD NAME	DESCRIPTION	NOTES
`Timestamp`	When the event occurred	Common syslog concepts
`ObservedTimestamp`	When the event was observed	
`SeverityText`	Log level	
`SeverityNumber`	Numeric value of log level	
`Body`	The message of the log record	

TABLE 4.2: Field names available to log records and what they mean *(CONTINUED)*

FIELD NAME	DESCRIPTION	NOTES
`Resource`	Source information	OTel concept; metadata
`Attributes`	Additional information	
`InstrumentationScope`	Scope that emitted the log record	
`TraceId`	Request trace ID	Used to enable trace correlation (covered in Chapter 6)
`SpanId`	Request span ID	
`TraceFlags`	W_3C trace flags	

Data Protocols

According to the OTel documentation, the OTel wire protocol or protocol, known as OTLP, "describes the encoding, transport, and delivery mechanism of telemetry data between telemetry sources, intermediate nodes, such as collectors, and telemetry backends. OTLP is a general-purpose telemetry data delivery protocol designed in the scope of the OpenTelemetry project."[18] OTLP is paramount to the OTel project, allowing it to be extensible and vendor-agnostic. *All data generated or received by OTel components is converted to OTLP.* As a result, any OTel component that can receive and/or export data must support an OTLP receiver and/or exporter. More information about OTLP exporting is available here: `https://opentelemetry.io/docs/specs/otel/protocol/exporter`. OTLP is implemented over gRPC (HTTP 2.0) and HTTP 1.1 transports and uses Protocol Buffers or Protobuf schema with either binary or JSON encodings for payloads. Regarding transport, OTLP must support no compression and gzip compression options. The data protocol specification defines the default ports and transport requests, including concurrency, responses, retries, and throttling.

In addition to OTLP, an agent management protocol, called OpAMP, is defined. This protocol was created to enable capabilities including status reporting, remote configuration, and auto-updating of the OTel Collector (or any agent). Especially at scale, these capabilities can be beneficial if you do not have another way to provide them. OpAMP is a specification whose client-side components have been implemented in the Collector. Extensive information and configuration of OpAMP will be covered in Chapter 6.

Data Semantic Conventions

Semantic conventions were covered in Chapter 1. In short, they define the names, known as *keys*, that describe commonly observed items used by applications. Semantic conventions are vast and can be grouped into signal- and area-specific categories. The data specification defines OTel reserved attributes and namespaces: `https://opentelemetry.io/docs/specs/otel/semantic-conventions`. A dedicated repository captures area- and signal-specific semantic conventions: `https://github.com/open-telemetry/semantic-conventions`. The contents of this repository are published in the OpenTelemetry website documentation: `https://opentelemetry.io/docs/specs/semconv`.

Semantic conventions are critical to telemetry sources, such as OTel instrumentation, and consumers of telemetry, such as observability platforms. Sources want to ensure standardization of metadata names, while consumers may need to depend on metadata names to support features such as querying and alerting. As a result, any modification to a semantic convention is a *breaking change*, which is something that changes the previous behavior. To address this, OTel supports the notion of a *telemetry schema* (`https://opentelemetry.io/docs/specs/otel/schemas`). A telemetry schema has a defined file format and URL and is versioned. In addition, it explicitly defines transformations required to convert data between different versions. Telemetry schemas are in development and only become applicable once semantic conventions are marked stable.

Telemetry sources include information about the schema consumers can monitor and react to. As demonstrated in Figure 4.4, schema-aware observability platforms can support changes to semantic conventions.

In addition, the Collector, which is a telemetry consumer, supports schema transformations via a processor (`https://github.com/open-telemetry/opentelemetry-collector-contrib/tree/main/processor/schemaprocessor`), as demonstrated in Figure 4.5. This processor is still in development.

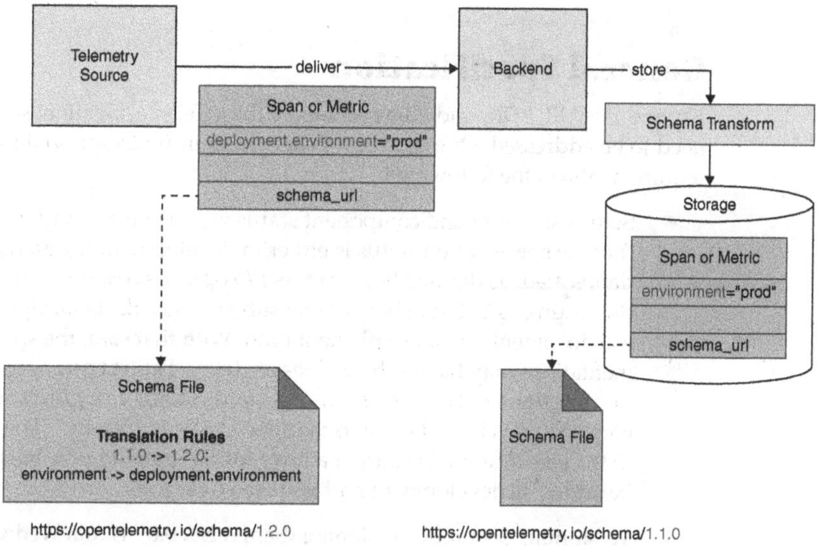

FIGURE 4.4 An example of an OTel telemetry schema version change and how a schema-aware observability platform supports the change.[19]
Source: [19] / OpenTelemetry Authors/ CC BY 4.0.

Data Compatibility

OTel's goal is to be the standard for telemetry data. To achieve this, it needs to be compatible with other open standards. A great example of the need for compatibility is the precursor projects to OTel, namely OpenTracing and OpenCensus. To provide a migration path to OTel, the project provides compatibility shims and defines specification requirements to support them. In addition, OTel provides signal-specific compatibilities, including:

- Traces: W_3C, B3, and Jaeger context propagation
- Metrics: Prometheus and OpenMetrics
- Logs: Trace context in non-OTLP formats

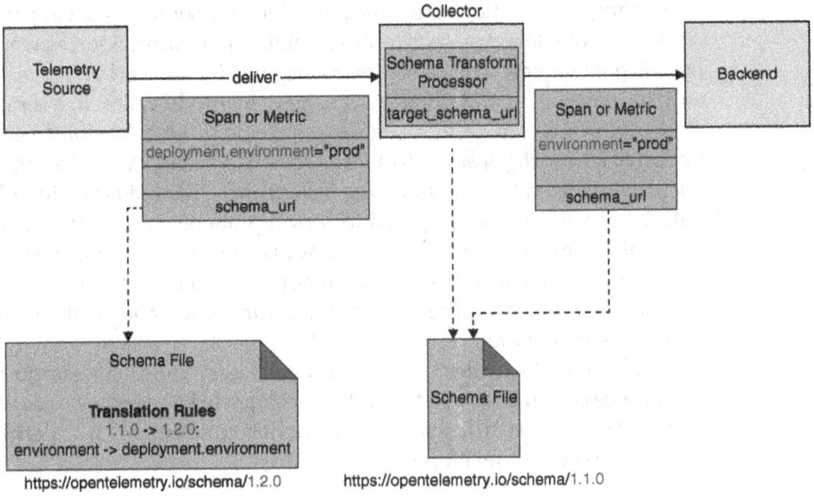

FIGURE 4.5 An example of an OTel telemetry schema version change and how the schema transform processor in the Collector supports the change.[20]
Source: [20] / OpenTelemetry Authors/ CC BY 4.0.

General Specification

Beyond the API, SDK, and data sections of the OTel specification, some cross-cutting concerns need to be addressed. One significant concern is around supportability. The specification defines requirements on the following:

- Statuses: Project and component status were covered in Chapter 2, but it is worth noting that the specification status is either in development (formerly experimental), stable, or deprecated, as defined here: `https://opentelemetry.io/docs/specs/otel/document-status`. There are no sub-statuses like beta, alpha, or RC, as the specification is a document, not an implementation. With that said, the specification states that implementations may have sub-statuses as defined at `https://opentelemetry.io/docs/specs/otel/versioning-and-stability/#experimental`, and there are conversations to add them to the specification officially.[21] The mixed status is also critical to the specification because it allows for the stability of some parts while other parts can be added as development and matured over time.
- Versioning: Semantic Versioning (SemVer) 2.0.0[22] is followed with some additional requirements as defined here: `https://opentelemetry.io/docs/specs/otel/versioning-and-stability/#version-numbers`.
- Stability guarantees: All stable components must ensure backward compatibility with themselves. A stable API must be supported for at least three years after the release of the next major version, while a stable SDK and contrib (OTel-supported extensions) must be supported for at least one year. Only forward compatibility is guaranteed between the API and SDK. For example, SDK version 1.3.0 is not guaranteed to work with API version 1.4.0 or newer. In addition, stable semantic conventions, once adopted, must be supported until a new schema version is made available, as defined here: `https://opentelemetry.io/docs/specs/otel/telemetry-stability`. See the "Data Semantic

Conventions" section earlier in this chapter for more information. In addition, information about long-term support is described here: `https://opentelemetry.io/docs/specs/otel/versioning-and-stability/#language-version-support`.

In addition, the specification defines many common terms and practices for builders of the OTel APIs and SDKs (not generally applicable to all readers), including:

- Common attributes: a form of metadata and introduced in Chapter 1 (`https://opentelemetry.io/docs/specs/otel/common`).
- Error handling (`https://opentelemetry.io/docs/specs/otel/error-handling`)
- Library design principles (`https://opentelemetry.io/docs/specs/otel/library-guidelines`)
- Performance and blocking of the API (`https://opentelemetry.io/docs/specs/otel/performance`)
- Performance benchmarking of the API (`https://opentelemetry.io/docs/specs/otel/performance-benchmark`)
- Upgrading approach (`https://opentelemetry.io/docs/specs/otel/upgrading`)

The Bottom Line

Distinguish between OpenTelemetry versioning and stability, including support guarantees. Understanding the OTel specification is helpful for effectively implementing and leveraging its capabilities in your observability practices. A key aspect of this is distinguishing between OTel versioning and stability. OTel follows a clear versioning strategy where different components, such as APIs, SDKs, and protocols, are versioned independently. This allows for gradual and nondisruptive upgrades. Stability guarantees are provided for versions 1.0 and greater, ensuring that once a version is marked stable, it will be supported and maintained with backward compatibility. This stability is essential for building reliable and predictable observability solutions.

Master It What are the long-term support guarantees for OTel?

Understand the OpenTelemetry data model, including protocol support and OTLP. OTel defines a data model, which standardizes how signals, including metrics, logs, and traces, are structured and transmitted. The OTel Protocol (OTLP) is a significant part of this model, providing a unified and efficient way to export telemetry data to various backends. Understanding the data model and protocol support helps to ensure that your telemetry data is consistent, interoperable, and can be effectively processed and analyzed across different systems and platforms.

Master It How is OTLP leveraged in OTel, and what value does it provide?

Differentiate between the OpenTelemetry API and SDK. The OTel API and SDK are intentionally separated given the concerns they address are different. The OTel API defines the standard interfaces and abstractions for generating telemetry data, ensuring a consistent way to instrument applications. The SDK implements these interfaces, including functionalities like data processing, exporting, and resource management.

Master It Who or what typically implements the OTel API and SDK?

Notes

1 https://opentelemetry.io/docs/specs/otel/library-guidelines/#opentelemetry-client-generic-design
2 https://en.wikipedia.org/wiki/API
3 https://en.wikipedia.org/wiki/Cross-cutting_concern
4 Public interfaces are ones that external third party libraries can interact with
5 https://opentelemetry.io/docs/specs/otel/overview/#api
6 https://opentelemetry.io/docs/specs/otel/context
7 https://opentelemetry.io/docs/specs/otel/context/api-propagators
8 https://opentelemetry.io/docs/specs/otel/context/api-propagators/#propagators-distribution
9 https://w3c.github.io/baggage
10 When creating a new baggage from an existing one, key conflicts are resolved with the new key/value being used
11 https://opentelemetry.io/docs/specs/otel/library-guidelines/#api-and-minimal-implementation
12 https://en.wikipedia.org/wiki/Java_Development_Kit
13 https://cloud.google.com/sdk
14 https://opentelemetry.io/docs/specs/otel/overview/#api
15 https://opentelemetry.io/docs/specs/otel/resource/sdk
16 https://github.com/open-telemetry/opentelemetry-specification/blob/main/specification/metrics/sdk.md#metricfilter
17 https://opentelemetry.io/docs/specs/otel/library-guidelines/#sdk-implementation
18 https://opentelemetry.io/docs/specs/otlp
19 https://opentelemetry.io/docs/specs/otel/schemas/#full-schema-aware
20 https://opentelemetry.io/docs/specs/otel/schemas/#collector-assisted-schema-transformation
21 https://github.com/open-telemetry/opentelemetry-specification/pull/4061#discussion_r1617910890
22 https://semver.org/spec/v2.0.0.html

Chapter 5

Managing the OpenTelemetry Collector

Now that you understand the OpenTelemetry specification and its contents, it is time to explore the reference implementations. In this chapter, you will explore the data collection aspects, primarily focusing on the OpenTelemetry Collector. In Chapter 6, "Leveraging OpenTelemetry Instrumentation," you will explore OpenTelemetry instrumentation. Docker and Kubernetes examples will be provided, along with extensive YAML configuration and various programming languages. By the end, you will have firsthand experience with OpenTelemetry!

The OpenTelemetry Collector, or just Collector, is a pivotal component in the OpenTelemetry ecosystem, designed to facilitate the efficient collection, processing, and exporting of telemetry data. As you continue your journey to mastering OpenTelemetry and observability, understanding how to manage the Collector effectively is essential. In this chapter, you will explore the architecture and functionalities of the Collector, providing you with the knowledge and tools to deploy, configure, and optimize its performance. You will learn about various deployment models, including agent and gateway modes, and delve into advanced configurations to tailor the Collector to your specific needs. By the end of this chapter, you will have a comprehensive understanding of how to manage the Collector, enabling you to harness its full potential to enhance your observability position and strategy.

Version 0.95.0 of the Collector was used to create this chapter and is the minimum recommended version to test against. Newer versions of the Collector may have changes in behavior, so check the OpenTelemetry documentation if anything does not work as expected. All code examples are available in the book's GitHub repository (`https://github.com/flands/mastering-otel-book`).

IN THIS CHAPTER, YOU WILL LEARN TO:

- Distinguish between agent and gateway mode
- Identify Collector components
- Configure and run the Collector
- Size, secure, observe, and troubleshoot the Collector

Background

What is data collection? As the name implies, data collection deals with collecting, or receiving, data. It may also include doing something with or to the data, known as processing data. What may not be clear is that most data collectors end up sending the data somewhere, known as exporting data, versus persisting it. For data collection to occur, either something needs to send data to a data collector in a supported format, or the data collector needs to perform some operation to generate the data that should be collected.

For telemetry data, data collection may reside anywhere between an application and the platform where the data will eventually reside:

- When data collection happens very close to the application, either beside, such as a sidecar, or on the same host, it is often referred to as an agent.
- When data collection happens in a clustered fashion within the same network boundary or environment, it may be referred to as a gateway, aggregator, forwarder, edge processor, or observability pipeline.
- When data collection happens close to the platform, it may be referred to as cloud collection, ingest processing, or simply ingest.

The OpenTelemetry (OTel) Collector, often abbreviated as otelcol and henceforth referred to as simply the *Collector*, is a data collector binary written in Golang, or Go for short. The Collector supports a variety of form factors, including running as an agent or as a gateway, either standalone or in a clustered fashion. The Collector supports being the central hub for all telemetry data, including applications and infrastructure (see Figure 5.1).

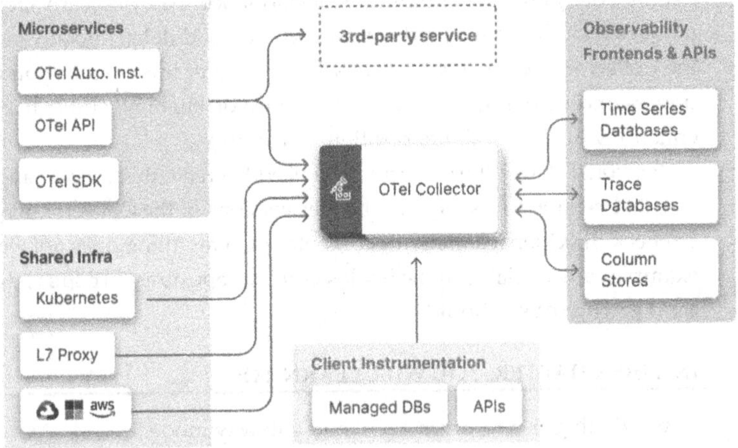

FIGURE 5.1 Different types of telemetry data the Collector supports.[1]
Source: [1] / OpenTelemetry Authors/ CC BY 4.0.

In this chapter, when the term *agent* is used, it is analogous to Collector and simply refers to the form factor of the Collector. While open source agents are commonplace, most are optimized for a single signal. In addition, it is common for agents to be optimized to receive a variety of open source formats but only export in a single, typically proprietary, format to support a single, typically vendor, platform. The Collector, whose origins come from the OpenCensus Service as discussed in Chapter 2, "Introducing OpenTelemetry!," takes a different approach. From the beginning, it was built to receive, process, and export all signal data in a vendor-agnostic way.

There are a few important things to note about the Collector:

- All data received by a receiver is converted to OpenTelemetry Protocol (OTLP) protobuf structs, a protocol discussed in Chapter 2, known as pdata (pipeline data).[2] This also means that all data exported by an exporter in a format other than OTLP is converted to that format before being exported. By leveraging a single internal format within the Collector, it is possible to create a single set of components that support all data. This also means that data can be received in one format but exported in another, allowing the Collector to be vendor-agnostic.
- By default, the Collector is stateless and keeps all data in memory. This means data may be lost on crash or if the Collector is restarted before all data has been flushed. Configuring the Collector in stateful ways, including persisting data, is possible.

Upon exploring the Collector architecture, one of your first questions may be why you would consider using it, especially if you already have one or more different types of collectors running in your environment. Here are some reasons:

- **Open source and vendor-agnostic:** The Collector can transform data from any available receiver format to any available exporter format.
- **Extensible:** The Collector supports observability data formats, including Jaeger, Prometheus, and OpenSearch, and can be extended to support future formats.
- **One agent for all signals:** The Collector is among the first to support trace, metrics, and logs in both agent and gateway modes.
- **Processing capabilities:** The Collector offers a rich set of processing capabilities, which can be leveraged by any data that the Collector can receive.
- **Multiple destinations:** One use case that most agents do not handle well is the ability to export the same data to two different platforms in parallel. The Collector fully supports this capability.
- **Fully OTel compliant:** Given the Collector exists in the OTel project, it fully supports all OTel concepts, including signals, resources, and schemas.

Historical information, including other collection approaches, donations, and mechanisms, are listed in the Appendix.

Deployment Modes

Data collectors come in various form factors but are stand-alone binaries at their core. These binaries are then packaged in some way. The most common form factor is an agent. Agents may be binaries that sit next to applications, sidecars to an application container, or host agents supporting one or more applications. While agents are the most common form factor, they are far from the only. Data aggregation and advanced scenarios, such as tail sampling, often require a cluster of data collectors. The Collector supports both deployment modes, as shown in Figure 5.2 and Figure 5.3.

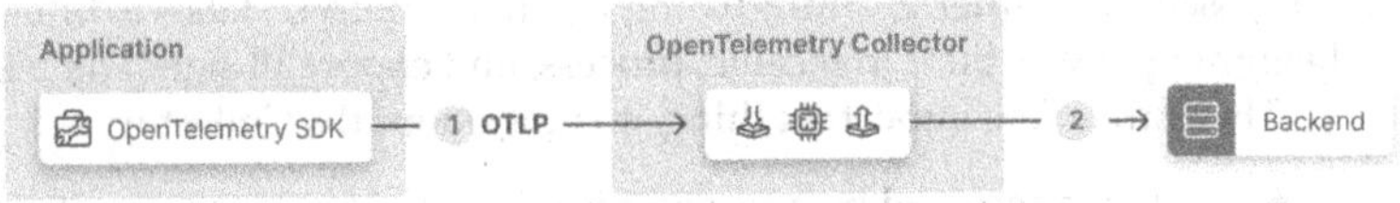

FIGURE 5.2 An example of the OTel SDK sending data to a Collector running in agent mode if you assume the application and Collector are on the same host.[3] By default, the OTel SDK is configured to send data to a local OTLP endpoint, optimizing it for agent mode. Deploying the Collector at least in agent mode is recommended for most environments. Of course, if desired, you can have the instrumentation SDK send directly to an observability platform.
Source: [3] / OpenTelemetry Authors/ CC BY 4.0.

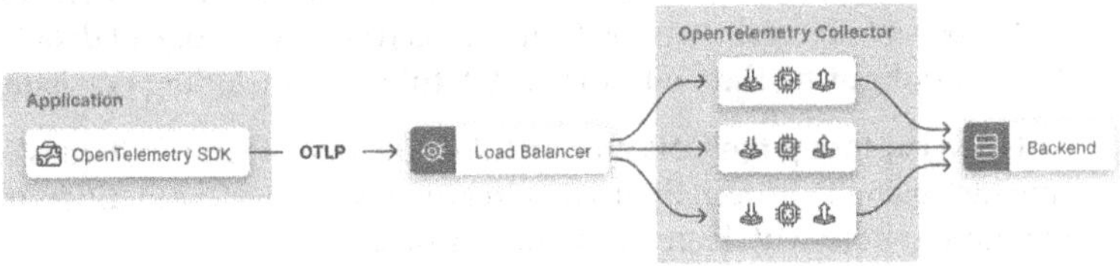

FIGURE 5.3 An example of the OTel SDK sending data to a Collector running in gateway mode.[4] The OTel SDK is configured to send data to a local OTLP endpoint by default. As such, appropriately changing the instrumentation configuration would be required to achieve this architecture. It is also possible to have a gateway cluster between an agent and backend (deploy the gateway cluster at 2 in Figure 5.2).
Source: [4] / OpenTelemetry Authors/ CC BY 4.0.

You may be wondering if you even need the Collector. Like most things, it depends. The value of the Collector is that it separates logical responsibility. For example, the instrumentation can focus on generating, while the Collector can focus on what to do with the data generated and everything required to get it to its destination. It also separates user responsibility. For example, developers could handle instrumentation, while site reliability engineers (SREs) could handle data collection. The primary benefits of the Collector are that it allows centralizing capabilities instead of requiring each instrumentation to implement the same functionality and offers more flexibility on what to do with generated data.

Agent Mode

Agent mode can be either per application, such as via a stand-alone binary or sidecar, or per host, meaning it can support all applications on a given host, as shown in Figure 5.4. The advantage of agent mode is that the Collector runs very close to the applications. As a result, it can offload certain capabilities, such as buffer and retry logic as well as processing capabilities, such as resource detection. The biggest benefit of agent mode is that it enables quickly getting the telemetry data out of the application, thus minimizing application resource requirements and overhead. On the flip side, agent mode requires sizing the Collector to support all the data being processed and does not support high availability (HA).

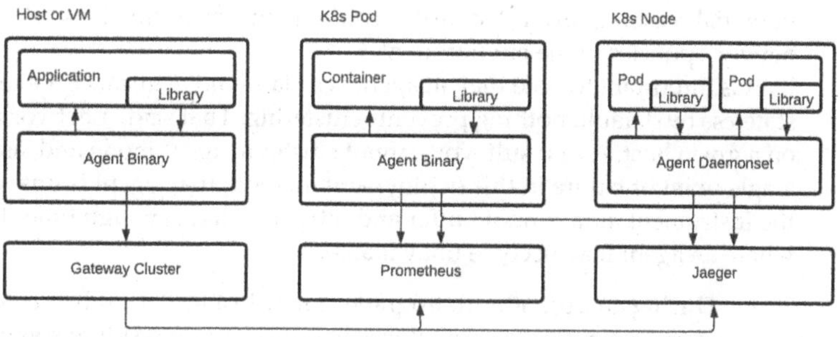

FIGURE 5.4 Common agent deployment architectures. The Agent Binary represents a stand-alone Collector instance. Note that the gateway architecture will be described in the next section.

A Collector running in agent mode typically needs more components than one running in gateway mode. The reason for this is that an agent typically needs to support a wide range of data formats, especially in brownfield environments where more than one mechanism is used to generate and emit telemetry data. For example, say you had a host running two applications that required gathering the following telemetry:

- **App1:** Zipkin traces, Prometheus metrics, and filesystem logs
- **App2:** OTel traces, OTel metrics, and syslog

In this example, you would need five different receivers (the Collector has an OTLP receiver that supports traces, metrics, and logs). If this host was running Docker, you may also want the Docker stats receiver, while on Kubernetes (K8s) you may want several additional components. Generally, in gateway mode, you primarily receive data from agents and typically perform a narrow set of processing, thus reducing the number of components required.

Do you need to run the Collector in agent mode? Like most things, it depends, but, in general, it is *highly recommended*. For example, collecting host metrics and reading log files are typical use cases that agent mode supports. In addition, separating processing and transmission from telemetry generation is a good practice. Using the previous example, perhaps you are migrating from Zipkin and Prometheus to OTel. By leveraging the Collector, you could start by supporting Zipkin and Prometheus, thus eliminating the need for whatever other agents were collecting this data. Alternatively, you would need to send the OTel data to a gateway cluster, directly to an observability platform, or deploy the Collector as another agent that runs side by side during the migration. Given that the Collector supports various receivers, the recommendation would be to standardize on the Collector as the primary agent versus running multiple different agents and the overhead this introduces.

Beyond agent consolidation, it comes down to business requirements. For example, how sensitive are your applications to overhead, and how critical is the telemetry data being collected? If no agent is used, it will likely require more processing and, thus, more resources in the aforementioned application. In addition, any processing capabilities required would need to be implemented in every instrumentation for every programming language in your environment and configured in a language-specific way instead of generally once in the agent. Yet another potential reason is around security requirements, including how to handle token rotation and the network policies in the environment.

It is important to note that an agent is a stand-alone instance. Given that the Collector is stateless by default, nothing prevents clustering. That said, a network port can only be used once on a given host. As a result, you cannot cluster in agent mode and, as such, the Collector is a single point of failure in this deployment method. If an agent is unavailable, data may be lost if the instrumentation cannot buffer and retry for a long enough time. There are a few situations where an agent may become unavailable:

- **During an upgrade:** To upgrade, a new instance must be deployed, and traffic must be cut over. Depending on how this is handled, it may result in some downtime. It is not possible to do an in-place, no down time upgrade of the Collector.
- **During a restart:** The Collector may also be restarted to apply a new configuration, though a SIGHUP[5] is sufficient.
- **Improperly sized:** The Collector will leverage the resources it is allocated, but it is possible that it either receives or needs to process more data than it can support. A Collector may restart if it is not appropriately sized for the amount of data it is handling. It is critical to properly configure Go environment variables as well as the memory limiter processor, as defined in the "Configuration" section. Benchmarking information for the Collector can be found at `https://opentelemetry.io/docs/collector/benchmarks` and scaling information at `https://opentelemetry.io/docs/collector/scaling`.
- **Improperly configured:** The Collector validates configuration on start, including SIGHUP, and will crash if improperly configured. If this happens during an upgrade or restart, it could result in extended downtime and data loss.

The easiest ways to minimize agent downtime are to test before rolling out changes and always perform a rolling upgrade or restart. A rolling upgrade refers to standing up a new instance, adding the destination to the load balancing pool or switching traffic to point to the new destination, and removing the old instance. Platforms, such as K8s, do this automatically.[6] In addition, if telemetry data is critical for an application, ensuring sufficient buffer and retry is configured so more data can be retained in case of agent downtime may be beneficial.

Gateway Mode

Gateway mode refers to one or more Collectors running within an environment, namespace, cluster, region, or network boundary. In this mode, the Collector acts as an aggregation tier and is deployed across hosts for HA, but not per host like agent mode. Typically, gateway mode is run clustered to support scale-out and HA via a load balancer. As a result, each instance in the cluster should be run on a separate host to ensure HA. In addition, gateway mode is typically run in the same location as the infrastructure and applications it supports. For example, say you were using a cloud-based platform, and your agents could not access the Internet for security reasons. You may opt to deploy a cluster of Collectors in gateway mode that can access the cloud-based platform and have your instrumentation or agents send data to this cluster, as shown in Figure 5.5. For most circumstances, there is no reason for Collectors in the same cluster to talk to each other. As a result, a simple round-robin load balancer is often sufficient. However, more advanced load balancing techniques can be used depending on the number of inbound connections and the length of each connection. All Collector instances in a gateway cluster should be configured identically.

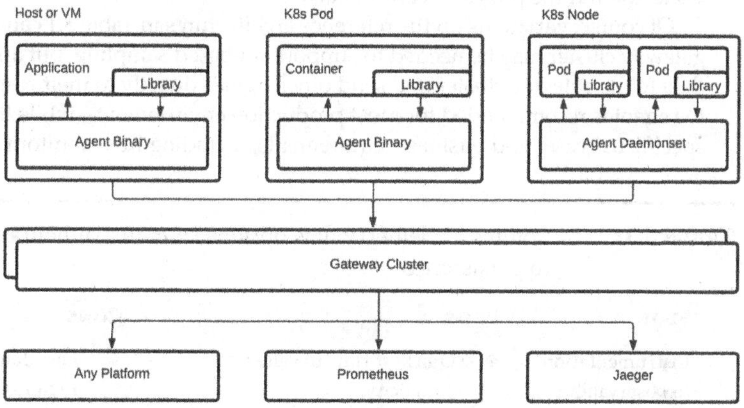

FIGURE 5.5 Common gateway deployment architecture. In this image, the Gateway Cluster represents multiple Collector instances configured identically and fronted by a load balancer.

Some situations require running a single Collector in gateway mode or a cluster deployed centrally but supporting multiple locations. For example, collecting data from the K8s API requires running a single instance of the Collector; otherwise, data would be collected more than once. Another example is supporting tail-based sampling, which requires that all spans for a given trace be received and processed by the same instance of the Collector. If spans for the same trace come from multiple locations, then this means a gateway cluster in one location may need to receive and process data from a different location to support tail-based sampling.

Gateway mode often requires fewer components than agent mode. For example, if a gateway cluster only receives data from other agents, it may only require the OTLP receiver. In addition, if the gateway cluster is dedicated to a specific purpose, say tail-based processing, then it may only require components necessary to perform that purpose. The importance of removing unnecessary components will be discussed in the "Distributions" section.

Do you need to run the Collector in gateway mode? Again, it depends on what you are trying to achieve and your business requirements. Here are some scenarios where you might want to run the Collector in gateway mode:

- You want to collect data from specific APIs, like the K8s API, or scrape a Prometheus server configured for federation.
- You want to leverage tail-based sampling.
- You want to receive data from applications that do not support sending to an agent. For example, some serverless environments do not allow the deployment of agents.
- Your network configuration prevents agents from accessing the Internet and you leverage a cloud-based observability platform.
- Your security team requires that API tokens be managed centrally and/or separated from agents.

Reference Architectures

With so many deployment options, you may be wondering how to get started or decide on the architecture right for you. Table 5.1 shows common reference architectures with and without the Collector and the pros and cons of each.

Of course, variations on the reference architectures in Table 5.1 can also be taken. For example, a gateway cluster may be needed to support tail-based sampling, but an agent may only send trace data to the gateway cluster and send other signals directly to their respective back ends. In general, the agent is recommended for most production environments, while the gateway is needed for specific use cases and business requirements, including K8s monitoring and tail-based sampling.

TABLE 5.1: Common telemetry flow options from instrumentation generation to persistence

FLOW	PROS	CONS
Instrumentation to observability platform	◆ Quickest time to value; simplicity. ◆ Lowest latency.	◆ Less data processing flexibility and requires language-specific components, such as resource detection and configuration. ◆ Operational complexity as each language and possibly each application needs to be independently configured. ◆ Added resource requirements to handle processing, and buffer and retry logic. ◆ Decentralized security controls.
Instrumentation to agent to observability platform	◆ Quick time to value, especially given that instrumentation sends data to a local OTLP destination by default. ◆ Separates telemetry generation from transmission, reducing application load. ◆ Enhanced data processing capabilities and dynamic configuration without redeploying applications.	◆ Agent is a single point of failure and must be sized and monitored properly.
Instrumentation to gateway to observability platform	◆ If a gateway cluster separates telemetry generation from transmission without a single point of failure. ◆ Supports advanced data processing capabilities, including metric aggregation and tail-based sampling. ◆ Useful in certain environments, such as serverless, where an agent deployment may not be possible.	◆ Cannot offload all application processing capabilities, including resource detection. ◆ Requires thought when configuring pull-based receivers to ensure proper load balancing and no data duplication. ◆ May introduce unacceptable latency, impacting applications.

FLOW	PROS	CONS
Instrumentation to agent to gateway to observability platform	◆ The pros of agent and gateway mode. Supports the most use cases and requirements while providing the most data flexibility and portability.	◆ Complex configuration and highest management costs.

Real World Scenario

RILEY'S INITIAL OTEL STRATEGY

Riley knew that she wanted to deploy the OTel Collector, but the question was how. Given that the new Jupiterian cloud native architecture leveraged primarily K8s and Prometheus metrics, she thought deploying the Collector in gateway mode might be the way to go. With this approach, Riley could experiment with the Collector and the Watchwhale platform without significant changes to the environment. She also knew that if additional metrics sources were needed or other signal data, such as traces, needed to be collected, she could deploy agent mode in the future.

As a result, she configured two separate gateway instances: one had the Prometheus receiver, and the other had the applicable K8s receivers. She could have deployed a single gateway instance to cover both use cases. Still, she was concerned that the Collector size would become untenable as the K8s cluster and Prometheus server grew. In addition, she liked the separation of responsibility to prevent issues such as a noisy neighbor.

The Basics

Now that you understand more about the Collector, it is time to learn more about what it contains, how it is configured, and how it works. Examples in this chapter were created with version 0.95.0. Most examples in this chapter will be based on running the Collector locally on a Linux or Unix-based operating system. Adjusting the examples for Windows should be straightforward. Given that Go is a statically compiled language, no dependencies are needed to get started. If you prefer and have experience using Docker or K8s, you can also perform the tasks in this chapter using those tools. The following are the most important aspects to keep in mind when using Docker or K8s:

- Knowing where the Collector config is located
- Ensuring that the endpoints in the Collector configuration are properly specified (default values will not work)
- Exposing the proper ports

One significant difference between running the Collector locally versus as a container is network connectivity. For example, locally you may connect to the Collector over `localhost` or `127.0.0.1`. By default, in Docker or K8s, you need to connect to the Collector via its container name. This means that the default OTel instrumentation exporter endpoint (`127.0.0.1`) must also be changed to receive data. (This will be covered in Chapter 6.) Of course, you can configure port mapping to overcome this limitation as shown next.

To get started with the Collector in Docker, you can run something like the following command. Note that you may want to expose one or more ports to interact with the container. OTel-specific ports, such as 4317, will be covered later in this chapter.

```
$ docker run -p 127.0.0.1:4317:4317 \
  otel/opentelemetry-collector-contrib:0.95.0
```

It is important to note that when starting the Collector, you must pass the `--config` flag and a valid YAML, short for Yet Another Markup Language,[7] configuration file to the Collector binary. The Docker containers for the Collector include the config flag (`https://github.com/open-telemetry/opentelemetry-collector-releases/blob/main/distributions/otelcol-contrib/Dockerfile`) and a YAML configuration (`https://github.com/open-telemetry/opentelemetry-collector-releases/blob/main/distributions/otelcol-contrib/config.yaml`)—thus, the previous command is valid. If you wanted to override the default configuration in the container, then you would need to mount a configuration YAML file in the same location the config flag has been specified, as demonstrated next. The Collector configuration file will be explored in the "Configuration" section.

```
$ docker run -p 127.0.0.1:4317:4317 \
  -v $(pwd)/otelcol-config.yaml:/etc/otelcol-contrib/config.yaml \
  otel/opentelemetry-collector-contrib:0.95.0
```

Similarly, for K8s, you cannot connect to the Collector over `localhost`. If the Collector is to be deployed as a DaemonSet, then you would want to connect to the Collector using the host IP. To do so, you need to configure an environment variable with the host IP in each application and then set the exporter endpoint. For example:

```
...
spec:
  env:
  - name: HOST_IP
    valueFrom:
      fieldRef:
        fieldPath: status.hostIP
  - name: OTEL_EXPORTER_OTLP_ENDPOINT
    value: http://$(HOST_IP):4318
...
```

In the case of K8s, the OTel Helm chart is recommended. To get started, you can run the following commands, replacing `<value>` with either `DaemonSet` (agent mode), `deployment` (gateway mode), or `statefulset`:

```
$ helm repo add open-telemetry \
  https://open-telemetry.github.io/opentelemetry-helm-charts
$ helm install my-opentelemetry-collector \
  open-telemetry/opentelemetry-collector --set mode=<value>
```

The Binary

As you may recall from Chapter 2, the Collector components reside in two repositories: core and contrib. In addition, there are other Collector repositories that handle packaging. This chapter will use Collector binaries published in the release package repository (`https://github.com/open-telemetry/opentelemetry-collector-releases`). It is worth noting that the Collector has three different tiers of support for platforms, as shown in Table 5.2.

TABLE 5.2: Tiers of Collector support, including guarantees and OS types supported[8]

TIER	GUARANTEED TO	OS TYPES
1	Work	Linux/amd64
2	Work with specified limitations	Windows/amd64
3	Build	Darwin and other flavors of Linux and Windows

Source: Adapted from [8].

Installation documentation for various operating systems and architectures can be found here: `https://opentelemetry.io/docs/collector/installation`. Unless you plan to run Docker or K8s for the examples in this chapter, you should get the Collector binary release from here: `https://github.com/open-telemetry/opentelemetry-collector-releases/releases`. Download the appropriate contrib (not core) binary for your system. Once downloaded and extracted, you should attempt to run it from the CLI by typing `./otelcol-contrib` (note that the core version is run by typing `./otelcol`) from within the directory hosting the binary. Note that on some operating systems, such as macOS, you may need to perform additional actions to run the binary, as it is unsigned and untrusted.[9]

Upon running the Collector, you should get an error like the following:

```
Error: at least one config flag must be provided
2024/01/14 21:08:21 Collector server run finished with error: at least one config
flag must be provided
```

As you will quickly discover, the Collector attempts to write relevant information to the console so that you can understand its behavior. The preceding error indicated that the Collector requires a configuration file to start. First, you will learn about the components. Then, you will begin building a configuration file to run the Collector.

Sizing

Beyond configuration, it is essential to understand how to size the Collector. Improper sizing can lead to various issues including host resource contention, Collector restarts, application back pressure, and dropped telemetry data. It is one of the most common issues experienced with the Collector. In general, a Collector's resources can be scaled up or out (concepts covered in Chapter 1, "What is Observability?") depending on its configuration. In agent mode, the only viable options are to scale up aspects such as CPU, memory, and disk space or reduce the amount of traffic sent to the Collector. In gateway mode, both scale-up and scale-out are available options, but all Collector instances behind the same load balancer should be configured with the same resources. Resources can also be controlled by setting limits. For example, K8s supports setting requests and limits.[10] Configuring these settings is highly recommended to prevent the Collector from causing noisy neighbor problems. In software, a noisy neighbor is when one or more parts of a system are impacted by another part of the system running on the same host.[11]

Other configuration options need to be considered beyond resources and the number of instances—for example, the `GOGC` and `GOMEMLIMIT` environment variables, which will be covered in the "Configuration" section next in this chapter. Even the YAML configuration file needs to be considered. For example:

- Running complex regular expressions via configured processors against a large volume of data may result in an excessive amount of CPU being consumed. Optimizing the configuration to be more efficient or load balancing the data across a larger pool of smaller Collectors could help offset this issue.
- Significant spikes in traffic, custom buffer and retry configurations, and the tail-based sampling processor may result in excessive amounts of memory being consumed, leading to the Collector restarting. Testing failure scenarios to understand Collector behavior and validating Collector configuration is vital.
- Excessive logging or configuring the storage extension may consume all disk space. Monitoring and alerting against disk space usage can help mitigate this issue.

Given all of this, you may be wondering how to determine the proper sizing of the Collector. You may even be looking for a specific metric to monitor. One fundamental way to monitor the Collector is based on the amount of data per signal being received. Assuming a consistent telemetry stream and an unchanged configuration, you should be able to determine the utilization of the Collector using this data. Of course, consistent telemetry streams are difficult to guarantee, and configurations will change over time. The best approach is often to test performance with your telemetry data and desired configuration. As the configuration or traffic changes, you should rerun the performance test to reduce the likelihood of issues. The "Relevant Metrics" section will cover metrics that can be used to measure utilization. You should also test performance after Collector version upgrades, whether major, minor, or patch, as the behavior may change.

Components

To understand the Collector configuration, you must first understand its components. The Collector supports the following components (as shown in Figure 5.6):

- **Receivers:** These are used to get data into the Collector. Other common names for receivers outside of OTel include sources and scrapers. Receivers can be either push- or pull-based and may support one or more signal types. For example, trace data is typically pushed from an application to the Collector, and the Collector supports common standards, including OTLP and Zipkin. Alternatively, Prometheus metrics are scraped or pulled from application endpoints via the Prometheus receiver available in the Collector. The OTLP receiver supports all signal types and is the recommended and default way to get OTel instrumentation data into the Collector. More than 90 receivers are available in the contrib repository (`https://github.com/open-telemetry/opentelemetry-collector-contrib/tree/main/receiver`) supporting a variety of open source and commercial solutions.

- **Processors:** These are used to perform specific actions based on received data. For example, filtering or CRUD, which stands for Create, Remove, Update, and Delete, operations. Other common names for processors outside of OTel include transformers.
- **Exporters:** These are used to get data out of the Collector. Other common names for exporters outside of OTel include routes or sinks. Like receivers, these can be either push- or pull-based. More than 45 exporters are available in the contrib repository (`https://github.com/open-telemetry/opentelemetry-collector-contrib/tree/main/exporter`) supporting a variety of open source and commercial destinations.
- **Connectors:** These are used to connect service pipelines, a component discussed in the "Configuration" section next in this chapter. A connector must be an exporter *and* a receiver; it may or may not alter data. Connectors are the newest component type supported by the Collector. Connectors either forward data to a new Collector pipeline or generate new data, which is picked up by a separate pipeline.
- **Extensions:** These are used to provide capabilities on top of the Collector's primary functionality. Generally, extensions do not require direct access to telemetry data and are not part of service pipelines. Extensions may be used independently of any pipeline component or in conjunction with them. For example, extensions may provide authentication capabilities required by receivers and exporters or service discovery capabilities necessary for receivers. In addition, they can assist with the health and troubleshooting of the Collector.

In addition to the components, the Collector has a configuration section, called *service*, which will be explored later in this chapter. It is used to enable components, define *pipelines*, and configure the Collector's own telemetry settings. Pipelines are a powerful capability in the Collector that enable signal-specific receivers, processors, and exporters, as well as define the order in which processors are run.

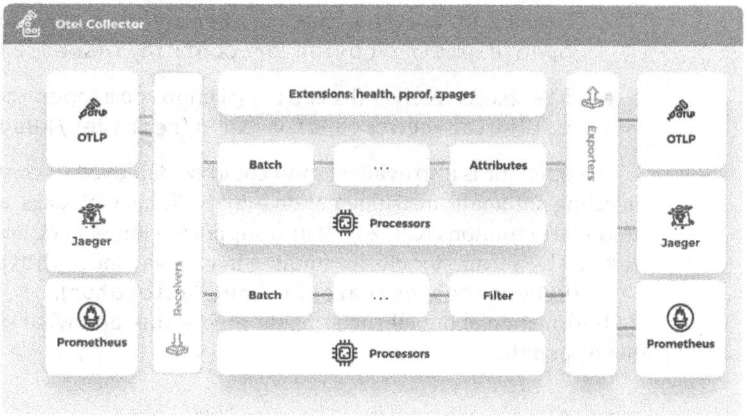

FIGURE 5.6 A high-level architecture diagram of the Collector. A trace service pipeline is represented by a line from OTLP through the batch and attributes processors and finally to the Jaeger exporter.[12] In addition, a metric service pipeline is represented by a line from OTLP through the batch and filter processor and finally dual-published to the OTLP and Prometheus.[13]
Source: [12] / OpenTelemetry Authors / CC BY 4.0.

The components required depend on the environment. For cloud native workloads, commonly leveraged components on the Collector include:

- **Receivers:** OTLP, Zipkin, Prometheus, Host Metrics, Filelog[14]
- **Processors:** Environment-specific but may include filtering, CRUD metadata, and resource detection
- **Exporters:** OTLP or observability platform–specific
- **Extensions:** Health check, zPages

For K8s observability, several additional components are needed. In general, it is recommended to use the OTel Helm chart (`https://github.com/open-telemetry/opentelemetry-helm-charts/tree/main/charts/opentelemetry-collector`) to observe K8s, but it is possible to deploy components manually. For example, an agent would require the following in addition to the aforementioned components:

- Kubelet stats receiver (`https://github.com/open-telemetry/opentelemetry-collector-contrib/blob/main/receiver/kubeletstatsreceiver/README.md`)
- K8s attributes processor (`https://github.com/open-telemetry/opentelemetry-collector-contrib/blob/main/processor/k8sattributesprocessor/README.md`)

A stand-alone gateway instance would also be required with the following receivers:

- K8s cluster receiver (`https://github.com/open-telemetry/opentelemetry-collector-contrib/blob/main/receiver/k8sclusterreceiver/README.md`).
- K8s events receiver (`https://github.com/open-telemetry/opentelemetry-collector-contrib/blob/main/receiver/k8seventsreceiver/README.md`). (Note that this receiver will be deprecated in favor of the K8s objects receiver. Check this issue for the latest information: `https://github.com/open-telemetry/opentelemetry-collector-contrib/issues/24242`).
- K8s objects receiver (`https://github.com/open-telemetry/opentelemetry-collector-contrib/blob/main/receiver/k8sobjectsreceiver/README.md`).

An operator is also available and could be deployed. If configured, the operator can support injecting automatic instrumentation into .NET, Java, Node.js, and Python applications via custom resource definitions (CRDs).[15] It also supports a target allocator so Prometheus targets can be scraped by a Collector cluster running in gateway mode (`https://opentelemetry.io/docs/kubernetes/operator/target-allocator`).

Information about all components, their status, and what signals they support is provided in the Appendix.

Configuration

Collector configuration is primarily handled via a YAML file, which is passed at runtime via command line interface (CLI) arguments. YAML is common for cloud native configurations and gained popularity in part due to the K8s project. In addition, the Collector supports other CLI arguments, like enabling feature flags, and respects some environment variables. Given that the Collector is written in Go, there are a couple of Go-specific environment variables to be aware of, as documented here: `https://pkg.go.dev/runtime#hdr-Environment_Variables`.

- `GOGC` (default=100): This option sets the garbage collection target percentage. Depending on Collector behavior and performance in your environment and with your configuration, this setting may need to be adjusted.
- `GOMEMLIMIT` (no default): This option sets a soft memory limit for the runtime. The recommended setting to start with is 80 percent of the hard memory limit of your Collector. *It is highly recommended that this value be set, especially in production environments.*

BALLAST EXTENSIONS

Prior to the `GOGC` and `GOMEMLIMIT` environment variables, the Collector provided a ballast extension[16] that offered the same capabilities. Using these environment variables makes the ballast no longer necessary or useful. As such, the ballast extension has been deprecated and will be removed. If you are using the ballast extension, it is highly recommended that you remove it and configure these environment variables instead.

Providing a basic configuration that can be explored is helpful in understanding how to configure the Collector. Within the Collector YAML file, the structure follows the components described previously. Every component is defined once as a top-level item, known as a *block sequence* in YAML, and may contain zero or more items supported by that component. At least one receiver, exporter, and signal-specific service pipeline must be defined. Now, you will try out the Collector configuration. All steps performed should be within the directory containing the Collector binary.

1. Create a file called `otelcol-otlp-debug.yaml` and add the following:

```
receivers:
  otlp:
    protocols:
      grpc:
        endpoint: 0.0.0.0:4317

processors:
  batch:
  # Not set as the limit_mib is not known
  # Highly recommended for production environments
  # If defined, ensure it is the first processor in *each* pipeline
  # Also, do not forget to set the GOMEMLIMIT environment variable
  #memory_limiter:
  #  check_interval: 1s
  #  limit_mib: <TODO>

exporters:
  debug:
```

```
      verbosity: detailed

service:
  pipelines:
    traces:
      receivers: [otlp]
      processors: [batch]
      #processors: [memory_limiter, batch]
      exporters: [debug]
```

2. Start the Collector with the YAML file:

```
$ GOMEMLIMIT=1600 ./otelcol-contrib --config otelcol-otlp-debug.yaml
```

Setting the GOMEMLIMIT is *strongly recommended* for production environments and demonstrated in the previous command. All other examples in this chapter will not specify this variable, as your memory settings may vary.

YAML SYNTAX

It is worth noting that YAML syntax matters. If something is not entered correctly, it will result in an error. One of the most important YAML aspects is the indentation or nesting of items. As you can see in the preceding example, `otlp` is nested under `receivers`, and `protocols` is nested under `otlp`. If `otlp` were not indented, the configuration would be invalid. Also worth noting, this chapter may refer to nested configuration using double colons. For example, `receivers::otlp::protocols::grpc::endpoint:0.0.0.0:4317` would be equivalent to the receivers section shown in the previous configuration example.

3. You are done. If everything is configured properly, you should see output like the following after executing the preceding commands:

```
2024-09-14T21:19:36.204-0500   info   service@v0.95.0/telemetry.go:86   Setting
up
own telemetry...
2024-09-14T21:19:36.206-0500   info   service@v0.95.0/telemetry.go:203   Serving
Prometheus metrics  {"address": ":8888", "level": "Basic"}
2024-09-14T21:19:36.206-0500   info   exporter@v0.95.0/exporter.go:275
Development
component. May change in the future.  {"kind": "exporter", "data_type": "traces",
"name": "debug"}
2024-09-14T21:19:36.208-0500   info   service@v0.95.0/service.go:145   Starting
otelcol...  {"Version": "0.95.0", "NumCPU": 8}
2024-09-14T21:19:36.208-0500   info   extensions/extensions.go:34   Starting
extensions...
2024-09-14T21:19:36.209-0500   warn   internal@v0.95.0/warning.go:40   Using the
0.0.0.0 address exposes this server to every network interface, which may
```

```
facilitate Denial of Service attacks  {"kind": "receiver", "name": "otlp",
"data_type": "traces",
"documentation": "https://github.com/open-telemetry/opentelemetry-
Collector/blob/main/docs/security-best-practices.md#safeguards-against-denial-of-
service-attacks"}
2024-09-14T21:19:36.210-0500  info  otlpreceiver@v0.95.0/otlp.go:83  Starting
GRPC server  {"kind": "receiver", "name": "otlp", "data_type": "traces",
"endpoint": "0.0.0.0:4317"}
2024-09-14T21:19:36.211-0500  info   service@v0.95.0/service.go:171
Everything
is ready. Begin running and processing data.
```

The Collector is now running, but the console messages are worth checking. You can confirm via the `info` messages what was configured on the Collector. Additional information may also be provided. For example, you will see a `warn` message, like the one in the preceding example, indicating a potential security concern. When configuring the gRPC OTLP receiver, you exposed the endpoint to all interfaces. As a result, the Collector listens for traffic on all interfaces. A more secure and production-like configuration would specify a custom endpoint limiting the interfaces the Collector listens on for that receiver. For example, you could update the configuration as shown next:

```
receivers:
  otlp:
    protocols:
      grpc:
        endpoint: 127.0.0.1:4317
```

Upon looking at a Collector config, your first question might be, what is the difference between components defined outside and inside the service section? Those outside the service section make a component available and define its configuration. For example, the batch processor has been made available and is using the default configuration, while the debug exporter has been made available and is configured to use a non-default verbosity level. Components must be defined outside of the service section, even if just using the default settings, in order to be usable in the service section. For example, the following configuration is invalid:

```
service:
  pipelines:
    traces:
      receivers: [otlp]
      processors: [batch]
      exporters: [debug]
```

If you were to run the Collector with only the preceding config, you would receive the following error:

```
Error: invalid configuration: no receiver configuration specified in config
2024/01/14 21:24:40 Collector server run finished with error: invalid
configuration: no receiver configuration specified in config
```

Some components have mandatory configuration parameters. For example, the `otlp` receiver requires that one or more supported protocols be defined; otherwise, the configuration is invalid. For example, change the `otlp` receiver to just the following, keeping the rest of the configuration the same:

```
receivers:
  otlp:
```

Upon starting the Collector with this configuration, the following error will be returned:

```
Error: invalid configuration: receivers::otlp: must specify at least one protocol
when using the OTLP receiver
2024/01/14 21:32:15 Collector server run finished with error: invalid
configuration: receivers::otlp: must specify at least one protocol when using
the OTLP receiver
```

Defining a component outside of the service section configures it but does not enable it. To enable a receiver, processor, exporter, or connector component, it must be defined in the `service::pipelines` section in a signal-specific way. In the first example in this section, a `service::pipelines::trace` was defined with a receiver, processor, and exporter. While not demonstrated in the examples in this section, extensions are enabled as a list under the `service::extensions` section and not in a service pipeline. While the `service` section is primarily for enabling components, it does offer some configuration capabilities. Specifically, it allows configuring the order in which processors are executed and setting Collector telemetry options. To configure telemetry settings, a telemetry option under the service section is used: `service::telemetry`.

Here are some important things to note about Collector configuration:

- The components available depend on the Collector distribution being run. For example, the core distribution offers only a small number of components, whereas the contrib distribution offers significantly more. See the "Distributions" section for more information.
- Every component has a GitHub README that details status, supported signals, defaults, and configuration options. For example, documentation for the OTLP receiver can be found here: `https://github.com/open-telemetry/opentelemetry-collector/tree/main/receiver/otlpreceiver`. Note that this configuration information is not available in the OTel documentation (though will be in the future).
- Within `service::pipelines`, one or more receivers and exporters and zero or more processors or connectors must be defined per signal.
- Not everything defined outside of the `service` section needs to be used in the `service::pipelines` section. For example, you can remove `batch` from any of the service::pipelines::<signal>::processors examples in this section, and the configuration will still be valid. Of course, configuring but not enabling components provides no value.
- The components specified in a service::pipelines::<signal> must support the signal type. For example, the `otlp` receiver supports traces, metrics, and logs, while the `prometheus` receiver supports only metrics.

- More than one configuration can be passed to the Collector, in which case configurations are merged. For example, ./otelcol-contrib --config config1.yaml --config config2.yaml. The configuration also supports capabilities such as including files via ${file:filename.yaml}, environment variables via ${env:VAR_NAME}, YAML bytes, and HTTP URI. Finally, one or more --set flags can be passed to override config properties. (Note that the --set flag is likely to be removed in the future in favor of --config with YAML, such as --config="yaml:receivers::otlp::protocols::grpc::endpoint:0.0.0.0:4317".) More information about the configuration can be found here: https://github.com/open-telemetry/opentelemetry-collector/tree/main/service.
- You can use something defined outside of the service section in multiple service::pipelines. For example, the otlp receiver could be used in multiple trace pipelines or a trace and a metric service pipeline.
- The order in which service::pipelines::<signal>::processors are defined determines the order in which processors are executed. For example, you could filter before performing a CRUD operation or vice versa. This only applies to processor components and not lists for other components. More information will be provided in the "Processors" section.
- The same component and the same service::pipelines::<signal> can be defined multiple times by adding a forward slash followed by one or more characters like <*component*>[/<*name*>]. For example, a second otlp receiver could be defined using a name, such as otlp/2, and a second trace pipeline could be defined using a name, such as service::pipelines::traces/2.

The last bullet is worth demonstrating to see the flexibility it provides. Every component can be defined multiple times with different configurations as long as unique names are used. You will now attempt to configure multiple instances of the same processor type as well as multiple trace pipelines. (Note that other examples of leveraging multiple components or pipelines are provided in the GitHub repository associated with this book.)

1. Start by creating a YAML configuration file called otelcol-multi-trace.yaml and add the following:

```
receivers:
  otlp:
    protocols:
      http:
        endpoint: 0.0.0.0:4318

processors:
  attributes/1:
    actions:
      - key: test
        action: insert
        value: 1
```

```
    attributes/2:
      actions:
        - key: test
          action: insert
          value: 2

  exporters:
    debug/1:
      #verbosity: detailed
    debug/2:
      #verbosity: detailed

  service:
    pipelines:
      traces/debug/1:
        receivers: [otlp]
        processors: [attributes/1]
        exporters: [debug/1]
      traces/debug/2:
        receivers: [otlp]
        processors: [attributes/2]
        exporters: [debug/2]
```

2. Start the Collector with the YAML file by running the following:

```
$ ./otelcol-contrib --config otelcol-multi-trace.yaml
```

3. Get the `otlphttp-trace.json` payload from Chapter 1 (it is also found in the book's GitHub repository) and save it locally.

4. Send this payload to the Collector in a separate window by running the following. (Note that the `Content-Type` header is required; otherwise, the operation will fail.)

```
$ curl -H "Content-Type: application/json" -d @otlphttp-trace.json \
  http://0.0.0.0:4318/v1/traces
```

5. You are done. You will receive a `{"partialSuccess":{}}%` response after running the previous command. In the window running the Collector, you should see an output like the following:

```
2024-01-14T11:54:28.615-0800   info   TracesExporter   {"kind": "exporter",
"data_type": "traces", "name": "debug/1", "resource spans": 1, "spans": 2}
2024-01-14T11:54:28.615-0800   info   TracesExporter   {"kind": "exporter",
"data_type": "traces", "name": "debug/2", "resource spans": 1, "spans": 2}
```

6. You can also repeat this scenario by uncommenting the `#verbosity: detailed` line in the Collector's YAML configuration for both attribute processors. In this scenario, you will see that a test attribute is added to each output with a specific value.

In the previous example, you did the following:

- Configured two separate instances of the attributes processor using unique names. Each instance added the same named attribute (test) to the payload but with different values (1 versus 2).
- Configured two separate trace service pipelines, using unique names. One was configured with the first attributes processor and the other with the second.

Connectors are a topic that will be covered later in this section, but for demonstration purposes, you could modify the previous example to use them. For example, the exporter list for the `traces/debug/1` pipeline could leverage the forward connector to feed `traces/debug/2`. With this configuration, data after running the `traces/debug/1` pipeline would be rerouted to the Collector to be processed a second time. To try this scenario, create a YAML configuration file called `otelcol-multi-trace-connector.yaml` and add the content shown next. Follow the rest of the steps in the previous example using this configuration file:

```
receivers:
  otlp:
    protocols:
      http:
        endpoint: 0.0.0.0:4318

processors:
  attributes/1:
    actions:
      - key: test
        action: insert
        value: 1

  attributes/2:
    actions:
      - key: test
        action: upsert
        value: 2

exporters:
  debug/1:
    #verbosity: detailed
  debug/2:
    #verbosity: detailed

connectors:
  forward:

service:
  pipelines:
    traces/debug/1:
      receivers: [otlp]
```

```
      processors: [attributes/1]
      exporters: [debug/1, forward]
    traces/debug/2:
      receivers: [forward]
      processors: [attributes/2]
      exporters: [debug/2]
```

Given that the OTLP components support JavaScript Object Notation (JSON) over HTTP, it is straightforward to test sending data and view the output, as shown in the previous two examples. By default, and for performance reasons, OTLP uses protocol buffers (protobuf). Understanding and generating protobuf requires more dependencies and is more advanced than using JSON. To try protobuf with OTLP, follow these steps:

1. Use the `otelcol-otlp-debug.yaml` configuration file created earlier.
2. Run the Collector with the YAML file:

   ```
   $ ./otelcol-contrib --config otelcol-otlp-debug.yaml
   ```

3. Install and run the `telemetrygen` Go utility to generate data in protobuf format:

   ```
   $ go install github.com/open-telemetry/opentelemetry-collector-
   contrib/cmd/telemetrygen@latest
   $ telemetrygen traces --otlp-insecure --duration 5s
   ```

As you can see, the Collector configuration is extremely flexible. With that said, reasoning through a YAML configuration file can be quite a task. While these examples are concise, it can already be difficult to visualize what the pipelines look like. In addition, it is easy to make configuration errors. The Collector provides a couple of ways to mitigate these concerns quickly.

First, the Collector binary offers a `validate` CLI option to ensure your configuration is valid. The command returns nothing if the configuration is valid and has a status code `0`. If the config is invalid, it will tell you what needs fixing. For example, you could define an OTLP receiver without a protocol by creating a YAML configuration file called `otelcol-invalid-otlp.yaml` and adding the following content:

```
receivers:
  otlp:

exporters:
  debug:

service:
  pipelines:
    traces:
      receivers: [otlp]
      exporters: [debug]
```

Now run the `validate` command, with the YAML file:

```
$ ./otelcol-contrib validate --config=otelcol-invalid-otlp.yaml
Error: receivers::otlp: must specify at least one protocol when using the OTLP
receiver
2024/01/14 20:35:26 Collector server run finished with error: receivers::otlp:
must specify at least one protocol when using the OTLP receiver
```

Additionally, the Collector core repository offers the zPages extension. While more information about this extension will be provided in the "zPages Extension" section, this extension can show the configured pipelines on the running Collector instances if enabled. For example, the `otelcol-connector.yaml` defined in the preceding code snippet could be viewed on the default zPages pipelines page (`http://localhost:55679/debug/pipelinez`), and would look like Figure 5.7.

FIGURE 5.7
An example of the zPages pipelines page provided by the Collector.

builtPipelines

FullName	InputType	MutatesData	Receivers	Processors	Exporters
traces/debug	traces	true	forward (connector)	→ batch →	debug
traces/router	traces	true	zipkin	→ batch →	forward (connector)

An interesting open source project that has been created is `https://www.otelbin.io`. This site helps validate and visualize Collector configurations. For example, if you enter the otelcol-multi-trace.yaml config created earlier, you will see output like that shown in Figure 5.8.

FIGURE 5.8
Visualization of a Collector configuration. This makes it easier to understand how data flows through the Collector.

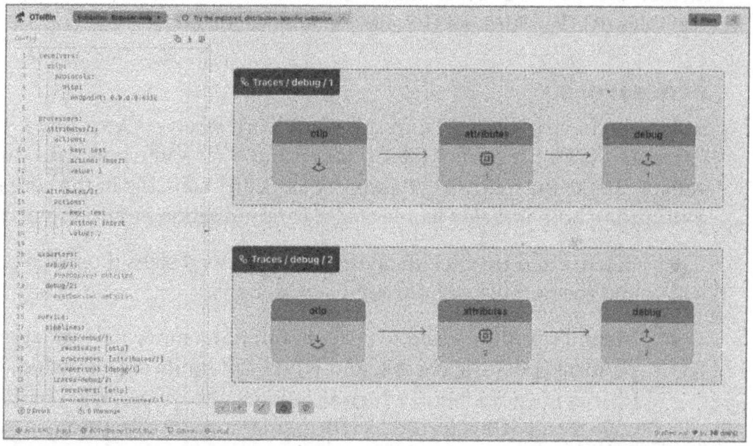

Receivers and Exporters

Receivers and exporters may support protocols, including REST and/or remote procedure call (RPC) as well as one or more serialization methods, including protobuf or JSON. The core repository offers reusable config modules (`https://github.com/open-telemetry/opentelemetry-collector/tree/main/config`) that receivers and exporters can take advantage of to handle aspects including authentication, encryption, buffers, compression, and security settings. These common configurations can be specified in the receiver or exporter configuration when non-default settings are required. For example, you can pass encryption settings like Transport Layer Security (TLS) to the OTLP receiver or exporter. The YAML configuration would look like the following:

```
receivers:
  otlp:
    protocols:
```

```
        grpc:
          endpoint: mysite.local:4317
          tls:
            cert_file: Collector.crt
            key_file: Collector.key

exporters:
  otlp:
    endpoint: myothersite.local:4317
    tls:
      cert_file: server.crt
      key_file: server.key
...
```

Beyond the common configuration required to establish a connection, receiver- and exporter-specific aspects are also often required. These aspects include things like endpoint, collection interval, indices, and time-out, to name a few. Receivers and exporters can also make use of extensions. Common extensions used with receivers include authentication mechanisms and observers that can dynamically discover additional data to collect. Extensions will be discussed further later in this chapter. Exporters that use the net/http package[17] respect proxy environment variables (`HTTP_PROXY`, `HTTPS_PROXY`, and `NO_PROXY`).

Processors

So far, you have played around primarily with receivers, exporters, and service pipelines. Processors are a big part of the Collector and offer some powerful capabilities. As of Collector version 0.95.0, the following two processors are available in the core repository and properly configuring both is *highly recommended* for production environments:

- **Batch:** Used to batch data, reducing payload sizes if used in conjunction with compression and the number of outbound connections.
- **Memory limiter:** Used to prevent out of memory (OOM) situations on the Collector. It performs periodic checks, and when soft limits are exceeded, it refuses data from the upstream component, which should be a receiver. When hard limits are exceeded, garbage collection (GC) is forced to reduce memory consumption.

Batch and Memory Limiter Processor Changes

As of Collector version 0.95.0, the batch and memory limiter processors are highly recommended for production environments. These processors will be deprecated in the future, and these capabilities will be made available to receivers and exporters through a shared helper library. In short, the Collector will one day support configuring batch and memory limiting settings through receiver and exporter settings, similar to how encryption is configured. Reasons for this change include the ability to better support back pressure use cases. *Back pressure* refers to a state where some component is not able to keep up with the amount of data being processed and needs to indicate to a downstream service to slow down to prevent data loss.

In addition, it is important to note that the `GOGC` and `GOMEMLIMIT` environment variables are separate from the memory limiter processor. These environment variables replace the memory ballast extension, which has been deprecated in the core repository. Configuring these environment variables *and* the memory limiter processor is *highly recommended* for production environments.

The rest of the processors live in the contrib repository. These processors can be grouped into a few major categories, as shown in Table 5.3.

TABLE 5.3: General categories and examples (not a complete list) of processors

CATEGORY	EXAMPLES
Metadata processing	◆ `k8sattributesprocessor` ◆ `resourceprocessor`
Filtering, routing, and sampling	◆ `filterprocessor` ◆ `routingprocessor` ◆ `tailsampling`
Enriching	◆ `k8sattributeprocessor` ◆ `resourcedetection`
Generating (primarily metrics)	◆ `metricsgenerationprocessor` (metrics only) ◆ `spanmetricsprocessor` (metrics only)
Grouping (helpful in batching and processing)	◆ `groupbyattrprocessor` ◆ `groupbytraceprocessor` (valid for tail-based sampling)
Transforming (primarily metrics)	◆ `cumulativetodeltaprocessor` (metrics only) ◆ `deltatorateprocessor` (metrics only) ◆ `schemaprocessor` (schemas only)

STABILITY AND FUTURE OF PROCESSORS

If you look through all the processors available in the Collector today, you will notice an overlap of capabilities. For example, the transform processor is a superset of the metrics transform, filter, resource, and attributes processors. In addition, both processors are in development. With that said, the transform processor is in alpha, while the metrics transform processor is in beta. In general, using the more mature component is recommended. The primary reason why the transform processor is alpha is that it is using the rapidly evolving OTTL package—which will be described later in this chapter. In the future, it is reasonable to assume that these processors will be consolidated into the transform processor.

Like all components, each processor has extensive configuration documentation available in GitHub. The primary difference between processors and other components is that the order in which they are defined matters, and some are recommended. As a result, OTel recommends enabling certain processors in a specific order:[18]

1. Memory limiter (highly recommended for production environments)
2. Any filtering or sampling processor (optional)

   Note that performing some metadata operations, especially enrichment, may be necessary to filter and sample data properly.

3. Any processor relying on sending source from context, such as the K8s attributes processor (optional)
4. Batch (highly recommended for production environments)
5. Any other processor, including CRUD metadata (optional)

The memory limiter processor was described earlier in this section and should be the first processor defined in production environments for every service pipeline. For example, if you had a Collector with 2 GB of memory configured, you might define the memory limiter as follows:

```
processors:
  memory_limiter:
    check_interval: 1s
    limit_mib: 1900
```

Two GB of memory is 2048 MB of memory, so you may be wondering why the `limit_mib` was set to `1900`. That is because the README for this configuration states that the memory usage will be about 50 MB higher than this value. This means setting the value to the actual limit would result in the processor not working as expected. Again, it is critical that you read the documentation, understand all the settings, and perform your own testing.

In general, the default settings for the batch processor are a good starting place. Of the remaining processing capabilities, there are a few that will apply to most environments and are worth discussing, including filtering, CRUD metadata processing, and resource detection. Filtering or sampling is almost always one of the first things you should do after receiving data. This is because any data that is not relevant should be discarded as early as possible to eliminate unnecessary resource utilization. For example, say you had two business units (BUs) sending trace data to a gateway cluster configured with an OTLP trace receiver but utilizing two different tracing platforms. In addition, assume that BU1 wanted to perform CRUD metadata processing on the trace data prior to exporting the data. In this scenario, if data between the BUs could be distinguished, such as via metadata added from instrumentation or an agent, then it would be possible to have a single OTLP receiver and two separate trace pipelines. To work properly, a filter processor would need to be configured for each pipeline to ensure that only the appropriate data were being processed and sent. In addition, a CRUD metadata processor, such as the attributes processor, would be needed for the BU1 pipeline. If the attributes processor were applied before the filter processor, then resources may unnecessarily be consumed for a portion of data that would later be filtered out.

To experience the power of processing, you will re-create the described scenario. To do so, perform the following steps:

1. Create a file called `otelcol-filter-attributes.yaml` and add the following contents:

```
receivers:
  zipkin:

processors:
  filter/bu1:
    error_mode: ignore
    traces:
      span:
        - 'attributes["bu"] != "bu_1"'
```

```
  filter/bu2:
    error_mode: ignore
    traces:
      span:
        - 'attributes["bu"] != "bu_2"'
  attributes/bu1:
    actions:
      - key: env
        value: dev
        action: insert
      - key: jdbc.query
        action: delete
      - key: db.request
        from_attribute: request
        action: insert
      - key: request
        action: delete
      - key: db.request
        pattern: .*limit=(?P<db_request_limit>.*)\}
        action: extract
      - key: db_request_limit
        converted_type: int
        action: convert

exporters:
  debug:
    verbosity: detailed
#  otlp:
#    endpoint: bu1.company.com:4317
#  zipkin:
#    endpoint: https://bu2.company.com:9411/api/v2/spans

service:
  pipelines:
    traces/bu1:
      receivers: [zipkin]
      processors: [filter/bu1, attributes/bu1]
      exporters: [debug]
 #     exporters: [otlp]
    traces/bu2:
      receivers: [zipkin]
      processors: [filter/bu2]
      exporters: [debug]
 #     exporters: [zipkin]
```

2. Run the Collector with the YAML file:

```
$ ./otelcol-contrib --config=otelcol-filter-attributes.yaml
```

Say now that both BUs want to send the data to the same platform, but BU1 still wants to perform metadata enrichment. In this case, filtering can be brought into the attributes processor. To test this scenario:

1. Create another file called `otelcol-attributes-include.yaml` and add the following contents:

```
receivers:
  zipkin:

processors:
  attributes/bu1:
    include:
      match_type: strict
      attributes:
      - key: bu
        value: bu_1
    actions:
      - key: env
        value: dev
        action: insert
      - key: jdbc.query
        action: delete
      - key: db.request
        from_attribute: request
        action: insert
      - key: request
        action: delete
      - key: db.request
        pattern: .*limit=(?P<db_request_limit>.*)\}
        action: extract
      - key: db_request_limit
        converted_type: int
        action: convert

exporters:
  debug:
    verbosity: detailed
#  otlp:
#    endpoint: bu1.company.com:4317
#  zipkin:
#    endpoint: https://bu2.company.com:9411/api/v2/spans

service:
  pipelines:
    traces:
      receivers: [zipkin]
      processors: [attributes/bu1]
```

```
        exporters: [debug]
#         exporters: [otlp]
```

2. Now run the Collector with the YAML file:

```
$ ./otelcol-contrib --config=otelcol-attributes-include.yaml
```

In order to see the power of CRUD metadata processing, you can test this scenario with an actual payload. To do so:

1. Create a JSON file called `trace-attributes.json` and add the following contents:


```
[
    {
      "traceId": "5982fe77008310cc80f1da5e10147517",
      "name": "get",
      "id": "bd7a977555f6b982",
      "timestamp": 1458702548467000,
      "duration": 386000,
      "localEndpoint": {
        "serviceName": "zipkin-query",
        "ipv4": "192.168.1.2",
        "port": 9411
      },
      "annotations": [],
      "tags": {
        "bu": "bu_1"
      }
    },
    {
      "traceId": "5982fe77008310cc80f1da5e10147517",
      "name": "get-traces",
      "id": "ebf33e1a81dc6f71",
      "parentId": "bd7a977555f6b982",
      "timestamp": 1458702548478000,
      "duration": 354374,
      "localEndpoint": {
        "serviceName": "zipkin-query",
        "ipv4": "192.168.1.2",
        "port": 9411
      },
      "tags": {
        "bu": "bu_1",
        "lc": "JDBCSpanStore",
        "request": "QueryRequest{serviceName=zipkin-query, spanName=null,
annotations=[], binaryAnnotations={}, minDuration=null, maxDuration=null,
endTs=1458702548478, lookback=86400000, limit=1}"
      }
    },
```

```
{
  "traceId": "5982fe77008310cc80f1da5e10147517",
  "name": "query",
  "id": "be2d01e33cc78d97",
  "parentId": "ebf33e1a81dc6f71",
  "timestamp": 1458702548786000,
  "duration": 13000,
  "localEndpoint": {
    "serviceName": "zipkin-query",
    "ipv4": "192.168.1.2",
    "port": 9411
  },
  "remoteEndpoint": {
    "serviceName": "spanstore-jdbc",
    "ipv4": "127.0.0.1",
    "port": 3306
  },
  "annotations": [],
  "tags": {
    "bu": "bu_1",
    "jdbc.query": "select distinct `zipkin_spans`.`trace_id` from `zipkin_
spans` join `zipkin_annotations` on (`zipkin_spans`.`trace_id` = `zipkin_
annotations`.`trace_id` and `zipkin_spans`.`id` = `zipkin_annotations`.`span_
id`) where (`zipkin_annotations`.`endpoint_service_name` = ? and `zipkin_
spans`.`start_ts` between ? and ?) order by `zipkin_spans`.`start_ts` desc
limit ?",
    "sa": "true"
  }
 }
]
```

2. With the Collector running, open a second window and pass the JSON file to the Collector by running the following:

```
$ curl -d @trace-attributes.json http://0.0.0.0:9411/api/v2/spans
```

3. The preceding command will return no result, but the Collector window will show a lot of output. From that output, you can confirm that the configured attribute changes were made to the payload:

```
2024-09-14T16:59:08.926-0500   info   TracesExporter   {"kind": "exporter",
"data_type": "traces", "name": "debug", "resource spans": 1, "spans": 3 }
2024-09-14T16:59:08.926-0500   info   ResourceSpans #0
Resource SchemaURL:
Resource attributes:
     -> service.name: Str(zipkin-query)
```

```
ScopeSpans #0
ScopeSpans SchemaURL:
InstrumentationScope
Span #0
    Trace ID       : 5982fe77008310cc80f1da5e10147517
    Parent ID      : ebf33e1a81dc6f71
    ID             : be2d01e33cc78d97
    Name           : query
    Kind           : Unspecified
    Start time     : 2016-03-23 03:09:08.786 +0000 UTC
    End time       : 2016-03-23 03:09:08.799 +0000 UTC
    Status code    : Unset
    Status message :
Attributes:
     -> sa: Str(true)
     -> bu: Str(bu_1)
     -> env: Str(dev)
     -> net.host.ip: Str(192.168.1.2)
     -> net.host.port: Int(9411)
     -> peer.service: Str(spanstore-jdbc)
     -> net.peer.ip: Str(127.0.0.1)
     -> net.peer.port: Int(3306)
Span #1
    Trace ID       : 5982fe77008310cc80f1da5e10147517
    Parent ID      : bd7a977555f6b982
    ID             : ebf33e1a81dc6f71
    Name           : get-traces
    Kind           : Unspecified
    Start time     : 2016-03-23 03:09:08.478 +0000 UTC
    End time       : 2016-03-23 03:09:08.832374 +0000 UTC
    Status code    : Unset
    Status message :
Attributes:
     -> bu: Str(bu_1)
     -> lc: Str(JDBCSpanStore)
     -> db.request: Str(QueryRequest{
        serviceName=zipkin-query, spanName=null, annotations=[],
        binaryAnnotations={}, minDuration=null, maxDuration=null,
        endTs=1458702548478, lookback=86400000,
        limit=1})
     -> net.host.ip: Str(192.168.1.2)
     -> net.host.port: Int(9411)
     -> env: Str(dev)
     -> db_request_limit: Int(1)
Span #2
    Trace ID       : 5982fe77008310cc80f1da5e10147517
    Parent ID      :
```

```
        ID             : bd7a977555f6b982
        Name           : get
        Kind           : Unspecified
        Start time     : 2016-03-23 03:09:08.467 +0000 UTC
        End time       : 2016-03-23 03:09:08.853 +0000 UTC
        Status code    : Unset
        Status message :
    Attributes:
         -> bu: Str(bu_1)
         -> net.host.ip: Str(192.168.1.2)
         -> net.host.port: Int(9411)
         -> env: Str(dev)
           {"kind": "exporter", "data_type": "traces", "name": "debug"}
```

As mentioned earlier, another capability to be aware of is resource detection. This allows the enrichment of telemetry data with environment information, such as `host.name` and `os.type`. While instrumentation supports some amount of resource detection via a processor in the SDK, doing it in the agent can help minimize the resource requirements in the application, and some detection, such as in cloud environments, may require detection in a Collector. Of course, using instrumentation-based resource detection together with Collector-based is possible, along with the ability to override metadata in the Collector if desired.

Resource detection can be configured in the Collector as a processor with one or more detectors defined (`https://github.com/open-telemetry/opentelemetry-collector-contrib/tree/main/processor/resourcedetectionprocessor`). It is important to note that the order in which detectors in this processor are specified matters. By default, the first detector to set resource information wins. In addition, the resource detector processor will override the received resource information by default, but this behavior can be changed with the `override` option (defaults to `true`). You generally want the most specific detector to set the resource information. The best practice is to list `env` first to allow for modification outside of the processor configuration. In addition, `system` should be listed last in case no other detectors provide context. Between `env` and `system`, detectors should be listed from more specific to least specific. For example, cloud provider K8s detectors should be listed before general cloud provider detectors. Note that the `docker` detector requires mounting the socket into the Collector container to access the Docker API and, as such, may not be used in all environments. An example of how you may configure the resource detection processor is shown next. (Remember that you need to enable it in one or more `service::piplines`).

```
processors:
 # Add or remove detectors as applicable to your environment
 # Important: By default, received resource metadata will be overridden.
 #            Set "override" to "false" if this is not desired.
 #            Remember: Order matters! The first detector to insert wins.
 resourcedetection:
   detectors: [env, eks, ecs, ec2, aks, azure, gcp, system]
```

If resource detection is configured as a processor in the Collector, it should generally be done in an agent, not a gateway cluster. The reason for this is because the resource detection needs information local to the application and, as such, needs to be running at least on the same host as the application to enrich with the correct information. While enabling in the gateway is possible, the enriching data would be incorrect for applications not residing on the same host as the gateway instance. The only exception is cloud provider detectors (not to be confused with K8s cloud provider detectors), which can be configured on a gateway instance. Enabling the system detector on a gateway cluster is not recommended for non-cloud provider detectors, as the local information would be incorrect for the majority, if not all, of the data received.

Real World Scenario

RILEY'S OTel VISION

One of the Collector's features that excited Riley the most was its various processors. She understood the power of filtering as well as creating, removing, updating, and deleting (CRUD) metadata operations. In addition, she had been researching Watchwhale's pricing and was concerned that custom metrics would cost Jupiterian a lot of money. As part of testing OTel in the Jupiterian environment, she noticed that some of the metadata in Prometheus was incorrect. With the Collector, she knew she could address this before sending it to the Watchwhale platform. With OTel, Riley felt like she had control over the telemetry data instead of a vendor having control over her.

Upon reviewing the available processors, Riley initially found the filter processor, and while it sounded like it met her requirements, she noticed it was marked as alpha. Upon further review, she found the metric transform processor, which supported filtering and CRUD metadata operations. This processor was marked as beta. As a result, she was inclined to configure the metric transform processor. She reached out to Niko to see if they had a recommendation. Niko stated that changes were underway with the metric transform processor, but it was the best option today. They suspected that changing to other processors, such as the filter processor, would be required in the future. Riley moved forward with configuring the metric transform processor and successfully resolved the metadata issues.

Another aspect of the Collector to be aware of is the OpenTelemetry Transformation Language, or OTTL (`https://github.com/open-telemetry/opentelemetry-collector-contrib/tree/main/pkg/ottl`). OTTL is a domain-specific language (DSL) that offers SQL-like configuration. It can be used to define processor configuration. For example, deleting an attribute in YAML using the standard configuration might look like this:

```
attributes/bul:
  actions:
    - key: http.request.header.authorization
      action: delete
```

While in OTTL it would look like this:

```
traces:
  delete(attributes["http.request.header.authorization"])
```

As of version 0.95.0 of the Collector, OTTL is under active development and rapidly evolving. Going forward, OTTL will be a primary configuration option with processors, such as the transform processor, relying on it.

Extensions

While typically not directly interacting with telemetry data, extensions are another critical component in the Collector. Multiple categories of extensions can be found in the Collector, as shown in Table 5.4. In general, authentication, observers, and storage extensions are environment specific. The storage extension gives the Collector a persistent store via a database or filesystem, allowing the Collector to keep telemetry data in case configured exporters are unavailable. Of the extensions, the `healthcheckextension` and `zpagesextension` are the extensions that should be enabled for most environments. These extensions will be discussed in the "Observing" section.

TABLE 5.4: Extensions grouped into categories and with examples

CATEGORY	EXAMPLES
Authentication—Used by receivers and exporters	◆ `basicauthextension` ◆ `bearertokenauthextension` ◆ `oidcauthextension`
Health and Troubleshooting	◆ `healthcheckextension` ◆ `pprofextension` ◆ `remotetapextension` ◆ `zpagesextension`
Observers—Used by receivers to discover and collect data dynamically	◆ `dockerobserver` ◆ `hostobserver` ◆ `k8sobserver`
Persistence—Via a database or filesystem	◆ `storage/dbstorage` ◆ `storage/filestorage`

Connectors

Connectors are one of the newest components in the Collector. They are unique in that they result in one or more additional service pipelines being run due to the completion of a service pipeline. For example, say you had a trace receiver `foo` that sent data to a trace exporter `bar`, and for this service pipeline, you wanted to create a count, or metric, of all spans sent to a metric exporter `baz`. You could achieve this with the following Collector configuration:

```
receivers:
  foo:
exporters:
  bar:
connectors:
  count:
service:
  pipelines:
    traces:
      receivers: [foo]
      exporters: [count, bar]
    metrics:
      receivers: [count]
      exporters: [baz]
```

If you did not create the `count` metric, the `foo` receiver would only send it to the `bar` exporter in the trace service pipeline. With the desire to create a `count` metric, a second service pipeline was needed, and the count connector was used as both an exporter and a receiver. It is important to note that when connectors are used, they must be used as both an exporter and a receiver.

While generating a metric is one example of what a connector can do, there are other use cases as well. For example, as you saw earlier, you can forward the data from one signal-specific service pipeline to a second service pipeline of the same signal type. While the earlier example was only demonstrative, there are real reasons for this functionality. For example, you could use this connector to send processed data to a platform but send the same processed data to a second platform with either metadata enrichment or metadata redacted. If two separate pipelines were used from the start, the same received data would need to be processed twice, with only one doing the final metadata mutation. For example:

```
service:
  pipelines:
    traces/1:
      receivers: [receiver1]
      processors: [processor1, processor2, processor3]
      exporters: [exporter1]
    traces/2:
      receivers: [receiver1]
      processors: [processor1, processor2, processor3, processor4]
      exporters: [exporter2]
```

Could instead be handled more efficiently by using a connector:

```
service:
  pipelines:
```

```
traces/1:
  receivers: [receiver1]
  processors: [processor1, processor2, processor3]
  exporters: [connector1, exporter1]
traces/2:
  receivers: [connector1]
  processors: [processor4]
  exporters: [exporter2]
```

Examples of other types of connectors include:

- **Exceptions:** Generating metrics or logs from span exceptions
- **Failover:** Allows for health-based routing between trace, metric, and log pipelines, depending on the health of target downstream exporters
- **Service graph:** Building a map representing the interrelationships between various services in a system

Observing

The Collector offers several components to track its health and performance. These aspects include:

- **Metrics:** The Collector uses OTel Go metric instrumentation internally and, by default, exposes a local Prometheus interface available at `http://127.0.0.1:8888`. If monitoring a Collector from a separate Collector instance, which is recommended for production environments, changing at least the endpoint configuration may be required. Telemetry settings for the Collector are configured under the `service::telemetry` section, as defined here: `https://opentelemetry.io/docs/collector/configuration/#telemetry`.
- **Health check extension:** This extension is beneficial for determining the health of the Collector. For example, when running in gateway mode, load balancers can use this endpoint to assess the health of the Collector instances.
- **zPages extension:** This extension shows configured pipelines and feature flag status and provides trace span exemplars. It is helpful in determining the running configuration as well as the result of receiver and exporter transactions.

The subsequent sections will cover examples of how to use these capabilities and what you can do with them.

Relevant Metrics

Prometheus metrics for the Collector offer some valuable insights into health and performance. For example:

- **Dropped data:** While alerting about all drops is likely undesirable, the following metrics can be a useful indicator that something is wrong, especially when the rate meaningfully changes over some time period:
  - `otelcol_processor_dropped_spans`

    - otelcol_processor_dropped_metric_points
    - otelcol_processor_dropped_log_records

- **Queue length:** The following metrics indicate the capacity of the retry queue (in batches) and the current size of the retry queue:
    - otelcol_exporter_queue_capacity
    - otelcol_exporter_queue_size

- **Enqueue failed:** The following metrics indicate that the signal data failed to be added to the sending queue. This may be caused by a full queue, meaning you may need to decrease your sending rate or horizontally scale the Collector.
    - otelcol_exporter_enqueue_failed_spans
    - otelcol_exporter_enqueue_failed_metric_points
    - otelcol_exporter_enqueue_failed_log_records

- **Receiver refused:** The following metrics indicate too many errors returned to clients. Depending on the deployment and the client's resilience, this may indicate data loss.
    - otelcol_receiver_refused_spans
    - otelcol_receiver_refused_metric_points
    - otelcol_receiver_refused_log_records

- **Exporter send failed:** Sustained rates indicate that the Collector cannot export data to the configured destination.
    - otelcol_exporter_send_failed_spans
    - otelcol_exporter_send_failed_metric_points
    - otelcol_exporter_send_failed_log_records

- **CPU cores against a known rate:** While monitoring CPU utilization may not be a good indication of health, measuring the number of cores against known safe rates can be a good way to gauge health—for example, `actual_rate/available_cores < safe_rate`. The `actual_rate` can be determined using the following metrics. Of course, you need to determine what the `safe_rate` is for your environment.
    - otelcol_receiver_accepted_spans
    - otelcol_receiver_accepted_metric_points
    - otelcol_receiver_accepted_log_records

The Collector can be configured to collect its own telemetry data. For example, given that a Prometheus interface is exposed by default, you can configure a Prometheus receiver to scrape the Collector's own endpoint. To test this locally, perform the following steps:

1. Create a configuration file called `otelcol-prometheus-debug.yaml` and add the following:

```
receivers:
  prometheus/internal:
    config:
      scrape_configs:
      - job_name: 'otel-collector'
        scrape_interval: 10s
        static_configs:
        - targets: ["127.0.0.1:8888"]
        metric_relabel_configs:
          - source_labels: [ __name__ ]
            regex: '.*grpc_io.*'
            action: drop

processors:
  # Add or remove detectors as applicable to your environment.
  # Important: By default, received resource metadata will be overridden.
  #            Set "override" to "false" if this is not desired.
  #            Remember: Order matters! The first detector to insert wins.
  resourcedetection:
    detectors: [env, eks, ecs, ec2, aks, azure, gcp, system]

exporters:
  debug:

service:
  pipelines:
    metrics:
      receivers: [prometheus/internal]
      processors: [resourcedetection]
      exporters: [debug]
```

2. Start the Collector with the YAML file:

```
$ ./otelcol-contrib --config otelcol-prometheus-debug.yaml
```

Of course, monitoring one's own telemetry data may not be the best decision because when the Collector has issues, it may not be able to collect or export its own telemetry data. As such, in production environments, it is recommended to create a dedicated gateway cluster whose job is only to collect the telemetry data of other Collectors. In most circumstances, this would require changing the default telemetry endpoint setting for all Collectors from which you wanted to scrape metrics. For example:

```
service:
  telemetry:
    metrics:
      address: 0.0.0.0:8888
```

Health Check Extension

The health check extension (`https://github.com/open-telemetry/opentelemetry-collector-contrib/blob/main/extension/healthcheckextension/README.md`) provides an HTTP URL that defaults to `http://0.0.0.0:13133/` and can be probed to check the status of the Collector. You can define, configure, and enable the extension as follows:

```
receivers:
  ...

exporters:
  ...

extensions:
  health_check:

service:
  extensions: [health_check]
  pipelines:
    ...
```

This extension can be used as a liveness and/or readiness probe on K8s or as a health check for a load balancer. For example, on K8s, the following could be added to the deployment YAML if the extension is enabled:

```
readinessProbe:
  initialDelaySeconds: 5
  httpGet:
    path: /
    port: 13133
livenessProbe:
  initialDelaySeconds: 5
  httpGet:
    path: /
    port: 13133
```

The health check extension provides the overall health of the Collector, not the health of pipelines. In the future, it will likely be able to report errors sending to destinations as well. As of version 0.102.1 of the Collector, it returns a parseable JSON response like the following:


```
{"status":"Server available","upSince":"2024-01-14T20:07:26.686831-
05:00","uptime":"8.385203625s"}
```


zPages Extension

The zPages extension (`https://github.com/open-telemetry/opentelemetry-collector/blob/main/extension/zpagesextension/README.md`) provides an HTTP URL that defaults to `http://localhost:55679/` and a dynamically generated set of HTML web pages (covered next) that display configuration and a lightweight way to display trace data from the running application without a database. The term zPages was created at Google. You can define, configure, and enable the extension as follows:

```
receivers:
  ...

exporters:
  ...

extensions:
  zpages:
    #endpoint: 0.0.0.0:55679

service:
  extensions: [zpages]
  pipelines:
    ...
```

To access zPages, especially in containerized environments, you may need to change the endpoint from `localhost:55679` to `0.0.0.0:55679`. You can uncomment the `endpoint` in the previous example if needed. After the extension is enabled, zPages makes build and configuration information available at `http://localhost:55679/debug/servicez` by default. The configuration information includes the following:

- A visualization of the defined pipelines (`http://localhost:55679/debug/pipelinez`)
- The enabled extensions (`http://localhost:55679/debug/extensionz`)
- The status of feature flags (`http://localhost:55679/debug/featurez`)

Trace data is available at `http://localhost:55679/debug/tracez` and is helpful in observing the Collector's health. The Collector must have processed some data for the Trace Spans table to show any data. Upon doing so, receiver and exporter trace spans will be shown. The data displayed is sampled and meant to provide exemplars of system behavior. To test this, start the Collector with the connector config created earlier: `./otelcol-contrib --config otelcol-connector.yaml`. Send the Zipkin payload created earlier in a separate window: `curl -d @trace-attributes.json http://0.0.0.0:9411`. In a browser, visit the trace data page, and you should see the number one entered in three separate sections, as shown in Figure 5.9.

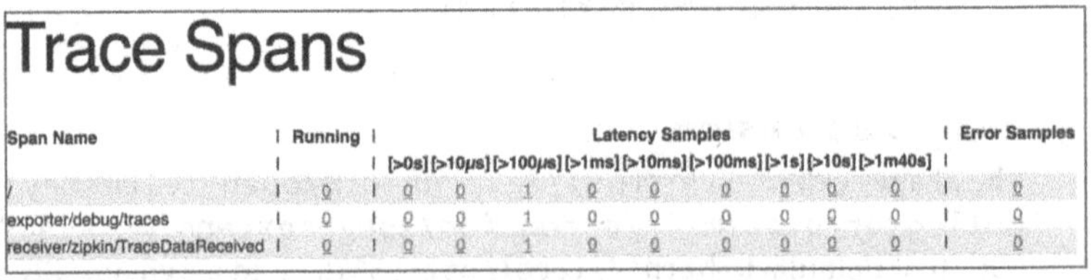

Trace Spans

Span Name	Running	Latency Samples									Error Samples
		[>0s]	[>10μs]	[>100μs]	[>1ms]	[>10ms]	[>100ms]	[>1s]	[>10s]	[>1m40s]	
/	0	0	0	1	0	0	0	0	0	0	0
exporter/debug/traces	0	0	0	1	0	0	0	0	0	0	0
receiver/zipkin/TraceDataReceived	0	0	0	1	0	0	0	0	0	0	0

FIGURE 5.9 An example of the zPages Trace Spans page after receiving a single payload.

You can click the number one to see additional information about the request. The row containing the path, in this case /, will give you information about the inbound request (see Figure 5.10).

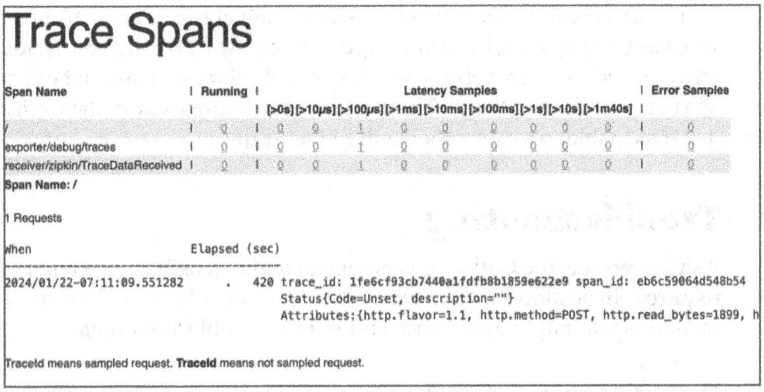

FIGURE 5.10 Selecting a non-zero number link next to the path will display information about the inbound request.

The row containing the receiver information will provide information about accepted and refused data, as shown in Figure 5.11.

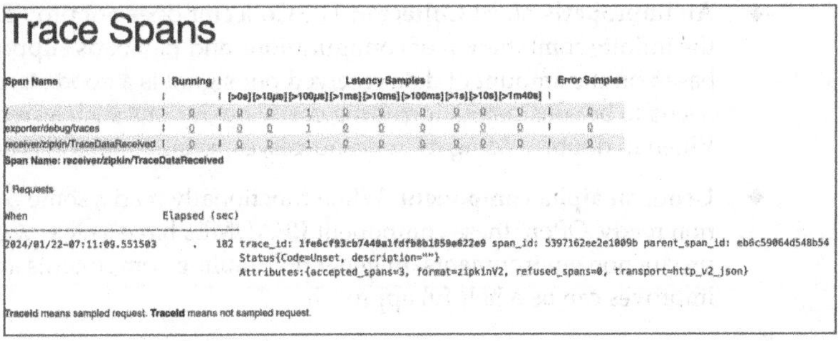

FIGURE 5.11 Selecting a non-zero number link next to the receiver will display information regarding data received or refused.

The row containing the exporter information will provide information about sent and failed data (see Figure 5.12).

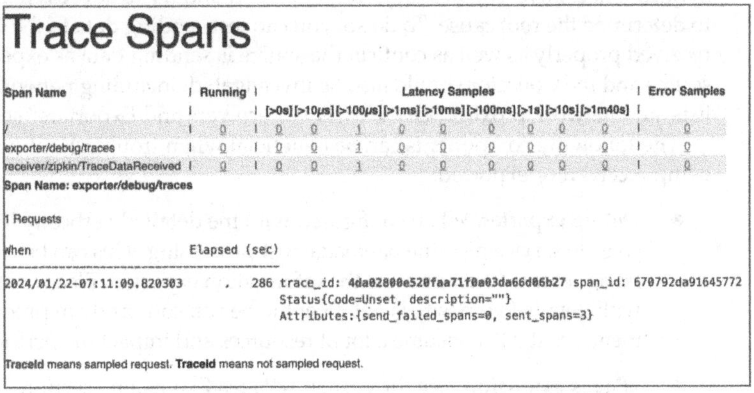

FIGURE 5.12 Selecting a non-zero number link next to the exporter will display information regarding data sent or failed.

The OTel specification also has information about zPages (`https://github.com/open-telemetry/opentelemetry-specification/blob/main/development/trace/zpages.md`). It even defines additional endpoints such as `/debug/traceconfigz`, `/debug/statsz`, and `/debug/rpcz`. These endpoints do not exist in the Collector as of version 0.95.0, but it is reasonable to assume they will in the future.

Troubleshooting

As you can see, the Collector is powerful and extensible. As a result, proper observing is required. In addition, you may run into a variety of issues. This section discusses some common scenarios you might experience and how to troubleshoot them.

Out of Memory Crashes

Out of memory (OOM) crashes are almost always the result of:

- **A misconfiguration:** This could be either the `GOGC` or `GOMEMLIMIT` environment variables or the memory limiter processor.
- **An improperly sized Collector:** The Collector does not provide sizing guidelines due to the infinite combination of configurations and payloads supported. In general, sizing based on the amount of data received per signal is a good starting place. Next, processing needs to be considered, including costly operations such as regular expression matching. When in doubt, adding more resources, especially memory, can help.
- **Using an alpha component:** While functionally ready, some components are not production ready. Often, these component READMEs have a clear warning about using them in production environments. In general, disabling components and seeing if the situation improves can be a helpful approach.

Data Not Being Received or Exported

A big issue experienced that may or may not be due to the Collector is that data is either not received or not exported. In this situation, you may expect to see an error from either the client, which may be another Collector or the instrumentation, or on the server, in this case, the Collector in question. If there is, you should understand it and try to address it. If there is not, then you need to determine the root cause. To do so, you can test sending data to the Collector to ensure that it is received properly as well as confirm the source is sending data as expected. Anything between the source and the Collector should also be investigated, including network connectivity, access control lists, and network proxies. See the earlier "Receivers and Exporters" section to learn more.

The following components can be beneficial when troubleshooting issues involving data being received or exported:

- **Debug exporter:** When configured with the detailed verbosity level, it can write to the console service pipeline payloads post-processing. This can be useful to ensure that data is being received and contains the information expected. Please note that the debug exporter with detailed verbosity is not meant to be run constantly in production or high-load environments, as it will consume a lot of resources and impact the performance of the Collector.
- **zPages extension:** See the earlier "zPages Extension" section.

Performance Issues

One problem often reported about the Collector is that it uses a lot of resources, especially memory. When memory pressure is seen, people will usually give the Collector more memory, expecting the utilization to decrease, but will find all memory remains consumed. This is by design, as the Collector is optimizing for the memory it is allocated. More memory offers more GC and buffer capacity. In short, all memory being used is not a problem, but OOM crashes are (see the earlier "Out of Memory Crashes" section). Properly setting Go environment variables and correctly configuring the memory limiter can often help with performance issues. It is common for resources on the Collector to be increased, but these settings are not adjusted to account for the additional capacity.

High CPU utilization is often the result of using an alpha component that has not been optimized or due to the configuration of processors that require a lot of CPU, such as those that utilize regular expressions. Minimizing the work it does and optimizing its configuration will go a long way in reducing utilization issues. Of course, if you are experiencing an issue, you should report it on GitHub with the appropriate steps to reproduce the problem.

You may run into other performance issues related to high resource utilization. For example, you may notice that the Collector's queue starts to grow, it may apply back pressure to inbound clients, or it may even drop data. While this may indicate a configuration, sizing, or resource issue, it may be a general performance issue. Looking at the relevant metrics and leveraging the zPages extension as outlined in the preceding section can help confirm a performance problem. Assuming adding resources does not address the issue or requires significantly more resources than expected, the first thing to check is whether in-development (formerly experimental) and especially alpha components are being used. Removing components and testing can help isolate the problem. When dealing with a very large Collector handling multiple signals, it may make sense to deploy Collectors per signal type to minimize noisy neighbor problems and the number of components that need to be leveraged.

If you believe the Collector itself is having performance issues that are code related, then the pprof extension can be used. pprof is a performance profiling tool initially developed for Go. It enables you to visualize and analyze profiling data. The use of pprof is an advanced use case typically reserved for Collector approvers and maintainers or software engineers who want to better understand the internal performance of the Collector code base. If a suspected performance issue is being experienced with the Collector, filing a support issue on GitHub with the relevant steps to reproduce is sufficient. Someone from the community can then run a pprof analysis if needed.

Beyond the Basics

By now, you should have a good understanding of critical Collector concepts, including deployment modes, components, and configuration. You should also be aware of some more advanced topics, including Collector distributions, sizing, security, and management.

Distributions

Distributions was a topic covered in Chapter 2. In short, distributions offer an OTel component with either a subset of capabilities or minor modifications. To see which components are included in a Collector distribution, you can run the Collector with the `components` command, which will list all the components and their status. An abbreviated output would look like the following:

```
$ ./otelcol-contrib components
otelcol components
buildinfo:
    command: otelcol
    description: OpenTelemetry Collector
    version: 0.95.0
receivers:
    - name: prometheus
      stability:
        logs: Undefined
        metrics: Beta
        traces: Undefined
...
```

The OTel project provides the following distributions of the Collector:

- Core (`https://github.com/open-telemetry/opentelemetry-collector`)
- Contrib (`https://github.com/open-telemetry/opentelemetry-collector-contrib`)
- K8s (`https://github.com/open-telemetry/opentelemetry-collector-releases/tree/main/distributions/otelcol-k8s`)

In addition, many vendors provide their own distribution of the Collector. They do this for various reasons—primarily for supportability and ease of use—and package only the required components. The OTel website ecosystem section has a page dedicated to available third-party (mainly vendor) distributions (`https://opentelemetry.io/ecosystem/distributions`).

Beyond the provided distributions, you may want to create your own. Reasons for this may include your desire to:

- Remove unused or unneeded components to reduce the security surface of the Collector, including the required dependencies
- Extend the Collector with additional capabilities
- Create custom packaging beyond what OTel provides

Distributions can either be created from scratch or by starting with an existing distribution and modifying it. A tool is provided to help with the process of building distributions called the OpenTelemetry Collector Builder, or OCB (`https://github.com/open-telemetry/opentelemetry-collector/tree/main/cmd/builder`). The process to use the tool is as follows:

1. Download or install OCB. For example, you can run the command, assuming you have Go installed. Please be advised that the version number tag listed after `@` should be the same version as the components in the manifest (described in step 2). Otherwise, the `builder` command will likely fail. This means using the `latest` version tag is not recommended. Given that version `0.95.0` is used in step 2, it will be used here.

   ```
   $ go install go.opentelemetry.io/collector/cmd/builder@0.95.0
   ```

2. Create an OCB YAML file that specifies the components and versions you want. For example, create a file named `otelcol-builder.yaml` and add the following:

```
dist:
  name: otelcol-custom
  description: Local OpenTelemetry Collector binary
  output_path: /tmp/dist
exporters:
  - gomod: github.com/open-telemetry/opentelemetry-collector-
contrib/exporter/alibabacloudlogserviceexporter v0.95.0
  - gomod: go.opentelemetry.io/collector/exporter/debugexporter v0.95.0

receivers:
  - gomod: go.opentelemetry.io/collector/receiver/otlpreceiver v0.95.0

processors:
  - gomod: go.opentelemetry.io/collector/processor/batchprocessor v0.95.0
```

3. Run the OCB tool (called `builder`) with the YAML file:

```
$ builder --config=otelcol-builder.yaml
```

4. Start the Collector distribution with the `otelcol-otlp-debug.yaml` configuration file you created in the "Configuration" section earlier in this chapter:

```
$ /tmp/dist/otelcol-custom --config=otelcol.yaml
```

Securing

Given that the Collector has the potential to receive, process, and export all telemetry data within an environment, the Collector must be hardened appropriately, especially in production environments. The Collector is secure by default, but configuration changes and operational concerns may result in potential security vulnerabilities. In this chapter, you already learned about important security aspects in receivers and exporters, including authentication, encryption, and exposing network ports. Other aspects need to be considered as well. The Collector repository captures security best practices here: `https://github.com/open-telemetry/opentelemetry-collector/blob/main/docs/security-best-practices.md`. For end users, it lists the following items. After each item, additional information is provided.

- Configuration
  - *SHOULD* only enable the minimum required components. As covered earlier, everything enabled is a potential attack vector.
  - *SHOULD* ensure sensitive configuration information is stored securely—for example, secrets should not be stored in plain text in the YAML configuration file.
- Permissions
  - *SHOULD NOT* run Collector as root/admin user. If the Collector is compromised and run as root/admin, then other systems may be at risk of being compromised.
  - *MAY* require privileged access for some components. Care should be taken in these circumstances.

- Receivers/exporters
  - *SHOULD* use encryption and authentication, as discussed earlier in this chapter.
  - *SHOULD* limit exposure of servers to authorized users, as discussed earlier in this chapter.
  - *MAY* pose a security risk if configuration parameters are modified improperly.
- Processors
  - *SHOULD* configure obfuscation/scrubbing of sensitive metadata. Security can also be of the telemetry data being processed.
  - *SHOULD* configure recommended processors. The recommended processor can help mitigate security concerns such as a distributed denial-of-service (DDoS) attack.
- Extensions
  - *SHOULD NOT* expose sensitive health or telemetry data. Any information made available could be used to compromise the system.

Beyond these considerations, aspects including upgrades for security fixes and token rotation also need to be considered.

Management

Configuring a single Collector is straightforward, but what if you need to configure dozens, hundreds, or even thousands of Collectors? At scale, configuration management becomes a genuine concern. For example, what if you need to rotate the API token used to export data or if you need to add or remove a new component? Most Collectors leave configuration management as a task to the end user. This is because various configuration management tools are available, and the end user may already use one or more. For example, Ansible,[19] Chef,[20] and Puppet[21] are all standard solutions. In addition, Terraform[22] and K8s[23] have been widely adopted, and both support capabilities in this space.

Although managing the configuration file is a big part of the configuration management story, it is not the only part. For example, upgrade rollout strategy also matters. Take, for example, a gateway cluster. Suppose a configuration management solution updates the configuration on all cluster nodes simultaneously. In that case, the gateway cluster will be unavailable for some time, causing back pressure and possibly leading to data loss. A rollout strategy is needed to ensure that enough of the cluster is running during the rollout to prevent data loss.

The OTel project has a solution to address this and other problems with managing at-scale. It offers a protocol called OpAMP, or Open Agent Management Protocol. OpAMP supports the following functionality:

- Remote configuration
- Status reporting
- Collector telemetry reporting
- Management of downloadable Collector-specific packages

- Secure auto-updating capabilities
- Connection credentials management

In short, OpAMP handles the complete Collector lifecycle. OpAMP is agent/collector agnostic and could be used to manage the lifecycle of any agent/collector, not just the OTel Collector. Beyond the protocol itself, which is currently in beta (`https://opentelemetry.io/docs/specs/opamp`), implementing OpAMP requires an OpAMP server, a client implementation, and, depending on the mode, a supervisor. The server tells a client implementation or supervisor what to do whereas, a supervisor oversees a Collector lifecycle, including deployment and configuration. A single server supports multiple client implementations and/or supervisors, while a supervisor always has a 1:1 relationship with a Collector. There are two modes of operation regarding OpAMP, as described next and shown in Figure 5.13.

- Read-Write (R/W): This mode offers full lifecycle capabilities. To work, a supervisor is required.
- Read-Only (R/O): This mode offers limited lifecycle capabilities—namely, viewing, but not changing, configuration and health details.

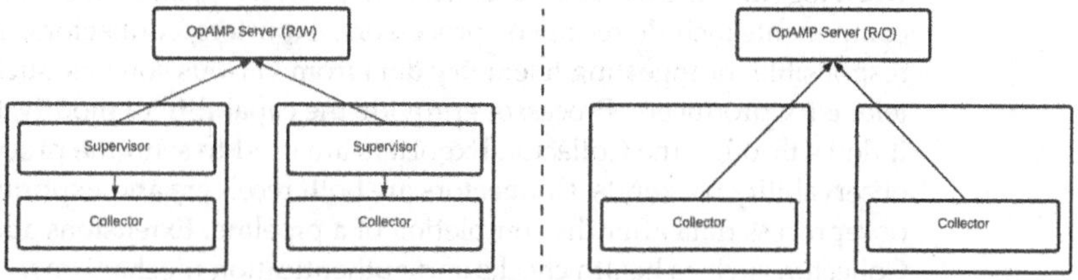

FIGURE 5.13 The two modes of operating OpAMP. On the left, the read-write mode architecture is shown. On the right, the read-only mode architecture is shown. A single server could support both modes in parallel.

The Collector has native integration with OpAMP. The client implementation is available via the OpAMP extension (`https://github.com/open-telemetry/opentelemetry-collector-contrib/tree/main/extension/opampextension`). This extension allows you to define the server endpoint and configuration options. To get started in read-only mode, you need to configure and enable the extension in a way similar to the following configuration example. In addition, the Collector repository includes a supervisor implementation that is currently in development (`https://github.com/open-telemetry/opentelemetry-collector-contrib/tree/main/cmd/opampsupervisor`). Collector releases do not publish a supervisor artifact as of version 0.95.0. See the previous link for information on how to build a supervisor as well as its current capabilities.

```
extensions:
  opamp:
    server:
      ws:
        endpoint: wss://127.0.0.1:4320/v1/opamp

service:
  extensions: [opamp]
```

OTel is also developing a Go implementation of an OpAMP server (`https://github.com/open-telemetry/opamp-go`). Of course, any end user, open source project, or vendor could implement one based on the OpAMP specification. Some vendors already offer server implementations that support OpAMP.

You can read more about how to get started with the OpAMP protocol here: `https://opentelemetry.io/docs/collector/management/#opamp`.

The Bottom Line

Distinguish between agent and gateway mode. The Collector comes in various packaging and can be deployed in two primary modes: agent and gateway. Each mode provides capabilities that may be beneficial when processing telemetry data. While using the Collector is not required, deploying at least the agent to separate telemetry generation from processing and exporting is highly recommended.

Master It What is the difference between agent and gateway mode?

Identify Collector components. The Collector is composed of several key components that work together to facilitate the collection, processing, and export of telemetry data. These components include receivers, processors, exporters, connectors, and extensions. Receivers are responsible for ingesting telemetry data from various sources, such as applications and other telemetry producers. Processors provide the capability to modify, filter, and enrich the data as it flows through the Collector. Exporters are used to send the processed data to different observability backends. Connectors are both receivers and exporters and are used to process or reprocess data after the completion of a pipeline. Extensions add functionality to the Collector, such as health checks and authentication mechanisms.

Master It When getting started, what are the most essential components to configure?

Configure and run the Collector. Configuring and running the Collector involves defining the appropriate settings for its components and ensuring that it operates efficiently within your environment. Configuration is typically done through YAML files. You define and configure receivers, processors, exporters, connectors, and extensions settings in each file. To run the Collector, you must ensure that it is properly installed and the configuration file is correctly set up. Depending on your infrastructure, you can run the Collector in various form factors, including a stand-alone application, Docker container, or K8s pod. By carefully configuring the Collector, you can ensure that it collects, processes, and exports telemetry data effectively, providing valuable insights into your system's performance and behavior.

Master It How are Collector components configured?

Size, secure, observe, and troubleshoot the Collector. Proper sizing, securing, observing, and troubleshooting of the OTel Collector are critical to maintaining its performance and reliability. Sizing involves allocating sufficient resources, such as CPU and memory, to handle the expected volume of telemetry data without bottlenecks. Securing the Collector includes implementing authentication and encryption to protect telemetry data in transit and at rest. Observing the Collector entails monitoring its performance metrics, such as throughput and latency, to ensure that it operates within acceptable parameters. Troubleshooting involves diagnosing and resolving issues, such as misconfigurations or resource constraints, that may impact the Collector's functionality. You can maintain a robust and secure observability infrastructure that meets your organization's needs by addressing these aspects.

Master It Which components can be used to observe and troubleshoot the Collector?

Notes

1 `https://opentelemetry.io/docs`
2 `https://pkg.go.dev/go.opentelemetry.io/collector/consumer/pdata`
3 `https://opentelemetry.io/docs/collector/deployment`
4 `https://opentelemetry.io/docs/collector/deployment`
5 `https://en.wikipedia.org/wiki/SIGHUP`
6 `https://kubernetes.io/docs/concepts/workloads/controllers/deployment/#strategy`
7 `https://yaml.org`
8 `https://github.com/open-telemetry/docs/platform-support.md`
9 `https://support.apple.com/guide/mac-help/open-a-mac-app-from-an-unidentified-developer-mh40616/mac`
10 `https://kubernetes.io/docs/concepts/configuration/manage-resource-containers`
11 `https://en.wikipedia.org/wiki/Cloud_computing_issues#Performance_interference_and_noisy_neighbors`
12 Note the Jaeger export has been removed in favor of native OTLP
13 `https://opentelemetry.io/docs/collector`
14 Note the Jaeger receiver may also be used. With that said, Jaeger supports and recommends receiving data in OTLP format. In the future, the Jaeger receiver may be deprecated and removed.
15 `https://opentelemetry.io/docs/kubernetes/operator/automatic`
16 `https://github.com/open-telemetry/opentelemetry-collector/tree/main/extension/ballastextension`
17 `https://pkg.go.dev/net/http`
18 `https://github.com/open-telemetry/opentelemetry-collector/tree/main/processor#recommended-processors`
19 `https://www.ansible.com`
20 `https://www.chef.io`
21 `https://www.puppet.com`
22 `https://www.terraform.io`
23 `https://kubernetes.io`

Chapter 6

Leveraging OpenTelemetry Instrumentation

Now, it is time for you to try instrumenting an application with OpenTelemetry! Before reading this chapter, you should be familiar with OpenTelemetry concepts, including signals, API, SDK, processors, and exporters, as discussed in Chapter 4, "Understanding the OpenTelemetry Specification." In addition, understanding how to use the OpenTelemetry Collector, as discussed in Chapter 5, "Managing the OpenTelemetry Collector," will allow you to configure a more production-like environment.

In this chapter, you will explore the powerful capabilities of OpenTelemetry instrumentation and how it can be leveraged to gain comprehensive insights into your applications and infrastructure. Instrumentation is at the heart of observability, enabling you to collect detailed telemetry data that illuminates the inner workings of your systems. The content in this chapter will be technical and cover language- and environment-specific aspects. Reading this chapter sequentially is highly recommended regardless of the signal type you are interested in. A containerized Python application will be primarily used, but differences between Python and other programming languages will also be explored. In addition, the examples in this chapter are optimized for Linux, but modifying them for operating systems such as Windows should be relatively easy. The OpenTelemetry Collector version 0.95.0 and Python instrumentation version 1.23.0/0.44.b0 were used to create this chapter and are the minimum recommended versions to test against. Newer versions of the Collector and instrumentation may have changes in behavior, so check the OpenTelemetry documentation if anything does not work as expected. All code examples are available in the book's GitHub repository (`https://github.com/flands/mastering-otel-book`). Regardless of your background or level of experience, the material in this chapter is designed to be approachable by everyone.

By the end of this chapter, you will have a clear understanding of how to implement and customize OpenTelemetry instrumentation to capture metrics, logs, and traces effectively. Whether your goal is to instrument a new application or enhance an existing one, this chapter will provide the practical guidance and best practices needed to make the most of OpenTelemetry instrumentation.

IN THIS CHAPTER, YOU WILL LEARN TO:

- Instrument an application in various ways
- Add production-ready instrumentation
- Enrich instrumentation with metadata

Environment Setup

OpenTelemetry (OTel) instrumentation documentation (`https://opentelemetry.io/docs/instrumentation`) includes getting started information and multiple examples. The application you will play with in this chapter is adapted from "The OpenTelemetry Documentation," by The OpenTelemetry Authors, used under CC BY 4.0 (`https://creativecommons.org/licenses/by/4.0`). It is based on the OTel instrumentation getting started documentation, such as `https://opentelemetry.io/docs/instrumentation/python/getting-started`, as well as instrumentation examples, such as `https://opentelemetry.io/docs/instrumentation/python/automatic/example`. The modifications in this chapter are to better demonstrate a production environment and test capabilities you will likely want to leverage to achieve observability. While some basic Python knowledge is helpful, the prescriptive steps that follow should work as long as the environment is properly configured with the following prerequisites:

- `curl`[1]
- Docker and Docker Compose 2.0.0+

The examples in this chapter will be defined and run via Docker Compose to simulate instrumenting a production containerized application. The following containers will be configured:

- (Optional but recommended to simulate a more production-like environment) The OTel Collector using a configuration created in Chapter 5. Version 0.95.0 (`https://github.com/open-telemetry/opentelemetry-collector-contrib/releases/tag/v0.95.0`) of the Collector was used for these examples. Newer versions should work with minimal to no modifications.
  - Alternatively, you can leverage the `console` exporter instead of the default `otlp` exporter for local testing.
  - A container running a supported version of Python 3+[2] with the following dependencies:
    - GCC and GCC-C++,[3] which is typically available in most distributions of Linux except slim versions, such as Alpine, CentOS, Debian, and Ubuntu, as defined here: `https://opentelemetry.io/docs/instrumentation/python/automatic/#python-package-installation-failure`
    - `pip`[4]

Alternatively, if you are comfortable testing locally, you can set up a Python virtual environment case using either venv[5] or `virtualenv`[6] and manually install the required modules. For example:

```
$ #cd /some/dir
$ python3 -m venv venv
$ source ./venv/bin/activate
$ pip3 install Flask Werkzeug requests paste waitress
```

Again, this chapter will simulate a production, containerized environment, so the following examples will be optimized for Docker. To configure the containerized environment, first create a file called `server.py` and add the following contents:

```
from random import randint
from flask import Flask, request
from paste.translogger import TransLogger
from waitress import serve
import logging
import os

SERVER_HOST = os.getenv('SERVER_HOST', '127.0.0.1')
SERVER_PORT = os.getenv('SERVER_PORT', 8080)

app = Flask(__name__)
appname = os.path.splitext(os.path.basename(__file__))[0]

logging.basicConfig(level=logging.INFO)
logger = logging.getLogger(__name__)


@app.route('/')
def return_hello():
    player = get_player('OTel Test')
    return 'Hello! Be sure to roll the dice at /rolldice'


@app.route("/rolldice")
def roll_dice():
    player = get_player()
    result = str(roll())
    logger.warning("%s is rolling the dice: %s", player, result)
    return result


def get_player(default=None):
    try:
        if default is None:
            default = 'Anonymous player'
            raise TypeError
    except TypeError:
        logger.warning("Player request arg not set")
    return request.args.get('player', default=default, type=str)



def roll():
    return [randint(1, 6), randint(1, 6)]
```

```
if __name__ == "__main__":
    serve(TransLogger(app), host=SERVER_HOST, port=SERVER_PORT)
```

As you can see, the preceding Flask application uses `waitress` as the production Web Server Gateway Interface (WSGI) server. As mentioned, the example application is meant to simulate a production environment. If you are using a different WSGI server or only want to test Flask locally, you can modify the example as needed.

Next, create a file called `Dockerfile` with the following contents:

```
# New versions of Python may be available
# Given OTel Python only supports supported version of Python,
# the version may need to be increased to a supported version.

FROM python:3.9-slim

# Default settings

ENV SERVER_APP=${SERVER_APP:-server.py}
ENV SERVER_HOST=${SERVER_HOST:-0.0.0.0}
ENV SERVER_PORT=${SERVER_PORT:-8080}
ENV OTEL_SERVICE_NAME=${OTEL_SERVICE_NAME}
WORKDIR /app

# Build commands

COPY . .

RUN apt-get update -y && apt-get install -y gcc
RUN pip3 install --upgrade pip # Optional, but recommended
RUN python3 -m pip install --upgrade setuptools wheel # Optional, but recommended

RUN pip3 install Flask Werkzeug requests paste waitress

# Run commands
# Note: execution form will not work due to dynamic variable
# Note: exec is required in order for Ctrl+C to be respected

CMD exec python3 ${SERVER_APP}
```

To simulate telemetry data collection in a production environment, the OTel Collector will be configured to receive the telemetry data generated from the application. Alternatively, you could test with the console exporter locally, but this would not simulate a production environment. To ease the configuration of multiple containers, create a file called `compose.yaml` and add the following contents:

```
services:
  server:
    build:
      context: .
```

```
      dockerfile: ${MY_DOCKERFILE}
    environment:
      - SERVER_APP
      - SERVER_HOST
      - SERVER_PORT
      - OTEL_SERVICE_NAME
    ports:
      - "${SERVER_PORT}:${SERVER_PORT}"
  otelcol:

    # Note: Using the latest tag is not recommended for production environments
    image: otel/opentelemetry-collector-contrib:0.95.0
    # This requires the YAML file you created in Chapter 5
    volumes:
      - ./otelcol-otlp-debug.yaml:/etc/otelcol-contrib/config.yaml
    ports:
      - "4317:4317"  # OTLP gRPC receiver
```

After saving the changes, the last thing you need to do is dynamically configure the containers in the compose Yet Another Markup Language (YAML) file. To do this, create a file called `.env`, short for "environment," and add the following environment variables:

```
SERVER_APP=server.py
SERVER_HOST=0.0.0.0
SERVER_PORT=8080
```

After saving the file, the last step is to copy the `otelcol-otlp-debug.yaml` file from Chapter 5 into the same directory. If you have not completed Chapter 5, you can find the file in the GitHub repository associated with this book. If you are in the `chapter6` directory of the repository, you can run the following command:

```
cp ../chapter5/otelcol-otelp-debug.yaml .
```

(Do not forget the ending period.)

Now everything is configured and you can start Docker Compose by running:

```
$ docker compose up --build --force-recreate --remove-orphans --detach
```

On the first run, whenever the `--build` flag is specified, or a new container version is specified, the containers will need to be fetched and built. As a result, it will take a while for the containers to start running. You only need to pass the `--build` flag when you have made changes that would impact a container—for example, changes to the Dockerfile or any of the `*.py` files. Given that this chapter is all about making changes, the `--build` flag will always be passed. Once the preceding command finishes, the containers will run in the background. To see the logs for the running containers, run:

```
$ docker-compose logs -f -t
```

Upon doing so, you should see output like the following (you will likely be running a newer version of the Collector, so the version number will be newer than `v0.95.0`):

```
server-1    | 2024-09-16T12:32:24.695492464Z INFO:waitress:Serving on
   http://0.0.0.0:8080
```

```
otelcol-1  | 2024-09-16T09:13:40.499830137Z 2024-06-24T09:13:40.498Z   info
   service@v0.95.0/telemetry.go:55   Setting up own telemetry...
otelcol-1  | 2024-09-16T09:13:40.499863096Z 2024-06-24T09:13:40.499Z   info
   service@v0.95.0/telemetry.go:97   Serving metrics
   {"address": ":8888", "level": "Basic"}
otelcol-1  | 2024-09-16T09:13:40.500743137Z 2024-06-24T09:13:40.499Z   info
   exporter@v0.95.0/exporter.go:275   Development component. May change in the
   future. {"kind": "exporter", "data_type": "traces", "name": "debug"}
otelcol-1  | 2024-09-16T09:13:40.501911721Z 2024-06-24T09:13:40.501Z   info
   service@v0.95.0/service.go:143   Starting otelcol-contrib...
   {"Version": "0.95.0", "NumCPU": 8}
otelcol-1  | 2024-09-16T09:13:40.502781304Z 2024-06-24T09:13:40.501Z   info
   extensions/extensions.go:34   Starting extensions...
otelcol-1  | 2024-09-16T09:13:40.503943596Z 2024-06-24T09:13:40.502Z   warn
   internal@v0.95.0/warning.go:42 Using the 0.0.0.0 address exposes this server
   to every network interface, which may facilitate Denial of Service attacks.
   Enable the feature gate to change the default and remove this warning.
   {"kind": "receiver", "name": "otlp", "data_type": "traces", "documentation":
   "https://github.com/open-telemetry/opentelemetry-collector/blob/main/docs/
   security-best-practices.md#safeguards-against-denial-of-service-attacks",
   "feature gate ID": "component.UseLocalHostAsDefaultHost"}
otelcol-1  | 2024-09-16T09:13:40.505334137Z 2024-06-24T09:13:40.503Z   info
   otlpreceiver@v0.95.0/otlp.go:102   Starting GRPC server {"kind":
   "receiver", "name": "otlp", "data_type": "traces", "endpoint": "0.0.0.0:4317"}
otelcol-1  | 2024-09-16T09:13:40.505407387Z 2024-06-24T09:13:40.505Z   info
   service@v0.95.0/service.go:169 Everything is ready. Begin running and
   processing data.
otelcol-1  | 2024-09-16T09:13:40.505410096Z 2024-06-24T09:13:40.505Z   warn
   localhostgate/featuregate.go:63 The default endpoints for all servers in
   components will change to use localhost instead of 0.0.0.0 in a future
   version. Use the feature gate to preview the new default. {"feature gate ID":
   "component.UseLocalHostAsDefaultHost"}
```

The default environment variables and settings to be aware of are as follows:

- Python application (`server.py`)
  - `SERVER_HOST` (listen interface): `127.0.0.1`
  - `SERVER_PORT` (listen port): `8080`
- Docker container
  - `SERVER_APP` (Python application to run): `server.py`
  - `SERVER_HOST` (listen interface): `0.0.0.0`
  - `SERVER_PORT` (listen port): `8080`
  - `OTEL_SERVICE_NAME` (`service.name` resource attribute): <None>

- Docker Compose server container
    - `SERVER_APP` (Python application to run): `server.py`
    - `SERVER_HOST` (listen interface): `0.0.0.0`
    - `SERVER_PORT` (listen port): `8080`
    - `OTEL_SERVICE_NAME` (`service.name` resource attribute): <None>

You can change the preceding by passing the appropriate environment variable. For example:

```
$ SERVER_PORT=8081 docker compose up --force-recreate --remove-orphans
```

With the container running and the container logs being tailed, test the Python server container using the `curl` command from a new window. Note that because the container is listening on all network interfaces (`0.0.0.0`) and local port `8080` is being mapped to the container port `8080`, you can `curl` the loopback interface to reach the container:

```
$ curl http://127.0.0.1:8080
Hello! Be sure to roll the dice at /rolldice
```

In the server-side window, you should see output like the following:

```
server-1    | 2024-09-16T13:12:30.126685720Z 192.168.65.1 - -
                [2024-09-16:13:12:30 +0000] "GET / HTTP/1.1" 200 6 "-" "curl/8.4.0"
```

As the output stated, there is a second route available. Try it out by running the following command:

```
$ curl http://127.0.0.1:8080/rolldice
[1, 2]
```

When calling the `/rolldice` route, you will notice a warning in the server window that says: `WARNING:__main__:Player request arg not set`. You can address this by passing a player name in the request like the following:

```
$ curl -G -d 'player=otel' 0.0.0.0:8080/rolldice
```

Congratulations, you have a working Python Flask application! When you are ready to shut down the containers, you can run:

```
$ docker compose down
```

You are now ready to add OTel instrumentation!

Python Trace Instrumentation

As you may recall, there are multiple ways to instrument an application, including automatic instrumentation, manual instrumentation, or via an instrumented library, also known as programmatic instrumentation. You will try all three mechanisms, focusing initially on the tracing signal. The goal will be to generate the exact same telemetry data regardless of the mechanism chosen. Next, you will instrument other signal data and play with more advanced scenarios. Along the way, you will learn about how to configure and extend the examples provided.

Version 1.23.0/0.44b0 (`https://github.com/open-telemetry/opentelemetry-python/releases/tag/v1.23.0`) of OTel Python instrumentation was used to create the output shown in this chapter. Newer versions should work with minimal to no modifications.

While it is easier to demonstrate non-production examples, such as just writing telemetry data to the console, to get a real feel for what is provided and how it works, it is better to attempt production-like scenarios. As a result, all scenarios provided in this chapter will be production-like (this is different than the OTel documentation). In addition, code comments will be provided to give additional context as there is more than one way to accomplish the same outcome. When possible, alternative approaches will be provided.

To get started with instrumentation, the basic steps are:

- Download the required dependencies.
- Update the configuration, primarily the OTel SDK.
  - Automatic instrumentation: set environment variables or runtime parameters
  - Manual instrumentation: add code interfaces
- Update the runtime parameters and start the application.

When updating instrumentation configuration, the following are important to keep in mind:

- Setting the `service.name` is critical and *highly recommended*, otherwise it will be hard to understand what service was impacted when analyzing data.
- Updating the exporter settings may be necessary. For example, when using protocols other than the OpenTelemetry protocol (OTLP) or sending to non-default locations.
- Changing at least the OTLP endpoint address will be necessary for most containerized environments.

Instrumentation is extremely flexible and offers a lot of configuration options. Most other configuration options would be a secondary concern and could be addressed after initial instrumentation has been added.

Automatic Instrumentation

The easiest way to instrument an application is via automatic instrumentation. In fact, it might be the only way for anyone who does not have access to or knowledge of the source code, such as operations teams or site reliability engineers (SREs). With that said, automatic instrumentation is not magic. It focuses on well-known frameworks and may not capture all telemetry required to achieve observability. In addition, it can be hard to control the data generated and might result in unacceptable performance overhead especially for latency-sensitive applications. You should consider using automatic instrumentation when instrumenting applications for the first time. You may also consider leveraging it with existing instrumentation to ease SDK configuration.

Automatic instrumentation works by injecting instrumentation during runtime and may be called bytecode instrumentation or monkey patching.[7] To get started with automatic trace instrumentation in Python, you need to install some dependencies, including:

- The opentelemetry-distro (`https://opentelemetry.io/docs/instrumentation/python/distro`), which contains the OTel API, SDK, `opentelemetry-bootstrap` command, and the `opentelemetry-instrument` command.

- The OTLP exporter, so telemetry data can be sent to the OTel Collector. By default, you can send telemetry data to the console, which is great for demo or debug purposes but unrealistic for a production environment. This can be installed independently or with the opentelemetry-distro.
- Instrumentation libraries for the frameworks your Python application leverages—in this case, `Flask`, `requests`, and `logging`. The `opentelemetry-bootstrap` command can handle this for you but will likely install more instrumentation packages than needed (more on this later).

Ready to try it out? Before continuing, follow the "Environment Setup" section earlier in this chapter! Create a copy of the Dockerfile you created earlier by running: `cp Dockerfile automatic.Dockerfile`. Then, add the following after the `RUN pip3 install` line in the automatic Dockerfile:

```
# The quotes are required or else the package will not be found with ZSH shells
# If the command still does not work, ensure straight quotes are being used
# as curly quotes will also not work.
# This command is equivalent to:
#   pip install opentelemetry-distro opentelemetry-exporter-otlp
RUN pip3 install "opentelemetry-distro[otlp]"

# If you only plan to use the console exporter (example: no OTel Collector),
# you can use this command instead:
#RUN pip3 install opentelemetry-distro

# Easiest to get started but installs more instrumentation packages than needed
#RUN opentelemetry-bootstrap -a install

# Requires manually determining which instrumentation packages are needed
# Instrumentation packages are available in the OTel Python Contrib repository
# https://github.com/open-telemetry/opentelemetry-python-
# contrib/tree/main/instrumentation
RUN pip3 install opentelemetry-instrumentation-flask
RUN pip3 install opentelemetry-instrumentation-requests
RUN pip3 install opentelemetry-instrumentation-logging
```

You may be wondering what the difference is between running the `opentelemetry-bootstrap` command and manually installing instrumentation packages. To see the differences, you could run the `bootstrap` command:

```
$ opentelemetry-bootstrap | sort
opentelemetry-instrumentation-aws-lambda==0.44b0 # not needed
opentelemetry-instrumentation-dbapi==0.44b0      # not needed
opentelemetry-instrumentation-flask==0.44b0
opentelemetry-instrumentation-grpc==0.44b0       # only if OTLP exporter
opentelemetry-instrumentation-jinja2==0.44b0     # not needed
opentelemetry-instrumentation-logging==0.44b0
opentelemetry-instrumentation-requests==0.44b0
opentelemetry-instrumentation-sqlite3==0.44b0    # not needed
```

```
opentelemetry-instrumentation-urllib3==0.44b0     # not needed
opentelemetry-instrumentation-urllib==0.44b0      # not needed
opentelemetry-instrumentation-wsgi==0.44b0
```

As you can see, the `opentelemetry-bootstrap` command, if run with the install action, will install the above instrumentation modules. While the above list includes required instrumentation modules, including `Flask` and `requests`, it also includes modules such as `AWS-Lambda` and `SQLite3`, which are unnecessary. These unneeded modules are known as default modules because they are included by default. You can see a list of detected versus default instrumentation modules here: `https://github.com/open-telemetry/opentelemetry-python-contrib/blob/main/opentelemetry-instrumentation/src/opentelemetry/instrumentation/bootstrap_gen.py`.

Ease-of-use Versus Production Readiness

Using `opentelemetry-bootstrap` versus manually installing the instrumentation packages required is an excellent example of ease-of-use versus production readiness. To ease adoption and quickly show value, OTel, like many other projects, offers mechanisms to make it easier to get started. For example, the `opentelemetry-bootstrap` command installs instrumentation packages that may be required for automatic instrumentation to work properly. While this is great, one drawback is that this command will likely install packages that are not required. These additional packages represent additional dependencies that need to be managed and secured. As such, care should be taken when moving from a development or proof of concept environment to a production environment as changes will likely be required to ensure proper hardening and that only required components are deployed.

Now that the required dependencies are installed, all you need to do is wrap your Python command with the `opentelemetry-instrument` command. By default, this command enables OTLP exporting of traces and metrics. For now, you will disable metric instrumentation as it will be covered in the next section. In the automatic instrumentation Dockerfile, comment out the `CMD` line by prefixing it with the pound symbol (#), then add the following after it:

```
#CMD exec python3 ${SERVER_APP}

CMD OTEL_SERVICE_NAME=${OTEL_SERVICE_NAME} \
    OTEL_EXPERIMENTAL_RESOURCE_DETECTORS=process \
    exec opentelemetry-instrument --metrics_exporter none \
         python3 ${SERVER_APP}
```

This example adds a few items above the bare minimum to get started. First, it sets an OTel `service.name` resource attribute based on the `OTEL_SERVICE_NAME` environment variable. If this step is skipped and two different Python applications send data from the same host, it would be difficult to determine which application it is coming from. Setting the `service.name` is *highly recommended* for production environments. As mentioned, the `service.name` is a resource attribute, which means the following command is also equivalent, though it takes lower precedence:

```
#CMD OTEL_RESOURCE_ATTRIBUTES=service.name=${OTEL_SERVICE_NAME} \
#    OTEL_EXPERIMENTAL_RESOURCE_DETECTORS=process \
```

```
#    exec opentelemetry-instrument --metrics_exporter none \
#         python3 ${SERVER_APP}
```

In addition, the preceding command enables the in development (formerly experimental) process resource detector. This processor enriches the telemetry data with process information, including process runtime and process ID (PID) details. While enabling this processor is not required, providing additional context makes the telemetry data more valuable. In short, this command demonstrates a more realistic production configuration. Of course, using an in development component in production is a business decision and comes with risks.

The preceding command can also be run in different ways depending on requirements. For example, the following commands are equivalent to the one in the previous code snippet:

```
# An equivalent and more specific way to run the command:
#CMD OTEL_SERVICE_NAME=${OTEL_SERVICE_NAME} \
#    OTEL_EXPERIMENTAL_RESOURCE_DETECTORS=process \
#    exec opentelemetry-instrument --traces_exporter otlp \
#         --metrics_exporter otlp python3 ${SERVER_APP}

# An equivalent way to run the command with only environment variables:
#CMD OTEL_SERVICE_NAME=${OTEL_SERVICE_NAME} \
#    OTEL_EXPERIMENTAL_RESOURCE_DETECTORS=process \
#    OTEL_METRICS_EXPORTER=none \
#    exec opentelemetry-instrument python3 ${SERVER_APP}

# If you wish to use the console exporter instead (example: no OTel Collector),
# use this command instead:
#CMD OTEL_SERVICE_NAME=${OTEL_SERVICE_NAME} \
#    OTEL_EXPERIMENTAL_RESOURCE_DETECTORS=process \
#    exec opentelemetry-instrument --traces_exporter console \
#         --metrics_exporter none python3 ${SERVER_APP}
```

The `opentelemetry-instrument` command supports a wide range of configuration options that can be specified via:

- Command-line interface (CLI) arguments: `./opentelemetry-instrument -h`
- Environment variables: `https://opentelemetry-python.readthedocs.io/en/stable/sdk/environment_variables.html`

Understanding the default options will make configuration and troubleshooting easier. For example, the default exporter configured for traces and metrics is OTLP, but what is the default endpoint address and port used? Default values are documented in the following locations:

- OTel Python instrumentation environment variables: `https://opentelemetry-python.readthedocs.io/en/stable/sdk/environment_variables.html#envvar-OTEL_EXPORTER_OTLP_ENDPOINT`
- OTel specification SDK configuration: `https://opentelemetry.io/docs/languages/sdk-configuration/otlp-exporter/#otel_exporter_otlp_endpoint`

The answer is `http://localhost:4317`, which may need to be changed in containerized environments since `localhost` refers to the user space of the container and thus cannot be used to communicate with a host-level agent.

Automatic Instrumentation Agent Versus Data Collection Agent

For many programming languages, automatic instrumentation contains what is referred to as an *agent*. For example, in Python, the `opentelemetry-instrument` command is called an *agent*. Perhaps a better example is that the automatic instrumentation Java archive (JAR) file that is passed to the Java application is done so via the `-javaagent` parameter. The use of the term *agent* may be confusing as it is a term also used for data collection, such as the OTel Collector running as an agent. It is important to note that an automatic instrumentation agent and a data collection agent are not the same thing. To distinguish, instrumentation can be referred to as language-based agents while data collection can be referred to as application- or host-based agents.

Given that you are running the Python application and Collector as Docker containers, the OTLP endpoint will need to be modified. While you could modify this in the code, leaving configuration outside the code can be easier and more flexible. As mentioned, there are environment variables that can handle this for you. The OTLP endpoint can either be configured per signal via `OTEL_EXPORTER_OTLP_TRACE_ENDPOINT` or centrally for all signals via `OTEL_EXPORTER_OTLP_ENDPOINT`. For this example, you will configure it centrally. In addition to the endpoint, the connection is secure by default unless an insecure protocol, such as `http://`, is used. While not advised for production environments, for this example you will use an insecure connection, which can also be specified per signal or centrally by an environment variable.

To configure these, add the following to the `.env` file (note that you must prefix the endpoint with something like `http://` (otherwise, the Docker build command will fail):[8]

```
$ echo OTEL_EXPORTER_OTLP_ENDPOINT=http://otelcol:4317 >>.env
```

Then, add the variable to the environment section of the server container in `compose.yaml`:

```
services:
  server:
    build: .
    environment:
      - SERVER_APP
      - SERVER_HOST
      - SERVER_PORT
      - OTEL_SERVICE_NAME
      - OTEL_EXPORTER_OTLP_ENDPOINT
...
```

With the automatic configuration in place, you can now build the new container and start everything up:

```
$ MY_DOCKERFILE=automatic.Dockerfile \
  OTEL_SERVICE_NAME=py-webserver \
  docker compose up --build --force-recreate --remove-orphans --detach
$ docker compose logs -f -t
```

Now, `curl` the endpoint again (`curl http://127.0.0.1:8080`) and you will see logs from the Collector (saved as `server-otelcol.log`). If you are testing locally with the console exporter, you will receive a JavaScript Object Notation (JSON) payload (saved as `server-local.json`).

```
otelcol-1  | 2024-09-16T13:56:18.592808964Z 2024-02-10T13:56:18.592Z   info
   TracesExporter{"kind": "exporter", "data_type": "traces", "name": "debug",
   "resource spans": 1, "spans": 1}
otelcol-1  | 2024-09-16T13:56:18.592942423Z 2024-02-10T13:56:18.592Z   info
   ResourceSpans #0
otelcol-1  | 2024-09-16T13:56:18.592956006Z Resource SchemaURL:
otelcol-1  | 2024-09-16T13:56:18.592963381Z Resource attributes:
otelcol-1  | 2024-09-16T13:56:18.592968923Z
   -> telemetry.sdk.language: Str(python)
otelcol-1  | 2024-09-16T13:56:18.592974631Z
   -> telemetry.sdk.name: Str(opentelemetry)
otelcol-1  | 2024-09-16T13:56:18.592989173Z
   -> telemetry.sdk.version: Str(1.22.0)
otelcol-1  | 2024-09-16T13:56:18.592996423Z
   -> process.runtime.description: Str(3.9.18 (main, Feb  1 2024, 05:34:35)
otelcol-1  | 2024-09-16T13:56:18.593002381Z [GCC 12.2.0])
otelcol-1  | 2024-09-16T13:56:18.593010506Z
   -> process.runtime.name: Str(cpython)
otelcol-1  | 2024-09-16T13:56:18.593015964Z
   -> process.runtime.version: Str(3.9.18)
otelcol-1  | 2024-09-16T13:56:18.593021381Z
   -> process.pid: Int(1)
otelcol-1  | 2024-09-16T13:56:18.593026631Z
   -> process.executable.name: Str(/usr/local/bin/python3)
otelcol-1  | 2024-09-16T13:56:18.593032089Z
   -> process.executable.path: Str(/usr/local/bin)
otelcol-1  | 2024-09-16T13:56:18.593037381Z
   -> process.command: Str(server.py)
otelcol-1  | 2024-09-16T13:56:18.593042673Z
   -> process.command_line: Str(server.py)
otelcol-1  | 2024-09-16T13:56:18.593047964Z
   -> process.command_args: Slice([])
otelcol-1  | 2024-09-16T13:56:18.593053214Z
   -> process.parent_pid: Int(0)
otelcol-1  | 2024-09-16T13:56:18.593058548Z
   -> service.name: Str(otel_book_demo)
otelcol-1  | 2024-09-16T13:56:18.593063881Z
   -> telemetry.auto.version: Str(0.44b0)
otelcol-1  | 2024-09-16T13:56:18.593069131Z ScopeSpans #0
otelcol-1  | 2024-09-16T13:56:18.593074173Z ScopeSpans SchemaURL:
otelcol-1  | 2024-09-16T13:56:18.593079339Z InstrumentationScope
   opentelemetry.instrumentation.flask 0.44b0
otelcol-1  | 2024-09-16T13:56:18.593084839Z Span #0
```

```
otelcol-1  | 2024-09-16T13:56:18.593089923Z
   Trace ID       : a4d85fd66744bc3ef8b427a033b17d56
otelcol-1  | 2024-09-16T13:56:18.593125048Z
   Parent ID      :
otelcol-1  | 2024-09-16T13:56:18.593129714Z
   ID             : be7466d201fc9fd0
otelcol-1  | 2024-09-16T13:56:18.593133506Z
   Name           : /
otelcol-1  | 2024-09-16T13:56:18.593137089Z
   Kind           : Server
otelcol-1  | 2024-09-16T13:56:18.593140714Z
   Start time     : 2024-02-10 13:56:18.205034214 +0000 UTC
otelcol-1  | 2024-09-16T13:56:18.593144548Z
   End time       : 2024-02-10 13:56:18.207003422 +0000 UTC
otelcol-1  | 2024-09-16T13:56:18.593148381Z
   Status code    : Unset
otelcol-1  | 2024-09-16T13:56:18.593151923Z
   Status message :
otelcol-1  | 2024-09-16T13:56:18.593155381Z Attributes:
otelcol-1  | 2024-09-16T13:56:18.593158923Z
   -> http.method: Str(GET)
otelcol-1  | 2024-09-16T13:56:18.593162714Z
   -> http.server_name: Str(waitress.invalid)
otelcol-1  | 2024-09-16T13:56:18.593166464Z
   -> http.scheme: Str(http)
otelcol-1  | 2024-09-16T13:56:18.593170089Z
   -> net.host.port: Int(8080)
otelcol-1  | 2024-09-16T13:56:18.593173756Z
   -> http.host: Str(0.0.0.0:8080)
otelcol-1  | 2024-09-16T13:56:18.593177423Z
   -> http.target: Str(/)
otelcol-1  | 2024-09-16T13:56:18.593181006Z
   -> net.peer.ip: Str(192.168.65.1)
otelcol-1  | 2024-09-16T13:56:18.593184631Z
   -> http.user_agent: Str(curl/8.4.0)
otelcol-1  | 2024-09-16T13:56:18.593188381Z
   -> net.peer.port: Str(62427)
otelcol-1  | 2024-09-16T13:56:18.593192048Z
   -> http.flavor: Str(1.1)
otelcol-1  | 2024-09-16T13:56:18.593195673Z
   -> http.route: Str(/)
otelcol-1  | 2024-09-16T13:56:18.593199298Z
   -> http.status_code: Int(200)
otelcol-1  | 2024-09-16T13:56:18.593203006Z
   {"kind": "exporter", "data_type": "traces", "name": "debug"}
```

As you can see, with a few commands, you were able to instrument a Python application! You can also test curling the `/rolldice` route to see the output. You can take this example one step further and test context propagation. You could pass a `traceparent:` header with a valid World Wide Web Consortium (W_3C) context in your `curl` command. For example: `curl -H "traceparent: 00-00000000000000000000000000000001-aaaaaaaaaaaaaaaa-01" http://127.0.0.1:8080/`. The output will then include the trace ID value from the `traceparent` (`00000000000000000000000000000001`) and the same for the parent ID (`aaaaaaaaaaaaaaaa`). If the `traceparent:` header is not passed, then the server assumes it is the root span and generates a unique trace ID and parent ID, which would be passed to downstream requests. More information about W_3C Trace Context can be found here: `https://www.w3.org/TR/trace-context`.

Manual Instrumentation

The most flexible way to add instrumentation is via manual instrumentation, which requires manually editing the code. The changes required include adding dependencies, instrumenting interfaces, and adding configuration details. Like any code change, care must be taken to minimize the overhead introduced by the instrumentation and ensure coding errors are properly caught. In addition, ongoing maintenance must be considered, including updating the code as well as increasing, reducing, or improving the telemetry data generated by the instrumentation.

Ready to try it out? Be sure to follow the "Environment Setup" section earlier in the chapter and configure at least `OTEL_EXPORTER_OTLP_ENDPOINT` environment variable as defined in the "Automatic Instrumentation" section before continuing!

To get started, create a copy of the `server.py` file created in the "Environment Setup" section earlier in this chapter and call it `server_trace_manual.py` by running: `cp server.py server_trace_manual.py`. Edit `server_trace_manual.py` and make the following changes (in bold text):

```
from random import randint
from flask import Flask, request
from paste.translogger import TransLogger
from waitress import serve
import logging
import os

# Trace-specific OTel modules
from opentelemetry.exporter.otlp.proto.grpc.trace_exporter import (
    OTLPSpanExporter,
)
from opentelemetry.propagate import extract
from opentelemetry.sdk.trace import TracerProvider
from opentelemetry.sdk.trace.export import (
    BatchSpanProcessor,
    ConsoleSpanExporter,
)
from opentelemetry.trace import (
    get_current_span,
    get_tracer_provider,
    set_tracer_provider,
    SpanKind,
```

```
    Status,
    StatusCode,
)

# Signal-agnostic OTel modules
from opentelemetry.instrumentation.wsgi import collect_request_attributes
from opentelemetry.sdk.resources import (
    get_aggregated_resources,
    ProcessResourceDetector,
    Resource,
)

SERVER_HOST = os.getenv('SERVER_HOST', '127.0.0.1')
SERVER_PORT = os.getenv('SERVER_PORT', 8080)

app = Flask(__name__)
appname = os.path.splitext(os.path.basename(__file__))[0]

logging.basicConfig(level=logging.INFO)
logger = logging.getLogger(__name__)

# One-time signal-agnostic OTel configuration
resource = get_aggregated_resources(
    [ProcessResourceDetector()],
    Resource.create({"service.name": appname}),
)

# One-time trace-specific OTel configuration
# Replace OTLPSpanExporter with ConsoleSpanExporter if not using the Collector
set_tracer_provider(TracerProvider(
    active_span_processor=BatchSpanProcessor(OTLPSpanExporter()),
    resource=resource,
))
tracer = get_tracer_provider().get_tracer(__name__)


@app.route("/")
def return_hello():
    # Signal-agnostic, function-specific OTel attributes creation
    attributes = collect_request_attributes(request.environ)

    # Trace-specific OTel span creation
    with tracer.start_as_current_span(
        "server_request",
        context=extract(request.headers),
        kind=SpanKind.SERVER,
        attributes=attributes,
    ):
```

```
        player = get_player('OTel Test')
        return "Hello! Be sure to roll the dice at /rolldice"


@app.route("/rolldice")
def roll_dice():
    # Signal-agnostic, function-specific OTel attributes creation
    attributes = collect_request_attributes(request.environ)

    # Trace-specific OTel span creation
    with tracer.start_as_current_span(
        "roll_dice_request",
        context=extract(request.headers),
        kind=SpanKind.SERVER,
        attributes=attributes,
    ):
        current_span = get_current_span()
        player = get_player()
        current_span.set_attribute("player", player)

        current_span.add_event("Rolling dice!")
        result = str(roll())
        current_span.add_event("Got a result!", attributes={"result": result})
        logger.warning("%s rolled a: %s", player, result)
        return result


def get_player(default=None):
    try:
        if default is None:
            default = 'Anonymous player'
            raise TypeError
    except TypeError as e:
        get_current_span().record_exception(e)
        logger.warning("Player request arg not set")
    return request.args.get('player', default=default, type=str)


def roll():
    return [randint(1, 6), randint(1, 6)]


if __name__ == "__main__":
    serve(TransLogger(app), host=SERVER_HOST, port=SERVER_PORT)
```

That was quite a few changes. Ready to walk through them? First, you imported some modules:

```
# Pull in the OTLP exporter
from opentelemetry.exporter.otlp.proto.grpc.trace_exporter import (
    OTLPSpanExporter,
)

# Required to extract header information
# Used to handled context propagation, which is critical to stitch spans together
from opentelemetry.propagate import extract

# TracerProvider was covered in Chapter 4
# It is part of the API but configured via the SDK
# It is one of the main components to generate signal telemetry data
from opentelemetry.sdk.trace import TracerProvider

# Instrumentation includes processors and exporters
# This example uses the batch processor which is common for production workloads
# This example uses the OTLP exporter which is common for production workloads
# For demo purposes, the BatchSpanProcessor could be removed
# For demo purposes, the ConsoleSpanExporter above could be used
from opentelemetry.sdk.trace.export import (
    BatchSpanProcessor,
    OTLPSpanExporter,
)

# Tracer was covered in Chapter 4 - it is part of the API
from opentelemetry.trace import (
    get_current_span,
    get_tracer_provider,
    set_tracer_provider,
    SpanKind,
    Status,
    StatusCode,
)

# Instrumentation-specific capability that collects request attributes
from opentelemetry.instrumentation.wsgi import collect_request_attributes

# A processor to detect resources which can be added to telemetry data
from opentelemetry.sdk.resources import (
    get_aggregated_resources,
    ProcessResourceDetector,
    Resource,
)
```

Next, you gathered resource information and configured the `TracerProvider`:

```
# Get the resources from the resource detector processor
# Also add the service name based on the application name
```

```
# Alternatively to defining the service.name in code an
# environment variable could be passed at runtime
resource = get_aggregated_resources(
    [ProcessResourceDetector()],
    Resource.create({"service.name": appname}),
)

# Initialize the TracerProvider
# Add the batch processor, span exporter and resource information
set_tracer_provider(TracerProvider(
    active_span_processor=BatchSpanProcessor(OTLPSpanExporter()),
    resource=resource,
))

# Get the global tracer
tracer = get_tracer_provider().get_tracer(__name__)
```

Finally, you generated spans within each route. For example:

```
    # Create a span with a name of "server_request",
    # Set the context based on request headers,
    # Set the SpanKind to SERVER,
    # And add a resource attribute with the request environment information
    with tracer.start_as_current_span(
        "server_request",
        context=extract(request.headers),
        kind=SpanKind.SERVER,
        attributes=collect_request_attributes(request.environ),
    ):
```

For the roll_dice function, you took the instrumentation one step further, adding another attribute as well as span status and span events:

```
        # Get the current span so it can be modified
        current_span = get_current_span()
        player = get_player()
        # Add another attribute with the player information
        current_span.set_attribute("player", player)

        # Add a span event denoting when the roll function is called
        current_span.add_event("Rolling dice!")
        result = str(roll())
        # Add a span event denoting when a result of the roll is known
        # Include the result as an attribute
        current_span.add_event("Got a result!",attributes={"result":result})
        logger.warning("%s rolled a: %s", player, result)
        return result
```

```
def get_player(default=None):
    try:
        if default is None:
            default = 'Anonymous player'
            raise TypeError
    except TypeError as e:
        get_current_span().record_exception(e)
        logger.warning("Player request arg not set")
    return request.args.get('player', default=default, type=str)
```

As you can see, all the concepts and steps are built from your knowledge about the OTel specification covered in Chapter 4. In summary, you:

- Added the OTel trace API to the application.
- Used the TracerProvider (https://opentelemetry.io/docs/specs/otel/trace/api/#tracerprovider) to create a Tracer (https://opentelemetry.io/docs/specs/otel/trace/api/#tracer).
- Created a Span (https://opentelemetry.io/docs/specs/otel/trace/api/#span) leveraging the SpanContext (https://opentelemetry.io/docs/specs/otel/trace/api/#spancontext).
- Added the OTel trace SDK and configured the BatchSpanProcessor (https://opentelemetry.io/docs/specs/otel/trace/sdk/#span-processor) and OTLPSpanExporter (https://opentelemetry.io/docs/specs/otel/trace/sdk/#span-exporter) to process and export the spans.

Of course, this is a simple example. More advanced trace instrumentation, including span links (https://opentelemetry.io/docs/specs/otel/trace/api/#link) and sampling (https://opentelemetry.io/docs/specs/otel/trace/sdk/#sampling), are also possible and may be desired. A visual representation of the architecture is available in Figure 6.1.

FIGURE 6.1
A diagram of how the OTel API and SDK are leveraged to provide trace instrumentation.

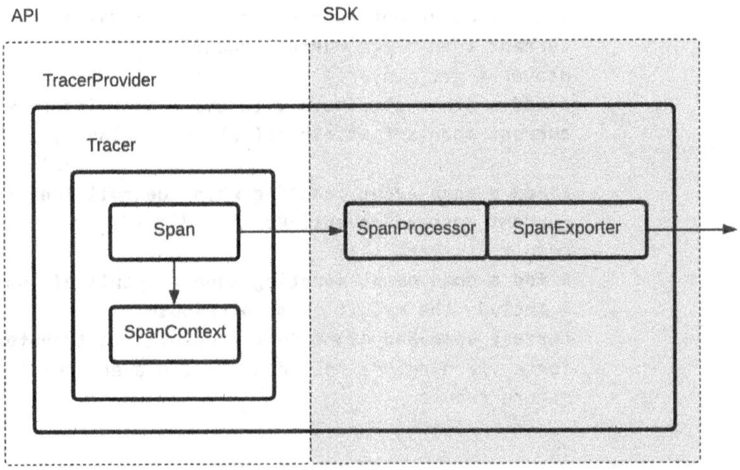

With the manual configuration in place, you can pass the new application name, build the new container, and start everything up with the original Dockerfile. This time, you defined the `service.name` based on the application name in code so setting the `OTEL_SERVICE_NAME` environment variable is unnecessary. You will use a different application name, so the `SERVER_APP` environment variable must be passed this time.

```
$ SERVER_APP=server_trace_manual.py \
  docker compose up --build --force-recreate --remove-orphans --detach
$ docker-compose logs -f -t
```

You should see output as you did in the earlier "Automatic Instrumentation" section. From a new window, test the server using the `curl` command: `curl http://127.0.0.1:8080`. How does the manual instrumentation output compare to the automatic instrumentation output? It is exactly the same except for dynamic variables such as `trace_id`, `start_time`, and `process_pid`! Just like in the automatic instrumentation example, you could pass a `traceparent:` header in the `curl` request to test context propagation.

You may be wondering why you would ever use manual instrumentation if the automatic instrumentation provides the same value. It comes down to factors, including what you are trying to instrument, how much customization is desired, and the performance overhead. For example, the scenario so far has been instrumenting a Flask application. What if you had custom code or a framework that was not widely adopted that you wanted to instrument? Manual instrumentation would be required unless the instrumentation supported instrumenting custom interfaces. Another scenario is if the automatic instrumentation supports the customization you desire. Customization may include adding or removing metadata or including or excluding interfaces or paths. While automatic instrumentation allows some customization, manual instrumentation may be required to support your use case. As it turns out, you can use automatic and manual instrumentation within the same application. More information on this topic is covered later in this chapter.

As mentioned earlier, adding initial manual instrumentation can be done with significantly less code than the examples you just tried. For example, resource detection is not required to generate telemetry data. However, reducing the manual instrumentation will also provide significantly less value in the telemetry data. The purpose of this section is to demonstrate the basics of manual instrumentation but also provide a more real-world example that would be necessary for production environments and helpful to achieve observability. The importance of adding context, such as resource detection, will be explored in Chapter 8, "The Power of Context and Correlation."

Another thing to note with Python manual instrumentation is that the programming language has the notion of decorators, which OTel supports. For example, you can use `@tracer.start_as_current_span("name")` before function calls instead of the `with tracer.start_as_current_span` wrapper within the function. If you `pip install otel-extensions`,[9] syntactic sugar[10] around decorators is possible. For example, `@tracer.start_as_current_span("name")` can be replaced with just `@instrumented`.

Programmatic Instrumentation

As you can see, there is a big difference between automatic and manual instrumentation regarding getting started and customization. For the most popular libraries, there is a middle ground known as an instrumentation library or programmatic instrumentation. This form of instrumentation is still manual instrumentation, but it reduces the amount of effort required to generate telemetry from supported libraries. Ready to try it out? Before continuing, follow the "Environment Setup" section earlier in this chapter and configure at least the `OTEL_EXPORTER_OTLP_ENDPOINT` environment variable as defined in the "Automatic Instrumentation" section before continuing!

To try this approach, create a copy of the `server.py` file created in the "Environment Setup" section and call it `server_trace_programmatic.py` by running: `cp server.py server_trace_programmatic.py`. Edit `server_trace_programmatic.py` and make the following changes (in bold text):

```
from random import randint
from flask import Flask, request
from paste.translogger import TransLogger
from waitress import serve
import logging
import os

# Trace-specific OTel modules
from opentelemetry.exporter.otlp.proto.grpc.trace_exporter import (
    OTLPSpanExporter,
)
from opentelemetry.sdk.trace import TracerProvider
from opentelemetry.sdk.trace.export import (
    BatchSpanProcessor,
    ConsoleSpanExporter,
)
from opentelemetry.trace import set_tracer_provider

# Signal-agnostic OTel modules
from opentelemetry.instrumentation.flask import FlaskInstrumentor
from opentelemetry.sdk.resources import (
    get_aggregated_resources,
    ProcessResourceDetector,
    Resource,
)

SERVER_HOST = os.getenv('SERVER_HOST', '127.0.0.1')
SERVER_PORT = os.getenv('SERVER_PORT', 8080)

app = Flask(__name__)
appname = os.path.splitext(os.path.basename(__file__))[0]

logging.basicConfig(level=logging.INFO)
logger = logging.getLogger(__name__)

# One-time signal-agnostic OTel configuration
resource = get_aggregated_resources(
    [ProcessResourceDetector()],
    Resource.create({"service.name": appname}),
)
```

```
# One-time trace-specific OTel configuration
# Replace OTLPSpanExporter with ConsoleSpanExporter
# if not using the OTel Collector
set_tracer_provider(TracerProvider(
    active_span_processor=BatchSpanProcessor(OTLPSpanExporter()),
    resource=resource,
))

# OTel programmatic instrumentation
instrumentor = FlaskInstrumentor()
instrumentor.instrument_app(app)

@app.route('/')
... (no additional changes)
```

With this approach, the module imports changed a bit and you do not need to worry about context propagation or `SpanKind`. In addition, while you still needed to set the `TracerProvider`, you no longer needed to worry about the `Tracer`. Finally, instead of constructing and generating spans with requests, you only need to create a `FlaskInstrumentor` and then tell it to instruct the application.

With the changes shown in the preceding code in place, create a copy of the Dockerfile by running: `cp Dockerfile programmatic.Dockerfile`. Then, add the following after the `RUN pip3 install` line in the programmatic Dockerfile:

```
# Requires manually determining which instrumentation packages are needed
# Instrumentation packages are available in the OTel Python Contrib repository
# https://github.com/open-telemetry/opentelemetry-python-
# contrib/tree/main/instrumentation
RUN pip3 install opentelemetry-instrumentation-flask
RUN pip3 install opentelemetry-instrumentation-requests
RUN pip3 install opentelemetry-instrumentation-logging
```

Now, you can pass the new application name, build the new container, and start everything up with the programmatic Dockerfile:

```
$ MY_DOCKERFILE=programmatic.Dockerfile \
  SERVER_APP=server_trace_programmatic.py \
  docker compose up --build --force-recreate --remove-orphans --detach
$ docker-compose logs -f -t
```

From a new window, test the server using the `curl` command: `curl http://127.0.0.1:8080`. How does the server-side window output compare to the automatic and manual instrumentation output? It is exactly the same except for dynamic variables such as `trace_id`, `start_time`, and `process_pid`! Three different approaches to achieve the same outcome. Just like in the automatic instrumentation example, you could pass a `traceparent:` header in the `curl` request to test context propagation.

You may be wondering why you would ever use manual instrumentation if programmatic instrumentation is available. The primary reason is that programmatic instrumentation is only available for well-known libraries and frameworks. For non-well-known or custom libraries and frameworks, programmatic instrumentation will not exist, necessitating manual instrumentation. In addition, programmatic instrumentation will also be more limited in customization than manual instrumentation.

Mixing Automatic and Manual Trace Instrumentation

As mentioned, automatic instrumentation is typically easier to get started with and does not require code changes. With that said, it is harder to customize, while manual instrumentation is typically harder to get started and does require code changes but is easier to customize. What if you could have the best of both worlds? Turns out, you can! For many languages, you can use automatic and manual instrumentation together. Ready to try it out? Be sure to follow the "Environment Setup" section earlier in the chapter and configure at least the `OTEL_EXPORTER_OTLP_ENDPOINT` environment variable as defined in the "Automatic Instrumentation" before continuing!

To try this approach, create a copy of the `server.py` file created in the "Environment Setup" section earlier in the chapter and call it `server_trace_mixed.py` by running: `cp server.py server_trace_mixed.py`. Edit `server_trace_mixed.py` and make the following changes (in bold text):

```
from random import randint
from flask import Flask, request
from paste.translogger import TransLogger
from waitress import serve
import logging
import os

from opentelemetry.trace import get_current_span

SERVER_HOST = os.getenv('SERVER_HOST', '127.0.0.1')
SERVER_PORT = os.getenv('SERVER_PORT', 8080)

app = Flask(__name__)
appname = os.path.splitext(os.path.basename(__file__))[0]

logging.basicConfig(level=logging.INFO)
logger = logging.getLogger(__name__)


@app.route('/')
def return_hello():
    current_span = get_current_span()
    player = get_player('OTel User')
    current_span.set_attribute("player", player)
    return 'Hello! Be sure to roll the dice at /rolldice'
... (no additional changes)
```

You added an attribute to an automatically created span via manual instrumentation. For this to work, the tracer needs to be configured and initialized. In addition, a span needs to be created for the route. To do this, pass the new application name, build the new container, and start everything up with the automatic Dockerfile:

```
$ MY_DOCKERFILE=automatic.Dockerfile \
  SERVER_APP=server_trace_mixed.py \
```

```
docker compose up --build --force-recreate --remove-orphans -detach
$ docker-compose logs -f -t
```

In a separate window, `curl` the endpoint (`curl http://127.0.0.1:8080/`). In the server-side window, you should see output similar to the previous examples, but a player attribute has been added to the telemetry data this time. As you can see, extending automatic instrumentation with manual instrumentation is straightforward. In addition, less manual instrumentation was required as automatic instrumentation handled several aspects for you.

Given that programmatic instrumentation instantiates a tracer and generates spans just like automatic instrumentation, combining both does not make sense. If you do attempt this, you will get a warning message on the server like:

```
WARNING:__main__:opentelemetry.instrumentation.flask:Attempting to instrument
Flask app while already instrumented.
```

Python Metrics Instrumentation

So far, you have only worked with trace instrumentation. It is time to add metric instrumentation! In Python, metric instrumentation, like trace instrumentation, can be added through automatic or manual instrumentation. The general approach for metric instrumentation is very similar to traces just with metric-specific concepts.

Before continuing, follow the "Environment Setup" section earlier in this chapter and configure at least the `OTEL_EXPORTER_OTLP_ENDPOINT` environment variable as defined in the trace instrumentation "Automatic Instrumentation" section before continuing! You should also read the entire "Python Trace Instrumentation" section in this chapter, which covers topics that also apply to metrics.

It is important to note that there is a significant difference between traces and metrics. Traces are generated per request and reported as they occur. Metrics are generated at a defined cadence and may or may not change values between each interval. By default, OTel metrics are exported once every 60 seconds. The `OTEL_METRIC_EXPORT_INTERVAL` environment variable defines this. You may wish to reduce this interval, for example to 5 seconds. To do this, add the following to the `.env` file:

```
$ echo OTEL_METRIC_EXPORT_INTERVAL=5000 >>.env
```

Then, add the environment variables to the `compose.yaml` under the `server.environment` section:

```
services:
  server:
    build: .
    environment:
      - SERVER_APP
      - SERVER_HOST
      - SERVER_PORT
      - OTEL_SERVICE_NAME
      - OTEL_EXPORTER_OTLP_ENDPOINT
      - OTEL_METRIC_EXPORT_INTERVAL
...
```

METRIC EXPORT INTERVAL

Changing the metric export interval may be necessary to ensure the right granularity of data necessary to achieve observability. For example, with the default setting of 60 seconds, it is possible that availability or performance issues may be missed. Alternatively, reducing the interval results in additional data that needs to be generated, processed, and stored resulting in additional costs. In general, an interval between 10 and 60 seconds may be appropriate depending on business requirements. Just remember that the metric export interval is a balance between having the data necessary to achieve observability and dealing with the complexity and cost of data that may not be valuable.

Automatic Instrumentation

Ready to try automatic OTel metric instrumentation? Be sure to read the important prerequisite information in the "Python Metrics Instrumentation" section before continuing! Start with the base `server.py` file and try using automatic metric instrumentation. To do this, start the containers with the automatic Dockerfile and tail the logs:

```
$ MY_DOCKERFILE= automatic.Dockerfile \
  docker compose up --build --force-recreate --remove-orphans --detach
$ docker-compose logs -f -t
```

Now, `curl` the endpoint again and soon metric data will be reported in the logs. After the telemetry data is reported, it will continue to be reported on a regular cadence even if you do not `curl` the endpoint anymore.

Real World Scenario

MAJOR OUTAGE AT JUPITERIAN

Riley received a page at 2 am on Thursday. After acknowledging the page, she groggily made her way to her work computer to see what was going on. Someone had messaged her a link to a web conference. She joined, and the incident manager quickly caught her up on the situation. An alert had triggered, indicating the number of checkouts was abnormally low. Upon investigation, it was discovered that the average time on the cart page was also significantly higher than usual. The on-call engineers feared something was wrong on the Jupiterian side. Riley checked the Prometheus metrics, looking for clues, but could not determine why the system behavior had changed.

While the rest of the engineers on the call continued looking into their services, Riley began looking for other possible causes outside the metrics. Upon checking the continuous integration and continuous delivery (CI/CD) system, she noticed that the weekly push happened about 12 hours earlier. Upon looking into the changes pushed, she saw that the feature flag for a new caching service was enabled. Riley knew the caching service was responsible for maintaining the state of the cart page. She interrupted the video conference to ask if people had looked into the new cache service. The on-call engineer for the cart service was unaware of the new service and could not find any dashboards with Prometheus metrics for it. Riley suggested turning off the feature flag to see if the system stabilized. The on-call engineer made the change, and the number of checkouts immediately returned to the expected numbers.

The outage lasted almost 90 minutes and cost the company millions of dollars in lost revenue. One week after the incident, the team did a post mortem. The root cause of the issue was determined to be a bug in the new caching service. The bug had gone undetected due to a lack of telemetry instrumentation in the new service. Riley suggested adding automatic metric instrumentation as an easy way to gain some visibility into the service and get it rolled back out to production.

Manual Instrumentation

Ready to try manual OTel metric instrumentation? Be sure to read the important prerequisite information in the "Python Metrics Instrumentation" section before continuing! Next, try adding manual instrumentation. To do this, create a new file called `server_metrics_manual.py` by running: `cp server.py server_metrics_manual.py`. Edit `server_metrics_manual.py` and make the following changes (in bold text):

```
from random import randint
from flask import Flask, request
from paste.translogger import TransLogger
from waitress import serve
import logging
import os

# Metric-specific OTel modules
from opentelemetry.exporter.otlp.proto.grpc.metric_exporter import (
```

```
    OTLPMetricExporter,
)
from opentelemetry.metrics import (
    get_meter,
    set_meter_provider,
)
from opentelemetry.sdk.metrics import MeterProvider
from opentelemetry.sdk.metrics.export import (
    ConsoleMetricExporter,
    PeriodicExportingMetricReader,
)

# Signal-agnostic OTel modules
from opentelemetry.instrumentation.wsgi import collect_request_attributes
from opentelemetry.sdk.resources import (
    get_aggregated_resources,
    ProcessResourceDetector,
    Resource,
)

SERVER_HOST = os.getenv('SERVER_HOST', '127.0.0.1')
SERVER_PORT = os.getenv('SERVER_PORT', 8080)

app = Flask(__name__)
appname = os.path.splitext(os.path.basename(__file__))[0]

logging.basicConfig(level=logging.INFO)
logger = logging.getLogger(__name__)

# One-time signal-agnostic OTel configuration
resource = get_aggregated_resources(
    [ProcessResourceDetector()],
    Resource.create({"service.name": appname}),
)

# One-time metric-specific OTel configuration
# Replace OTLPMetricExporter with ConsoleMetricExporter
# if not using the OTel Collector
exporter = OTLPMetricExporter()
#exporter = ConsoleMetricExporter()
reader = PeriodicExportingMetricReader(exporter)
provider = MeterProvider(
    metric_readers=[reader],
    resource=resource,
)
set_meter_provider(provider)

# OTel way to create a meter and a counter
meter = get_meter(
```

```
    "roll-dice",
    "0.1.2"
)
counter = meter.create_counter(
    "counter",
    description="count of dice rolls since start"
)


@app.route('/')
def return_hello():
    player = get_player('OTel Test')
    return 'Hello! Be sure to roll the dice at /rolldice'


@app.route("/rolldice")
def roll_dice():
    player = get_player()

    # Function-specific OTel metric creation
    attributes = collect_request_attributes(request.environ)
    attributes.update({"player": player})

    result = str(roll(attributes))
    logger.warning("%s is rolling the dice: %s", player, result)
    return result


def get_player(default=None):
    try:
        if default is None:
            default = 'Anonymous player'
            raise TypeError
    except TypeError:
        logger.warning("Player request arg not set")
    return request.args.get('player', default=default, type=str)


def roll(attributes):
    counter.add(
        1,
        attributes=attributes
    )

    return [randint(1, 6), randint(1, 6)]


if __name__ == "__main__":
    serve(TransLogger(app), host=SERVER_HOST, port=SERVER_PORT)
```

Again, there were quite a few changes. Ready to walk through them? First, you imported some modules:

```
# Metric-specific OTel modules
from opentelemetry.exporter.otlp.proto.grpc.metric_exporter import (
    OTLPMetricExporter,
)
from opentelemetry.metrics import (
    get_meter,
    set_meter_provider,
)

# MeterProvider was covered in Chapter 4
# It is part of the API but configured via the SDK
# It is one of the main components to generate signal telemetry data
from opentelemetry.sdk.metrics import MeterProvider

# Metric instrumentation requires a reader to export data
# This example uses the PeriodicExportingMetricReader
# which is common for production workloads
# By default, this reader only exports on shutdown
# For production environments, setting a value for export_interval_millis
# is recommended
# For demo purposes, the ConsoleMetricExporter could be used
from opentelemetry.sdk.metrics.export import (
    ConsoleMetricExporter,
    PeriodicExportingMetricReader,
)

# Signal-agnostic OTel modules
# Same as the tracing section above
from opentelemetry.instrumentation.wsgi import collect_request_attributes
from opentelemetry.sdk.resources import (
    get_aggregated_resources,
    ProcessResourceDetector,
    Resource,
)
```

Next, you configured the `MeterProvider`:

```
# Configure the exporter
# If testing locally, the console exporter can be used
exporter = OTLPMetricExporter()
#exporter = ConsoleMetricExporter()

# Configure the reader which requires at least the exporter configuration
# If the export_interval_millis is not specified then metrics will only
# be exported on shutdown. Specified via environment variable.
reader = PeriodicExportingMetricReader(exporter)
```

```
# Get the resources from the resource detector processor
# Also add the service name based on the application name
# Alternatively to defining the service.name in code an
# environment variable could be passed at runtime
resource = get_aggregated_resources(
    [ProcessResourceDetector()],
    Resource.create({"service.name": appname}),
])

# Initialize the provider with reader and resource information
provider = MeterProvider(
    metric_readers=[reader],
    resource=resource,
)
set_meter_provider(provider)
```

Then, you created a meter and a counter:

```
# Create a meter and specify the name and version
meter = get_meter(
    "roll-dice",
    "0.1.2"
)

# Create a counter and specify the name, units, and description
counter = meter.create_counter(
    "counter",
    description="count of dice rolls since start"
)
```

Finally, you generated metrics within the `roll` function. You did this by creating and extending attributes and passing them to the `roll` function:

```
attributes = collect_request_attributes(request.environ)
attributes.update({"player": player})

result = str(roll(attributes))
```

Then you generated the metric to be reported with the associated attribute data:

```
def roll(attributes):
    counter.add(
        1,
        attributes=attributes
    )

    return [randint(1, 6), randint(1, 6)]
```

With the manual configuration in place, pass the new application name, build the new container, and start everything up using the original Dockerfile:

```
$ SERVER_APP=server_metric_manual.py \
  docker compose up --build --force-recreate --remove-orphans --detach
$ docker-compose logs -f -t
```

With the current configuration, you will need to `curl` the `/rolldice` route to see metric data. Test it out! As you can see, the general flow for metric instrumentation is similar to traces and outlined in Figure 6.2. In summary, you:

- Added the OTel metric API to the application and used the `MeterProvider` (`https://opentelemetry.io/docs/specs/otel/metrics/api/#meterprovider`) to create a `Meter` (`https://opentelemetry.io/docs/specs/otel/metrics/api/#meter`).
- Associated the `Meter` with an `Instrument` (`https://opentelemetry.io/docs/specs/otel/metrics/api/#instrument`) and configured it to create a series of `Measurements` (`https://opentelemetry.io/docs/specs/otel/metrics/api/#measurement`) with attributes.
- Added the OTel metric SDK and configured the `PeriodicExportingMetricReader` (`https://opentelemetry.io/docs/specs/otel/metrics/sdk/#metricreader`) and `OTLPMetricExporter` (`https://opentelemetry.io/docs/specs/otel/metrics/sdk/#metricexporter`) to observe and export the metrics.

Of course, this is a simple example. More advanced metric instrumentation, including asynchronous instruments (`https://opentelemetry.io/docs/specs/otel/metrics/api/#synchronous-and-asynchronous-instruments`), exemplars (`https://opentelemetry.io/docs/specs/otel/metrics/sdk/#exemplar`), and aggregating measurements into views (`https://opentelemetry.io/docs/specs/otel/metrics/sdk/#view`), are also possible and may be desired.

FIGURE 6.2 A diagram of how the OTel API and SDK are leveraged to provide metric instrumentation.

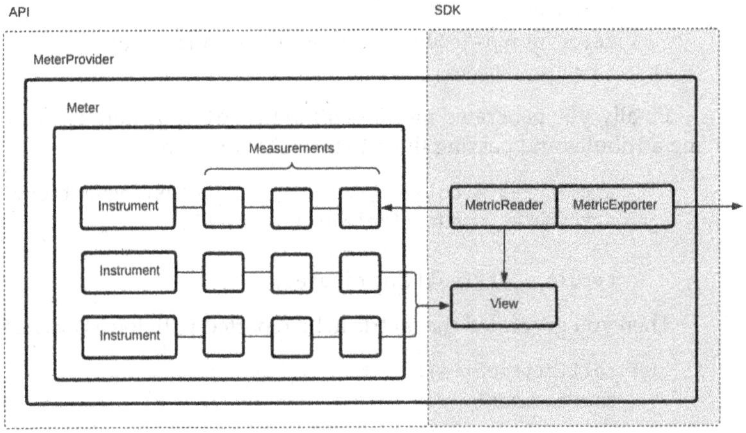

Programmatic Instrumentation

Ready to try programmatic OTel metric instrumentation? Be sure to read the important prerequisite information in the "Python Metrics Instrumentation" section before continuing! Just like with traces, metrics can support programmatic instrumentation. To test this, create a new file called `server_metrics_programmatic.py` by running: `cp server.py server_metrics_` programmatic.py. Edit server_metrics_programmatic.py and make the following changes (in bold text):

```
from random import randint
from flask import Flask, request
from paste.translogger import TransLogger
from waitress import serve
import logging
import os

# Metric-specific OTel modules
from opentelemetry.exporter.otlp.proto.grpc.metric_exporter import (
    OTLPMetricExporter,
)
from opentelemetry.sdk.metrics import MeterProvider
from opentelemetry.sdk.metrics.export import (
    ConsoleMetricExporter,
    PeriodicExportingMetricReader,
)
from opentelemetry.metrics import set_meter_provider

# Signal-agnostic OTel modules
from opentelemetry.instrumentation.flask import FlaskInstrumentor
from opentelemetry.sdk.resources import (
    get_aggregated_resources,
    ProcessResourceDetector,
    Resource,
)

SERVER_HOST = os.getenv('SERVER_HOST', '127.0.0.1')
SERVER_PORT = os.getenv('SERVER_PORT', 8080)

app = Flask(__name__)
appname = os.path.splitext(os.path.basename(__file__))[0]

logging.basicConfig(level=logging.INFO)
logger = logging.getLogger(__name__)

# One-time signal-agnostic OTel configuration
resource = get_aggregated_resources(
    [ProcessResourceDetector()],
    Resource.create({"service.name": appname}),
)

# One-time metric-specific OTel configuration
# Replace OTLPMetricExporter with ConsoleMetricExporter
# if not using the OTel Collector
exporter = OTLPMetricExporter()
```

```
#exporter = ConsoleMetricExporter()
reader = PeriodicExportingMetricReader(exporter)
provider = MeterProvider(
    metric_readers=[reader],
    resource=resource,
)
set_meter_provider(provider)

# OTel programmatic instrumentation
instrumentor = FlaskInstrumentor()
instrumentor.instrument_app(app)


@app.route('/')
... (no additional changes)
```

With the programmatic configuration in place, you can pass the new application name, build the new container, and start everything up with the programmatic Dockerfile:

```
$ MY_DOCKERFILE=programmatic.Dockerfile \
  SERVER_APP=server_metric_programmatic.py \
  docker compose up --build --force-recreate --remove-orphans --detach
$ docker-compose logs -f -t
```

With programmatic metric instrumentation, you can `curl` either the / or `/rolldice` route to generate metric data. Test it out!

Mixing Automatic and Manual Metric Instrumentation

Ready to try mixing automatic and manual OTel metric instrumentation? Be sure to read the important prerequisite information in the "Python Metrics Instrumentation" section before continuing! Just like traces, you can mix automatic and manual instrumentation. To try this approach, create a copy of the `server.py` file created in the "Environment Setup" section earlier in this chapter and call it `server_metrics_mixed.py` by running: `cp server.py server_metrics_mixed.py`. Edit `server_metrics_mixed.py` and make the following changes (in bold text):

```
from random import randint
from flask import Flask, request
from paste.translogger import TransLogger
from waitress import serve
import logging
import os

from opentelemetry.instrumentation.wsgi import collect_request_attributes
from opentelemetry.metrics import get_meter

SERVER_HOST = os.getenv('SERVER_HOST', '127.0.0.1')
SERVER_PORT = os.getenv('SERVER_PORT', 8080)
```

```
app = Flask(__name__)
appname = os.path.splitext(os.path.basename(__file__))[0]

logging.basicConfig(level=logging.INFO)
logger = logging.getLogger(__name__)

meter = get_meter(
    "roll-dice",
    "0.1.2"
)
counter = meter.create_counter(
    "counter",
    description="count of dice rolls since start"
)


@app.route('/')
def return_hello():
    player = get_player('OTel User')
    return 'Hello! Be sure to roll the dice at /rolldice'


@app.route("/rolldice")
def roll_dice():
    player = get_player()

    # Function-specific OTel metric creation
    attributes = collect_request_attributes(request.environ)
    attributes.update({"player": player})

    result = str(roll(attributes))
    logger.warning("%s is rolling the dice: %s", player, result)
    return result


def get_player(default=None):
    try:
        if default is None:
            default = 'Anonymous player'
            raise TypeError
    except TypeError:
        logger.warning("Player request arg not set")
    return request.args.get('player', default=default, type=str)


def roll(attributes):
    counter.add(
        1,
        attributes=attributes
```

```
        )

        return [randint(1, 6), randint(1, 6)]


if __name__ == "__main__":
    serve(TransLogger(app), host=SERVER_HOST, port=SERVER_PORT)
```

With these modifications, you added attributes to a custom metric via manual instrumentation. For this to work, the `MeterProvider` needs to be configured and initialized. This can be achieved by running the server with automatic instrumentation. Pass the new application name, build the new container, and start everything up with the automatic Dockerfile:

```
$ MY_DOCKERFILE=automatic.Dockerfile \
  SERVER_APP=server_metrics_mixed.py \
  docker compose up --build --force-recreate --remove-orphans -detach
$ docker-compose logs -f -t
```

If you `curl` the `/rolldice` route, you will now get automatically generated metrics, such as `http.server.active_requests` as well as the manually created metric `roll-dice`. Given the automatic instrumentation configured the `MeterProvider` as well as the OTel SDK, including the exporter, adding the metric was as simple as running `get_meter` and then creating the desired metric.

Python Log Instrumentation

For logs, OTel leverages existing loggers, or objects that trigger log events, but enriches the data. The two primary enrichments would be metadata, including resource information, and trace correlation, including the trace ID. The value of metadata has been covered extensively, but why would trace correlation provide value? A single log record represents what happened but typically does not have the context of what led up to the log record being generated. In short, it is missing context. By enriching log records with trace data, you can associate the record in the context of a transaction. Of course, to enable trace correlation in log, trace instrumentation needs to be configured. More information about the value that trace ID correlation provides will be discussed in Chapter 8.

OTel log instrumentation supports both automatic and manual methods and is in development. In-development OTel modules in Python are prefixed with an underscore. To try automatic log instrumentation without traces and metrics, create a copy of the automatic Dockerfile by running: `cp automatic.Dockerfile automatic-logs.Dockerfile`. Edit the automatic logs Dockerfile, commenting out the `CMD` line by prefixing it with the pound symbol (#), then add the following after it:

```
#CMD OTEL_SERVICE_NAME=${OTEL_SERVICE_NAME} \
#    OTEL_EXPERIMENTAL_RESOURCE_DETECTORS=process \
#    exec opentelemetry-instrument --metrics_exporter none \
#         python3 ${SERVER_APP}

CMD OTEL_SERVICE_NAME=${OTEL_SERVICE_NAME} \
   OTEL_EXPERIMENTAL_RESOURCE_DETECTORS=process \
```

```
OTEL_PYTHON_LOGGING_AUTO_INSTRUMENTATION_ENABLED=true \
exec opentelemetry-instrument --traces_exporter none --metrics_exporter none \
    --logs_exporter otlp python3 ${SERVER_APP}
```

After saving the changes, you can now build the new container, and start everything up with the automatic logs Dockerfile:

```
$ MY_DOCKERFILE=automatic-logs.Dockerfile \
  docker compose up --build --force-recreate --remove-orphans --detach
$ docker-compose logs -f -t
```

With the current configuration, you will need to `curl` the `/rolldice` route to see logs data. Test it out! From the output, you will see metadata enrichment and trace correlation.

Manual Metadata Enrichment

Now, you are ready to add manual log instrumentation, which provides metadata enrichment. To try this approach, create a copy of the `server.py` file created in the "Environment Setup" section and call it `server_logs_enrichment.py` by running: `cp server.py server_logs_enrichment.py`. Edit `server_logs_enrichment.py` and make the following changes (in bold text):

```
from random import randint
from flask import Flask, request
from paste.translogger import TransLogger
from waitress import serve
import logging
import os

# Log-specific OTel modules
# Note the underscore means the component is currently in development
from opentelemetry._logs import set_logger_provider
from opentelemetry.exporter.otlp.proto.grpc._log_exporter import (
    OTLPLogExporter,
)
from opentelemetry.sdk._logs import (
    LoggerProvider,
    LoggingHandler,
)
from opentelemetry.sdk._logs.export import BatchLogRecordProcessor

# Signal-agnostic OTel modules
from opentelemetry.sdk.resources import (
    get_aggregated_resources,
    ProcessResourceDetector,
    Resource,
)

SERVER_HOST = os.getenv('SERVER_HOST', '127.0.0.1')
SERVER_PORT = os.getenv('SERVER_PORT', 8080)
```

```
app = Flask(__name__)
appname = os.path.splitext(os.path.basename(__file__))[0]

logging.basicConfig(level=logging.INFO)
logger = logging.getLogger(__name__)

# One-time OTel log configuration
exporter = OTLPLogExporter()
resource = get_aggregated_resources(
    [ProcessResourceDetector()],
    Resource.create({"service.name": appname}),
)
logger_provider = LoggerProvider(resource=resource)
set_logger_provider(logger_provider)
logger_provider.add_log_record_processor(BatchLogRecordProcessor(exporter))
handler = LoggingHandler(level=logging.NOTSET, logger_provider=logger_provider)

# Attach OTLP handler to root logger
logging.getLogger().addHandler(handler)


@app.route('/')
... (no additional changes)
```

Assuming you have completed the "Python Trace Instrumentation" and "Python Metrics Instrumentation" sections, you will notice that the general process of adding log instrumentation is very similar. The big difference with logs is that once the initial configuration is completed, all that needs to be done is to add the OTel log handler to the existing logger. After that point, any logger statement in the code will automatically be enriched with OTel information.

You can now build the new container, and start everything up with the original Dockerfile:

```
$ SERVER_APP=server_logs_enrichment.py \
  docker compose up --build --force-recreate --remove-orphans --detach
$ docker-compose logs -f -t
```

Even without curling a route, you will immediately get a log record. Given that this log record is outside of a function call, the missing trace information is probably unsurprising. If you want to test with `curl`, you will need to hit the `/rolldice` route. Try it out! Upon curling the endpoint, you will see that the trace information is missing. This is because trace instrumentation has not been added.

In summary, you:

- Added the OTel log API to the application and used the `LoggerProvider` (`https://opentelemetry.io/docs/specs/otel/logs/bridge-api/#loggerprovider`) to create a `Logger` (`https://opentelemetry.io/docs/specs/otel/logs/bridge-api/#logger`).
- As a result, Log Records (`https://opentelemetry.io/docs/specs/otel/logs/bridge-api/#emit-a-logrecord`) were created by the `Logger`.

- Added the OTel SDK and configured the `BatchLogRecordProcessor` (`https://opentelemetry.io/docs/specs/otel/logs/sdk/#logrecordprocessor`) and `OTLPLogExporter` (`https://opentelemetry.io/docs/specs/otel/logs/sdk/#logrecordexporter`) to process and export the log records.

A visual representation of the architecture is available in Figure 6.3.

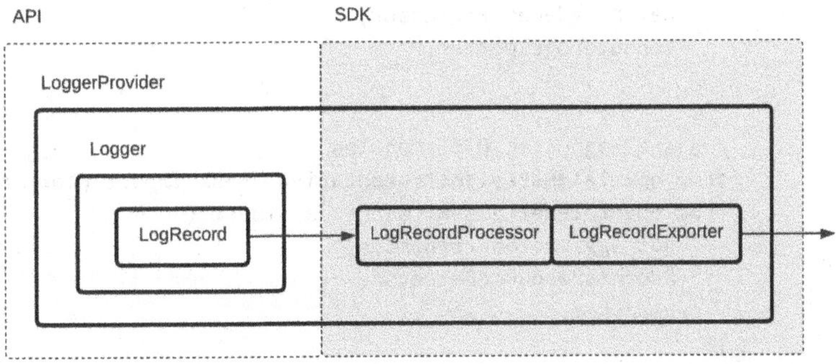

FIGURE 6.3
A diagram of how the OTel API and SDK are leveraged to provide log instrumentation.

Trace Correlation

In addition to metadata enrichment, you can also add trace correlation to the manual log instrumentation. To try this approach, create a copy of the `server_logs_enrichment.py` file created in the earlier "Environment Setup" section and call it `server_logs_correlation.py` by running: `cp server_logs_enrichment.py server_logs_correlation.py`. Edit `server_logs_correlation.py` and make the following changes (in bold text):

```
from random import randint
from flask import Flask, request
from paste.translogger import TransLogger
from waitress import serve
import logging
import os

# Trace-specific OTel modules
from opentelemetry.exporter.otlp.proto.grpc.trace_exporter import (
    OTLPSpanExporter,
)
from opentelemetry.sdk.trace import TracerProvider
from opentelemetry.sdk.trace.export import (
    BatchSpanProcessor,
    ConsoleSpanExporter,
)
from opentelemetry.trace import set_tracer_provider

# Log-specific OTel modules
from opentelemetry._logs import set_logger_provider
from opentelemetry.exporter.otlp.proto.grpc._log_exporter import (
```

```
    OTLPLogExporter,
)
from opentelemetry.sdk._logs import (
    LoggerProvider,
    LoggingHandler,
)
from opentelemetry.sdk._logs.export import (
    BatchLogRecordProcessor,
    ConsoleLogExporter,
)

# Signal-agnostic OTel modules
from opentelemetry.instrumentation.flask import FlaskInstrumentor
from opentelemetry.sdk.resources import (
    get_aggregated_resources,
    ProcessResourceDetector,
    Resource,
)

SERVER_HOST = os.getenv('SERVER_HOST', '127.0.0.1')
SERVER_PORT = os.getenv('SERVER_PORT', 8080)

app = Flask(__name__)
appname = os.path.splitext(os.path.basename(__file__))[0]

logging.basicConfig(level=logging.INFO)
logger = logging.getLogger(__name__)

# One-time signal-agnostic OTel configuration
resource = get_aggregated_resources(
    [ProcessResourceDetector()],
    Resource.create({"service.name": appname}),
)

# One-time trace-specific OTel configuration
# Replace OTLPSpanExporter with ConsoleSpanExporter
# if not using the OTel Collector
set_tracer_provider(TracerProvider(
    active_span_processor=BatchSpanProcessor(OTLPSpanExporter()),
    resource=resource,
))

# OTel programmatic instrumentation
instrumentor = FlaskInstrumentor()
instrumentor.instrument_app(app)

# One-time logs-specific OTel configuration
# Replace OTLPLogExporter with ConsoleLogExporter
```

```
# if not using the OTel Collector
exporter = OTLPLogExporter()
#exporter = ConsoleLogExporter()
logger_provider = LoggerProvider(resource=resource)
set_logger_provider(logger_provider)
logger_provider = logger_provider.add_log_record_processor(
    BatchLogRecordProcessor(exporter)
)

# Attach OTLP handler to root logger
handler = LoggingHandler(level=logging.NOTSET, logger_provider=logger_provider)
logging.getLogger().addHandler(handler)


@app.route('/')
... (no additional changes)
```

Given this example leverages programmatic instrumentation, you will need to use the programmatic Dockerfile by running:

```
$ MY_DOCKERFILE=programmatic.Dockerfile \
  SERVER_APP=server_logs_correlation.py \
  docker compose up --build --force-recreate --remove-orphans --detach
$ docker-compose logs -f -t
```

If you `curl` the `/rolldice` route this time, you will get both trace and log telemetry data. In addition, the log record will have trace correlation information. The above example shows how you can add instrumentation for multiple signals. As you can see, signal-specific items need to be added and signal-agnostic items can be shared across signals.

Language Considerations

By now, you have a good understanding of how OTel instrumentation works using the Python programming language, but what about other languages? While the general concepts are the same, thanks to OTel's open standard, there are language-specific aspects to be aware of. OTel supports instrumentation for all popular languages. The instrumentation methods supported vary by language as do the instrumentation steps, given the differences between how languages operate. For example, automatic instrumentation for Java requires adding the `-javaagent` flag with a JAR file containing the automatic instrumentation. This is different from Python, which requires prefixing the startup command with the `opentelemetry-instrument` command. In addition, some languages do not support automatic instrumentation and require some amount of code modification.

Regardless of the language being instrumented, one common consideration is around the exporter endpoint. By default, the exporter endpoint is configured to send data to `localhost`. In many cases, this default configuration needs to be changed. Examples of when the default endpoint needs to be changed include containerized environments, sending data to a gateway cluster instead of a local agent, and sending data directly to an observability platform.

.NET

.NET automatic instrumentation can be installed and enabled on Windows via a PowerShell module. For example:

```
# PowerShell 5.1 or higher is required
# Download the module
$module_url = "https://github.com/open-telemetry/opentelemetry-dotnet-
instrumentation/releases/latest/download/OpenTelemetry.DotNet.Auto.psm1"
$download_path = Join-Path $env:temp "OpenTelemetry.DotNet.Auto.psm1"
Invoke-WebRequest -Uri $module_url -OutFile $download_path -UseBasicParsing

# Import the module to use its functions
Import-Module $download_path

# Install core files
Install-OpenTelemetryCore

# Set up the instrumentation for the current PowerShell session
Register-OpenTelemetryForCurrentSession -OTelServiceName "MyServiceDisplayName"

# Run your application with instrumentation
.\MyNetApp.exe
```

Java

Java offers some of the best support for OTel. As mentioned above, Java leverages an instrumentation JAR file to provide automatic instrumentation. A wide range of libraries and frameworks support automatic instrumentation: `https://opentelemetry.io/ecosystem/registry/?s=&component=instrumentation&language=java`. This means getting started with OTel instrumentation in Java is as easy as downloading the JAR and passing the JAR, as well as any needed environment variables. For example:

```
# Download required dependencies
$ curl -L -O https://github.com/open-telemetry/opentelemetry-java-
          instrumentation/releases/latest/download/opentelemetry-javaagent.jar

# Update configuration - Forward slash required otherwise must prefix with export
# Update runtime parameters and start the application
$ OTEL_SERVICE_NAME=your-service-name \
  java -javaagent:path/to/opentelemetry-javaagent.jar -jar myapp.jar

# Also possible by passing -D runtime parameter instead of or in addition to
# environment variables
#java -javaagent:path/to/opentelemetry-javaagent.jar \
#     -Dotel.service.name=your-service-name -jar myapp.jar
```

Go

The Golang or Go programming language does not support native automatic instrumentation. As a result, OTel programmatic instrumentation is provided in addition to manual instrumentation (`https://opentelemetry.io/docs/instrumentation/go/libraries`). For example, instrumentation libraries (called packages in Go), such as the OTel instrumentation library for net/http,[11] can be added to existing code. It acts like middleware to provide instrumentation capabilities. You can see an example of this functionality here: `https://pkg.go.dev/go.opentelemetry.io/contrib/instrumentation/net/http/otelhttp#pkg-examples`. One thing to know about Go OTel instrumentation is that much of it is hosted outside of the OTel GitHub org: `https://opentelemetry.io/ecosystem/registry/?s=&component=instrumentation&language=go`.

For an example on how to add OTel instrumentation for `net/http`, see `https://opentelemetry.io/docs/languages/go/getting-started`. As an alternative to programmatic instrumentation, it is possible to achieve the equivalent of automatic instrumentation for Go using eBPF technology. An in-development approach is shown here: `https://github.com/open-telemetry/opentelemetry-go-instrumentation`. This approach requires Linux, x64 or ARM processor, a kernel version of 4.19+, and for the application to run with elevated privileges (integrity mode disabled). To allow eBPF instrumentation to propagate trace context, elevated privileges are required. With these prerequisites satisfied, it is possible to enable a form of automatic instrumentation for Go.

Node.js

Node.js OTel instrumentation supports both JavaScript and TypeScript. Adding automatic instrumentation is very similar to Python:

```
$ npm install --save @opentelemetry/api
$ npm install --save @opentelemetry/auto-instrumentations-node
$ node --require @opentelemetry/auto-instrumentations-node/register app.js
```

Deployment Models

This chapter has focused primarily on deploying applications either containerized or standalone. Other deployment models exist, including via orchestration engines such as Kubernetes (K8s) or function-as-a-service (FaaS) providers. OTel provides packaging and tooling for these environments:

- A K8s Helm operator is available, which can be used to inject automatic instrumentation into .NET, Java, Node.js, Python, and Go: `https://opentelemetry.io/docs/kubernetes/operator/automatic`.
- AWS Lambda layers are available to provide automatic instrumentation for Java, Node.js, and Python, and manual instrumentation for all languages: `https://opentelemetry.io/docs/kubernetes/operator/automatic`. Other cloud providers also support OTel automatic instrumentation in serverless environments, including Azure.[12]

Distributions

After learning about Collector distributions in Chapter 5, you may be wondering whether distributions are applicable to instrumentation. The answer is yes, but unlike the Collector, they are often only leveraged by commercial vendors. The reasons for instrumentation distributions are mostly the same as the Collector, including ease-of-use and better supportability. The major differences are that only minimal tooling exists to create them and removing components is typically not applicable given the decoupled nature of the OTel API and SDK.

As you may recall, the Collector bundles a variety of different components depending on the distribution leveraged. With instrumentation, in general, you choose which components to leverage. Given this flexibility, potential concerns around maintenance and security are reduced. With that said, automatic instrumentation libraries are a potential component you may not wish to leverage or only wish to leverage selectively. Some languages, such as Java, bundle all automatic instrumentation together, which could be a potential concern depending on business requirements. Others, like Python, offer the ability to control which automatic instrumentation libraries to install.

The decoupled nature of the instrumentation does bring up an important difference from the Collector. Some instrumentation components are being built and supported outside of the OTel project versus being primarily contained within the project. For example, if you query the OTel registry for Go instrumentation (`https://opentelemetry.io/ecosystem/registry/?s=&component=instrumentation&language=go`), you will find that many of the items listed are not hosted within the OTel GitHub organization. Most components are located in the contrib repository for the Collector, but not all. This difference is important because it means leveraging these components may require working with people outside of the OTel community.

Over time and as OTel continues to evolve, you should expect more and more components, including those for the Collector, to be hosted outside of the OTel project. This is because OTel's vision is for telemetry to be built in (`https://opentelemetry.io/community/mission/#telemetry-should-be-built-in`). This means library owners should include or expose OTel natively where possible. As such, you should have a strategy for when and how to adopt components hosted outside of the OTel project.

The Bottom Line

Instrument an application in various ways. Successfully instrumenting an application involves understanding and utilizing the different methods available to collect telemetry data. OTel offers versatile options for instrumentation, including automatic, manual, programmatic, and mixed approaches. You can choose the approach that best fits your application's architecture and observability needs, ensuring comprehensive data collection with minimal overhead.

Master It What is the difference between the automatic, manual, programmatic, and mixed methods of instrumentation?

Add production-ready instrumentation. Transitioning from initial instrumentation, like what can be found in the OTel getting started guides, to a production-ready state requires a focus on robustness, scalability, and minimal performance impact. Production-ready instrumentation involves ensuring that your telemetry setup can handle the load and complexity of real-world environments. This includes optimizing data collection to manage data volume, configuring error handling to ensure reliable data collection even under failure conditions, and validating that the instrumentation does not introduce significant latency or resource consumption. Implementing secure practices, such as encrypting telemetry data in transit and applying appropriate access controls is also essential. By rigorously testing and refining your instrumentation setup, you can achieve a balance between detailed observability and system performance, providing valuable insights while maintaining a seamless user experience.

Master It After the basics of generating telemetry data that is exported to the console, what are some additional capabilities you should add in preparation for production?

Enrich instrumentation with metadata. Enriching your instrumentation with metadata is crucial for providing context to the raw telemetry data collected, enabling more meaningful analysis and troubleshooting. Metadata can include information such as service names, environment tags, version numbers, and user-specific identifiers. Adding this contextual information allows you to filter, aggregate, and correlate data across different dimensions, making it easier to identify patterns, trends, and anomalies. OTel supports the inclusion of metadata through attributes and resources, which can be attached to signals. By systematically enriching your telemetry data with relevant metadata, you enhance its usability and effectiveness, empowering your team to gain deeper insights into system behavior and quickly pinpoint the root causes of issues.

Master It What are some ways you can enrich telemetry data with metadata?

Notes

1. `https://curl.se`
2. `https://www.python.org`
3. `https://gcc.gnu.org`
4. `https://pypi.org/project/pip`
5. `https://docs.python.org/3/library/venv.html`
6. `https://pypi.org/project/virtualenv`
7. `https://en.wikipedia.org/wiki/Monkey_patch`
8. `https://github.com/moby/moby/issues/46129`
9. `https://pypi.org/project/otel-extensions`
10. `https://en.wikipedia.org/wiki/Syntactic_sugar`
11. `https://pkg.go.dev/net/http`
12. `https://learn.microsoft.com/en-us/azure/azure-functions/opentelemetry-howto`

Chapter 7

Adopting OpenTelemetry

With hands-on experience instrumenting and collecting data, you may now be wondering what parts of OpenTelemetry to adopt to get the optimal return. As should be clear, adopting OpenTelemetry is a transformative step toward achieving comprehensive observability in your systems. This chapter will guide you through the process of integrating OpenTelemetry into your organization, from initial planning to full-scale implementation. You will learn about strategic considerations necessary for successful adoption, including setting clear objectives, understanding organizational readiness, and securing stakeholder buy-in. You will also learn about the technical aspects of deploying OpenTelemetry, such as configuring the Collector, instrumenting applications, and integrating with existing observability tools.

By the end of this chapter, you will have a clear roadmap for adopting OpenTelemetry in any environment, enabling you to leverage its powerful capabilities to enhance your monitoring and observability practices, drive operational excellence, and ultimately improve system reliability and performance. This chapter includes examples of Collector configuration, so reviewing Chapter 5, "Managing the OpenTelemetry Collector," is recommended before continuing. In addition, the information in the "Brownfield Deployment" section is relevant to the "Greenfield Deployment" section, so reading this chapter sequentially is recommended. All code examples are available in the book's GitHub repository (`https://github.com/flands/mastering-otel-book`).

IN THIS CHAPTER, YOU WILL LEARN TO:

- Prepare to adopt OpenTelemetry
- Approach adopting OpenTelemetry in brownfield deployments
- Approach adopting OpenTelemetry in greenfield deployments

The Basics

When introducing new technology, such as OpenTelemetry (OTel), within an environment, it is crucial to understand both the objectives you aim to achieve and the requirements necessary for a successful implementation. For observability solutions, this may include:

- Data portability and sovereignty, with a goal of gaining deeper insights into application availability and performance. Examples of requirements may include removing proprietary instrumentation and data collection components as well as gaining more control of your data.

- Reduced complexity, with a goal of ensuring compliance with industry standards. Examples of requirements may include consolidating observability tools and using a single open standard to simplify management.
- Improved observability, with a goal of reducing mean time to detection (MTTD) and mean time to recovery (MTTR). Examples of requirements may include consistent metadata tagging on all telemetry data and context and correlation across signal types.

You must assess your current observability needs to determine your objectives and requirements. This includes identifying the types of telemetry data that are most valuable for your organization, understanding the existing infrastructure, and determining the level of integration required with your current systems. Of course, to move to the implementation phase, you either need to have or get buy-in from relevant stakeholders. The easiest way to get this buy-in is by clearly communicating why this investment is necessary now and the expected return on investment (ROI).

Why OTel and Why Now?

OTel has rapidly gained traction as the de facto standard for observability due to its robust, flexible, and vendor-neutral approach. One of the primary reasons for adopting OTel now is the growing complexity of modern distributed systems. As applications increasingly rely on microservices, containers, and serverless architectures, traditional monitoring tools struggle to provide the necessary visibility across these dynamic environments. By leveraging OTel, organizations can benefit from a consistent and comprehensive view of their systems. OTel supports a wide range of programming languages and frameworks, making it a versatile choice for diverse technology stacks. Additionally, it offers extensive support for various observability platforms, ensuring that you can continue using your preferred ones while reducing vendor lock-in.

As shown in Table 7.1, OTel provides everything you need to generate and collect the telemetry data required to achieve observability. In addition, OTel has an active and vibrant community backing the project. Continuous improvements, regular updates, and a wealth of community-driven resources make OTel a forward-thinking choice that will evolve alongside industry needs.

TABLE 7.1: Example of the components that need to be supported for each telemetry signal. OTel provides a single solution for everything in this table. While traces, metrics, and logs are the most commonly used signals, additional signals, including profiling, are also being added to the project.

	TRACES, METRICS, AND LOGS
Instrumentation API	Defines how to create and manage telemetry data per programming language
Instrumentation SDK	Provides an implementation for telemetry operations, including processing and exporting, per language
Data Collection	A single binary supporting various form factors to receive, process, and export telemetry data
Interoperability Formats	Data models, communication protocols, context propagation, and semantic conventions

OTel does not stop with just a single way to capture data. It also defines a standard and provides capabilities to ensure consistency. Examples of the standard and provided capabilities include:

- Semantic conventions, which provide standardized names for objects, including HTTP calls, databases, and message queues, to name a few. The net result is data consistency across systems and data portability regardless of the observability platform you are using.
- Processors and telemetry pipelines, which allow end users to control the data generated, what it contains, and where it goes. For example, the OTel Collector grants complete control of telemetry data through a flexible Yet Another Markup Language (YAML) configuration.
- Context and correlation, which help end users reduce MTTR by enabling problem isolation and root cause analysis. While more details on context and correlation will be provided in Chapter 8, "The Power of Context and Correlation," a good example is OTel's ability to enrich existing logs with trace context, thus bringing traces and logs closer together.

Once stakeholders understand why OTel is the right technology to adopt, they next need to understand the urgency of the change. The easiest way to demonstrate urgency is to answer the *why now* question. Generically, the question can be answered by explaining the significant benefits OTel provides organizations aiming to enhance their observability stack. These include:

- Standardized and comprehensive observability, including a single instrumentation per programming language capable of supporting multiple signal types and a single binary deployable in various form factors to receive, process, and export this signal data
- Vendor neutrality, giving you data control and portability
- A vibrant community to ensure that you can take advantage of the latest developments in a rapidly evolving technological landscape while getting the support you need

In addition, adopting OTel now ensures that organizations are equipped with a future-proof observability framework that can handle the demands of modern, complex applications. It is also important to answer the *why now* question for your specific environment and business requirements. For example, maybe you are in the process of deploying or migrating to a new observability platform, or perhaps you have been experiencing resiliency issues and need better visibility into how your environment is behaving. Using your defined objectives, you can put forth a proposal on why OTel is the right investment now. As part of the proposal, it would be helpful if you could demonstrate success. For example, doing a proof of concept (PoC) for an application or small environment that demonstrates the value provided.

Where to Start?

Once you have buy-in to adopt OTel and have clearly defined your objectives and requirements, you need to assess your environment and what it contains. This is especially important when introducing observability technology, as it will touch a large portion of the environment. Examples of environmental information you should be able to answer include the following:

- What infrastructure is used and what versions?
- What telemetry data is captured from the infrastructure and by what?
- What programming languages are used and what versions?

- What major frameworks are used for each programming language and what versions?
- What are the security requirements in the environment?

In addition, if there are existing observability solutions already in use, you should be able to answer the following questions:

- Is automatic or manual instrumenting being used?
- What telemetry data is captured per programming language?
- What agents or collectors are used?
- What monitoring or observability platforms are used?
- What charts and alerts are configured and used in these platforms?

Begin by identifying a small, noncritical application or service as a pilot project. This will allow your team to experiment with OTel in a controlled environment, gain hands-on experience, and address any challenges without impacting critical operations. Instrument this pilot application to collect traces, metrics, and/or logs and integrate these with your observability platform of choice. Next, gradually expand the scope of your OTel implementation. Roll out instrumentation across additional services and applications, focusing on high-impact areas where observability can drive the most significant improvements. Throughout this process, ensure that you maintain clear communication with all stakeholders, providing training and support to help your team understand and embrace the new observability practices. Be sure to review and refine your OTel deployment regularly. Collect feedback, analyze telemetry data, and adjust your instrumentation and configuration as needed to optimize performance and achieve your observability goals. By taking a measured, iterative approach, you can ensure a successful and sustainable adoption of OTel within your organization.

Examples of companies that have successfully adopted OTel include GitHub[1] (traces), Cloudflare[2] (logs), and eBay[3] (metrics).

General Process

The general process for OTel adoption is captured in Figure 7.1. Items to consider include:

- Deploying the Collector in either agent or gateway mode. While using the Collector is not required, it would enable some pull-based collection and allow you to tap into any existing telemetry data. In addition, the Collector is configurable and extensible, giving you complete control over your telemetry data. Deploying the Collector in agent mode is recommended for most environments.

- Adding, if not already present, or replacing, if present, automatic instrumentation. While automatic instrumentation is more common in enabling tracing, OTel automatic instrumentation allows easy configuration of the OTel SDKs and provides instrumentation for other signals depending on the programming language. If you decide to enable traces, ensuring that the same context propagation mechanism is used throughout the environment is critical. After enabling tracing, consider enriching logs with trace context, as they provide value beyond what you are likely getting in your environment today. If enabling tracing is not desired, automatic instrumentation should still be considered, as the tracing signal can be turned off.

- Adding or replacing manual instrumentation service by service. Manual instrumentation provides more control and can be used with or without automatic instrumentation. In addition, it may be required to support custom libraries and frameworks. Programmatic instrumentation can be used to ease manual instrumentation adoption. Like automatic instrumentation, starting with a single signal and ensuring items like context propagation for traces are properly configured are important. While multiple different manual instrumentation libraries can usually be used on the same application, it is recommended to consolidate onto a single for various reasons, including maintenance.

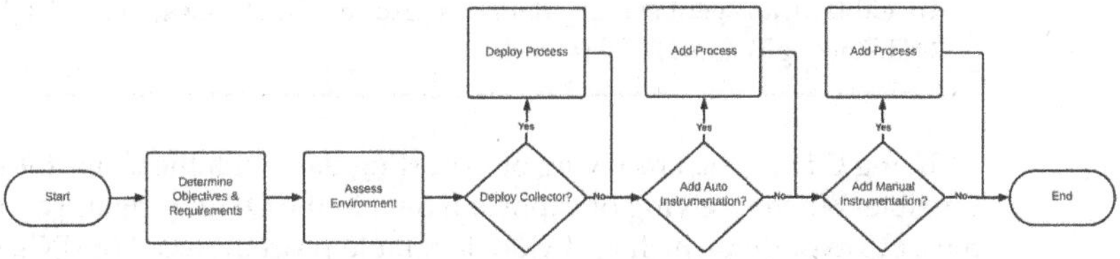

FIGURE 7.1 Flow chart of the general approach for OTel adoption. While every component is optional, deploying the Collector in agent mode is recommended for most environments. In addition, if an OTel automatic instrumentation is added, any non-OTel automatic instrumentation should be removed beforehand. Having two automatic instrumentation mechanisms in the same application can cause various issues. Multiple manual instrumentation libraries are usually okay, though they add to the operational complexity.

Data Collection

You will likely find that leveraging the OTel Collector is the easiest way to start adopting OTel. For most environments, the contrib distribution of the Collector will be used, at least initially. Over time, you may want to create or leverage a custom distribution to best support your requirements. (Distributions were covered in Chapter 5.) Reasons why you might opt to use the contrib distribution instead of the core distribution include the desire to:

- Receive or collect telemetry data other than or beyond what OTel instrumentation provides. Examples include collecting host metrics instead of or in addition to metric instrumentation, or collecting metrics from non-OTel sources, such as Prometheus or collected.[10]
- Process, enrich, or modify telemetry data, such as leveraging resource detectors, attribute processors, or platform-specific processing.
- Export or send data to a destination that does not support OTLP.
- Extend or take advantage of additional capabilities not available in the core distribution, such as the health check extension or connectors.

Since every environment is different and the Collector supports many components, it is impossible to demonstrate a configuration applicable to most environments. Instead, an example of a Collector configuration when using the core distribution and OpenTelemetry Protocol (OTLP), as well as one for the contrib distribution, is provided in the "Greenfield Deployment" section later in this chapter. These examples can be modified as needed but should serve as a good starting place.

OTLP Is Recommended

The use of OTLP is highly recommended whenever possible. As you may recall from Chapter 5 and Chapter 6, "Leveraging OpenTelemetry Instrumentation," everything generated from OTel instrumentation is in OTLP format, and everything the Collector receives is converted internally into the OTLP format via pdata. This is true even if the receiver and exporter formats are identical and not in OTLP format. If the observability platform supports OTLP, it is recommended to use the OTLP exporter over a custom exporter in order to reduce resource utilization and overhead in the Collector. Most vendors support receiving OTLP (`https://opentelemetry.io/ecosystem/vendors`). In addition, an agent sending data to a gateway should always use OTLP. It does not matter whether OTLP over gRPC or HTTP is used.

Using OTLP when receiving or exporting data with the Collector is *highly recommended* when possible. When receiving or exporting data in the OTLP format, you must decide whether to use the `otlp` exporter, which uses Google remote procedure call (gRPC), or the `otlphttpexporter`, which uses the HTTP protocol. The decision about which protocol to use is mostly yours, but factors include:

- **Instrumentation leveraged**: Per the OTel specification, OTel instrumentation *should* implement both but *must* implement at least one (`https://opentelemetry.io/docs/specs/otel/protocol/exporter/#specify-protocol`). As such, depending on your implementation, you may need one or both.
- **Protocols leveraged**: For example, if gRPC is not used anywhere in your environment, you may not be comfortable using it. Of course, if you use a protocol other than gRPC or HTTP, such as Apache Thrift, you will need to introduce a new protocol regardless.
- **The amount of data expected**: For environments generating a large amount of telemetry data, gRPC might perform better, but to date, there are no accurate benchmarks in OTel to confirm this. Most instrumentation libraries now default to HTTP/protobuf, but the question remains: *what is the best option for the Collector?*[4]

Some people may prefer HTTP over gRPC because of their comfort with REST. It is important to note that the payload is protocol buffers (protobuf), a binary format, by default. The `otlphttpexporter` also supports changing the encoding to JSON with a configuration like the following:

```
exporters:
  otlphttp:
    ...
    encoding: json
```

Changing Default Settings

OTel comes with default settings to make it easier to get started and ensure best practices are followed. These settings should be generally applicable to most environments. Of course, every environment is different, so it may be necessary to change the default settings. Care should be taken when changing the default settings to understand the impact. For example, changing the encoding on the `otlphttpexporter` from protobuf to JSON may result in different payload sizes and resource requirements. Ensure that any changes are necessary and adequately tested before rolling out to a production environment.

The primary differences between gRPC and HTTP are as follows:

- **The number of dependencies:** gRPC usually has many more dependencies than HTTP. The net result is that gRPC and its dependencies may need to be upgraded more often to address vulnerabilities, and the package size is often larger.
- **The HTTP version used:** gRPC uses HTTP 2.0, whereas HTTP defaults to 2.0 and can fallback to 1.1 if needed. It can also be explicitly configured only to use 1.1, though this is not recommended.

Finally, if you decide to deploy the Collector, you should configure and collect its own telemetry data so that it can be observed appropriately. A Collector instance *can* collect its own telemetry, but this approach is *not recommended* for production environments. As such, standing up and configuring at least a Collector running in gateway mode dedicated to collecting telemetry data from other Collectors is recommended. For more information, see Chapter 5.

ADVANCED SCENARIO: COLLECTOR PER SIGNAL

One Collector per signal may make sense when deploying the Collector in high-volume telemetry environments. When this architecture is deployed, it is often just for gateway mode. This deployment model isolates responsibilities and helps address noisy neighbor problems, which might otherwise result in telemetry data for one signal being dropped due to a different signal being processed by the same Collector instance. Deploying a Collector per signal would likely require more resources because any shared responsibilities, such as resource detection, would need to occur per signal.

Deploying a Collector per signal is more complex to manage and secure, so it should only be deployed independently if deemed necessary. Looking at the utilization and telemetry rate of the existing Collectors, in addition to the types of operational issues experienced, can help in decision-making. Being clear on business requirements can also help. For example, is one signal's data more important than another? Alternatively, is a subset of one signal's data more important? When possible, unimportant data should not be generated or should at least be filtered out. Some data collection may be contractually required. For example, it is common for logs to be needed for compliance reasons. Data that must be collected may be a good candidate for a Collector per signal architecture.

Instrumentation

How to start with instrumentation depends on various factors, including time, experience, and priorities. Automatic instrumentation is an easy way to get started, but manual instrumentation is often needed too. Determine which signal or signals you want to instrument and start small. In the case of traces, remember that you *do not* need to add trace instrumentation to every operation within an application to get value. Still, you *do* need to instrument every application in a transaction and ensure that context propagation is appropriately configured. When determining which operations to instrument with tracing, focus first on network operations, such as HTTP requests or RPC calls, including calls to databases and message queues.

Regardless of whether you are using automatic or manual instrumentation, there are some things you should perform and validate, including:

- Extensive performance tests to understand the impacts on the application, including resource utilization and startup time.
- Configuration validation to ensure that items such as context propagation and tagging are correctly set. Also, note that changes in the data received may result in the need to create or update charts and alerts to ensure that they work correctly—topics covered in the "Dashboards and Alerts" section.
- Metadata enrichment to help provide observability and ensure parity with any previous instrumentation. Note that enrichment may also be possible from the Collector instead of or in addition to the instrumentation.

The following are some important aspects to keep in mind when configuring OTel instrumentation:

- The exporter endpoint may need to be updated, especially for containerized environments or when the Collector is not deployed in agent mode. By default, instrumentation exports? to localhost (`127.0.0.1`).
- The service name should be set to distinguish applications from one another. This is necessary to understand the behavior, health, and performance of different services.
- You should determine how you want additional resource information to be added. Options include instrumentation, Collector, or both, and implementation depends on requirements. Leveraging Collector instances running in agent mode is the recommended default option.
- You should consider abstracting configuration and instrumentation where it makes sense. For example, multiple services written in the same language may be able to leverage a shared library to configure OTel instrumentation.

Production Readiness

As you introduce observability solutions in your environment, it is vital to perform extensive testing before rolling them out to production. You will want to ensure that the following are well understood and documented to prevent production issues:

- **Performance:** If performance issues are experienced, you will need to determine if they are because of the configuration, the application, or because of a new component being leveraged. Often, performance issues are due to a lack of understanding of how the new component operates. For example, configuring either the OTel Collector or instrumentation without batching or setting the correct number of workers on the sending queue will likely result in suboptimal performance.
- **Reliability:** Both the stability of the application and Collectors will be critical. Like performance, many reliability issues are due to a lack of understanding of how OTel works. For example, the Collector may crash if not sized and configured to support the traffic it receives. Properly configuring aspects such as the `GOGC` and `GOMEMLIMIT` environment variables, as covered in Chapter 5, is critical to ensuring reliability.

- **Security:** It is important to ensure that all components are properly hardened. For example, configuring encryption and using authentication when sending or receiving data is recommended. In addition, ensuring that components are regularly updated to address vulnerabilities is also critical.

Maturity Framework

When adopting or using an observability framework, it is essential to take a structured approach to assess and improve your organization's observability capabilities. One recommended step is to define and measure maturity levels, including a progression from basic instrumentation and data collection to advanced, automated observability capabilities. What follows is a maturity framework that could be implemented and modified as needed. It consists of five levels: Initial Implementation, Basic Instrumentation, Advanced Instrumentation, Integrated Observability, and Proactive Observability.

Level 1: Initial Implementation: At this foundational level, organizations begin their OTel journey by setting up the basic infrastructure necessary for collecting telemetry data. This includes installing OTel components and ensuring initial data flows. Key aspects include:

- Deployment of the Collector and basic configuration to start collecting and forwarding data to an observability platform
- Installation of OTel SDKs in select applications

Level 2: Basic Instrumentation: This step involves expanding the use of OTel by adding instrumentation to critical parts of the application. This level focuses on generating meaningful telemetry data from key services and components. Key aspects include:

- Identifying and instrumenting critical services and application components using OTel SDKs
- Utilizing OTel APIs to generate custom telemetry data specific to your application's needs
- Ensuring that essential signals are being collected through an environment

Level 3: Advanced Instrumentation: This step involves comprehensive instrumentation across the entire application stack, including third-party services and dependencies. This level emphasizes the detailed collection and analysis of telemetry data. Key aspects include:

- Full-stack instrumentation, including external dependencies and third-party services
- Signals enriched with contextual metadata such as service names, environment tags, and user identifiers (IDs)
- Enhanced use of OTel APIs to capture fine-grained telemetry data for detailed analysis

Level 4: Integrated Observability: This step focuses on the seamless integration of OTel with existing observability and monitoring tools. This level aims to provide a unified view of system health and performance through comprehensive data aggregation and visualization. Key aspects include:

- Complete integration with existing monitoring and observability tools
- Centralized dashboards that aggregate and visualize telemetry data from multiple sources for unified visibility

- Advanced querying and visualization techniques to gain deeper insights into system performance and health

Level 5: Proactive Observability: This step represents the highest level of OTel adoption, where telemetry data is used to drive proactive monitoring and automated responses. This level focuses on predictive analytics and automated remediation to maintain optimal system performance. Key aspects include:

- Predictive analytics and machine learning (ML) for anomaly detection and potential issue forecasting
- Incident response with automated remediation workflows to address incidents and performance bottlenecks in real time
- Continuous improvement through feedback loops and performance tuning

Brownfield Deployment

Often, when working on an observability project, you will be in an environment that has been around for a while and may have various monitoring or observability solutions in use. Adding something to such environments is known as a *brownfield deployment* or *brownfield project*.[5] When adopting an open standard such as OTel in a brownfield deployment, you must first understand the landscape and what technology is in play. Next, you must determine how telemetry data is used in the environment. With the environmental information, the general process for OTel adoption includes adding OTel components, including the Collector or instrumentation, or replacing proprietary collectors and instrumentation with OTel equivalents.

Data Collection

For brownfield deployments, the Collector can be either deployed in gateway mode and configured to collect data from other solutions, such as K8s and Prometheus, or deployed as an agent with the goal of making it the central Collector in the environment over time. If a commercial platform is used, it is often a prime candidate to introduce the Collector into the environment. The idea would be to replace any proprietary Collector and ensure the Collector is responsible for processing and routing all telemetry data to its destination, as shown in Figure 7.2. When this milestone is achieved, you will gain data portability and have a migration path to the OTel open standard. Of course, this requires the commercial platform to support one of the Collector exporters, but today, most do. Injecting the Collector between your applications and commercial platform, typically in gateway mode, is a good place to start.

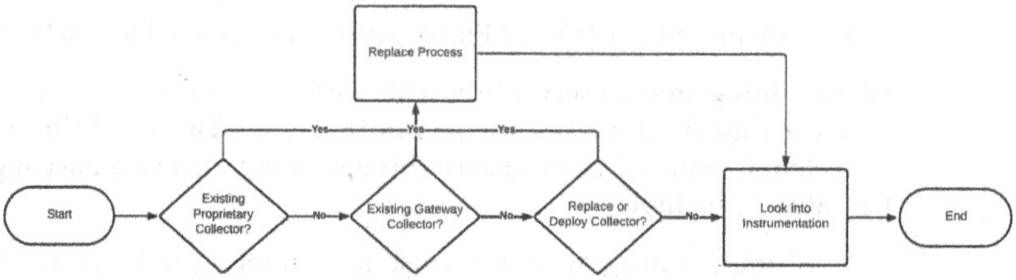

FIGURE 7.2 Example of how to initially approach adopting OTel in a brownfield deployment. Starting with data collection components first is recommended. Instrumentation will be handled next.

With the agent approach, you likely need to deploy it alongside other agents you may eventually want to replace, as shown in Figure 7.3. Alternatively, testing and preparing a rip-and-replace strategy may be easier or more desirable. With this approach, the OTel Collector replaces another agent in a single action.

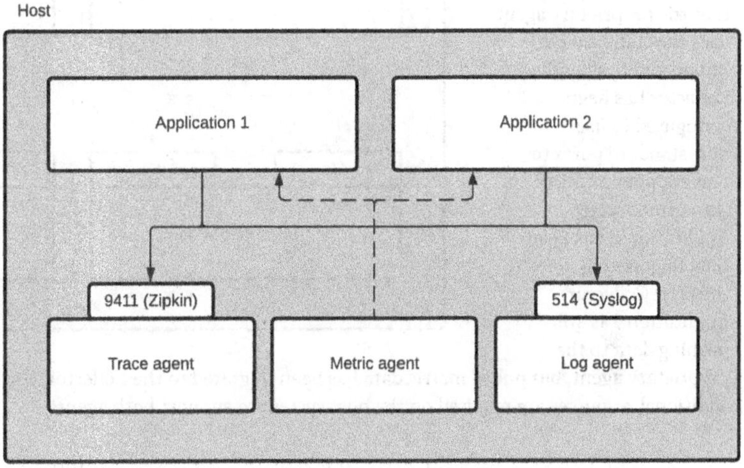

FIGURE 7.3 Common agent architecture for brownfield deployments. Typically, one or more agents are deployed to support one or more signals. In this example, Application 1 and 2 push traces and logs to dedicated agents while a metric agent pulls metrics from them. The OTel Collector has not been deployed. To deploy the OTel Collector, it either needs to be deployed alongside the other agents, or a rip-and-replace strategy needs to be implemented to migrate functionality.

For side-by-side migration, you will migrate parts of the collection to the Collector. An example of a transition state is shown in Figure 7.4. In addition, several considerations must be taken into account, including:

- **Resource usage and constraints:** As discussed in Chapter 5, proper resource constraints must be configured so that deploying a new agent does not result in resource contention or scheduling issues. If resource usage is not configured correctly, it may impact observability solutions and applications running in the environment. In addition, running another agent requires more resources on the host system.
- **Port conflicts:** When deploying in agent mode, you will want to determine whether port conflicts are an issue. If yes, you must decide how you want to handle them. Options include using a non-standard port, attempting to mirror or forward the traffic to the new destination, or opting for the rip-and-replace strategy.
- **Network configuration:** Beyond the agent's configuration, network access control lists or ACLs and network proxies may also need to be reconfigured to allow traffic to the new agent. Proxy settings were discussed in Chapter 5.
- **Effects of migration:** When making changes to the way telemetry data is collected, it is possible that errors will be seen, configured alerts may trigger, and some amount of telemetry data may be dropped. As a result, properly communicating with teams and potentially muting alerts may be desired during the migration.

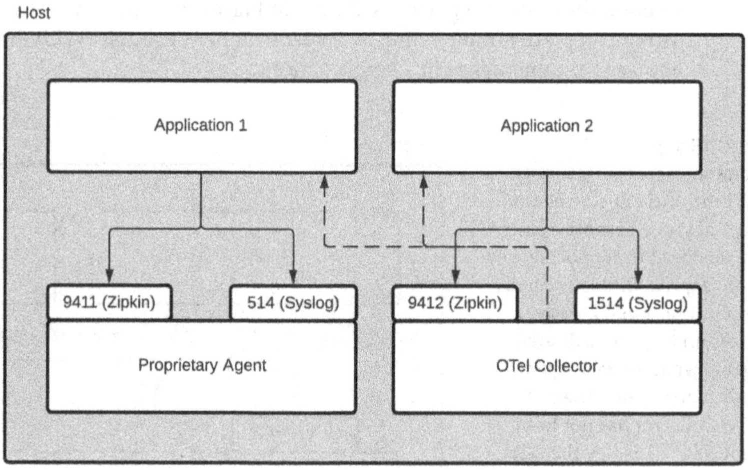

FIGURE 7.4
One possible side-by-side agent migration state. In this example, a proprietary agent is being replaced by the OTel Collector. Given that the proprietary agent uses the standard ports for Zipkin and Syslog, the Collector has been configured to use non-standard ports to prevent port conflicts. In the current state, Application 2 has been fully migrated to point to the OTel Collector. Application 1 is still pushing data to the proprietary agent, but pulled metric data has been migrated to the Collector. Until the migration is complete, additional resources are required on the host system to support both agents.

In the rip-and-replace model, you would perform all the testing and document the procedure for replacing the previous agent before rolling out the changes. In general, the flow would be to remove the old agent and deploy the new one once done. Like the side-by-side migration, the effects need to be appropriately considered. In addition, if the new agent deployment does not work correctly, you will want the ability to revert to the previous agent again. Beyond configuration testing, performance and failure testing beforehand are critical to ensuring a successful rollout.

Instrumentation

Instrumentation, especially manual instrumentation, is often a bigger lift when migrating than data collection. With that said, the process is relatively similar. For example, say your environment is already using an automatic instrumentation library. Adding a second automatic instrumentation library in the same application is *never recommended* as the two libraries will likely conflict and have unexpected behaviors. Instead, the previous automatic instrumentation needs to be removed, and the new one needs to be added as shown in Figure 7.5. This is the same as the rip-and-replace strategy discussed in the "Data Collection" section. Using different automatic instrumentation libraries across different services is OK if the same context propagation mechanism is used. While replacing automatic instrumentation may be straightforward as it only requires dependencies and runtime changes, it will require extensive testing and may impact observability during the transition.

When adopting OTel in a brownfield deployment, you should be aware of the following:

- Replacing manual instrumentation is not required for any instrumentation formats supported by the Collector but may be considered to reduce the number of technologies used and maintained in an environment. Other reasons to consider switching to OTel instrumentation include it being the most adopted open standard and that it can handle multiple signals with the same SDK. At the very least, proprietary instrumentation should be removed over time. One way to approach this is to ensure every new service introduced into the environment leverages the new instrumentation standard.

- While automatic instrumentation is most commonly used to generate trace data, in OTel, it supports more, including OTel SDK configuration and possibly other signals. Even if automatic instrumentation is not used in the environment, it should be considered in brownfield deployments. Considerations for new deployments of automatic instrumentation are covered in the "Greenfield Deployment" section.
- The same context propagation mechanism must be used when replacing trace instrumentation, regardless of whether it is via automatic or manual instrumentation. Otherwise, traces will be broken, impacting observability. OTel supports common open source propagators (`https://opentelemetry.io/docs/specs/otel/context/api-propagators/#propagators-distribution`) and even supports the ability to pass more than one propagation format at a time. This means that only when migrating off proprietary propagators must care be taken to ensure observability is not negatively impacted.

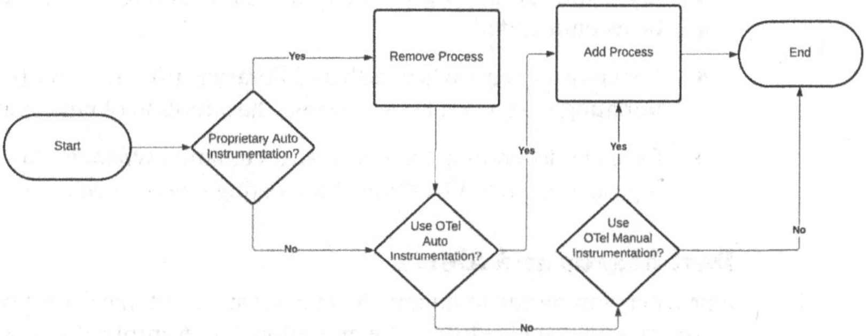

FIGURE 7.5
Example of how to approach adopting OTel in a brownfield deployment. Automatic instrumentation can be beneficial regardless of the signal, but using more than one automatic instrumentation mechanism per application is not recommended. Manual instrumentation can be approached after automatic instrumentation.

As mentioned earlier, manual instrumentation is usually more involved to replace. Unlike automatic instrumentation, which is primarily dependency and runtime changes, manual instrumentation requires code changes. These changes may require several iterations to properly configure items such as context propagation and metadata enrichment. While manual instrumentation is more work, you usually have more flexibility when switching instrumentation. For example, you can generally configure two manual instrumentation libraries in the same application. While this may have performance implications, beyond dependency management, both should be able to generate and emit telemetry data. Of course, the end state should only run a single instrumentation framework.

For brownfield deployments, there is an expectation by end users of the amount and type of telemetry data as well as a dependency on that data in the observability platform. When migrating to different instrumentation, it is important to maintain a similar level of observability otherwise, stakeholders may be upset—more on this in the "Dashboards and Alerts" section.

Beyond deciding on automatic, manual, or both types of instrumentation, you need to decide which signals to prioritize, what telemetry to generate, and how to enrich it. Given your existing telemetry, you may replicate the same behavior as a starting place. Alternatively, you may have some known issues or improvements you want to make, and you can use this migration as an opportunity to address them. Regardless, you should not try to take on too much at once. Start by choosing a single signal on a single service. Then, define how you want telemetry data to be generated. For example, what metadata should it contain, and how should it be exported? When adopting OTel in a brownfield deployment, leveraging the default OTLP exporter and sending data to the Collector is *highly recommended*. Beyond this, resource detectors (covered in Chapters 5 and 6) are a great starting place for metadata enrichment. Over time, you can choose to make additional enhancements if needed.

Given the difficulty in changing instrumentation, the question of whether migrating is worth the effort may be raised. The benefit of adopting an open standard is the promise of not needing to learn or adopt a different standard or format in the future. While even after adoption changes may be required, these changes will typically be more minor and follow the same basic concepts versus needing to learn something completely new. In addition, the value is the ability to leverage OTel constructs and abilities, including resources and attribute processing. What follows are some common approaches to take when changing instrumentation:

- If you are using any proprietary instrumentation, then at least migrating it to OTel would be recommended.
- For environments where a shared library is used for a particular language, consider updating the shared library to ease the adoption of new instrumentation:
- Consider leveraging the new instrumentation when deploying new services or rearchitecting existing ones. Over time, the existing ones can be migrated if desired.

Dashboards and Alerts

If or when you decide to migrate to an open standard like OTel, you need to determine what the experience will be like during the migration. For example, if you were collecting metrics with specific names and relied on those names to create multiple charts or alerts, then when migrating to OTel, you need to decide how to handle metric name changes. The same applies to metadata changes, including semantic conventions. In general, you have the following options:

- **Send the new name and make it a platform problem:** while this is easiest from a client perspective, this will break existing charts and alerts. Platform options to fix the breakage depend on platform capabilities. Options include configuring mapping rules at ingest or query time, updating all charts and alerts to use both names, or creating a second set of charts and alerts that use the new metric names and waiting for the migration to complete. The last option offers the worst end-user experience as it requires knowing about and looking at two sets of dashboards or alerts. The Prometheus query language (PromQL) can be used to demonstrate updating queries to use two different metric names. It supports selecting time series with different names via the `__name__` pseudo-label.[6] For example, you could use the following syntax:

  ```
  <aggregation>({__name__=~"<metric1>|<metric2>"})
  ```

- **Send the original name and wait for the migration to complete before cutting over:** if using the Collector, you could change metric names using the metric transform processor. Depending on the rules configured, this would add load to the Collector and not achieve the goal of fully migrating to an open standard, but it might serve as a good stopgap during migration. Once the migration is completed, you can remove the processor and use updated charts and alerts. For example, the metric transform processor in the OTel Collector might be configured like this:

```
...
processors:
  # rename system.cpu.usage to system.cpu.usage_time
  # for all system.cpu metrics, rename the label state to cpu_state
  # changes like this would need to occur for every metric impacted
  metrictransform:
    - include: system.cpu.usage
      action: update
      new_name: system.cpu.usage_time
    - include: ^system\.cpu\.
      action: update
      operations:
        - action: update_label
          label: state
          new_label: cpu_state

service:
  pipelines:
    metrics:
      receivers: [otlp]
      processors: [metricstransform]
      exporters: [otlp]
```

- **Send both the original and the new name and wait for the migration to complete before cutting over:** if you are using the Collector, you could also choose to send both metric names to the same platform. Of course, there is a platform cost associated with this, and once the migration is done, you will want to remove this double publishing. For example, a forward connector could be used in conjunction with the metric transform processor in the previous example:

```
...
connectors:
  # instead of using the forward connector, it may be possible to
  # use the insert action of the metrictransform processor depending
  # on the rules required
  forward:

processors:
  # rename system.cpu.usage to system.cpu.usage_time
  # for all system.cpu metrics, rename the label state to cpu_state
  # changes like this would need to occur for every metric impacted
  metrictransform:
    - include: system.cpu.usage
      action: update
      new_name: system.cpu.usage_time
```

```
        - include: ^system\.cpu\.
          action: update
          operations:
            - action: update_label
              label: state
              new_label: cpu_state

service:
  pipelines:
    metrics/new:
      receivers: [otlp]
      processors: []
      exporters: [otlp, forward]
    metrics/original:
      receivers: [forward]
      processors: [metricstransform]
      exporters: [otlp]
```

As you can see, leveraging the OTel Collector may be necessary to ensure the proper experience during the migration, depending on the option you choose. You might be wondering whether you could migrate all instrumentation simultaneously instead of needing to configure potentially extensive YAML in the Collector for a temporary state. It might be possible depending on your environment. For example, if all applications are written in the same language and the rollout could be released or feature flagged simultaneously, then it might be possible. Reasons why you might not be able to include polyglot architectures, rollout strategies, and different teams with different priorities, to name a few.

Greenfield Deployment

Sometimes, you get the opportunity to add observability to a new environment. These situations may arise due to a new company, department, or team being formed or because of a switch to a new technology stack. The migration from on-premises to the cloud is a potential example of the latter. While some have opted to create new workloads in the cloud, others have decided to deploy existing on-premises software to the cloud, with minimal changes to its architecture, known as lift and shift. Regardless of the approach taken, migration offers the opportunity to introduce change more easily.

Any environment for which observability or monitoring does not exist and you can add it would be considered a *greenfield deployment* or *greenfield project*.[7] The approach for a greenfield deployment is very similar to that of a brownfield, and many of the same considerations must be taken into account. As such, reading the "Brownfield Deployment" section is highly recommended before continuing.

Data Collection

Starting with the OTel Collector is highly recommended as the first step. Unless in an unsupported environment, such as many serverless environments, deploying the Collector as an agent on each host provides a great foundation for generating and collecting telemetry data. In addition, the Collector can generate some amount of metric data without modifying applications. For greenfield deployments, you can even standardize on the OTLP format from the very beginning, eliminating the number of additional protocols, wire formats, and dependencies that need to be configured, supported, and maintained.

If you plan to receive only OTLP data and can send all data to destinations that support OTLP, it is entirely possible to leverage the core version of the Collector. To start with the core distribution, you must configure at least an OTLP receiver and exporter. An example of a core distribution configuration file for a greenfield deployment may look like the following:

```
receivers:
  otlp:
    protocols:
      grpc:
        endpoint: 0.0.0.0:4317

processors:
  batch:

  # Assumes the Collector has 2GB of memory - adjust as needed
  # Also remember to set the GOMEMLIMIT environment variable
  # See Chapter 5 for more information

  memory_limiter:
    check_interval: 1s
    limit_mib: 1900

exporters:
  otlp:
    endpoint: mycluster:4317

service:
  pipelines:
    traces:
      receivers: [otlp]
      processors: [memory_limiter, batch]
      exporters: [otlp]
    metrics:
      receivers: [otlp]
      processors: [memory_limiter, batch]
      exporters: [otlp]
    logs:
      receivers: [otlp]
      processors: [memory_limiter, batch]
      exporters: [otlp]
```

If different endpoints are required for different signals, then the configuration will be a little more complex:

```
receivers:
  otlp:
    protocols:
      grpc:
        endpoint: 0.0.0.0:4317
```

```
processors:
  batch:

  # Assumes the Collector has 2GB of memory - adjust as needed
  # Also remember to set the GOMEMLIMIT environment variable
  # See Chapter 5 for more information
  memory_limiter:
    check_interval: 1s
    limit_mib: 1900

exporters:
  otlp:
    traces_endpoint: traces.mycluster:4317
    metrics_endpoint: metrics.mycluster:4317
    logs_endpoint: logs.mycluster:4317

service:
  pipelines:
    traces:
      receivers: [otlp]
      processors: [memory_limiter, batch]
      exporters: [otlp]
    metrics:
      receivers: [otlp]
      processors: [memory_limiter, batch]
      exporters: [otlp]
    logs:
      receivers: [otlp]
      processors: [memory_limiter, batch]
      exporters: [otlp]
```

If more than just the OTLP receiver or exporter are needed, or if additional capabilities, such as processors or extensions, are needed, then the contrib version of the Collector would be needed. To get started with the contrib distribution, you can start with a similar configuration as just outlined. Still, you will probably want more components, such as the host metric receiver, resource detector processor, and health check extension. For example, your configuration might look like the following:

```
extensions:
  healthcheck:

receivers:
  hostmetric:
    scrapers:
      cpu:
      disk:
      memory:
```

```
  otlp:
    protocols:
      grpc:
        endpoint: 0.0.0.0:4317

processors:
  batch:

  # Assumes the Collector has 2GB of memory - adjust as needed
  # Also remember to set the GOMEMLIMIT environment variable
  # See Chapter 5 for more information
  memory_limiter:
    check_interval: 1s
    limit_mib: 1900

  # Add or remove detectors as applicable to your environment
  # Important: By default, received resource metadata will be overridden.
  #            Set "override" to "false" if this is not desired.
  #            In addition, order matters, the first detector to insert wins.
  resourcedetection:
    detectors: [env, eks, ecs, ec2, aks, azure, gcp, system]

exporters:
  otlp:
    traces_endpoint: traces.mycluster:4317
    metrics_endpoint: metrics.mycluster:4317
    logs_endpoint: logs.mycluster:4317

service:
  extensions: [healthcheck]
  pipelines:
    traces:
      receivers: [otlp]
      processors: [memory_limiter, batch, resourcedetection]
      exporters: [otlp]
    metrics:
      receivers: [otlp]
      processors: [memory_limiter, batch, resourcedetection]
      exporters: [otlp]
    logs:
      receivers: [otlp]
      processors: [memory_limiter, batch, resourcedetection]
      exporters: [otlp]
```

Of course, if you are running on a particular platform such as those discussed in the "Brownfield Deployment" section, you will likely want to configure additional components. Remember that setting the GOGC and GOMEMLIMIT environment variables for the Collector is *highly recommended*. In addition, when deploying the contrib distribution using something like the preceding example, you may start receiving data immediately. This is different from the core distribution, which requires applications to be instrumented to receive pushed data. For example, if receiver components such as `hostmetrics` or `k8scluster` are configured and enabled, they will begin searching for and collecting data.

Instrumentation

If you decide to deploy the Collector, you can turn to instrumentation once it is in place. Alternatively, you can start with instrumentation and deploy the Collector later or use instrumentation without the Collector. With instrumentation, it is common for people to want to start by instrumenting metrics. The reasons why people often start with metrics is severalfold, including:

- Developers are often more comfortable troubleshooting with metrics.
- Service owners care more about their services than those they are dependent on or that depend on them.
- Tracing requires context propagation, meaning services must be instrumented end-to-end to provide value. Instrumenting all services in a transaction can take time, depending on the number of services, the types of languages and frameworks used, and the teams involved.

As should be clear by now, automatic instrumentation is an easy way to get started, but manual instrumentation is often needed as well. The type of automatic instrumentation available depends on the programming language and signal, as discussed in Chapter 2, "Introducing OpenTelemetry!," It is common for people to associate automatic instrumentation with traces. As such, considering automatic instrumentation for metrics or even logs is often overlooked. If the goal is to start with metrics, automatic instrumentation can help even if it does not currently support automatic metric instrumentation. For example, it can be used to configure the OTel SDK outside the application code. As such, starting with automatic instrumentation can be a good strategy even if tracing is not desired initially or automatic metric instrumentation is not currently supported. For manual instrumentation, care should be taken not to over-instrument. Being intentional about what and how to instrument can go a long way in providing value while avoiding unnecessary overhead and costs. Examples of how to get started with automatic and manual instrumentation were covered in Chapter 6.

Other Considerations

Now that you understand how to approach an OTel adoption project, it is time to explore other considerations, including administration, maintenance, and changes to OTel over time.

Administration and Maintenance

Three separate OTel components may need to be deployed and managed. These components are typically deployed by one of two different administrators, as outlined in Table 7.2. Understanding who the administrator is is important because it often drives behaviors. For example, it is common for companies that have a site reliability engineering (SRE) team to make them responsible for observability solutions, including their deployment and management. In these scenarios, it is typical for the SRE team to opt to deploy automatic instrumentation or manual instrumentation. The reasons for this include the SRE team's ability to control the outcome and minimize the required coordination between teams.

TABLE 7.2: The types of OTel components that may need to be deployed and managed, as well as who typically administrates them

COMPONENT	ADMINISTRATOR
Collector	SRE
Automatic instrumentation	SRE
Manual instrumentation	Developer

Adopting OTel is not a one-time effort; it requires ongoing administration and maintenance—just like any other dependency—to ensure continuous, effective observability. One of the first administrative tasks is to establish clear ownership and governance for your OTel implementation. It is recommended to designate a team or individual responsible for managing the deployment, overseeing configuration changes, and ensuring that the system remains up-to-date with the latest releases and best practices. Regular maintenance includes updating OTel components to the latest versions to benefit from new features, performance improvements, and security patches. You should be aware of the following regarding OTel project upgrades:

- Semantic Version (SemVer) 2.0.0 is followed, and breaking changes are only allowed between major versions.
- Versions less than 1.0 are in development (previously called experimental) and may experience breaking changes with any release until reaching 1.0.
- Versions 1.0 or higher are stable but may contain in-development components.
- A release may contain new features, bug fixes, and/or security updates.
- In general, bug fixes and security updates are not backported to older versions; upgrading to the latest version is recommended.
- Release cadences vary by project.

OTel RELEASES

Releases of OTel are repository specific. In general, bug fixes and security updates are only available by upgrading to the latest minor or patch version; backporting to older versions is typically not done. Newer minor versions may also include new features or changes in behavior. While stable versions will not introduce breaking changes for stable components, changes in the new minor version need to be considered and tested. As a result, it is *highly recommended* to read the release notes and upgrade to the latest version when experiencing a bug or when validating whether a vulnerability has been addressed. In addition, it is critical to do testing, including performance testing, prior to upgrading in case of regressions or changes in behavior.

The people responsible for maintaining observability initiatives should keep a close watch on the OTel community's release notes and roadmap to stay informed about upcoming changes and plan for updates accordingly. Additionally, they should ensure that code instrumentation and configurations are regularly reviewed and optimized to minimize performance overhead and maintain data accuracy. Other administrative tasks include managing the storage and retention policies of telemetry data. Clear data retention policies that balance the need for historical data with storage costs and compliance requirements should be defined. In addition, it may be necessary to implement data aggregation and downsampling techniques to reduce storage costs while preserving the granularity needed for effective analysis.

Real World Scenario

ADOPTING OTel AT JUPITERIAN

Riley obtained elevated permissions on K8s and owned all agents and collectors as part of being the DevOps lead at Jupiterian. As such, it was easy for her to deploy the contrib distribution of the OTel Collector, configure it to collect data from Prometheus, and send it to the Watchwhale platform. In addition, she recently took over ownership of the Prometheus server from IT. As such, she could easily configure federation, allowing the OTel Collector to scrape data from Prometheus. After extensively testing in the development environment, she followed the appropriate steps to roll the Collector out to production. These steps included going through a legal and security review, creating runbooks, and configuring appropriate monitoring. Once everything was rolled out and validated, she prepared training material for the team so they could begin to adopt the Watchwhale platform. With production data now in the Watchwhale platform, she was ready to open access to the engineering team to get feedback from others regarding Watchwhale's capabilities.

In addition to deploying the Collector, Riley also decided to deploy OTel automatic instrumentation to the caching service involved in the most recent outage. She enabled resource detection processing in the Collector, which enriches the OTel instrumentation with infrastructure metadata, including where the service is running and relevant application information. Since automatic instrumentation only requires dependency and runtime parameter changes, she could test in development quickly and easily. In addition to testing, Riley created relevant dashboards, alerts, and runbook updates in preparation for production rollout. Since she had only deployed the Collector in gateway mode, she needed to decide where to send the telemetry data. Since both gateway instances were stand-alone, Riley did not want to deploy agent mode at this time and did not want to manage a third gateway instance. Instead, she opted to send the metric data directly to Prometheus.

With the bug responsible for the outage fixed and the appropriate telemetry data now being generated, the feature flag was re-enabled for the caching service. This time, everything worked as expected, with the latency on the cart page being reduced by over 60 percent. Less than a week after deploying the automatic instrumentation, the on-call received a page about high memory usage on caching service pods running in Jupiterian's largest production environment. Upon investigation, it appeared as though a couple of the pods were experiencing a memory leak. The impacted pods were quarantined to prevent a service outage and allow time to get a memory dump. The memory dump analysis confirmed a memory leak, which was quickly patched. The telemetry data from OTel had saved Jupiterian from another major outage.

Environments

With a better understanding of how to take advantage of OTel, you may also be wondering about environment-specific considerations. Here are some common environments and how to approach them:

- **Development, staging, and production:** Each environment has unique requirements and constraints that will influence your observability strategy. You should strive for consistency across environments to minimize issues due to differences. As such, you should adopt OTel in all environments.
- **Kubernetes (K8s):** In K8s environments, using the OTel Helm chart is *highly recommended* for the Collector, and the OTel K8s Operator can help you decrease your OTel adoption time by providing auto-instrumentation capabilities.[8] Instrumentation and Collector considerations for K8s were covered in Chapter 5 and Chapter 6.
- **Functions-as-a-service (FaaS):** OTel supports AWS Lambda. In addition, there are examples of other cloud providers supporting OTel, including Google Cloud Functions and Azure Functions. One important thing to consider in serverless environments is startup time. Given that cold start time for short-lived functions is important and automatic instrumentation often increases the cold start time, manually instrumenting is usually a better approach than automatic instrumentation. Also, using the Collector in serverless environments is often more challenging. While AWS Lambda offers Collector support, some serverless environments do not. In addition, deploying a Collector in a serverless environment may not be desired due to resource utilization. A Collector running in gateway mode outside of the serverless environment could also be leveraged if needed.
- **Internet of Things (IoT):** The primary difference between IoT and embedded environments is the low-resource footprint requirement. Due to this requirement, it is better to

have telemetry built into the technologies used versus using automatic instrumentation. In addition, a lightweight and custom version of the Collector may also be required. Creating a custom distribution of the Collector was covered in Chapter 5.

- **Air-gapped:**[9] Air-gapped environments often have strict security requirements. If an application is air-gapped, instrumentation may need to be sent directly to its destination, or a Collector binary would need to be installed alongside the application. If an environment's local area network (LAN) is air-gapped, then it comes down to security requirements and proxy configurations.

The underlying infrastructure also plays a role. For example, you will likely want to configure and enable platform-specific receivers and processors if running applications on top of a platform such as Docker, K8s, OpenShift, or Heroku. In addition, platform-specific configuration, such as making the host IP address available to the application in K8s (covered in Chapter 6) or mounting the socket to access the Docker API (covered in Chapter 5), may be required.

Semantic Conventions

One of the powerful aspects of OTel is its commitment to semantic conventions. The value they offer is the ability to provide context, which helps with performing problem isolation as well as understanding root cause and remediation, a topic that will be covered in Chapter 8. The problem in brownfield deployments is that these conventions likely differ from what is currently used. In addition, OTel is still maturing these conventions, with only the HTTP category being stable at the time this book was published. (For the latest information, see `https://opentelemetry.io/docs/concepts/semantic-conventions`.) Like signal name changes, changing semantic conventions can break charts and alerts, impacting observability. Minimizing the impact of the changes, whether during migration or upgrade, requires understanding which you depend on and testing upgrades to see whether changes were introduced. Given the various components and maturity levels in OTel, testing each upgrade is beneficial beyond semantic conventions.

One way to gain visibility into OTel telemetry changes is by using the console exporter for instrumentation and the debug exporter for the Collector. These exporters allow you to collect the output, which can then be used to compare different versions. What is missing is a utility to generate the telemetry that could be emitted. If you identify changes that impact your existing charts or alerts, you need to determine how to handle those changes. Options to handle these types of changes were covered in more detail, including Collector configuration options, in the "Brownfield Deployments" section.

As you can see, changes to signal names and semantic conventions can be highly disruptive. This is why OTel worked to stabilize the signals and is now actively working to stabilize the semantic conventions. Once stable, breaking changes would be handled through schema versioning, a topic covered in Chapter 4, "Understanding the OpenTelemetry Specification." With schema versioning, any observability platform that supports OTel schemas would be able to handle translations, or the Collector could handle it via the schema processor. The net result is a native way to support changes without needing to determine and handle changes manually.

In addition to the official conventions, consider defining organization-specific conventions that address your unique requirements and use cases. Using a unique namespace is *highly recommended*. Document these conventions and ensure that they are communicated and enforced across all development teams. This practice not only enhances the consistency and quality of your telemetry data but also fosters a culture of observability within your organization.

The Future

While OTel has focused primarily on the three pillars of observability to date, several additional forms of telemetry are important and on the roadmap (`https://opentelemetry.io/community/roadmap`), including:

- Profiling to provide code-level telemetry data helpful in investigating performance issues in an application. This data is similar to a trace but contains deeper information from within a service. In the first quarter of 2024, OTel announced that profiling would be the next signal type (`https://opentelemetry.io/blog/2024/profiling`).
- Client instrumentation, which is required to support Real User Monitoring (RUM). Initial support for client instrumentation is already present for the browser via Node.js instrumentation. In addition, mobile instrumentation is available for Android (Java) and iOS (Swift). While client instrumentation can be considered a form of trace, it differs in several ways. First, it contains user-agent information and is more likely to contain personally identifying information (PII). Second, it will eventually support session replay capabilities and crash analytics reporting, which are typically binary-formatted data, which differs significantly from what a trace provides.
- eBPF telemetry for observability, which is already available in parts of OTel, including the eBPF Collectors (`https://github.com/open-telemetry/opentelemetry-network`) and Go automatic instrumentation (`https://github.com/open-telemetry/opentelemetry-go-instrumentation`). eBPF enables a new way to collect telemetry data through the kernel and support additional use cases such as developer security operations (DevSecOps) in the future.

As these areas mature, you may also want to adopt them. In many cases, this will require upgrading and configuring the existing components, including instrumentation and the Collector. In some cases, such as eBPF telemetry, new components may need to be deployed. Beyond OTel, the future of observability generally is also changing. More details will be provided in Chapter 12, "The Future of Observability."

The Bottom Line

Prepare to adopt OpenTelemetry. Preparation is key to a successful adoption of OTel. Start by setting clear objectives for what you aim to achieve with enhanced observability, such as reducing MTTD and MTTR, improving performance monitoring, or gaining deeper insights into user behavior. Next, assess your current observability maturity and identify gaps that OTel can fill. In addition, stakeholders across development, operations, and business units should be engaged to secure buy-in and align on goals. Finally, develop a detailed implementation plan that includes timelines, resource allocation, and training requirements.

Master It Preparation will ensure that your OTel adoption is strategic, well-supported, and aligned with organizational goals. What are some reasons why you might want to adopt OTel?

Approach adopting OpenTelemetry in brownfield deployments. Adopting OTel in brownfield deployments, or environments that already contain observability tools, requires careful planning to integrate new observability practices without disrupting current operations. Begin by conducting an inventory of your existing monitoring and observability solutions and identify how OTel can complement or replace these tools. Start with a pilot project, selecting a noncritical application to instrument and test the integration. Gradually expand the scope to more critical systems, ensuring that each step is thoroughly tested and that the team is comfortable with the new tools and processes. Focus on interoperability and backward compatibility to minimize disruptions and provide continuous training and support to help your team adapt to the new observability framework.

Master It What are the recommended steps to adopt OTel in a brownfield deployment?

Approach adopting OpenTelemetry in greenfield deployments. Greenfield deployments, or environments without existing observability tools, offer a unique opportunity to build observability into your infrastructure from the ground up. In these deployments, you can leverage OTel's capabilities to design a robust observability strategy that is integrated into your development lifecycle. Instrument your applications from the start, incorporating telemetry data collection as a fundamental aspect of your system architecture. Start with a single signal and use OTel's components, including semantic conventions, to ensure consistent and comprehensive data collection across all services. Expand instrumentation and data collection over time and be careful not to over-instrument. If telemetry generation is implemented correctly, you will establish a strong observability foundation, enabling you to quickly identify and address issues, optimize performance, and maintain high system reliability as your applications evolve.

Master It What are the recommended steps to adopt OTel in a greenfield deployment?

Notes

1 `https://github.blog/engineering/infrastructure/why-and-how-github-is-adopting-opentelemetry`
2 `https://blog.cloudflare.com/adopting-opentelemetry-for-our-logging-pipeline`
3 `https://opentelemetry.io/blog/2022/why-and-how-ebay-pivoted-to-opentelemetry`
4 `https://github.com/open-telemetry/opentelemetry-Collector/discussions/4102`
5 `https://en.wikipedia.org/wiki/Brownfield_(software_development)`
6 `https://prometheus.io/docs/prometheus/latest/querying/basics/#time-series-selectors`
7 `https://en.wikipedia.org/wiki/Greenfield_project`
8 `https://medium.com/cloud-native-daily/opentelemetry-operator-decreasing-your-otel-adoption-time-through-auto-instrumentation-and-more-da37f73b9490`
9 `https://en.wikipedia.org/wiki/Air_gap_(networking)`
10 `https://www.collectd.org`

Chapter 8

The Power of Context and Correlation

Context and correlation are powerful tools for observability that transform raw telemetry data into actionable insights. By enriching telemetry data with contextual information and correlating related signals, you can uncover more profound insights into system behavior, diagnose issues more efficiently, and gain a holistic view of your application's health. This chapter will pull from topics covered in Chapters 1 through 3 and delve into the importance of context and correlation and how they can be leveraged to enable observability. You will explore techniques for adding context to your telemetry data, such as metadata enrichment and context propagation, as well as methods for correlating data across different services and components. By the end of this chapter, you will appreciate the value of OpenTelemetry and see how the power of context and correlation can significantly elevate your observability capabilities. In addition, you will have greater confidence and precision in observing complex systems.

IN THIS CHAPTER, YOU WILL LEARN TO:

- Differentiate between context and correlation
- Identify the types of context and the value each provides
- Explain the value proposition of correlation

Background

Two terms that have been mentioned multiple times throughout this book are *context* and *correlation*. The reason for this is that in order to achieve observability, you need both. As a result, the OpenTelemetry (OTel) project leverages these two concepts extensively. At this point, you may still be wondering what these terms mean and how they differ. The Merriam-Webster dictionary defines these terms as follows:

- Context is "the interrelated conditions in which something exists or occurs."[1] For the tracing signal, a span contains a trace ID and associated metadata. This additional information on the span would be an example of context.
- Correlation is "a phenomenon that accompanies another phenomenon, is usually parallel to it, and is related in some way to it."[2] A single HTTP request, which would be represented by a metric, being associated with a transaction or trace ID would be an example of correlation.

In observability, context follows the thread of execution and provides a "you are here" pointer. It is created by metadata associated with a particular request or operation as it propagates through a distributed system. This metadata provides information about the data, such as where it originated from, when it occurred, and any relevant attributes. In OTel, context is used to pass information between different components of an application. This information may include metadata like request, trace, and span identifiers (IDs) as well as application, business, and user information. An easily recognizable example of context can be found in the tracing signal. For example, when a request enters a system instrumented with tracing, it will be assigned a unique trace ID. As the request propagates through various services, this contextual information is carried along with it. The net result is the ability to link spans from the original request through the complete transaction into a single trace. As you will see next, sometimes contextual information can also be used to enrich other signals, allowing for correlation.

Contextual information is crucial for understanding and interpreting metrics, logs, and traces within a distributed system. It helps associate telemetry data with specific components, services, or transactions, aiding in monitoring, troubleshooting, and performance analysis. For example, OTel resource metadata can provide infrastructure- and application-related information, as shown in Figure 8.1. As a result, telemetry can specify which host and container an application is running on as well as the application's version number. This information makes it possible to determine if issues are happening in specific contextual situations.

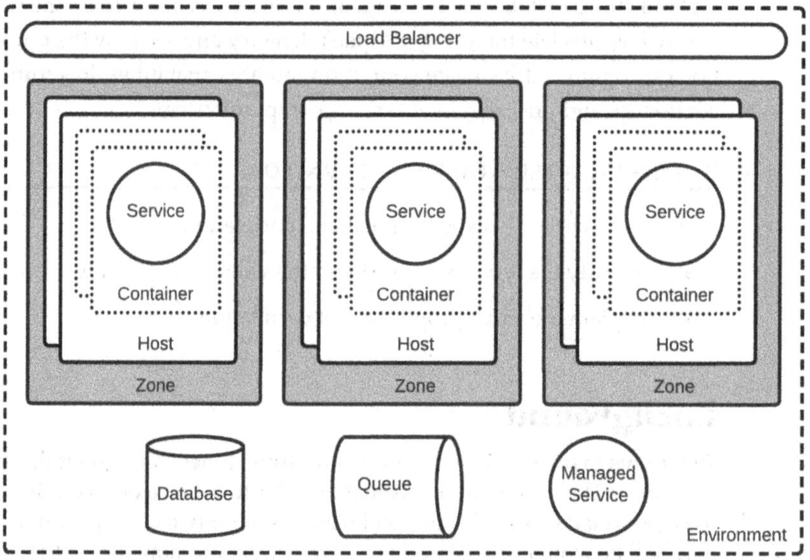

FIGURE 8.1 An example of the context that may be helpful when troubleshooting service availability and performance. In production environments and in cloud native environments, multiple instances of a service are usually deployed to provide availability. These services would typically be deployed to different hosts in different zones. In addition, calls between different services are expected. Attaching this contextual information to telemetry data through metadata is valuable. It can assist in problem isolation, such as determining whether an issue is service, host, or zone specific.

In observability, correlation refers to the ability to connect related events or pieces of data to understand their relationships and dependencies. Correlation is about recognizing patterns, associations, or connections between different pieces of data. In OTel, correlation can involve linking signals that are part of the same operation or transaction. For example, suppose a user makes an HTTP request to a web server, which in turn triggers a series of downstream requests to various microservices. By correlating the spans generated by each request, OTel can provide a comprehensive view of the entire transaction, from the initial user request to the final response.

Another example of correlation in OTel is an exemplar. An *exemplar* is a specific instance of a piece of telemetry data chosen to represent or exemplify a particular characteristic or behavior within a dataset. For example, the web server discussed previously generated metric data about the HTTP request. Typically, only aggregated metric data would be exported, thus containing information about multiple requests. To supplement the aggregate data, a related trace, or even a few traces, could be provided to give a comprehensive view of the system behavior. An exemplar may even provide additional context about the data itself, such as attributes that may have been aggregated away from the metric during measurement. In short, an exemplar serves as a representative example within the dataset. It helps identify and highlight significant events or anomalies within the data, aiding in analysis and decision-making.

As you can see, context and correlation are related concepts, but they are not the same thing. They play complementary roles in providing visibility and insights into the behavior of distributed systems, as shown in Figure 8.2. In summary, while context travels with a request and provides the metadata necessary to track and monitor the flow of requests through a distributed system, correlation involves linking together related telemetry data to provide a coherent view of system behavior. Focusing on context first is common, as it is often easier to add and can quickly assist with problem isolation. Adding correlation is a natural evolution, as it helps bring together multiple sources of information. In terms of OTel:

- Context is attached to signals either implicitly or explicitly using concepts including attributes (`https://opentelemetry.io/docs/concepts/glossary/#attribute`) and resources (`https://opentelemetry.io/docs/concepts/glossary/#resource`).
- Context is passed using the concepts of baggage (`https://opentelemetry.io/docs/concepts/signals/baggage`) and propagation (`https://opentelemetry.io/docs/concepts/context-propagation`).
- Correlation is expressed through concepts including span links (`https://opentelemetry.io/docs/concepts/signals/traces/#span-links`) and metric exemplars (`https://opentelemetry.io/docs/specs/otel/metrics/data-model/#exemplars`).

Context

In a perfect world, no service would be uninstrumented, but sometimes, instrumenting a service is not possible. For example, third-party managed databases, such as cloud provider databases, often cannot be instrumented. Gaining visibility into uninstrumented objects is a significant value add. While OTel semantic conventions allow for easier correlation and consumption of data, they can also be used to provide some visibility into uninstrumented objects. For example, when an OTel instrumented application makes a call to an uninstrumented database, it supports a standardized way to denote that it is calling a database:

- Trace semantic conventions for databases: `https://opentelemetry.io/docs/specs/semconv/database/database-spans`
- Metric semantic conventions for databases: `https://opentelemetry.io/docs/specs/semconv/database/database-metrics`

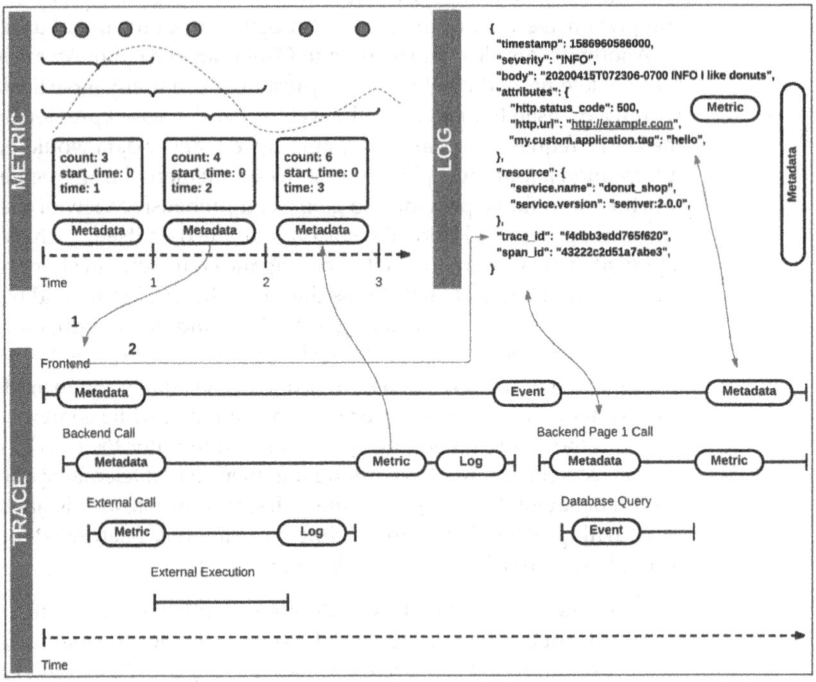

FIGURE 8.2 An example of the types of information different signals provide and the correlation possible. Each signal supports metadata, which can provide contextual information, such as a trace or span ID. This contextual information can be used to correlate data across signals, such as going from a metric to an exemplar trace (1) or a log to its associated trace (2).

Database semantic conventions are in development and include the ability to define context, including:

- `db.name`: A name for the database being accessed. Required and similar to `service.name` used for applications.
- `db.operation`: What operation was executed, such as `SELECT`. Required unless `db.statement` is specified.
- `db.statement`: The entire command executed. Note that this may contain sensitive information. In addition, unless normalized, indexing this value would result in high cardinality.
- `db.system`: The type of database called, such as `CASSANDRA`, `REDIS`, or `SQL`; required.
- `db.user`: The user who executed the command.

An example of the power of context can be demonstrated through what is often referred to as an *inferred service*. For example, say an instrumented application is calling an uninstrumented database. Usually, this would result in telemetry data only for the instrumented application.

One issue with this is that if the uninstrumented service is experiencing problems, then it will likely manifest as the instrumented service experiencing problems. OTel can be used to properly denote when an instrumented service is calling an uninstrumented service. For example, the tracing signal can be configured to set the `span.kind` to `client` when calling an uninstrumented database. In addition, database semantic conventions, like those described previously, can be set by the instrumented application to enrich the span. An observability platform can then use this data to represent an inferred service. For example, maybe the observability platform requires `db.name` to be set because OTel also requires it to be set, or perhaps it uses some combination of `db.name` and `db.system`, given that OTel requires both pieces of metadata. The net result is that a service map could be constructed, as shown in Figure 8.3, and RED (requests, errors, and duration) metrics for instrumented calls would become known.

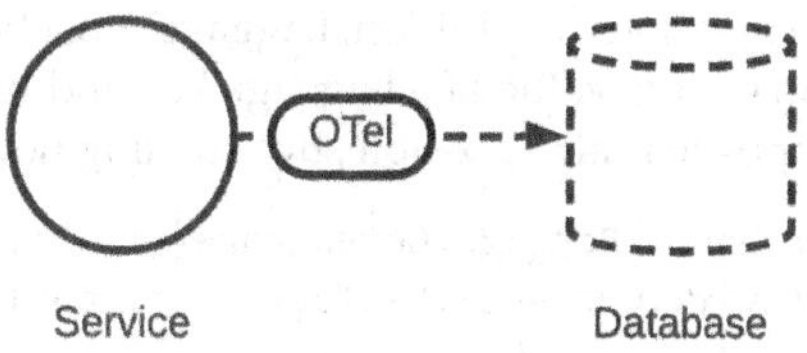

FIGURE 8.3 An example of an OTel instrumented service calling an uninstrumented service, such as a cloud provider database.

INFERRED SERVICES AND PARTIAL OBSERVABILITY

While features such as semantic conventions and inferred services provide value to uninstrumented services, it is important to remember that the observability provided is only partial. For example, RED metrics you receive from inferred services would only contain information that could be deduced from instrumented applications. It is possible that other uninstrumented applications could be calling the third-party database. In addition, while database errors returned to instrumented applications could be reported, database errors that are not returned may not be available. When possible, instrumentation should be added to provide internal observability, as discussed in Chapter 1, "What is Observability?" This advice is valid for all objects, not just databases.

OTel Context

OTel context is essentially key-value pairs, or metadata, used to propagate information across the lifecycle of a request. When a request is initiated, a context is created and associated with that request. As the request flows through different parts of the system, the `Context` is passed along, either explicitly in the code or implicitly, through frameworks that support context propagation. This context ensures that all parts of a system can contribute to and access the same set of telemetry information, facilitating end-to-end visibility and observability. Given the power of context, OTel has created a specification for it (`https://opentelemetry.io/docs/specs/otel/context`). One important thing to note about OTel `Context` is that it is *immutable*, meaning it cannot be changed. This means that modifications to a context require creating and passing a new context. Other concepts in OTel are also immutable, including baggage, resources, and spans. In addition, propagation in OTel is typically handled by instrumentation libraries and transparent to the user. With that said, it is possible to manually propagate context using the OTel `Propagators` API (`https://opentelemetry.io/docs/specs/otel/context/api-propagators`).

Baggage is a specific type of OTel context that is designed to be shared within and propagated across service boundaries. While the OTel baggage signal was discussed in Chapter 1 and Chapter 4, "Understanding the OpenTelemetry Specification," it has not been explored in depth. This concept originated from the tracing signal and applies to all signals in OTel. Baggage contains key-value pairs that carry additional information about the request. Unlike other forms of metadata, which may only be relevant within a specific service, baggage is intended to be globally available and consistent throughout an entire request or lifecycle. While baggage is used to attach metadata to signals dynamically, it is not the same as OTel's concept of attributes. Baggage is unique in that it is metadata stored in a context, and it can be passed between services via propagation. In addition, baggage must be explicitly added to signals. For example, in .NET, you can get the value of a baggage key and use it to set an attribute on a signal, as shown next. The opposite is also possible, but creating new baggage is required since baggage is immutable.

```
var bar = Baggage.GetBaggage("foo");
Activity.Current?.SetTag("foo", bar);
```

W_3C Baggage Specification

The concept of baggage is not unique to OTel. In fact, W_3C has a baggage specification (`https://www.w3.org/TR/baggage`). It is worth noting that the OTel specification has some requirements that are different from W_3C (`https://opentelemetry.io/docs/specs/otel/baggage/api/#overview`). One significant difference is that in OTel all keys must have a single value.

Similar to how trace context is passed, any metadata following the requirements of the OTel specification can be passed either within or across applications and signals via baggage. Like the tracing signal, an HTTP header is used when passing baggage between services. The baggage signal uses the `Baggage` header with a comma-separated list of key-value pairs. Here is an example of what the header may look like using metasyntactic,[3] or generic, variables:[4]

```
Baggage: foo=bar,hoge=fuga,aap=noot
```

Examples of metadata that you may want to add to baggage include account, customer, product, and user IDs. The benefit of baggage is that metadata can be generated in one part of a system but made available to another completely unrelated part of the system or even a completely different application. Some examples of when baggage is helpful include:

- When you need the ability to add a customer ID to all spans in a trace, but the metadata is only available in the initial request
- When one signal has metadata that another signal needs

You might still be wondering why you would want to add metadata to signals like the previous examples. The answer is context. To demonstrate the power of baggage, assume you have the situation depicted in Figure 8.4. In that situation, the service owner for the currency service may not be able to troubleshoot the issue if they do not have the proper context. Say that the errors seen are the result of a single customer ID and that customer ID only exists in the checkout service. The service owner would not have this context without the baggage that was explicitly added to the currency service.

> **IMPORTANT BAGGAGE CONSIDERATIONS**
>
> While baggage is powerful, care must be taken not to overwhelm applications with the burden of processing and passing this context. This means only the minimal required baggage to achieve observability should be passed. In addition, it is important to note that baggage is not secure. Given it is sent as a header, it can easily be read or modified. In addition, instrumentation has no way to validate the source of baggage.

Trace Context

Tracing is powerful because it allows you to take telemetry data from different services and stitch them together. Each span in a trace can also provide rich information, including:

- Golden signals or RED metrics (covered in Chapter 1): At a minimum, requests, error, and duration information can be extracted from traces.
- Metrics: Beyond golden signals or RED metrics, additional metrics may also be available that are library specific or developer added.
- Logs: Typically in the form of span events, but log correlation can also bring traces and logs together.
- Metadata: While additional signal information may be valuable, especially if it can be extracted from a trace, metadata is one of the most important pieces of context. Metadata may include library, business, application, or environment information. Application and environment information is typically provided by resource metadata, while library and business are usually defined by attribute metadata.

Chapter 1 provided a waterfall view representation of a trace. While individual traces are helpful, especially after problem isolation occurs, aggregate data is also critical in identifying patterns and trends. In addition, trace data can be used to visualize environments and follow context throughout a transaction. For example, say you had a checkout transaction similar to the Astronomy demo application covered in Chapter 3, "Getting Started with the Astronomy Shop." The flow for such a transaction could be described as follows:

1. An authenticated user is on the UI (frontend) and selects the Checkout option.
2. The checkout service calls the cart, currency, payment, and shipping services to execute the checkout operation.
3. Each downstream service calls its respective database to retrieve or persist data.

The service architecture or service map for this flow could be represented visually, as shown in Figure 8.4. This service map can be constructed using purely trace data.

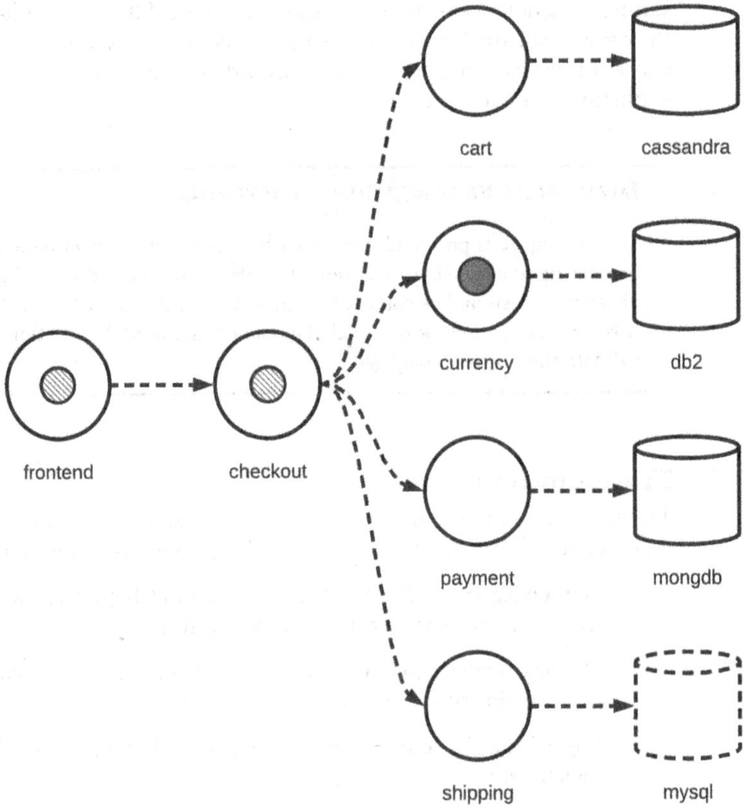

FIGURE 8.4
An example of what is possible when analyzing trace data provided by the OTel standard. As you can see, the checkout service calls various downstream services. The darker circle within the service represents errors. The solid dark circle indicates an error's root cause or origin. In contrast, the shaded less dark circles indicate an error received or propagated from a different service—in this case, the currency service.

When you think about context in the scope of observability, you may think it only applies to the trace signal. This is because traces are one of the few signals that have context by default. In addition, initially, application performance monitoring, or APM, was often referred to as observability, and it stressed the importance of context and correlation because it is often missing in metrics and logs. Given that the trace signal has context and correlation natively, you may wonder why observability is not just tracing. While it could be, there are several challenges to overcome, as covered in Chapter 1, including:

- Metrics and logs have been around for a long time, are easier to add, and are more commonly used to monitor environments.
- Tracing is more challenging to add than metrics and logs. Adding the appropriate metrics, logs, and metadata is nontrivial, even if context can be passed.
- Most tracing platforms cannot fully leverage metrics and logs attached to spans. Problems here include dimensionality and cardinality of the data.
- Traces are often heavily sampled, meaning metrics and logs must be appropriately handled at sample time to provide proper observability.
- Additional context and correlation, including business, user, and application logic is needed and may only be available from other signals.

CONTEXT ACROSS SIGNALS

Given that each signal provides its own value, what is usually better than trying to consolidate or overload one is to enrich all—for example, ensuring consistent logic and resource information across signals. While, in general, telemetry data supports enrichment via metadata, consistency across signal types has been an issue. OTel is the only open source and vendor-agnostic solution that provides a consistent way to do it through concepts, including semantic conventions and resources. In addition, OTel has been optimized for resources. For example, data can be batched based on resource information. Beyond this, OTel provides semantic conventions that normalize the names of objects. As a result, business, user, and environment metadata is consistently tagged across signals.

Resource Context

An environment is made up of various components commonly referred to as a *stack* and may include:

- Client-side devices
- Server-side runtimes
- Orchestration engines
- Operating systems
- Virtualization technology
- Bare metal hardware

These components can be grouped into various categories, including:

- End users: This category can consist of browsers, mobile applications, or API calls.
- Applications or services: First-party applications are those you have written, while third-party applications are those you manage or depend on. Examples of third-party applications include open source software such as Cassandra or Kafka, as well as cloud provider services such as object storage and databases.
- Orchestration or platform: This category can include container orchestration, such as Kubernetes (K8s), or serverless.
- Infrastructure: This category can include compute, network, and storage on bare metal or through virtualization.

Each category represents different layers of the stack that contain rich information that may be useful to provide observability. The signals collected from each of these layers vary:

- End users: Metrics, logs, sessions (instead of traces), and profiling
- Applications: Metrics, logs, traces, profiling, and synthetic tests
- Orchestration and infrastructure: Metrics and logs

Enriching signals with stack information provides a lot of insight and capabilities. A basic example would be the ability to distinguish between an application issue and an infrastructure issue. For example, say your application was experiencing performance problems. While your telemetry may alert you of the performance degradation, the infrastructure metadata may indicate that the issue is specific to a particular environment, host, or pod, as shown in Figure 8.5.

k8s.io/cluster/name	us-west-1-cluster
k8s.io/pod/name	currency-49hd95hsj382hp
region	us-west-1

FIGURE 8.5 An example of metadata analysis of telemetry data for a particular service. Metadata names are on the left, while metadata values are on the right. In addition, the metadata values are shaded with the darker shade representing root cause errors and the lighter shade representing inherited errors. This example shows that all root cause errors are coming from the same K8s pod. With this information, you could decide how to proceed. For example, you may choose to quarantine the pod in question to mediate the issue and buy time to determine the root cause.

OTel believes that metadata about the entity producing the telemetry is critical to observability. As such, it introduced the concept of a *resource* and optimized the project around it, as described in Chapter 2, "Introducing OpenTelemetry!," It is highly recommended that OTel signals be enriched with resource information. Resource processors are available for instrumentation as well as the Collector and are covered in Chapter 5, "Managing the OpenTelemetry Collector," and Chapter 6, "Leveraging OpenTelemetry Instrumentation."

Logic Context

Focusing on context, including resources and tracing, is common when starting with telemetry data. In many cases, it will be apparent very quickly that additional context is necessary to achieve observability. Examples of additional metadata include:

- Business logic, such as an organization ID and environment. For example, setting `deployment.environment`, which is the OTel semantic convention for environment business logic (`https://opentelemetry.io/docs/specs/semconv/resource/deployment-environment`), would allow you to distinguish between a development versus production environment. This distinction would allow you to avoid conflating similar telemetry from unrelated deployments, reducing the mean time to recovery (MTTR).
- User logic, such as a customer ID and geolocation. For example, setting a `user.id` would allow you to understand which users are impacted during availability or performance issues. Note that OTel does not have a semantic convention for a user ID, so you need to ensure that whatever standard you come up with is applied consistently throughout your environment.
- Application logic, such as version number and feature flag status. For example, setting `service.version`, which is the OTel semantic convention for version application logic (`https://opentelemetry.io/docs/specs/semconv/resource/#service`), would allow you to determine if issues experienced were version specific.

> **Custom Semantic Conventions**
>
> You may discover that you need to define semantic conventions beyond what OTel provides. An example of such a scenario may include adding a user ID to telemetry data. It is important in such scenarios to define a standard and ensure that it is consistently applied throughout your environment. Using a namespace, such as your company domain, is a good way to ensure that custom semantic conventions are unique. After you have defined custom semantic conventions, you may need to change them. Like any semantic convention change, you need to determine the impact on your ability to observe your systems. For example, dashboards and alerts may need to be updated to support semantic convention changes, as discussed in Chapter 7, "Adopting OpenTelemetry."

Correlation

In addition to context, it is critical to be able to correlate telemetry data to achieve observability. For example, suppose you are experiencing availability or performance issues with a service. In that case, you may need to correlate the service telemetry data with code deployment events to determine if a code change introduced an application issue. While both the application and code deployment systems can generate telemetry data, correlating these two disparate telemetry sources allows you to get to the root cause and remediation more easily. Of course, this is one of many examples of the power of correlation. Correlation can be achieved through various means, which will be explored next.

Time Correlation

One fundamental way to correlate information is by viewing different data sources together and visually correlating on the dimension of time. For example, a dashboard like the one shown in Figure 8.6 could be created, containing charts from trace, metric, and log data. Based on a given time, it would be possible to see what happened across data sources before or around that time. In general, this type of correlation is not recommended, as it is a form of manual correlation, often requires subject matter expertise, and takes more time to get to the root cause and remediation. In addition, the data shown from time-based correlation is cause, not effect.

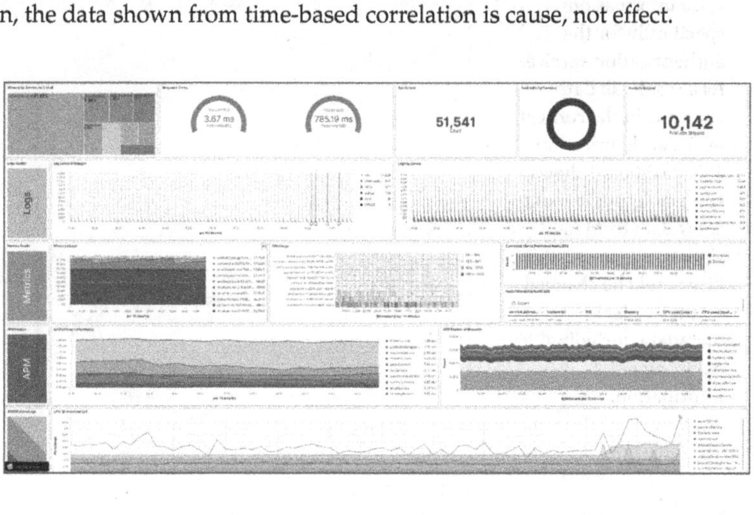

Figure 8.6
An example of a Kibana dashboard containing multiple signals and requiring time-based correlation.
Source: elastic content share / `https://elastic-content-share.eu/downloads/observability-kibana-dashboard`, last accessed 17 July 2024.

Another problem with time correlation is that it is prone to *false positives*.[5] A false positive is when an incorrect result is reached based on specific data. For example, a dashboard may indicate a code deployment happened shortly before a service's performance degraded. As such, it may be concluded that the code push caused the issue. The dashboard may not show that there was a sudden burst of customer traffic shortly before, which is the actual cause of the problem. Other limitations of time-based correlation include:

- Missing data: It is difficult to determine whether all data is being collected and visualized.
- Noise: Variable amounts of error and latency are possible even in healthy environments. Quickly distinguishing between noise and signal can decrease MTTR.
- Assumptions: Multiple investigations are often needed to test hypotheses and learn more about the system's behavior.

Context Correlation

A significant improvement to time correlation is context correlation. Context correlation is when metadata is used to perform problem isolation. Going back to Figure 8.6, you may notice that there was no ability to modify the queries on the dashboard based on metadata. As will soon become apparent, understanding what the data looks like based on metadata can be extremely useful. One manual way to do this is through filtering. For example, you may receive an alert about a specific service and, as such, decide to filter based on that service, as shown in Figure 8.7. Filtering is powerful for all signals and is typically done via metadata. Resource metadata, which includes service and environment information, and attribute metadata, which includes application and possibly business information, can be used for filtering. Capabilities, including autocomplete of metadata keys and values, depend on observability platform capabilities, including indexing of metadata. Indexing can make querying faster and easier but may result in additional costs, especially for high cardinality data.

FIGURE 8.7 An example of a service dashboard from OpenSearch displaying trace information specifically for the authentication service. As a result, all data shown is in the context of the authentication. This dashboard shows trace data, but it could show data from multiple signals. Of course, this filter could be changed to any available metadata, including environmental information.

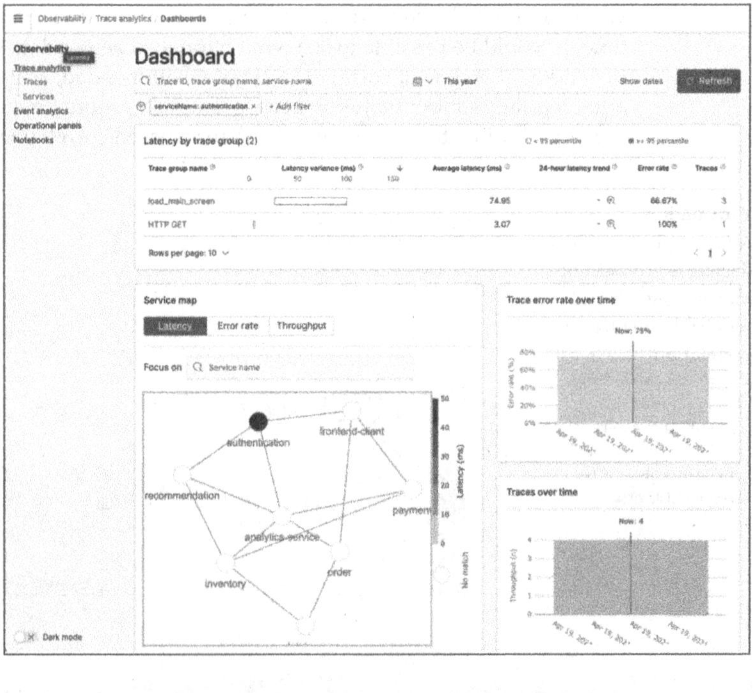

Real World Scenario

CONTEXT CORRELATION AT JUPITERIAN

Jupiterian had not standardized on semantic conventions such as setting the environment or customer ID. As a result, querying in Prometheus and Watchwhale was more challenging as the search strings varied across services and environments. Riley had firsthand experience with this problem and was interested in solving it. While the engineering team was busy adopting Watchwhale, Riley used some of her free time to read up on the topics of context and correlation in OTel. She was initially excited about the potential for trace and log correlation but knew it would be a while before Jupiterian had adopted enough OTel instrumentation to realize the potential. Riley quickly decided it was best to adopt OTel semantic conventions where possible. Riley wrote a naming standards proposal for Jupiterian-specific metadata, including business and user logic, and brought it to an architectural review meeting. After incorporating feedback and receiving approval, she quickly configured the Collector to rename any metadata that did not adhere to the standard. With the conventions defined, documented, and configured, Riley indexed them in Watchwhale so the team could leverage them. She knew she could deploy the Collector in agent mode to modify the data going into Prometheus if needed.

Even better than manual filtering would be the ability to do an analysis of the metadata for a particular service. For example, say a specific service instrumented with tracing was experiencing errors. If you could analyze the metadata from spans generated from that service, you might be able to determine what was causing it, as shown in Figure 8.8.

Automatic analysis of metadata could be used to reduce MTTR even further. Instead of manually needing to filter or perform visual analysis of metadata, the analysis could be done via the observability platform. The results could be presented to the user either visually or through a notification. The biggest challenge with this approach is trust. The user would need proof that the analysis provided was accurate. For the analysis to be correct, all necessary telemetry data would need to be generated, collected, and correlated. Artificial intelligence (AI) and AI for information technology (IT) operations (AIOps) enable this type of analysis. AI will be discussed further in Chapter 12, "The Future of Observability."

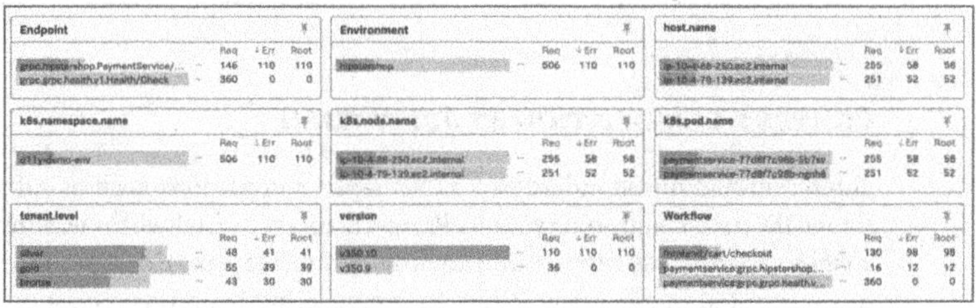

FIGURE 8.8 An example of metadata analysis of traces from a specific service. Each table represents a metadata key found in the span data for the given service. The rows within the tables represent values for these keys. The darker shaded bars on the values indicate root cause errors, while the lighter shaded bars represent inherited errors. Visually, it is clear that multiple metadata keys are experiencing some errors, but version v350.10 of the version key experiences 100 percent of the errors. As a result, it appears that something is wrong with that version of the application, and it may need to be rolled back.

Trace Correlation

Similar to trace context, when you think about correlation in the scope of observability, you may initially think about the trace signal. Correlation in a trace is provided by trace context propagation, a concept covered in Chapter 1. Trace context propagation allows for a transaction to be followed from the beginning to the end, assuming the context is passed every step of the way. Other examples of correlation found in relation to the trace signal also exist. For instance, log correlation, which is defined in the OTel logs bridge API (`https://opentelemetry.io/docs/specs/otel/logs/bridge-api`), allows trace information, including trace ID, span ID, and trace flags (`https://opentelemetry.io/docs/specs/otel/logs/data-model/#trace-context-fields`) to be implicitly or explicitly (`https://opentelemetry.io/docs/specs/otel/logs/supplementary-guidelines/#context`), depending on the language, added to log records. Log correlation provides context to logs and enables capabilities, including querying associated logs for a given trace, as shown in Figure 8.9.

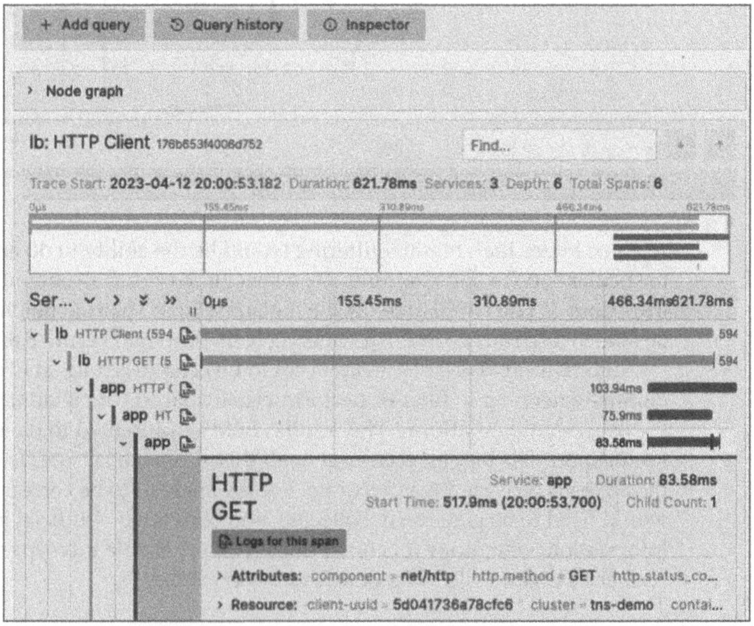

FIGURE 8.9 An example in Grafana Tempo of being able to query for logs associated with a given trace. This is possible by enabling log correlation, which adds trace information to log records.

Another example is span events, which are defined in the OTel trace API (`https://opentelemetry.io/docs/specs/otel/trace/api/#add-events`) and allow adding zero or more time-stamped and named events with optional metadata to spans. Span events provide information beyond what a traditional trace contains and allow correlating trace data with other telemetry data. For example, a span event may indicate that an uninstrumented task or operation was completed, as shown in Figure 8.10. OTel also defines a record exception (`https://opentelemetry.io/docs/specs/otel/trace/api/#record-exception`), which is a specific type of event to facilitate the recording of exceptions.

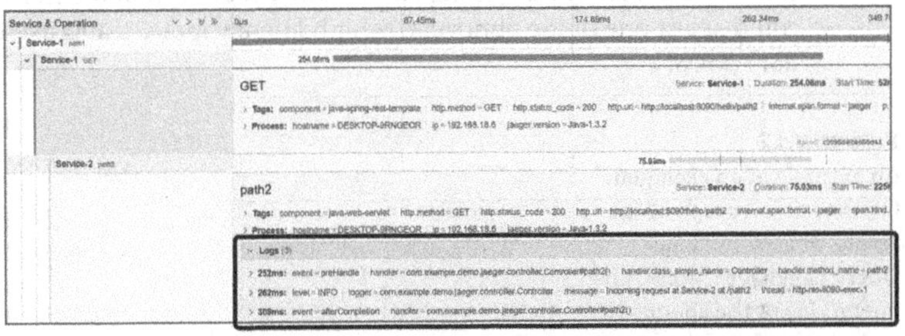

FIGURE 8.10
An example of OTel span events shown in Jaeger. Jaeger records OTel span events as logs. In this example, events were recorded before and after the controller handler was executed. The incoming request was also captured.

Span links, which are also defined in the OTel trace API (`https://opentelemetry.io/docs/specs/otel/trace/api/#link`), are another example and allow a span to link to zero or more other spans that are causally related (`https://opentelemetry.io/docs/specs/otel/overview/#links-between-spans`). An example of when span links may be helpful is a batch processing job.[6] In this scenario, a trace or request may result in a batch job being executed asynchronously. In this example, the batch job cannot be represented in a parent-child relationship with the initial request, but a link could be created between the requests to provide correlation.

These additional correlation methods should be added in the order explained. Log correlation can be enabled in OTel instrumentation. Span events can be automatically added via OTel instrumentation or with manual instrumentation. Span links are typically created with manual instrumentation. Observability platform support for these methods will also vary. For example, log correlation may be powered by linking or launching in context, as shown in Figure 8.11. Span event processing is platform specific, and span links would be a feature of the APM platform being leveraged.

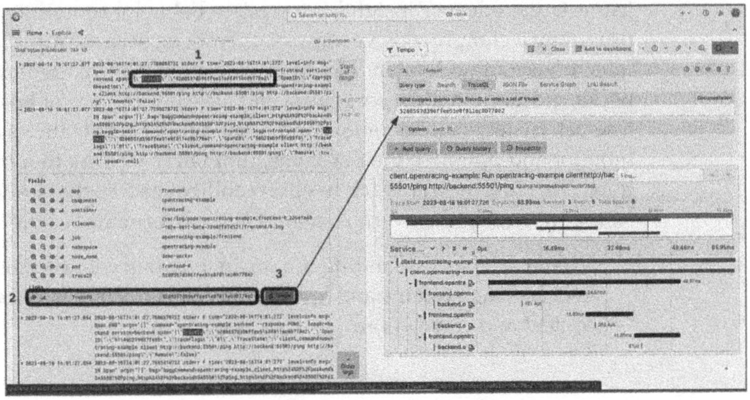

FIGURE 8.11
An example of linking or launch in context between logs and traces. This example has Grafana Loki on the left side with a log containing a trace ID (1) that has been indexed as a field (2). Upon selecting the Tempo link (3) in Loki for this trace ID, the trace could be pulled up in Tempo, as shown on the right side.

Metric Correlation

Similar to how traces and logs can be correlated, it is possible to correlate metrics with traces. A common way to provide metric correlation is through an exemplar. An exemplar is a trace representation or example of a measurement taken at a specific time. A simple example demonstrating the power of exemplars would be looking at a latency graph such as the one in Figure 8.12. Typically, latency would fall into a normal distribution[7] where most data is within a small range and some data could be above or below this range. Say, for example, a few customers reported delays on your website. If you capture latency information, then you may notice that some of the latency results are significantly higher than the norm. If you had exemplars, you could select one of the abnormally high latency metrics and ask to see a trace exemplar for that data point.

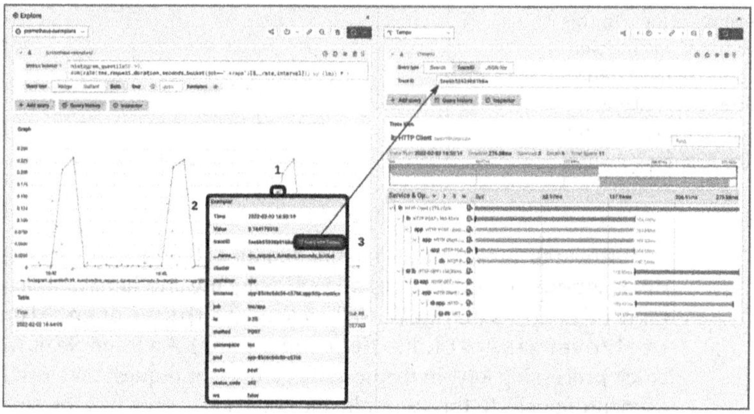

FIGURE 8.12 An example of an exemplar. On the left is a graph of the results of a Prometheus Query Language (PromQL) query. One of the abnormally high value points on the graph has been selected (1), and the value and metadata for one exemplar in that set is shown (2). The trace ID is one piece of metadata provided. If the Query with Tempo link is selected (3), then the trace can be pulled up in Tempo, as seen on the right.

The Bottom Line

Differentiate between context and correlation. Context and correlation play a pivotal role in enhancing the effectiveness of observability in complex, distributed systems. They enable teams to gain deeper insights into system behavior by connecting various data points and providing a comprehensive view of operations across multiple services and components. This interconnected understanding allows for more precise identification of performance bottlenecks, quicker diagnosis of issues, and a clearer picture of how different parts of the system interact. By leveraging context and correlation, organizations can improve their ability to monitor and optimize their systems, ultimately leading to more reliable and efficient operations. This holistic approach to observability ensures that issues are detected and resolved faster, enhancing the overall stability and performance of the system.

Master It Understanding the distinction between context and correlation is fundamental to observing systems and leveraging OTel effectively. What is the difference between context and correlation?

Identify the types of context and the value each provides. Several types of context can be added to telemetry data, each providing unique value. Temporal context includes timestamps and durations, allowing you to track when events occur and how long processes take. Environmental context encompasses details like the deployment environment, such as development or production, and infrastructure information, such as host or container, which helps you understand the operational conditions. User context includes identifiers and session data, enabling analysis of user behavior and experiences. Service context involves metadata such as service names, versions, and dependencies, which aids in mapping out service interactions and performance. Each type of context enhances the clarity and usefulness of telemetry data, making it easier to diagnose issues, understand user impacts, and optimize system performance.

> **Master It** In OTel, context is available through concepts including attributes, resources, and baggage. What is the difference between these concepts?

Explain the value proposition of correlation. The value proposition of correlation lies in its ability to provide a holistic view of system behavior and performance. By linking related telemetry data across different services and components, correlation helps to identify patterns and dependencies that are not immediately apparent when looking at isolated data points. This interconnected view is essential for diagnosing complex issues that span multiple services or layers of the stack. Correlation enables more effective root cause analysis by tracing the flow of requests through the system and highlighting where bottlenecks or failures occur. It also enhances the accuracy of anomaly detection by considering the broader context in which events happen.

> **Master It** Correlation transforms disparate telemetry data into a coherent narrative, empowering teams to make informed decisions and maintain robust, high-performing systems. What are some examples of correlation?

Notes

1 `https://www.merriam-webster.com/dictionary/context`
2 `https://www.merriam-webster.com/dictionary/correlate`
3 `https://en.wikipedia.org/wiki/Metasyntactic_variable`
4 The example provided uses common variables for English (foo=bar), Japanese (hoge=fuga), and Dutch (aap=noot)
5 `https://en.wikipedia.org/wiki/False_positives_and_false_negatives`
6 `https://en.wikipedia.org/wiki/Batch_processing`
7 `https://en.wikipedia.org/wiki/Normal_distribution`

Chapter 9

Choosing an Observability Platform

Data generated and transmitted by OpenTelemetry is only as powerful as the observability platforms to which the data is sent. This means selecting the right observability platform is a critical decision that can significantly impact your organization's ability to observe, troubleshoot, and optimize its systems. In this chapter, you will explore the key considerations and criteria for choosing an observability platform that aligns with your specific needs and goals. You will delve into the features and capabilities that differentiate leading platforms, including data collection, storage, and analysis capabilities. In addition, you will read about strategies on how to evaluate platforms based on factors such as scalability, ease of integration, cost, and support for open standards like OpenTelemetry. By the end of this chapter, you will be equipped with the knowledge and frameworks needed to make an informed decision, ensuring that your chosen platform enhances your ability to achieve comprehensive and effective observability across your systems.

IN THIS CHAPTER, YOU WILL LEARN TO:

- Distinguish between observability platform capabilities
- Decide which observability platform is right for you
- Get a quick return on your observability platform investment

Primary Considerations

When deciding on an observability platform, assessing your current monitoring and observability capabilities is important. In addition, clear business requirements and constraints should be gathered from relevant stakeholders throughout the organization. These requirements and constraints should be used to define key use cases and scenarios for observability. In general, you will find that the requirements will fall into the following two primary categories:

- Functional requirements,[1] or what you need the system to support, including signal, anomaly detection, data retention, real-time analysis, historical data analysis, machine learning (ML) and artificial intelligence (AI) capabilities
- Non-functional requirements,[2] or how you need a system to perform, including cost, scalability, performance, reliability, security, compliance, usability, documentation, and support

In addition, you may find that where or how the observability platform can be run may be just as important as the capabilities the platform provides. Examples of this include requirements for:

- **Data residency:** Where telemetry data is stored or processed, or multi-cloud support,[3] which may restrict the platform choices available to you.
- **Heterogeneous versus unified observability:** Whether multiple solutions or a single observability platform is used to achieve observability. Note that there is a distinction here between the platform and the back end. Either solution may have unique persistent stores or back ends, though a unified platform could have a single back end. What matters more is the experience to the user. For example, Prometheus and OpenSearch are unique back ends. If queried from Grafana and OpenSearch Dashboards, respectively, then heterogeneous observability is enabled. If queried only from Grafana, then unified observability could be achieved. A hybrid approach would be a Grafana dashboard linking to an OpenSearch dashboard.
- **Security and compliance, including for regulated industries and government agencies:** Various compliance certifications may be required, including System and Organization Controls 2 (SOC 2), Health Insurance Portability and Accountability Act (HIPAA), Payment Card Industry (PCI), and Federal Risk and Authorization Management Program (FedRAMP). Dedicated environments may be necessary to support these requirements. Some companies, especially in industries such as financial services, are even starting to require similar guidelines as those mandated by government agencies. Security and compliance may impact data residency, multi-cloud support, and heterogeneous versus unified observability.

When deciding on an observability platform, you must determine what is most important for your use cases. For example, say a multi-cloud observability platform was something you weighted heavily because your SaaS solution was already hosted on multiple clouds. In this case, you may decide to remove cloud provider observability platforms from consideration, given that they are optimized for a single cloud. Alternatively, if your solution was only running in one cloud and multi-cloud support was a long-term roadmap item, then you may consider cloud provider observability platforms. One way to do this is to create a prioritized checklist of requirements, like Table 9.1.

TABLE 9.1: A simplified example of a prioritized checklist of requirements. In the example, P0 items, which is short for priority 0 items, are the most important, while P2 is the least. Priorities may also be mapped to words. For example, a P0 may be called a "high" priority or "must have," while a P1 could be called a "medium" priority or a "nice to have." A full checklist to assess an observability platform may contain dozens of requirements.

REQUIREMENTS	EXAMPLES	PRIORITY
Data collection for specific environments	K8s, OpenShift, Cloud Foundry	P0
Platform integration to specific applications	ServiceNow, Slack, PagerDuty	P0
Platform compliance	SOC 2 Type II, PCI, FedRAMP	P0

REQUIREMENTS	EXAMPLES	PRIORITY
Important platform capabilities	SLIs/SLOs, Session replay (RUM)	P1
Nice to have platform capabilities	Auto-discovery, built-in content	P2

OTel Is Observability Platform Agnostic

OTel is an open source observability framework that does not provide an observability platform. While it embraces open standards and supports a wide range of open source and commercial observability platforms, it will always be vendor agnostic. While OTel is hosted in the Cloud Native Computing Foundation (CNCF) with observability platforms, including Prometheus and Jaeger, these platforms are not the recommended or standard way to consume OTel data—they are one of the many options available.

Many examples that demonstrate the power of OTel, including the Astronomy Shop discussed in Chapter 3, "Getting Started with the Astronomy Shop," leverage open source projects, such as Prometheus and Jaeger. As a result, you may believe OTel is optimized for these platforms. Although OTel supports these platforms, they are not OTel preferred platforms—no platform is. This distinction is important because commercial vendors support running managed versions of open source observability platforms. You should not conflate OTel demonstrating capabilities with open source observability platforms as OTel preferring certain observability platforms over others. If an open source project or vendor claims they are the preferred observability platform for OTel, that is marketing and not reality. If you are looking for observability platforms that are compatible with OTel, have a look at the OTel vendors' list (`https://opentelemetry.io/ecosystem/vendors`) or the CNCF observability landscape guide (`https://landscape.cncf.io/guide#observability-and-analysis-observability`).

Also note that if every observability platform fully supported the OTel standard, then, at the very least, you would have data portability, allowing you to choose the platform that best meets your needs. Of course, reality is always more complex. For example, legacy technology solutions may or may not be supported by OTel. In addition, aspects beyond trace, metrics, and logs are important and in development in OTel today. The general guidance is that you should be cautious when introducing or expanding the use of proprietary instrumentation and data collection components. In addition, you should know that OTel can only help prevent vendor lock-in based on telemetry data, and the observability platform may have capabilities that still result in vendor lock-in. Put another way, while OTel provides a vendor-agnostic solution, it is possible that the observability platform selected results in vendor lock-in due to using non-OTel–compliant instrumentation or data collection or due to proprietary dashboard, alert, and query capabilities.

Platform Capabilities

When deciding on an observability platform, requirements are often compared against platform capabilities. While there is a long tail[4] of capabilities you may care about, some of the most common ones may include the following:

- **OTel support:** As discussed in the "OTel Compatibility and Vendor Lock-in" section later in this chapter, while many open source and commercial solutions claim OTel support, the amount of support varies. You need to determine which aspects are important to you. Examples may include supporting pure OTLP ingestion or OTel's opinionated definition of histogram metrics.

- **Integrations:** What mechanisms are provided to collect and process data? While projects such as OTel make it easier to support a wide range of integrations, there may be specific requirements that you will need to ensure your chosen platform supports.
- **Ease of setup, migration, and use:** Time-to-Value (TTV) is critical when rolling out or migrating to an observability platform. It is not uncommon for commercial products to have an advantage here, especially for large-scale deployments. Features may include built-in content, such as dashboards and alerts, service discovery, and inventory service capabilities.
- **Troubleshooting ease:** Once data is stored in an observability platform, you need to determine how easy it is to troubleshoot issues. In observability, having the ability to ask questions is important—for example, analyzing metadata and determining whether a problem is infrastructure or application related.
- **Scalability and performance:** The platform's performance can impact the ability to provide observability. As more data is ingested and more content is created, how does the platform scale and does it continue to perform well? What happens to the cost as the scale is increased or metadata is indexed? Chapter 11, "Observability at Scale," will deep dive into this topic.
- **Support and community:** When things go wrong, how can you get assistance and how quickly will issues be resolved? These issues may be bugs or security concerns. In addition, how quickly are feature requests handled?
- **Security and compliance:** Security and compliance requirements may include data residency, privacy, and role-based access control (RBAC) capabilities as well as SOC 2 Type II, HIPAA, PCI, and/or FedRAMP certification.
- **Cost and licensing model:** Understanding what visibility you have into costs as well as having cost control mechanisms will be important as your usage increases over time. More on this topic later in the chapter.
- **Platform differentiating features:** While base features such as dashboarding and alerting will exist across platforms, understanding what value propositions the platform provides beyond the marketing hype is also critical.

In addition, many capabilities rely on or impact other capabilities. Examples include:

- Troubleshooting use cases may require real-time capabilities (feature) in the observability platform that can chart and alert on telemetry data in seconds. Real-time processing is more expensive (cost) than less real-time systems. In addition, real-time systems must be able to support your scale with reasonable performance (feature).
- Generating, processing, and storing telemetry comes at a price. *If* the data provides value, *then* the cost may be justified. If the data collected is never queried, it is likely not worth the cost. This means even if the platform has the required integrations (feature) and is easy to configure (feature), the value provided may not justify the price (cost).

Marketing Versus Reality

Upon reviewing all the observability platforms on the market, you may notice that many of them claim to support the same capabilities. It is important to test the capabilities that you care about the most to validate that you can achieve the desired level of observability. Examples of the types of things to look out for include:

- Startup companies claiming to support massive scale. While startup companies often have an agility advantage and take advantage of industrial shifts, they usually are less tested and mature than larger companies. In general, startups can usually provide great point solutions but generally lack a unified observability platform. Another consideration is the startup's future, including whether you believe it will be able to secure additional funding or if it might be acquired.
- Enterprise companies claiming to support new generation trends or solutions. While enterprise companies have often solved the scale and maturity aspects, they usually suffer from the need to sustain their cash cows[5] or steady income streams. In addition, larger companies move much slower, leading to innovator's dilemma,[6] or the inability to keep up with the competition. One way enterprise companies attempt to overcome this is to add marketing that claims to support new generation trends. While marketing can work for a time, eventually the gap becomes too noticeable. While some enterprise companies attempt to serve both customer bases, generally this is nontrivial without acquiring a new technology stack.
- Any companies offering significant cost savings for similar capabilities. In general, the cost of providing observable products is roughly the same. Those that are significantly more expensive than the competition usually offer some differentiating capabilities. You need to decide whether those differentiating capabilities justify the cost. Those that are significantly less expensive than the competition usually provide those cost savings by impacting the amount of observability possible. Sampling strategies are a great example of where you can see price differences compared to the ability to observe. If a price comes in significantly less than competitors, you should take the time to understand where those savings are coming from.

When researching observability platforms or talking to vendor sales teams, it may sound like platforms all offer the same capabilities. While there may be similarities between platforms, they are often architected for specific use cases and may or may not offer differentiating features. For example, application performance monitoring (APM) platforms have evolved from supporting primarily monolithic, on-premises software environments to supporting primarily cloud-based, distributed microservices architectures (as described in Chapter 2, "Introducing OpenTelemetry!"). APM platforms created during the previous generation will often market that they support cloud-based, distributed microservices architectures, but they often are missing critical capabilities such as the ability to handle highly dynamic environments or high-cardinality data.

It is highly recommended that observability platform capabilities be tested before deciding on which to adopt. Vendors offer the ability to do trials and proofs of concept (PoCs), and self-managed platforms can be manually tested. Some software-as-a-service (SaaS) solutions even offer the ability to create trial accounts for manual testing. Regardless of the approach, defining success criteria and testing with real data from your environment when doing a PoC is critical. Vendor-based PoCs are often driven by a sales team and time based, so advanced planning is required to vet the solution provided properly. It is impossible to test every scenario or use case; instead, you should be clear on your goals and what you want to validate. Examples of the types of scenarios you might want to test are covered in Table 9.2.

TABLE 9.2: Example scenarios that could be used to test the capabilities of an observability platform. In addition, the goals for each scenario are provided. Scenarios may be environment or business use case specific. Constraints could also be added, including the type of signal or product tested. In addition, a scoring system could be used to compare platforms.

SCENARIO	GOALS
Monitor the performance of a distributed application under heavy load.	Instrument and collect data from applications, and identify performance and latency issues.
Respond to and diagnose an incident affecting application availability.	Receive alerts, troubleshoot with real-time dashboards, and determine the root cause.
Plan and execute scaling operations based on observed workload patterns.	Monitor resource utilization and set automatic scaling policies.
Validate the performance and stability of a new application release.	Correlate deployment events with other signals, monitor KPIs, and use anomaly detection.
Monitor and maintain service levels defined by SLOs for critical services.	Define SLIs, alert against SLOs, and analyze historical data.

Price, Cost, and Value

When deciding on an observability platform, price versus total cost of ownership (TCO) is an often overlooked consideration. While vendors list pricing, calculating TCO requires understanding capital expenditure, or CapEx,[7] and operational expenditure, or OpEx.[8] CapEx is the money spent to purchase an asset, such as a vendor observability platform. OpEx is the money paid to support running a system, such as a vendor observability platform. In most companies, CapEx and OpEx are separate budgets that are tracked differently. Given that CapEx and OpEx are often tracked separately, the TCO may be much higher for an observability platform than you may realize. Here are some examples of the types of expenses that you need to be properly tracking:

- Integrations: Say you configured your SaaS-based observability platform to collect data from AWS CloudWatch. As you may know, CloudWatch charges you money to list and get metric data. These charges would be part of your monthly AWS bill. You must associate these charges with your observability platform to understand the true TCO.
- Where the processing occurs: Some observability platforms push the processing responsibility down to the customers. For example, tail-based sampling usually happens on the customer side. As such, the customer pays the processing cost instead of the vendor. In this scenario, the infrastructure costs required to support the tail-based sampling processing would need to be added to the TCO. In addition, the customer is responsible for managing the distributed system required to support tail-based sampling. This includes

scaling, securing, load balancing, and more. Maintaining a distributed system is an example of OpEx. Calculating the OpEx may be tricky, but it is necessary to determine TCO.

- Network egress: If all processing happens in the SaaS, all data must be sent to the SaaS. As a result, for cloud-based workloads, you need to pay for network egress, whereas the vendor pays the processing costs. While network egress is typically expensive, telemetry data compresses very well. Of course, even if processing is done on the customer side, eventually, the data needs to be sent to the observability platform. With self-managed observability platforms, network egress costs are usually significantly lower than SaaS-based observability platforms.

It should go without saying that the pricing structure of the observability platform needs to be carefully evaluated. Examples of pricing models for observability platforms include:

- Ingestion or usage: Where you pay based on the amount of data ingested. Some pricing structures also support a pool or bucket where a fixed amount of data is paid beforehand.
- Host or service: Where you pay based on the number of hosts or active services.
- User or seat: Where you pay based on the number of users provisioned in the observability platform.
- Feature or query: Where you pay based on the features enabled, the number of queries performed, or the amount of data queried over.

In reality, most observability platforms have complex pricing structures that depend on various aspects, including data cardinality (see Chapter 1, "What is Observability?"), tiering, and retention policies. In addition, every vendor also has pricing nuances you need to be aware of. For example, pricing per host usually only includes a fixed number of containers and custom metrics. If your environment exceeds these fixed numbers, then you will pay an additional fee. If you are not careful, these additional fees can result in a bill significantly higher than expected. For example, custom metrics are notorious for costing customers a lot of money.

Observability Spend Versus COGS

Regarding how much you should spend on observability, mature organizations typically look at the percentage spent against the cost of goods sold, or COGS.[9] COGS is the amount of money spent to serve paid customers, including cloud provider and observability spending. With revenue and COGS data, you can compute the gross margin, typically represented as a percent, for a product or business using the following formula:

$$(\text{revenue} - \text{COGS}) \div \text{revenue} \times 100$$

Observability spending generally is in the range of 1–15 percent of COGS, depending on the size and maturity of the organization. Large organizations are more likely to see spending in the 10 percent range, though mature or cost-conscious organizations typically target 5 percent or less.

Various factors can impact observability spend, including adding more telemetry data, introducing more microservices, or expanding the geographic footprint of an offering. In addition, self-managed versus vendor-managed platforms can have vastly different COGS implications. It is common for startups to initially leverage open source components, such as Prometheus and Jaeger, for observability purposes. This approach incurs some CapEx (infrastructure) and some OpEx (operations) spend. As a company grows, it is common for it to eventually purchase a vendor-based solution for observability purposes. Reasons for this include focusing on the company's core competencies and addressing security concerns. For very large companies spending a million or more a year on vendor-based observability platforms, eventually a tipping point will be reached where it is more economical to hire full-time staff to run observability platforms then to purchase one. Regardless of the approach taken, understanding observability spend, including TCO, CapEx versus OpEx, and observability spend versus COGS is essential.

Finally, when evaluating observability platforms, you should assess how much time is needed to get a return on investment (ROI). For example, deploying instrumentation and collection takes time, and if the correct data is not collected or enriched, then observability can be impacted. The same goes for the observability platform, where an investment in dashboards and alerts is often needed. Over time, these dashboards and alerts will need to be modified and can grow from dozens to hundreds to thousands. How much of an investment is required and what value or return you will get from this investment are important questions to answer.

Real World Scenario

THE WATCHWHALE BILL

Six months after rolling out Watchwhale at Jupiterian, Riley met with the account team for their quarterly meeting. They informed her that Jupiterian had already used 75 percent of their annual contract. They suggested renewing the Watchwhale contract early to avoid any additional charges. The account team offered a 3-year contract instead of the current annual contract and increased the discount from 40 percent to 55 percent. In addition, they offered to waive any overages throughout the rest of the current contract if the new contract was signed within 60 days.

Riley was surprised by the account team's update. During the meeting, she requested more information about what accounted for the overages. The account team said they would get back to her. After the meeting, she immediately logged into Watchwhale to find the answer. After wasting about an hour, she realized she could not answer the question quickly through the UI. As such, she decided to wait for the account team. In the meantime, she contacted the VP of Engineering to inform him about the overage. He stated that the account team had already been in touch. He asked for Riley's advice on how to proceed. Riley said she would make a recommendation after hearing back from the account team.

A week later, the account team provided a report with a breakdown of the billing data. In the report, she could see that custom metrics from the checkout service accounted for a significant portion of the usage. She asked how she could find this information in the Watchwhale UI. The account team stated that it was impossible to do this today and that either she could request the report from support or use the API to download and parse the usage data herself. With the usage report data, Riley tracked down the development team responsible for generating the custom metrics. She inquired about how these custom metrics were being used and learned the team had not created any dashboards or alerts from them. She requested the custom metrics be removed and worked with the team's product manager to add a story to the next sprint's backlog. In the meantime, Riley worked on a merge request to change the Collector configuration and drop the custom metrics before exporting to the Watchwhale platform. She successfully rolled out the change later that day. The following week, she requested an updated report from the Watchwhale support team. The data showed a significant drop in ingested data.

While the current billing issue had been resolved, the damage had already been done and could easily happen again. Riley needed to figure out a way to prevent these overages in the future. As a starting point, she advised the VP of Engineering to hold off on the renewal and to be prepared to pay for the overages. She suggested using the lack of automated reporting of custom metrics as leverage during the negotiation in order to get a better deal at the end of the year.

Observability Fragmentation

A problem, especially for larger companies, is when different teams use different observability platforms. In this situation, only partial observability may be possible in each platform, and correlation would require the ability to query against similar data in both platforms. In general, maintaining multiple platforms can add significant overhead and costs. Even when using a single vendor, the number of platforms matters. For example, say a vendor supports both logs and metrics but in different back ends. If data needs to be collected either from a cloud provider, such as AWS CloudWatch, or an environment, such as Kubernetes (K8s), does it require one collection mechanism or two? Does it need one API integration or two? Does it make one call to the third-party API or two? Using CloudWatch as an example, you are charged for API requests, including querying and requesting metrics, as well as the amount of data you are extracting. If you analyze your AWS bill, you may find that your CloudWatch expenses are high due to your observability platform's API usage. Beyond this, you may incur these costs multiple times if the data goes to separate back ends.

Given that each signal may be sent to a different observability platform, or the same signal could be sent to two or more observability platforms, the number of platforms and the ability to correlate must also be considered. As discussed in Chapter 8, "The Power of Context and Correlation," correlation is critical to providing observability, and sometimes that requires the ability to correlate across signals. If one signal is sent to one vendor but a second signal is sent to a second vendor, the way correlation is provided must be determined. In some circumstances, it is possible to link between different platforms. With that said, the user experience (UX) will differ across different platforms, which may impact the ability to provide observability and increase the mean time to recovery (MTTR). In addition, when using different platforms, some data duplication may be required. For example, correlating via metadata would not be possible if the same metadata does not exist on both platforms. Storing the same data twice means doubling the CapEx cost as well.

Primary Factors

In addition to the primary considerations described in the previous section, several factors emerge as pivotal considerations that influence decision-making and implementation strategies. From evaluating the merits of building versus buying an observability solution to navigating the complexities of licensing and operational implications, each factor holds significant implications for the ability to integrate observability into organizational workflows. Compatibility with existing systems and tools, coupled with concerns over vendor lock-in, further underscore the need for a nuanced approach. Equally critical is the alignment of stakeholders' expectations and the organizational culture, ensuring that the adoption of an observability platform not only meets technical requirements but also harmonizes with broader business objectives and operational practices. These factors will be explored next, including insights and strategies to empower organizations to make informed decisions and maximize the benefits of adopting an observability platform.

Build, Buy, or Manage

Build versus buy is a common phrase in the software industry. It refers to the approach taken to deliver a solution. The term *build* typically refers to creating something new and in-house, while the term *buy* typically refers to purchasing an existing solution. A third possible option is to run open source solutions yourself. While this could be considered a subset of the build approach, running open source solutions yourself will be referred to as *manage* in this section. For most companies today, the decision is really between buy or manage. This is because various open source and commercial observability platforms exist. Unless a company competes in the observability platform market, investing substantial effort into something that is not core to the business does not make sense.

Managing open source observability platforms is often the default choice for most startups and smaller companies. The primary reasons for this are usually cost and ease of getting started. Smaller companies often have a smaller budget and typically do not have the scalability challenges of larger companies, which often require more complex observability platform deployments. For example, a startup running a K8s cluster with a dozen hosts and a dozen microservices may be able to collect all metrics in a single Prometheus instance. While this deployment is not highly available, it could be more than sufficient for the initial operational needs. While running observability platforms is usually outside the scope of the smaller company's expertise, the overhead of managing the platform is low, considering the price of commercial products. In addition, with the introduction of concepts such as DevOps and technologies, including K8s, developers have become comfortable running open source software (OSS), including Prometheus. Of course, large companies may also choose to run self-managed open source observability platforms. This is especially true if they have in-house expertise and can maintain costs and operational concerns.

Problems arise when the operational cost of running an observability platform exceeds the cost of paying for a vendor solution. For example, as a company grows, it may run into challenges, including scalability—a topic that will be explored in Chapter 11. As a result, operational challenges for the deployed observability platform often increase over time. Say a large company has dozens of K8s clusters with hundreds, if not thousands, of microservices. Collecting metrics in this scenario may require a Prometheus cluster per region configured with a highly available long-term storage solution like Thanos[10] and possibly cross-cluster query federation. To sustain this observability platform architecture, additional people would be needed to scale, secure, and maintain it. These people need to have or gain expertise on the technology solutions used in the observability platform as well as the technology the company is developing. In addition, if long-term considerations such as automation are not invested in, the number of people may need to grow linearly according to the scale of the telemetry data. Given that running an observability platform is usually not core to the company's business at some point, it may be worth considering a change to a buy mentality. Of course, other scenarios may also require moving to a buy decision, such as certain business requirements, including compliance or tool consolidation.

While most companies will not build their own proprietary observability platform, some large companies that have been around for a while may have previously built a proprietary platform for their observability data. With the growth, maturity, and popularity of open standards, including OTel, companies with their own proprietary observability platform may choose to switch to a different, more commonly used observability platform. The reasons for this are the same as the buy versus manage decisions. Alternatively, some large companies relying on vendor-managed observability platforms may eventually face a crossroads due to the ever-increasing costs incurred. Either these companies will mandate more visibility and levers to control the amount of data, and thus the cost incurred, or they will need to turn to alternative solutions such as reconsidering the buy versus manage decision. For example, at some price point (usually several million dollars), hiring a team to manage an observability platform is cheaper than paying a vendor.

In practice, it is rarely a straightforward either-or decision. It is common for companies to take a dual approach, where some amount of observability data is handled internally while a vendor handles the same or different data. For example, a self-managed open source observability platform may deal with non-production data, while a vendor-managed platform may handle production data. The various approaches are covered in Table 9.3.

TABLE 9.3: The different approaches when choosing an observability platform and the major pros and cons

APPROACH	PROS	CONS
Build	Flexibility and choice	Distraction from the business value proposition
Buy	Reduced OpEx	Vendor lock-in and increased CapEx over time
Manage	Infrastructure CapEx only	Increased CapEx and OpEx over time
Combination	Flexibility and choice	Multiple systems to manage; inconsistency

Licensing, Operations, and Deployment

While it is possible to have a decision factor on whether the observability platform is open source or proprietary, typically, the more important question is whether the platform's capabilities meet your requirements. For example, if your requirements included the ability to run a self-managed, on-premises observability platform, then some proprietary platforms would not be an option. Alternatively, if your requirements included the ability to easily control costs by having quick insights into what telemetry data was being used or what data generated the most costs, then most open source solutions would not be an option without modification.

In general, it is the capabilities the platform provides that matter most. Still, there may be reasons why the platform technology matters, including vendor lock-in, a topic covered in Chapter 7, "Adopting OpenTelemetry." If being vendor agnostic is a consideration, then the platform supporting open standards, such as OTel, may be an important consideration. Another example of vendor lock-in is content compatibility. When combining build versus buy or migrating to a buy solution, it may be desirable to ensure compatibility between the platforms. For example, say that developers have invested in Prometheus queries and alerts for their internally managed Prometheus server. When migrating to or adding a different observability platform, the ability to reuse that content natively or through migration tools may be an important consideration.

Regardless of the observability platform licensing model, you must also decide on the operations and deployment model, as shown in Table 9.4. There may be reasons, including data sensitivity, or specific compliance requirements, such as where the observability platform must be hosted, that influence your decision. In the observability era, most platforms you manage are built internally or deployed from open source software. Most vendors, at least for cloud native workloads, primarily offer managed software-as-a-service (SaaS) solutions. This is different from the monitoring era, in which most solutions were managed by the customer on-premises. If you plan to manage an observability platform, it is important to consider factors including security patching and scaling. Of course, even when leveraging a managed platform, you still need to manage components, such as instrumentation libraries and collectors.

TABLE 9.4: Some critical decisions that need to be made when choosing an observability platform

DECISION	OPTIONS	NOTES
Licensing	Open source or proprietary	Capabilities are usually more important than the licensing model.
Operations	Self or vendor-managed	Open source vendor-managed may not be the same as open source self-managed.
Deployment	On-premises or SaaS	Most vendor-managed observability platforms are SaaS-based today.

OTel Compatibility and Vendor Lock-In

If you are adopting or have adopted OTel, one of the most significant considerations from an observability platform perspective is its compatibility with OTel. Many open source and commercial observability platforms support OTel today (`https://opentelemetry.io/`

`ecosystem/vendors`). However, even if a vendor supports native OTel Protocol (OTLP), that does not mean it fully endorses the OTel standard. In addition, just because a vendor states OTLP support does not mean they default to sending data via OTLP or encourage their customers to take advantage of OTel conventions. If they do not default to OTLP, why not? And does that matter to you?

In general, extensive testing is required to fully understand which parts of the OTel specification are supported by an observability platform. OTel-specific decision factors that you may want to consider when evaluating an observability platform are covered in Table 9.5.

TABLE 9.5: Some OTel decision factors that may influence the observability platform selected

FACTOR	NOTES
OTLP ingestion	In addition to yes, is it the default setting—and if not, why?
Distribution	If one is offered, does it contain proprietary components?
API and SDK	What versions and features are supported?
Instrumentation	Which languages are supported?
Collector	Which components are supported?
Semantic conventions	Does the platform support semantic conventions?
General support	If vendor-managed, is OTel support provided?
Contributions	What commitment, influence, and ability to support is provided?

Going back to vendor lock-in, projects such as OTel help reduce this problem by replacing the need to deploy proprietary instrumentation and data collection mechanisms. With that said, an observability platform that supports ingesting OTel data does not necessarily ensure a vendor-agnostic solution. Simply generating content, such as dashboards or alerts, may lead to vendor lock-in. While a small number of dashboards or alerts could be re-created, thousands or even tens of thousands of dashboards or alerts may be created over time. In addition, it is important to note that even vendor-managed open source observability platforms may not be the same as self-managed open source observability platforms. It is not uncommon for vendors of managed open source solutions to offer proprietary capabilities, which may result in vendor lock-in.

Stakeholders and Company Culture

As an engineering team grows from a single scrum team to groups, departments, and business units (BUs), it becomes harder and harder to ensure consistency and limit the platforms in use. Some companies control this through top-down mandates, where someone in the executive team or C-suite usually enforces standards or tools. Other companies provide agency and allow BUs and teams to make their own decisions. As a company grows, tool sprawl becomes a real issue. In addition, business or external factors can drive behaviors. For example, a security breach at a company may result in a top-down mandate to consolidate tools or vendors as well as focus on security use cases.

As an employee attempting to sway internal people to support an observability platform, it is important to consider stakeholders like those listed in Table 9.6 and what they care about. Stakeholders include the decision-makers who buy, manage, and use the technology. In addition, it would consist of influencers of the decision-makers, including finance and security. Vendor sales teams spend a lot of time understanding a company's organizational structure and requirements. It is this understanding that ultimately results in a signed deal.

TABLE 9.6: Key stakeholders to engage when making an observability platform decision. For commercial offerings, the buyer is the most important stakeholder to bring in the technology. For open source solutions, the administrator is usually the most important stakeholder.

STAKEHOLDER	EXAMPLE	INFLUENCED BY
Buyer	CTO or VP of Engineering	Legal, Finance, and Security
Administrator	SRE Team	Development Team
User	Development Team	SRE Team

Implementation Basics

Once a decision to use an observability platform is made, work must be put into realizing its value. For large companies where the executive teams make decisions, software is sometimes purchased from a vendor and then either partially or never implemented. A common term in the software industry is *shelfware*,[11] which refers to software that has been purchased but is not used. The net result is CapEx with no ROI. The reasons for shelfware extend well beyond a disconnect between the executive team and those closer to the problems requiring observability solutions. As an example, implementation consists of steps, including deploying instrumentation and data collection mechanisms, configuring identity providers and roles, and creating dashboards and alerts. Each of these steps has multiple substeps. Data collection and instrumentation were covered in Chapter 5, "Managing the OpenTelemetry Collector," and Chapter 6, "Leveraging OpenTelemetry Instrumentation," respectively, and included steps such as architecture and security review as well as authentication, configuration management, and performance testing. Implementing and adopting an observability platform at any point may become too challenging, resulting in shelfware or partial implementation. In addition, company priorities can also shift, impeding the adoption of an observability platform.

To help ensure success during implementation, it is usually best to start small and show value quickly. This is true for both greenfield and brownfield deployments (concepts covered in Chapter 7). Starting small might include identifying a single team to onboard or choosing a set of services for which observability has previously proven challenging. As mentioned in Chapter 6, starting with the metric signal is often the most impactful and straightforward way to show value in an observability platform. Of course, if you are coming from a brownfield environment, then you may already have existing signal data that you want to send to the new observability platform. In this case, starting with data collection and, more specifically, deploying the Collector as a gateway, as discussed in Chapter 5, can be an easy way to get started. No matter where you start, the recommendation is to pick a single signal or component for a subset of your environment and expand over time.

Using different phases or milestones is one way to approach implementation. In project management and software development, it is common to refer to each phase as a day even though each phase takes more than a day. In addition, the phase or day starts at zero instead of one. What follows next is a definition of phases that could be used to approach implementation.

Day 0: Establishing Observability: The initial phase of setting up observability practices and tools within a software system. Activities would include:

- Choosing and setting up observability tools such as instrumentation frameworks, data collectors, and observability platforms
- Instrumenting the application code to emit relevant signals (usually one at first)
- Configuring dashboards, alerts, and other monitoring settings based on initial requirements and expectations
- Providing training to the team on how to use observability tools effectively

Day 1: Initial Monitoring and Analysis: Focuses on the initial implementation and use of observability data to monitor and analyze one or more environments. Activities would include:

- Monitoring key signals to ensure that the system is performing as expected
- Using observability data to diagnose issues and understand system behavior during normal operations
- Establishing baseline metrics and performance indicators to measure against future changes
- Gathering feedback from initial observations to refine monitoring configurations and improve understanding of the system's behavior

Day 2: Continuous Improvement and Optimization: Involves the ongoing enhancement and optimization of observability practices to better understand and manage the software system. Activities would include:

- Implementing automation for monitoring setup, alerting, and response
- Performing deeper analysis using aggregated metrics, anomaly detection, and correlation across different observability data sources
- Scaling observability solutions to handle larger volumes of data and more complex systems
- Integrating observability into the development lifecycle (DevOps practices) to ensure continuous feedback and improvement

Instrumentation and data collection were covered in previous chapters. This section will discuss considerations beyond those when implementing a new observability platform.

Administration

Authentication is usually one of the first configuration settings to configure on the administration side. Beyond identity providers, users and roles are critical for proper access to the observability platform. Approaches for authentication and permissions vary based on the company.

Larger and more mature companies usually have a centralized identity provider that will need to be integrated. These types of companies usually also have requirements around users with administrator permissions and those without. Other companies may have multiple identity providers or no identity provider. Some companies may choose to give all users administrator permissions, at least initially. Regardless of how identity and access management is handled in your environment, the recommendation is to carefully consider the initial implementation, as it sets the precedence for users and lays the foundation upon which others will build. As an example, if everyone is initially granted administrator permissions and later this permission is removed, then users may become frustrated by the time it takes to make changes, reducing adoption and usage of the platform.

Usage

Beyond administrative configuration, observability platform capabilities, including dashboards and alerts, are also important. Some observability platforms come with built-in dashboards and alerts. All allow for the creation and modification of dashboards and alerts. At the very least, naming standards for dashboards and alerts can be helpful when adopting an observability platform. In addition, ensuring that the alerts enabled are tuned and actionable is also critical; otherwise, they can burn out people on-call and result in actual issues being missed. Given that the environment changes over time, the dashboards and alerts in observability platforms must change as well. To support changes in the environment, regular cleanup is necessary to reduce duplication and irrelevant data from being accessible.

Even after the initial configuration is done, there is still more work to ensure that value is realized, including:

- Training and onboarding for team members.
- Establishing and maintaining best practices and governance processes.
- Monitoring the observability platform. For example, how do you know the observability platform is working as intended, and what do you do when it is not functioning properly?
- Minimizing disruption to operation during a transition to a new observability platform. This usually means implementing phased rollouts and fallback mechanisms.
- Measuring and monitoring adoption and migration progress.
- Continuously identifying areas for optimization and improvement to provide and improve observability.

Maturity Framework

When implementing an observability platform, taking a structured approach to assess and improve your organization's observability capabilities is important. One recommended way is to define and measure maturity levels, including the depth and breadth of observability practices. These could range from basic monitoring to proactive insights into system performance and behavior. Each level could build on the previous one, introducing more sophisticated techniques and tools. An example of a framework you might create could consist of five levels: Basic Monitoring, Enhanced Monitoring, Proactive Observability, Predictive Observability, and Autonomous Observability.

Level 1: Basic Monitoring: At this level, organizations have basic monitoring in place, focusing primarily on uptime and system health. Monitoring is often manual and limited to simple metrics like CPU usage, memory utilization, and disk space. Key aspects of this level include:

- Basic system metrics collection (CPU, memory, disk)
- Basic monitoring capabilities, including initial dashboards, with manual telemetry review
- Simple alerting for critical system metrics and failures

Level 2: Enhanced Monitoring: This level introduces more detailed metrics and some level of automation. It includes application-level monitoring and the initial use of more than one signal for diagnosing issues. Key aspects of this level include:

- Application-level metrics and log collection, including the initial usage of a methodology, such as requests, errors, and duration (RED) or golden signals, as covered in Chapter 1
- Automated alerting and notifications based on predefined thresholds
- Basic aggregation, filtering, and search capabilities

Level 3: Proactive Observability: Organizations move from reactive monitoring to proactive observability at this stage. This includes advanced metrics, comprehensive logging, and the widespread use of tracing to understand system behavior. Key aspects of this level include:

- Comprehensive metrics collection (infrastructure and applications)
- Centralized logging with advanced search and analysis
- Distributed tracing for understanding request flows
- Dashboards and visualization for real-time insights and correlation across signals

Level 4: Predictive Observability: This level leverages ML and advanced analytics to predict potential issues before they impact the system. This level focuses on proactive problem resolution and optimization. Key aspects of this level include:

- ML models for anomaly detection
- Predictive analytics for identifying potential failures
- Automated root cause analysis
- Continuous improvement through feedback loops

Level 5: Autonomous Observability: This level represents the pinnacle of observability maturity, where systems are self-healing and capable of automatic adjustments. Human intervention is minimal, and the system can adapt to changing conditions dynamically. Key aspects of this level include:

- Self-healing infrastructure and applications, including things like K8s operators and chaos engineering[12]
- Automated remediation and response using tools like runbook automation[13]
- Use of AI/ML to dynamically adjust monitoring and alerting thresholds
- Fully integrating observability practices with continuous integration and continuous delivery (CI/CD) pipelines

The Bottom Line

Distinguish between observability platform capabilities. Understanding the varied capabilities of observability platforms is essential for making an informed choice. Observability platforms offer a range of features, including signal collection, real-time data processing, and advanced analytics and visualization tools. Evaluating these capabilities in relation to your organization's unique needs will help you determine which platform can best support your observability goals, ensuring that you have the right tools to gain deep insights into your systems.

Master It What are some of the primary differences among observability platforms?

Decide which observability platform is right for you. Observability can be achieved in many ways depending on your requirements. Choosing the right observability platform requires a thorough assessment of your current and future requirements. By aligning the platform's strengths with your specific use cases and organizational goals, you can make a decision that will provide long-term value and effectiveness.

Master It What are some of the key considerations and decision factors that need to be decided to choose the right observability platform?

Get a quick return on your observability platform investment. Even after deciding on an observability platform, implementation and adoption takes time. Without proper planning and reporting, observability may not be achieved. Maximizing the ROI for your observability platform involves leveraging its features to achieve quick and tangible benefits. By demonstrating early successes and improvements, you can build momentum and support for further observability initiatives, ensuring that the platform delivers sustained value and drives continuous operational enhancements.

Master It How can you get a quick return on your observability platform investment?

Notes

1 https://en.wikipedia.org/wiki/Functional_requirement
2 https://en.wikipedia.org/wiki/Non-functional_requirement
3 https://en.wikipedia.org/wiki/Multicloud
4 https://en.wikipedia.org/wiki/Long_tail
5 https://en.wikipedia.org/wiki/Cash_cow
6 https://en.wikipedia.org/wiki/The_Innovator%27s_Dilemma
7 https://en.wikipedia.org/wiki/Capital_expenditure
8 https://en.wikipedia.org/wiki/Operating_expense
9 https://en.wikipedia.org/wiki/Cost_of_goods_sold
10 https://thanos.io
11 https://en.wikipedia.org/wiki/Shelfware
12 https://en.wikipedia.org/wiki/Chaos_engineering
13 https://en.wikipedia.org/wiki/Runbook#Runbook_automation

Chapter 10

Observability Antipatterns and Pitfalls

Observability antipatterns and pitfalls are common mistakes or ineffective practices that hinder the successful implementation and utilization of observability in software systems. While antipatterns represent specific recurring patterns of behavior, pitfalls are more generalized challenges or shortcomings. Either can happen at any step in an observability journey, be it telemetry generation and collection or telemetry querying and alerting. In addition, company culture can play a big role in antipatterns or pitfalls occurring or being overcome.

In the realm of observability, understanding and avoiding common antipatterns and pitfalls is essential to maintaining a robust and effective system. Observability, by its nature, aims to provide deep insights into system performance and behavior, enabling rapid identification and resolution of issues. However, certain practices and approaches can undermine these goals, leading to inefficiencies, missed symptoms, and operational headaches. This chapter delves into the most prevalent antipatterns and pitfalls encountered in observability practices, from over-monitoring and alert fatigue to neglecting the importance of contextual metadata. By exploring these issues and offering practical guidance on how to avoid them, this chapter equips you with the knowledge to refine your observability strategy and ensure that it delivers meaningful and actionable insights. Through scenarios and recommendations, you will learn how to recognize these pitfalls in your own systems and adopt best practices to enhance the effectiveness of your observability efforts.

IN THIS CHAPTER, YOU WILL LEARN TO:

- Distinguish between observability antipatterns and pitfalls
- Recognize and overcome common observability antipatterns and pitfalls
- Describe the impacts of company culture on observability goals

Telemetry Data Missteps

Observability is powered by telemetry data, and that data can come from a vast number of sources. Each source can emit various forms of telemetry known as *signals*. The amount of telemetry data per source and signal varies, but it has the potential to be massive. Generating, processing, transmitting, and storing telemetry data comes at a cost at each step. As a result, it is critical to get value out of the data collected; otherwise, it should not be generated, processed, transmitted, or stored. On the flip side, not generating the right or enough telemetry data may result in blind spots or the inability to achieve observability. Ensuring that telemetry data is consistently collected, properly tagged, and relevant to the key performance indicators (KPIs) of your system is essential for maintaining a robust observability practice.

Common antipatterns and pitfalls in managing telemetry data can significantly undermine its effectiveness. Examples of telemetry data antipatterns include:

- **Incomplete instrumentation and blind spots:** Neglecting to instrument all relevant components of the system, such as third-party dependencies or error-prone areas, leading to gaps in visibility and difficulty in troubleshooting. This can also occur when attempting to instrument an entire system at once without a clear strategy or prioritization. In short, you cannot alert against or analyze data you do not have.
- **Over-instrumentation, or Big Bang[1] instrumentation:** Too much instrumentation can overburden sources and observability platforms as well as significantly increase costs. In addition, collecting excessive amounts of observability data without a clear storage, retention, and analysis plan can overwhelm teams. It is important to focus on collecting relevant telemetry data that provides actionable insights rather than collecting everything indiscriminately.
- **Ignoring sampling or sampling bias:** Failing to use sampling techniques for high-volume telemetry data can strain observability platforms and lead to increased costs. However, improper sampling strategies can introduce bias and affect analysis accuracy, impacting the ability to provide observability.
- **Inconsistent naming conventions:** Inconsistent naming conventions for telemetry data, which is especially common for logs, can lead to confusion and difficulty correlating data across different systems or components. Standardizing naming conventions helps maintain clarity and consistency in observability data.

Examples of telemetry data pitfalls include:

- **High-cardinality data:** While rich in detail, high cardinality can significantly increase the complexity and volume of the data being collected. Examples include performance and resource strain, difficulty in data management and noise versus signal, challenges in visualization and analysis, and increased observability platform costs.
- **Lack of data validation:** Failing to validate telemetry data for accuracy, completeness, and consistency can result in unreliable insights and incorrect conclusions about system performance. Implementing data validation checks ensures the reliability of telemetry data.
- **Misconfigured aggregation:** Improper aggregation of telemetry data can obscure important details and trends, leading to incorrect conclusions about system behavior and performance. Properly configuring aggregation methods is essential for accurate analysis.
- **Failure to evolve:** Neglecting to update telemetry data collection and processing practices to accommodate changes in system architecture, workload patterns, or user requirements can lead to obsolescence and inefficiency. Continuous improvement and refinement of telemetry data practices are necessary for maintaining effective observability over time.

Given these potential antipatterns and pitfalls, what should you do? First, it is important to understand your observability challenges and what problems you are trying to solve. Next, you need to determine the telemetry data required to address these challenges. Instead of trying to instrument everything or just the sources with known issues, consider establishing governance processes on the type of telemetry data that needs to be collected. For example, RED metrics or golden signals, covered in Chapter 1, "What is Observability?," can serve as a good starting point. In addition, host metrics and infrastructure metadata can provide additional information necessary to solve availability and performance problems. OpenTelemetry (OTel) provides a great initial set of telemetry data that can be consumed and queried against to address observ-ability challenges. Starting with automatic instrumentation and basic data collection, as covered in Chapter 5, "Managing the OpenTelemetry Collector," and Chapter 6, "Leveraging OpenTelemetry Instrumentation," is a good starting place. Over time, you can begin to look into advanced configurations to improve observability capabilities.

You may be wondering how telemetry data antipatterns and pitfalls would manifest. Examples of the scenarios that could lead to telemetry data antipatterns and pitfalls will be covered next.

Mixing Instrumentation Libraries Scenario

An organization's development teams use a mix of different instrumentation libraries, including OTel and proprietary vendor or custom-built solutions, within the same application. This results in inconsistent data formats, propagation contexts, and sampling strategies across different components. Recommendations to mitigate include:

- Standardization: Standardize on a single, vendor-agnostic instrumentation framework, such as OTel, to ensure consistency and interoperability across all applications and services.
- Migration plan: Develop a migration plan to gradually replace legacy or proprietary instrumentation with OTel, providing guidance, tools, and support to development teams during the transition.
- Compatibility layers: Implement compatibility layers or wrappers, like the Prometheus receiver in the OTel Collector, to bridge between legacy or proprietary instrumentation and OTel, allowing for phased adoption and minimizing disruption to existing workflows.

One way to categorize the implications of this scenario and the potential impact is as follows. It will be used in the "Prioritization Framework" section later in this chapter.

- Standardization: Medium
- Reliability: Low
- Performance: Medium
- Security: Low
- Troubleshooting Efficiency: High
- Developer Productivity: High

Automatic Instrumentation Scenario

An organization relies heavily on automatic instrumentation capabilities to instrument its applications. However, automatic instrumentation may not cover all application components or custom code paths, leading to gaps in telemetry data and incomplete observability coverage. Recommendations to mitigate include:

- Manual instrumentation: Supplement automatic instrumentation with manual instrumentation for critical components, custom frameworks, or specialized use cases to ensure comprehensive observability coverage.
- Code reviews and testing: Conduct code reviews and testing to identify areas that may require manual instrumentation and ensure that all relevant code paths are instrumented appropriately.
- Continuous improvement: Evaluate and enhance automatic instrumentation capabilities to address limitations and edge cases, incorporating user feedback and real-world use cases.

One way to categorize the implications of this scenario and the potential impact is as follows. It will be used in the "Prioritization Framework" section later in this chapter.

- Standardization: Medium
- Reliability: High
- Performance: High
- Security: Low
- Troubleshooting Efficiency: High
- Developer Productivity: Low

Custom Instrumentation Scenario

An organization's applications rely heavily on custom-built frameworks, libraries, or proprietary components that lack native support for observability instrumentation. As a result, telemetry data from these components may be missing or incomplete, hindering visibility into system behavior. Recommendations to mitigate include:

- Custom instrumentation frameworks: Develop custom instrumentation frameworks or libraries tailored to the organization's specific technology stack or domain, providing built-in support for observability signals.
- Community contributions: Encourage collaboration and contributions from the developer community to develop and maintain open source instrumentation libraries for popular frameworks and technologies, ensuring broad coverage and adoption.
- Vendor collaboration: Work closely with open source projects, technology vendors, or third-party providers to advocate for native observability support in their products and services, driving standardization and interoperability across the ecosystem.

One way to categorize the implications of this scenario and the potential impact is as follows. It will be used in the "Prioritization Framework" section later in this chapter.

- Standardization: High
- Reliability: Low
- Performance: Medium

- Security: Low
- Troubleshooting Efficiency: High
- Developer Productivity: High

Component Configuration Scenario

An organization misconfigures components of its observability platform, such as instrumentation libraries, collectors, or processing layers, leading to dropped data, delayed processing, or incorrect interpretation of telemetry data. Recommendations to mitigate include:

- Configuration management: Implement robust configuration management practices to ensure consistency and accuracy in configuring observability components, including version control, change tracking, and automated testing.
- Validation and testing: Validate configuration changes in a staging environment before deploying them to production, leveraging tools and techniques such as integration testing, regression testing, and canary deployments.
- Monitoring and alerting: Set up monitoring and alerting mechanisms to detect and alert on configuration errors or anomalies in observability components, enabling proactive resolution and preventing potential issues from impacting system operation.

One way to categorize the implications of this scenario and the potential impact is as follows. It will be used in the "Prioritization Framework" section later in this chapter.

- Standardization: Medium
- Reliability: High
- Performance: Medium
- Security: Medium
- Troubleshooting Efficiency: High
- Developer Productivity: High

Performance Overhead Scenario

An organization deploys observability components without considering the performance overhead introduced by instrumentation, data collection, or processing activities. As a result, telemetry data may impose significant resource overhead, impacting application performance or scalability. Recommendations to mitigate include:

- Performance profiling: Conduct performance profiling and benchmarking exercises to identify performance bottlenecks and resource-intensive operations in observability components, enabling optimization and tuning efforts.
- Fine-tuning parameters: Adjust configuration parameters, such as sampling rates, retention policies, or processing thresholds, to optimize resource utilization and minimize performance overhead without sacrificing observability coverage.
- Scalability testing: Perform scalability testing under realistic production conditions to ensure that observability components can handle anticipated workloads and data volumes without degradation in performance or stability. Alternatively, test corner cases to better understand and document system behavior.

One way to categorize the implications of this scenario and the potential impact is as follows. It will be used in the "Prioritization Framework" section later in this chapter.

- Standardization: Low
- Reliability: High
- Performance: High
- Security: Low
- Troubleshooting Efficiency: High
- Developer Productivity: High

Resource Allocation Scenario

An organization underestimates resource requirements for telemetry generating, processing, and exporting activities, allocating insufficient central processing unit (CPU), memory, or storage resources. This results in performance degradation, data loss, or system instability during peak usage. Recommendations to mitigate include:

- Capacity planning: Conduct thorough capacity planning exercises to estimate resource requirements for observability components based on anticipated workloads, data volumes, and growth projections.
- Resource scaling: Implement dynamic resource scaling and auto-scaling mechanisms in observability platforms to adapt to fluctuating demand and ensure adequate resource availability during peak usage periods.
- Monitoring and alerting: Set up monitoring and alerting mechanisms to track resource utilization metrics, such as CPU usage, memory consumption, and storage capacity, and proactively respond to resource constraints or saturation conditions.

One way to categorize the implications of this scenario and the potential impact is as follows. It will be used in the "Prioritization Framework" section later in this chapter.

- Standardization: Low
- Reliability: High
- Performance: High
- Security: Low
- Troubleshooting Efficiency: High
- Developer Productivity: High

Security Considerations Scenario

An organization neglects to incorporate security best practices, such as encryption, authentication, or access controls, into its observability platform. As a result, telemetry data could be exposed to unauthorized access, interception, or tampering. This can lead to data breaches, compliance violations, or the compromise of sensitive information. Recommendations to mitigate include:

- Redaction: Redact sensitive information at the data collection layer to prevent such information from being persisted within observability platforms where it is difficult to remove.
- Data encryption: Implement end-to-end encryption mechanisms to protect telemetry data both in transit and at rest, safeguarding it from interception or unauthorized access by external parties.
- Access controls: Enforce strong access controls and authentication mechanisms to restrict access to observability data based on user roles, privileges, and least privilege principles, preventing unauthorized users from accessing sensitive information.
- Audit logging: Enable audit logging and activity monitoring features in observability platforms to track and record access to telemetry data, configuration changes, and administrative actions, facilitating forensic analysis and compliance reporting.

One way to categorize the implications of this scenario and the potential impact is as follows. It will be used in the "Prioritization Framework" section later in this chapter.

- Standardization: Medium
- Reliability: Low
- Performance: Low
- Security: High
- Troubleshooting Efficiency: Low
- Developer Productivity: Low

Monitoring and Maintenance Scenario

An organization neglects to monitor and maintain its observability components, resulting in undetected issues, performance degradation, or system failures over time. In addition, troubleshooting efforts may be hindered and operational overhead may grow over time. Recommendations to mitigate include:

- Dashboard and alerts: Create and maintain dashboards and alerts for telemetry data, including instrumentation and data collection.
- Health checks: Implement health checks and self-monitoring capabilities in observability components to detect and report on operational status, resource availability, and performance metrics, enabling proactive maintenance and troubleshooting.
- Regular maintenance: Establish regular maintenance schedules and procedures for updating, patching, and upgrading observability components to address security vulnerabilities, performance optimizations, and feature enhancements, ensuring ongoing reliability and resilience of the platform.

One way to categorize the implications of this scenario and the potential impact is as follows. It will be used in the "Prioritization Framework" section later in this chapter.

- Standardization: Low
- Reliability: High
- Performance: High
- Security: Low
- Troubleshooting Efficiency: High
- Developer Productivity: High

Observability Platform Missteps

Telemetry data is sent to one or more observability platforms, where it may undergo additional processing and is finally stored. The stored data may be queried multiple times over its retention period, or the time the data is persisted, in the observability platform. Queries are primarily used to populate dashboards and power alerts. Assuming the telemetry data is queried, it may be valuable and worth the cost to generate, process, and store it. Any data that is not queried or is only queried for a small part of the retention period is likely not valuable and costs you money without providing value. In addition, dashboard and alert value can vary greatly depending on implementation and maintenance. To maximize the value of an observability platform, it is crucial to customize it to your specific use cases, ensure seamless integration with other systems, and regularly monitor its own performance.

An observability platform is a critical component for aggregating, analyzing, and visualizing telemetry data, but there are several antipatterns and pitfalls to avoid in its deployment and use. Examples of observability platform antipatterns include:

- Vendor lock-in: Over-reliance on proprietary observability platforms without considering interoperability, migration costs, or vendor lock-in risks can limit flexibility and hinder future scalability.
- Non-OTel–native: Like vendor lock-in, observability platforms that do not natively support OTel are either legacy, non-extensible, or do not align with OTel's vision of vendor-neutral telemetry.
- Poor integration support: Selecting observability platforms with limited or inadequate support for integrating with existing tools, systems, or custom applications can impede the organization's ability to achieve comprehensive observability across its infrastructure.
- Underestimating scalability requirements: Choosing observability platforms that lack scalability features or cannot handle the organization's growing data volume and velocity can lead to performance issues, increased latency, and diminished observability effectiveness over time.
- Tool sprawl: Using multiple observability tools without integration or a coherent strategy can result in increased complexity, maintenance overhead, and difficulty correlating data.
- Alert storms: Configuring alerting systems with excessive or poorly defined thresholds can cause teams to be inundated with a high volume of alerts, many of which are false positives.

- Static dashboards: Creating static dashboards that fail to adapt to changing system conditions or user needs can result in outdated or irrelevant information.
- Ignoring latency: Focusing solely on system availability metrics and neglecting latency measurements can lead to blind spots in performance monitoring and user experience (UX).
- Ignoring context: Analyzing observability data without considering contextual information, such as deployment changes or business events, can lead to incomplete or incorrect conclusions.

Examples of observability platform pitfalls include:

- Complex deployment: Implementing observability platforms with complex deployment requirements or dependencies can hinder adoption and increase the likelihood of configuration errors, leading to delays and operational inefficiencies.
- Data silos: Using multiple observability platforms that do not integrate seamlessly with each other can create data silos, making it difficult to correlate data and gain a holistic view of system performance and behavior.
- Inadequate security measures: Selecting observability platforms with inadequate security features or compliance certifications can pose risks to sensitive data and regulatory compliance, exposing the organization to potential security breaches and legal liabilities.
- Insufficient customization options: Adopting observability platforms that lack customization options or flexibility to adapt to the organization's unique requirements can limit the effectiveness of observability initiatives and hinder innovation.
- High total cost of ownership (TCO): Underestimating the total cost of ownership, a topic covered in Chapter 9, "Choosing an Observability Platform," can lead to budget overruns and financial strain on the organization. An observability platform's TCO includes licensing fees, infrastructure costs, training, and support.
- Alert fatigue: Excessive or poorly configured alerts can result in alert fatigue and desensitization to critical issues.
- Failure to monitor key business metrics: Neglecting to monitor metrics related to business objectives can lead to misalignment between technical performance and business outcomes.

Given these potential antipatterns and pitfalls, what should you do? Consider grouping observability platform antipatterns and pitfalls into relevant categories. For example, you may decide on categories such as:

- Understanding present and predicting future observability requirements: The focus here would be on planning and predicting now to reduce problems later.
- Defining and maintaining observability processes and best practices: The focus here would be on guardrails to help administrators and users configure and use observability platforms properly.
- Following the "keep it simple, stupid" (KISS) principle:[2] The focus here would be minimizing complexity and preventing data silos to help ensure correlation and reduce MTTR.

Of course, all of this is easier said than done. In practice, observability vendors are incentivized to try and lock you in. In addition, it is difficult to align a company on a single observability platform and enforce governance processes to ensure consistency. Finally, end users typically only care about a subset of the data available in an observability platform, and they do not have much time to spend optimizing an observability platform's configuration. Ensuring ownership of any observability platform being used and continuously improving observability within a company is essential to ensuring that observability can be achieved and maintained.

You may be wondering how observability platform antipatterns and pitfalls would manifest. Examples of the scenarios that could lead to observability platform antipatterns and pitfalls will be covered next.

Vendor Lock-in Scenario

An organization relies heavily on a single proprietary observability platform. Over time, the vendor increases prices or changes licensing terms. Migrating is difficult due to reliance on proprietary components. Recommendations to mitigate include:

- Standardize data formats: Adopt open standards like OTel for instrumentation and data collection to ensure interoperability and facilitate migration between platforms.
- Prioritize automation: Ensure that observability platform configuration, such as administration, dashboards, and alerts, are done programmatically, such as via Terraform. While automation will be vendor-specific, it will contain a blueprint of what needs to be migrated and how it should be laid out.
- Evaluate alternatives: Regularly assess alternative observability platforms and providers to maintain leverage and negotiate favorable terms.

One way to categorize the implications of this scenario and the potential impact is as follows. It will be used in the "Prioritization Framework" section later in this chapter.

- Standardization: High
- Reliability: High
- Performance: Medium
- Security: Low
- Troubleshooting Efficiency: Medium
- Developer Productivity: Medium

Fragmented Tooling Scenario

Different teams within an organization use disparate observability tools and platforms, leading to fragmented data silos and inconsistent monitoring practices. This results in difficulty correlating data, sharing insights, and collaborating on troubleshooting efforts. Recommendations to mitigate include:

- Centralize data sources: Consolidate observability data sources into a centralized platform or data lake to create a single source of truth for monitoring and analysis. Note that leveraging a centralized platform does not mean storing all signals the same way as the requirements and usage patterns of signals vary. In fact, be wary of observability platforms that treat all telemetry data the same way.

- Standardize tooling: Establish standardized observability tooling and practices across teams to promote consistency, streamline collaboration, and reduce duplication of efforts.
- Invest in integration: Invest in integrations or middleware solutions that enable seamless data sharing and interoperability between different observability tools and platforms.

One way to categorize the implications of this scenario and the potential impact is as follows. It will be used in the "Prioritization Framework" section later in this chapter.

- Standardization: High
- Reliability: Medium
- Performance: Medium
- Security: Low
- Troubleshooting Efficiency: High
- Developer Productivity: High

Tool Fatigue Scenario

Operators within an organization are inundated with alerts, dashboards, and monitoring tools, leading to cognitive overload and alert fatigue. They struggle to prioritize alerts, distinguish between critical issues and noise, and maintain focus on meaningful insights. Recommendations to mitigate include:

- Streamline alerting: Implement intelligent alerting mechanisms that prioritize critical issues, reduce false positives, and minimize unnecessary noise to prevent alert fatigue.
- Customize dashboards: Customize dashboards and visualization tools to display relevant metrics and insights tailored to specific roles or use cases, reducing information overload.
- Invest in integration: Integrate observability platforms with incident response workflows to automate routine tasks and streamline resolution processes.

One way to categorize the implications of this scenario and the potential impact is as follows. It will be used in the "Prioritization Framework" section later in this chapter.

- Standardization: High
- Reliability: Medium
- Performance: Medium
- Security: Low
- Troubleshooting Efficiency: High
- Developer Productivity: High

Inadequate Scalability Scenario

An organization experiences rapid growth in data volumes or system complexity, causing its observability platform to struggle with scalability and performance. This leads to increased latency, dropped data, or system instability during peak usage. Recommendations to mitigate include:

- Self-managed solutions: Implement scalable architectures that support horizontal scaling of observability components, such as collectors, storage layers, or processing pipelines, to handle increasing data volumes and workloads.
- Software-as-a-service (SaaS) solutions: Leverage cloud native observability platforms or managed services that offer elastic scalability, auto-scaling capabilities, and pay-as-you-go pricing models to accommodate dynamic resource demands.
- Performance testing: Conduct regular performance testing and capacity planning exercises to identify bottlenecks, optimize resource allocation, and ensure that observability platforms can scale effectively with growing demands.

One way to categorize the implications of this scenario and the potential impact is as follows. It will be used in the "Prioritization Framework" section later in this chapter.

- Standardization: Low
- Reliability: High
- Performance: High
- Security: Low
- Troubleshooting Efficiency: High
- Developer Productivity: High

Data Overload Scenario

An organization collects excessive telemetry data from its applications and infrastructure without implementing proper sampling, filtering, or aggregation mechanisms. This results in overwhelming data volumes, increased storage costs, and degraded performance of observability systems. Recommendations to mitigate include:

- Sampling strategies: Consider implementing intelligent sampling strategies to selectively collect representative data samples while reducing data volumes and preserving observability coverage.
- Filtering techniques: Employ filtering mechanisms to discard irrelevant or redundant data points, focus on high-value metrics and events, and minimize noise in observability data.
- Data retention policies: Use aggregation techniques and data retention policies to summarize and condense telemetry data into meaningful aggregates or statistical summaries, reducing storage requirements and improving query performance.

One way to categorize the implications of this scenario and the potential impact is as follows. It will be used in the "Prioritization Framework" section later in this chapter.

- Standardization: Low
- Reliability: Low
- Performance: Medium

- Security: Low
- Troubleshooting Efficiency: Low
- Developer Productivity: Medium

Real World Scenario

Alert Fatigue at Jupiterian

Riley had been hearing from engineers on call at Jupiterian that the number of on-call pages were too high, many of the runbooks for the alerts were out of date, and many of the pages were not actionable. Upon reviewing the reports from the on-call product Jupiterian used, Riley saw some concerning data. Over the last 6 months, the number of pages had grown linearly. As of today, on-callers were averaging almost five pages a day. The growth in pages correlated with the rollout and adoption of Watchwhale. Riley wondered whether there was a causal relationship. Upon investigating, she found that the bulk of the pages were indeed coming from Watchwhale.

While Riley was pleased with the adoption of Watchwhale, she was concerned about on-call burnout and the potential of missing critical alerts due to alert fatigue. She believed Jupiterian might be suffering from an observability antipattern and that better governance processes were needed. As a start, she collected relevant on-call data, including pages per team over time, the last runbook modification date, and outage mean time to recovery (MTTR). She presented the findings at the next architecture review meeting and proposed starting a monthly operation review meeting. The architects were unaware of the operational burden the on-callers were experiencing and supported creating an operation review meeting. Next, Riley presented the data to the VP of Engineering and asked for engineering capacity to improve operations. He supported the proposal. Over the next quarter, Riley worked with engineering teams to reduce pages by 50 percent while also reducing MTTR by 5 percent. Her manager awarded her a one-time bonus as a result of the outcome.

Company Culture Implications

Company culture is another critical piece of the observability ecosystem that may be overlooked. How a company operates and behaves can significantly impact how it implements and achieves observability. As a result, understanding and leveraging the positive aspects of your company culture can help accelerate your observability journey. At the same time, you should be aware of the negative aspects of your company culture, as they can hinder your observability journey. Fostering a culture of collaboration, continuous learning, and proactive problem-solving is essential for leveraging observability to its fullest potential and driving sustained improvements in system performance and reliability.

The success of observability initiatives is heavily influenced by company culture and several antipatterns and pitfalls can hinder effective implementation. In addition, symptoms, such as low developer velocity and employee churn, which are indicative of issues, are often overlooked. Examples of company culture antipatterns specific to observability include:

- Silos and lack of collaboration: A culture characterized by silos and departmentalism can impede collaboration and knowledge sharing, making it difficult to implement observability initiatives effectively across teams and departments. In addition, operating observability tools in isolated silos within different teams hinders collaboration, knowledge sharing, and collective problem-solving.
- Lack of ownership and accountability: A culture that lacks ownership and accountability for observability practices can result in a lack of initiative and responsibility for monitoring and troubleshooting issues. Without clear ownership and accountability, observability efforts may lack direction and follow-through.
- Short-term thinking: A culture focused on short-term results and immediate firefighting can neglect long-term observability goals and investments. Organizations may prioritize quick fixes over proactive measures to improve observability, leading to recurring issues and technical debt. In addition, short-term thinking may result in short-term fixes, such as relying on manual interventions and ad hoc troubleshooting processes, causing inefficiencies and delays in incident resolution.

Examples of company culture pitfalls specific to observability include:

- Underestimating the importance of observability culture: Neglecting cultural and organizational factors, such as resistance to change or lack of collaboration, can hinder observability initiatives.
- Misalignment of incentives: A lack of alignment between individual and organizational incentives can undermine observability efforts. If employees are not incentivized to prioritize observability practices or share observability data, they may prioritize other tasks or activities more directly tied to their incentives.
- Complexity of distributed systems: Challenges associated with monitoring and troubleshooting distributed systems, such as increased interdependencies and diverse technology stacks, can result in operational issues impacting the business and observability practices. Distributed system complexity will be explored in Chapter 11, "Observability at Scale."
- Lack of training and education: Failing to provide adequate training and education on observability principles and tools can result in low adoption rates and underutilization of

observability practices. As a result, employees may lack the necessary skills and knowledge to leverage observability tools effectively.

- Lack of continuous improvement: Failing to foster a culture of continuous improvement in observability practices can lead to complacency and stagnation. Organizations may miss opportunities to evolve and optimize their observability efforts over time, resulting in suboptimal outcomes.

Given these potential antipatterns and pitfalls, what should you do? First, get to know your company culture very well. Determine which aspects you should leverage and which aspects you need to watch carefully. For items you can control, such as training and education, ensure that they are prioritized. Remember, many items required to set up an observability platform are not one-time efforts. This is true for most software development projects as well. As such, it is important to understand and measure the progress of any observability project even after it is released. You can likely leverage many existing engineering practices on your observability journey.

You may be wondering how company culture antipatterns and pitfalls would manifest. Examples of the scenarios that could lead to company culture antipatterns and pitfalls will be covered next.

Lack of Leadership Support Scenario

The organization's leadership fails to recognize the importance of observability as a strategic initiative, viewing it as a technical concern rather than a business imperative. Consequently, there is limited investment in observability tools, resources, and initiatives, hindering the organization's ability to achieve comprehensive visibility and understanding of its systems. Recommendations to mitigate include:

- Educate leadership: Provide educational sessions and presentations to senior leadership, highlighting the benefits of observability in driving business outcomes, improving customer experience (CX), and reducing operational risk. Demonstrate how observability aligns with strategic objectives and contributes to the organization's overall success.

- Quantify impact: Quantify the impact of observability initiatives in terms of cost savings, revenue generation, risk mitigation, and customer satisfaction (CSAT). Use data-driven metrics and case studies to illustrate the tangible benefits of investing in observability capabilities.

- Engage stakeholders: Engage stakeholders from different business units (BUs) and departments in discussions about observability's role in achieving organizational objectives and key results (OKRs). Solicit input and feedback from executives, managers, and frontline staff to ensure alignment of observability initiatives with business priorities and operational needs.

One way to categorize the implications of this scenario and the potential impact is as follows. It will be used in the "Prioritization Framework" section later in this chapter.

- Standardization: High

- Reliability: High

- Performance: Medium
- Security: Low
- Troubleshooting Efficiency: High
- Developer Productivity: Medium

Resistance to Change Scenario

There is resistance to change among teams and individuals who are accustomed to either traditional monitoring practices and tools or the current observability platform and its capabilities. Employees may perceive observability initiatives or migration as disruptive or unnecessary, leading to inertia issues, skepticism, and reluctance to adopt new tools or practices. Recommendations to mitigate include:

- Communicate benefits: Clearly communicate the benefits of observability, such as improved system reliability, faster incident resolution, and enhanced CX. Highlight how observability complements existing monitoring practices and addresses the limitations of legacy tools.
- Provide training and support: Offer comprehensive training and support programs to help teams transition to observability tools and practices. Provide hands-on workshops, tutorials, and coaching to build confidence and proficiency in using new observability technologies.
- Address concerns: Address concerns and misconceptions about observability through open dialogue and transparent communication. Listen to employees' feedback, address their questions and reservations, and involve them in decision-making processes to foster buy-in and ownership.

One way to categorize the implications of this scenario and the potential impact is as follows. It will be used in the "Prioritization Framework" section later in this chapter.

- Standardization: High
- Reliability: High
- Performance: Medium
- Security: Low
- Troubleshooting Efficiency: High
- Developer Productivity: Medium

Collaboration and Alignment Scenario

There is a lack of collaboration and alignment between different teams and departments involved in observability initiatives, resulting in fragmented approaches, duplication of efforts, and missed opportunities for synergy and knowledge sharing. Recommendations to mitigate include:

- Establish cross-functional teams: Form cross-functional teams or working groups comprising members from different departments, such as engineering, operations, and DevOps, to collaborate on observability initiatives. Encourage diverse perspectives, skills, and expertise to drive holistic and integrated solutions.
- Define shared goals and objectives: Define shared goals and objectives for observability initiatives that align with organizational priorities and strategic objectives. Ensure that all stakeholders understand their roles, responsibilities, and contributions to achieving these goals.
- Align incentives and recognition: Align incentives and recognition programs to promote collaboration and alignment around observability initiatives. Reward teams and individuals who demonstrate collaboration, knowledge sharing, and contributions to achieving observability goals.

One way to categorize the implications of this scenario and the potential impact is as follows. It will be used in the "Prioritization Framework" section later in this chapter.

- Standardization: Medium
- Reliability: Medium
- Performance: Low
- Security: Low
- Troubleshooting Efficiency: Medium
- Developer Productivity: Medium

Goals and Success Criteria Scenario

An observability initiative lacks clear goals and success criteria, making it difficult to measure progress, track performance, and demonstrate value to stakeholders. Teams may struggle to prioritize efforts, allocate resources effectively, and assess the impact of observability investments. Recommendations to mitigate include:

- Define SMART[3] goals: Establish Specific, Measurable, Achievable, Relevant, and Time-bound goals for observability initiatives, outlining what success looks like and how it will be measured. Align goals with business OKRs, customer needs, and operational priorities.
- Identify KPIs:[4] Identify KPIs to track progress, assess performance, and evaluate the effectiveness of observability initiatives. Choose KPIs that are meaningful, actionable, and aligned with desired outcomes.
- Track and monitor progress: Implement mechanisms to track and monitor progress toward observability goals and KPIs. Use dashboards, reports, and metrics to visualize data, identify trends, and identify areas for improvement.

One way to categorize the implications of this scenario and the potential impact is as follows. It will be used in the "Prioritization Framework" section later in this chapter.

- Standardization: Medium
- Reliability: Medium
- Performance: Medium
- Security: Low
- Troubleshooting Efficiency: Medium
- Developer Productivity: Medium

Standardization and Consistency Scenario

Observability practices and tools are not standardized or consistent across teams and departments, resulting in fragmentation, inefficiency, and difficulty in aggregating and analyzing telemetry data. Recommendations to mitigate include:

- Standardization guidelines: Develop standardized guidelines, best practices, and templates for observability instrumentation and data collection across the organization. Document and communicate these standards to ensure consistency and alignment with organizational goals and requirements.
- Tool rationalization: Conduct a comprehensive review and rationalization of observability tools and technologies used across the organization to eliminate redundancies, reduce complexity, and streamline operations. Consolidate tools where possible to minimize overhead and facilitate integration and interoperability.
- Centralized platforms: Invest in centralized observability platforms or solutions that provide a unified view of telemetry data from different sources and environments. Standardize on a common set of tools and platforms to enable seamless collaboration, data sharing, and analysis across teams.

One way to categorize the implications of this scenario and the potential impact is as follows. It will be used in the "Prioritization Framework" section later in this chapter.

- Standardization: High
- Reliability: Medium
- Performance: Medium
- Security: Low
- Troubleshooting Efficiency: Medium
- Developer Productivity: Medium

Incentives and Recognition Scenario

Employees lack incentives and recognition for their contributions to observability initiatives. This leads to a lack of motivation, engagement, and commitment to driving observability maturity and excellence. Recommendations to mitigate include:

- Recognition programs: Implement recognition programs and rewards to acknowledge and celebrate individuals and teams who demonstrate excellence in observability practices, tools, and outcomes. Recognize achievements, milestones, and innovative solutions that contribute to improved system reliability and performance.
- Performance metrics: Incorporate observability-related performance metrics and objectives into employee performance evaluations and assessments. Tie performance metrics to rewards, bonuses, and career advancement opportunities to incentivize employees to prioritize observability initiatives and invest in their success.
- Team incentives: Establish team-based incentives and rewards for achieving observability goals, such as reducing incident response times, improving system availability, and enhancing CX. Encourage collaboration, teamwork, and collective ownership of observability outcomes.

One way to categorize the implications of this scenario and the potential impact is as follows. It will be used in the "Prioritization Framework" section later in this chapter.

- Standardization: Low
- Reliability: Medium
- Performance: High
- Security: Low
- Troubleshooting Efficiency: Medium
- Developer Productivity: Medium

Feedback and Improvement Scenario

There is a lack of feedback mechanisms and processes for gathering input, insights, and suggestions from employees about observability initiatives, resulting in missed opportunities for learning, innovation, and improvement. Recommendations to mitigate include:

- Post-incident reviews: Conduct post-incident reviews (PIRs) and retrospectives (retros) to analyze the effectiveness of observability tools, practices, and responses during incidents. Capture lessons learned, identify opportunities for improvement, and implement corrective actions to prevent similar incidents in the future.
- Continuous improvement culture: Foster a culture of continuous improvement by encouraging experimentation, innovation, and learning from failures. Embrace a growth mindset wherein employees are empowered to take risks, try new approaches, and challenge the status quo to pursue excellence in observability practices.
- Feedback loop closure: Close the feedback loop by communicating outcomes, actions, and resolutions resulting from employee feedback and suggestions. Demonstrate responsiveness to employee input by implementing changes, addressing concerns, and providing updates on progress and outcomes.

One way to categorize the implications of this scenario and the potential impact is as follows. It will be used in the "Prioritization Framework" section later in this chapter.

- Standardization: Medium
- Reliability: Medium

- Performance: Medium
- Security: Low
- Troubleshooting Efficiency: Low
- Developer Productivity: Medium

Prioritization Framework

There are many potential antipatterns or pitfalls you could experience on your observability journey. As such, it is essential to have a strategy for prioritizing and addressing them. One approach is to define and categorize the areas impacted and by how much. For each scenario in this chapter, the following categories were used:

- Standardization
- Reliability
- Performance
- Security
- Troubleshooting Efficiency
- Developer Productivity

In addition, an impact score of low, medium, and high was assigned to each category. In order to prioritize, you need to calculate a score based on the categories and impact. For example, you could decide to assign a score of 1 for low impact, 2 for medium impact, and 4 for high impact. In addition, you need to determine whether you want to give a higher weight to specific categories. For example, if operational excellence is most important, you might assign a weight of 2x for the security, troubleshooting, and reliability categories. Alternatively, if adoption is most important, you might assign a weight of 2x for the standardization and developer productivity (DevProd) categories. Once you have a formula, you can calculate a score. Finally, you can assign an amount of effort required to address the scored item. With this information, you can assign a priority based on score and effort.

In summary, a prioritization framework for addressing antipatterns and pitfalls could be achieved by:

1. Creating a list of antipattern and pitfall scenarios
2. Creating a list of categories significant to you
3. Assigning a category and impact to each scenario
4. Defining a scoring system based on the impact
5. Defining a weighting system based on what is important to you
6. Calculating the score for each scenario
7. Assigning an amount of effort for each scenario
8. Assigning a priority based on the score and effort

Using the "Mixing Instrumentation Libraries Scenario," you will now calculate a score and determine the priority based on the prioritization framework. As you may recall, the categories and impact listed for that scenario were as follows:

- Standardization: Medium
- Reliability: Low
- Performance: Medium
- Security: Low
- Troubleshooting Efficiency: High
- Developer Productivity: High

If the impact were scored on a 1, 2, 4 score system, then the scenario would have a total score of:

- 14 if unweighted: (2 + 1 + 2 + 1 + 4 + 4)
- 20 if an operational excellence weight were added: (2 + (2 * 1) + 2 + (2 * 1) + (2 * 4) + 4)
- 20 if an adoption weight were added: ((2* 2) + 1 + 2 + 1 + 4 + (2 * 4))

Next, you need to determine the amount of effort required to address the situation. If a low, medium, high scale is used, the "Mixing Instrumentation Libraries Scenario" effort rating would be a high. Based on the total score and effort, you could assign a priority. For example, the highest score and lowest effort scenarios could be assigned priority zero (P0), while the lowest score and highest effort scenarios could be assigned priority two (P2). An example of a priority mapping based on score and effort is shown in Table 10.1.

TABLE 10.1: A 2×2 matrix that could be used to determine priority. On the left is the score, and on the top is the amount of effort. P0 (priority zero) represents the highest priority, while P2 (priority two) represents the lowest priority.

		EFFORT	
		HIGH	**LOW**
Score	**High**	P1	P0
	Low	P2	P1

Using this framework, the unweighted score can be computed for all scenarios in this chapter. A priority can also be determined with the unweighted score and effort, as shown in Table 10.2. The GitHub repository associated with this book has a link to a spreadsheet containing all the calculations.

TABLE 10.2: The results of the prioritization framework for scenarios in this chapter. The unweighted score has been calculated and is the primary sort key. Effort is the secondary sort key. In addition, a priority has been assigned.

SCENARIO	UNWEIGHTED SCORE	EFFORT TO FIX	PRIORITY
Automatic Instrumentation	19	Low	P0
Component Configuration	18	Low	P0
Resource Allocation	18	Low	P0
Performance Overhead	18	Medium	P0
Monitoring and Maintenance	18	Medium	P0
Inadequate Scalability	18	High	P1
Tool Fatigue	17	Medium	P1
Fragmented Tooling	17	High	P1
Lack of Leadership Support	17	High	P1
Resistance to Change	17	High	P1
Custom Instrumentation	16	High	P1
Vendor Lock-in	15	High	P1
Mixing Instrumentation Libraries	14	High	P1
Standardization and Consistency	13	Medium	P2
Incentives and Recognition	12	Low	P2
Goals and Success Criteria	11	Low	P2
Feedback and Improvement	11	Medium	P2
Security Considerations	10	Medium	P2
Collaboration and Alignment	10	Medium	P2
Data Overload	8	Medium	P2

The Bottom Line

Distinguish between observability antipatterns and pitfalls. Observability antipatterns and pitfalls are common mistakes or ineffective practices that hinder the successful implementation and utilization of observability in software systems. By distinguishing between these two concepts, organizations can better identify and address systemic issues and specific errors that hinder their observability objectives.

Master It Understanding the difference between observability antipatterns and pitfalls is crucial for building effective observability practices. What is the difference between an antipattern and a pitfall?

Recognize and overcome common observability antipatterns and pitfalls. Observability antipatterns and pitfalls can happen at any step in the observability journey, be it telemetry generation and collection or telemetry querying and alerting. Remediation depends on the issue being experienced. To avoid over-monitoring and alert fatigue, teams should prioritize key metrics and implement strategic alerting thresholds. Addressing the pitfall of insufficient resource allocation involves ensuring that observability tools and infrastructure are adequately funded and maintained. Overcoming the challenge of inconsistent tagging and metadata application necessitates adopting standardization practices across the organization. Regularly reviewing and updating observability practices, fostering collaboration between development and operations teams, and investing in training can help mitigate these issues, leading to more robust and effective observability solutions.

Master It What is an observability antipattern that the OTel project is helping to mitigate?

Describe the impacts of company culture on observability goals. Company culture has a profound impact on the success of observability initiatives. A culture that values transparency, continuous learning, and cross-functional collaboration will support the effective implementation of observability practices. In contrast, a siloed or reactive culture can hinder these efforts, leading to fragmented observability data and delayed problem resolution. Encouraging open communication and shared responsibility for system health can help integrate observability into the fabric of the organization. By fostering a proactive mindset and prioritizing observability as a critical aspect of operational excellence, companies can achieve their observability goals more effectively, ensuring system reliability and performance.

Master It How can you use company culture to help achieve your observability goals?

Notes

1 `https://en.wikipedia.org/wiki/Big_Bang`
2 `https://en.wikipedia.org/wiki/KISS_principle`
3 `https://en.wikipedia.org/wiki/SMART_criteria`
4 `https://en.wikipedia.org/wiki/Performance_indicator`

Chapter 11

Observability at Scale

Observability in complex systems presents unique challenges that require careful consideration and strategic planning. As systems grow in size and complexity, the volume and velocity of telemetry data increase exponentially, making it challenging to capture, store, and analyze relevant information effectively and inexpensively. Moreover, the distributed nature of modern applications adds layers of complexity as interactions between microservices, containers, and infrastructure components become more intricate. Infrastructure constraints, such as limited resources and scalability bottlenecks, further exacerbate the challenges of scaling observability.

In this chapter, you will explore scalability challenges indepth and learn strategies for overcoming them to achieve comprehensive observability at scale. Many technical concepts will be covered along with the links to additional information.

IN THIS CHAPTER, YOU WILL LEARN TO:

- Identify observability scalability challenges
- Implement strategies to overcome observability scalability challenges
- Describe best practices to scale observability at every step

Understanding the Challenges

To effectively scale observability, you must first understand what makes observability complex and the underlying challenges posed by complex systems. Examples include:

- The sheer volume and velocity of telemetry data generated by distributed applications and infrastructure components. As systems grow in size and complexity, the amount of data produced can overburden traditional observability tools and platforms, making it challenging to extract meaningful insights in real time and cost-effectively.
- The complexity of distributed systems introduces challenges related to understanding and tracing the flow of data and requests across various components and services. This distributed system complexity can hinder visibility and make it challenging to identify and diagnose issues effectively.
- Infrastructure and resource constraints, such as limited storage capacity and processing power, pose significant challenges to scaling observability, as organizations must balance the need for comprehensive data collection with resource limitations and cost constraints.

Volume and Velocity of Telemetry Data

The volume of telemetry data refers to the total amount of data generated by all observability signals across an entire system or environment. As the number of monitored components grows or the load on an environment increases, so does the volume of telemetry data generated. For example, when decoupling a monolith into microservices, the amount of telemetry data will increase. In addition, if the architecture is deployed per region, then as new regions are provisioned, the amount of telemetry data will increase. Of course, this is on top of increases due to more traffic or the need to add more instances.

High data volume, which includes increased metadata, can lead to several issues, including:

- **Processing and storage costs:** Processing and storing large volumes of data can be expensive, especially if real-time analysis or long-term retention is required for analytical or compliance purposes.
- **Data management:** Managing and organizing vast amounts of data to ensure it is accessible and useful for analysis can be complex. Parsing unstructured or semi-structured data is resource intensive and error prone. In addition, enriching and correlating data is non-trivial. Then comes the complexity of managing tiered storage to balance cost and value.
- **Performance impact:** High data volume can affect the performance of observability platforms, potentially causing delays in data ingestion, processing, and query execution, including alerting.

To address these challenges, organizations can implement data retention policies to define how long different types of telemetry data should be stored. For instance, detailed trace data might be retained for a shorter period compared to aggregated metrics. Additionally, techniques such as data compression and efficient storage formats, such as columnar storage,[1] can help reduce the storage footprint. Of course, these strategies are for after the observability platform has consumed the data. Alternatively, data collection strategies, such as filtering, sampling, and aggregation, can be used to reduce the amount of data sent to the observability platform. Regardless of the approach taken, collecting data at the fidelity required to achieve observability and retaining it long enough to handle active troubleshooting and historical analysis is crucial.

DATA LAKES

A data lake is a central place where all data is stored.[2] Typically, raw data is stored in a data lake though processed or transformed data may also be stored. What is more important is that all data from all sources is stored in the same place. Given the volume of data, it is common for a data lake to be an object store, such as Amazon S3 or Apache Hadoop distributed file system (HDFS). A data lake can be thought of as an intermediary between the sources of the data and a platform which can do something with the data. Data lakes provide data flexibility. For example, data can be pulled out of a data lake for processing or transformation multiple times for different use cases. One use case might be for data science purposes while another could be to enrich the data with metadata. While data lakes may be useful, they are also an additional system to maintain, secure, and finance. At the very least, care must be taken to ensure proper data management policies, otherwise the data lake may become a data swamp.

Another consideration is the velocity of telemetry data, which refers to the speed at which data is generated and needs to be processed. In high-velocity environments, telemetry data must be ingested, processed, and analyzed in real time or near real-time to provide timely insights and support rapid decision-making. Key challenges associated with data velocity include:

- **Real-time processing:** Ensuring that data pipelines can handle high-throughput ingestion and real-time processing without introducing significant latency is often vital and difficult to achieve.
- **Scalability:** Scaling the infrastructure, sometimes ahead of time, to accommodate spikes in data velocity, such as during traffic surges or large-scale deployments, is fundamental and sometimes time-consuming.
- **Observing and alerting:** Implementing real-time observability and alerting mechanisms that can keep pace with the speed of data generation to detect and respond to issues promptly is pivotal and often overlooked, at least initially.

To manage data velocity, observability platforms can leverage stream processing technologies like Apache Kafka, Apache Flink, or Amazon Kinesis, which are designed to handle high-throughput data streams. Additionally, edge or ingest processing can be employed to filter and aggregate data, reducing the volume of data that needs to be transmitted and stored. Elasticity of data collection and observability platforms is paramount to handle changes in the amount of telemetry data that needs to be processed. As such, leveraging cloud native strategies, including containerization, and orchestration is *highly recommended*.

In the end, *what matters is the value provided by the data collected*, especially when compared to cost, as shown in Table 11.1. In practice, the value changes based on the amount of time that has passed. For example, retaining minimally aggregated data for hours or days may be essential to performing real-time troubleshooting, while retaining highly aggregated data for weeks or months may be sufficient for historical data analysis. This means that observability platforms must be able to query large amounts of data quickly at various levels of granularity and in a cost-effective way. Most observability platforms handle this by offering tiered data storage with multiple levels of aggregation and different retention periods. To balance costs, different types of persistent stores and caching layers may be required, which can complicate the architecture of the observability platform.

TABLE 11.1: A 2x2 matrix suggesting the order in which to instrument telemetry data and the operation to perform based on the cost of generating the data and the value the generated data provides. Cost includes the overhead and resources required to generate the data, while value indicates the relevance to help achieve observability.

		VALUE	
		LOW	**HIGH**
Cost	**Low**	Instrument later; aggregate or filter	Instrument first; keep
	High	Do not instrument; drop	Instrument next; aggregate or filter

Distributed System Complexity

In the era of cloud native applications and microservice architectures, distributed systems, which refer to multiple components running on different machines that work together as a single system, have become the norm. While these architectures offer numerous benefits, including scalability, resilience, and flexibility, they also introduce significant complexity. Understanding and managing the complexity of distributed systems is an essential challenge for achieving effective observability at scale. Distributed system considerations include:

- Heterogeneity of components
- Service interdependencies
- Latency, reliability, and error handling
- Data consistency and synchronization
- Scalability and performance
- Security and compliance

Distributed systems often comprise a diverse array of components, including microservices, databases, caches, message queues, and third-party services. Each component may be developed in a different programming language, use different frameworks, and have distinct performance characteristics. This heterogeneity complicates the task of collecting, correlating, and analyzing telemetry data. This task is further complicated by:

- **Diverse data sources:** Telemetry data comes from various sources, each with its own data format and semantics. Integrating and normalizing this data for coherent analysis requires sophisticated data processing capabilities.
- **Inconsistent instrumentation:** Different teams may use different instrumentation libraries and standards, leading to inconsistencies in the data collected. Ensuring uniformity and completeness of instrumentation across the entire system is essential for accurate observability—this is where OpenTelemetry (OTel) can help!

In a distributed system, services are interdependent, and the failure or performance degradation of one service can cascade and affect other services. Understanding and mapping these dependencies is crucial for diagnosing issues and understanding system behavior. This requires:

- **Dependency mapping:** Identifying and visualizing the relationships and dependencies between services helps understand the overall system architecture and identify potential points of failure.
- **Chaining failures:** An issue in one service can propagate through the system, causing cascading failures. Detecting and mitigating these chains of failures requires real-time analysis and alerting mechanisms. Even with these mechanisms, identifying the root cause can be challenging.

The communication between distributed components relies on network connections, which introduce latency and potential points of failure. Network issues can significantly impact the performance and reliability of the system. This requires:

- **Latency monitoring:** Measuring and monitoring network latency is critical for understanding the impact of performance on distributed interactions. High latency can degrade the user experience (UX) and system efficiency.

- **Network reliability:** Ensuring reliable communication between components requires monitoring network health and implementing redundancy and failover mechanisms to handle network failures gracefully.
- **Buffer and retry logic:** Applications should implement capabilities including buffer and retry logic to help reduce end user–facing errors or dropped data due to transient issues between services whether network related or otherwise.

Maintaining data consistency across distributed components, especially in conjunction with availability, is a significant challenge. Different parts of the system may have different views of the same data, leading to inconsistencies and potential errors. The CAP theorem,[3] which describes the relationship between consistency, availability, and partitioning tolerance, highlights the challenges. Addressing these challenges requires:

- **Eventual consistency:**[4] Many distributed systems adopt an eventual consistency model, where data is eventually synchronized but may be temporarily inconsistent. Observability tools must account for this. For example, OTel provides instrumentation for popular asynchronous libraries and frameworks. Amongst other things, this instrumentation can ensure that spans within a trace consisting of asynchronous calls are not disconnected with the parent ID.
- **Synchronization mechanisms:** Implementing and monitoring synchronization mechanisms, such as distributed transactions[5] or conflict resolution protocols, is essential for maintaining data integrity.

Scaling a distributed system to handle increasing load involves adding more components and resources, which in turn increases complexity. Ensuring a system scales efficiently without degrading performance requires careful planning and monitoring. Things to consider include:

- **Horizontal scaling:** Adding more instances of services to distribute the load requires observability tools to track and manage these instances dynamically.
- **Performance bottlenecks:** Identifying and addressing performance bottlenecks in a distributed system is more challenging due to the interaction between multiple components. Continuous performance monitoring and profiling are necessary to maintain optimal performance.

Distributed systems spread data across multiple components and locations, increasing the attack surface and complicating compliance, security, and regulatory requirements. Things to consider include:

- **Access control:** Implementing and monitoring fine-grained access control policies across distributed components ensures that only authorized entities can access sensitive data.
- **Data Privacy:** Ensuring data privacy and compliance with regulations such as the General Data Protection Regulation (GDPR) or the Health Insurance Portability and Accountability Act (HIPAA) requires monitoring data flows and implementing safeguards to protect sensitive information.

The easiest way to deal with distributed system complexity is to avoid, or at least minimize, it when possible. For example, the complexity of stateful versus stateless services is significantly different. Stateful services[6] maintain a persistent state across multiple requests from the same or different clients. The state can be stored in memory or external storage systems like a database.

Stateful services are typically required for applications where the context or session data needs to be preserved between interactions. With stateful services, you must ensure consistency, manage state replication and synchronization, handle failover, and ensure data integrity. Stateless services do not retain any state between requests. As such, each request is independent and self-contained, allowing the service to treat every interaction as new. With stateless services, managing distributed transactions and request context is difficult. Still, the main operational concerns include fault tolerance, duplicating data, and idempotency, or the ability to run the same operation multiple times and get the same result.

If a distributed system architecture is required and issues are experienced, the next most straightforward thing to do is throw resources at the problem. Scaling up and scaling out, also referred to as vertical and horizontal scaling, is a tactic that often addresses issues experienced with distributed system architectures, at least temporarily. The primary problems with this strategy are time and cost. While stateless services can quickly be scaled, stateful services may take hours or days, especially when scaling out. For example, Apache Cassandra is a highly scalable, distributed NoSQL database. It can be scaled out by adding new nodes to the cluster. Scaling out often requires adding more than one node depending on the replication factor. When new nodes are provisioned, they are bootstrapped, and then data needs to be rebalanced across the cluster. For large clusters, rebalancing can take a lot of time and put strain on the cluster itself as well as the network. Beyond time, scaling also incurs costs and those costs can be substantial. For example, Apache Kafka can be scaled out by adding more producers, however, for some use cases, the number of producers should be an even number to the number of consumers. If scaling from 4 producers, this means moving to 8, but scaling from 256 producers means moving to 512.

To address distributed system complexity, it is essential to spend time to understand the system and its hot spots or the locations where an architecture is reaching its limits. With this information, you can make the necessary changes to better support the workloads and scale. In summary, the types of required changes may include:

- **Changing how data is sent or ingested:** Schema changes or repartitioning of the data are examples of this approach.
- **Upgrading, especially to new major versions:** New versions are likely to have bug fixes, efficiencies, and new features that can be used to scale better.
- **Using a different technology:** Sometimes, a different technology choice is better suited for the needs of the data being ingested or processed. This may be due to changes in the requirements or the introduction of a better piece of technology for the use case.

LEARNING MORE ABOUT DISTRIBUTED SYSTEMS

Distributed systems are the backbone of modern computing, enabling large-scale applications to function efficiently, reliably, and seamlessly across multiple servers or even across the globe. The intricacies of distributed systems encompass a broad and complex field of study and only a few will be mentioned in this book. Gaining a deeper understanding of distributed systems is essential to designing or maintaining robust and resilient software solutions and is outside the scope of this book. With that said, there is a wealth of knowledge available on the topic, including free articles and videos, such as those on `freecodecamp.org`.[7]

Observability Platform Complexity

Observability platforms take different approaches to deal with distributed systems' complexity. Some optimize around a single persistent store and treat all telemetry data in a similar manner. While this can reduce operational complexity, it often comes at the cost of functionality and performance of the observability platform. For example, not all metrics are of equal importance, so storing them with trace data in a columnar store such as Apache Druid incurs significant and unnecessary costs. Even if cost is not a concern, which it always is at scale, operating Druid at scale is also no small feat and must be considered. Of course, all of these considerations are true of any distributed system, not just observability platforms. Some of these considerations can be mitigated through the use of application performance monitoring (APM) solutions. Others require following best practices for cloud native architectures and DevOps practices.

Distributed system complexity can also exist on the data collection side. For example, some aggregation and sampling techniques require maintaining state and routing data to the appropriate location to function correctly. Taking tail-based sampling as an example, a sampling decision is made after the completion of a trace. This means all spans for a given trace must be routed to the same Collector instance. In addition to routing, the length, size, and duration of a given trace are unknown and, as such, retaining data, usually in memory, for some period of time is required before analysis of the trace can occur. As such, enough resources must exist to store and process the data, and data loss scenarios need to be considered, given only a single Collector instance can be used. In the case of tail-based sampling, strategies including trace ID–based routing and in-memory storage solutions such as Redis can be used to help mitigate the concerns. Of course, adding these features introduces further complexity and considerations to the environment.

Infrastructure and Resource Constraints

As organizations scale their applications and infrastructure, observability platforms must also scale to keep pace with the increased complexity and volume of telemetry data. However, this growth introduces significant challenges related to infrastructure and resource constraints, including:

- **Hardware and resource limitations:** Scaling observability platforms involves managing hardware and resource limitations, including compute power, memory, storage, and network bandwidth. As the volume of telemetry data grows, the demands on these resources increase, potentially leading to bottlenecks and performance issues.
- **Cost considerations:** Scaling infrastructure to support observability can be costly. Organizations must balance the need for comprehensive observability with budget constraints. Key cost considerations include cloud or on-premises infrastructure costs as well as licensing and subscription fees.
- **Elasticity and scalability:** To effectively handle infrastructure and resource constraints, observability platforms must be designed for elasticity and scalability. Key strategies include auto-scaling, distributed processing, and edge or ingest processing.

Optimizing the performance of observability platforms is essential to manage infrastructure and resource constraints effectively. Techniques include:

- **Efficient data processing pipelines:** Designing pipelines capable of handling high-throughput data streams minimizes resource consumption and processing delays.

- **Data retention policies:** Implementing data retention policies that define the duration for which different types of telemetry data are stored helps manage storage costs and resource utilization.
- **Compression and serialization:** Using compression algorithms and efficient serialization formats reduces the storage footprint and speeds up data transmission and processing.
- **Throttles and limits:** Configuring capabilities, such as throttles and limits, can be used to control the amount of data being processed.

While scaling systems is an easy way to overcome many challenges, it is sometimes impossible due to infrastructure or resource constraints. These constraints may be because of the technology being used or the environment in which the technology is being run. In most cloud native environments, infrastructure and resource constraints are often not the bottleneck. Instead, cost and performance are the primary concerns. As such, infrastructure resource maintenance is required, including proper capacity management and financial operations (FinOps) practices.[8]

Strategies for Scaling Observability

Scaling observability requires adopting strategies that address the unique challenges posed by complex and dynamic systems. One key strategy is prioritizing elasticity, which involves deploying observability tools and platforms that can dynamically scale to handle increasing data volumes and processing demands. Relatedly, leveraging cloud native technology can make it easier to address scale. Outside of infrastructure, another strategy is to implement data aggregation, filtering, and sampling features, which involve selectively collecting and aggregating telemetry data to reduce storage and processing overhead while still capturing relevant information.

Elasticity, Elasticity, Elasticity!

Elasticity[9] is a fundamental concept in modern cloud native environments. It refers to the ability of a system to adapt to workload changes by provisioning and de-provisioning resources in an automatic and dynamic manner. In doing so, elasticity ensures that a system can handle peak loads and scale back during low-demand periods ideally without manual intervention. For example, the telemetry data generated may vary based on the environment workload. The workload pattern may change based on the time of day or day of the week. Increased telemetry data in an environment would likely result in increased CPU (central processing unit) usage on systems processing that telemetry data. For elastic systems, this increase in utilization could be detected and trigger a horizontal scaling event.

Automatic horizontal scaling, or just auto-scaling, refers to the automatic adjustment of the number of resources allocated to an application, typically compute and memory. To increase or decrease the number of resources, instances of the application are added or removed. Of course, auto-scaling is a reactive behavior; failure to scale in advance of increased load can result in application issues, including dropped telemetry data. If the seasonality[10] of traffic patterns is known, you can scale an environment proactively before the additional load.

As mentioned previously in the "Distributed System Complexity" section, scaling up or scaling out can be a way to address complexity. For stateless services, leveraging an auto-scaler is highly recommended. For Kubernetes (K8s) environments, the HorizontalPodAutoscaler (HPA) can dynamically scale workloads based on defined metrics, such as CPU utilization (`https://kubernetes.io/docs/tasks/run-application/horizontal-pod-autoscale`). For example, you may implement a simple HPA like the following: `kubectl autoscale deployment my-app --cpu-percent=75 --min=3 --max=10`. This HPA would then attempt to maintain an average CPU utilization of all pods of `my-app` to 75% while ensuring a minimum of three pods, likely for availability reasons, and a maximum of ten pods, likely for cost reasons. Of course, cloud providers, including AWS,[11] also offer auto-scaling capabilities.

Auto-scalers are great for environments where the load may vary for periods of time within reasonable bounds. Typically, auto-scalers are configured with limits (`--min=3 --max=10`) in addition to thresholds (`--cpu-percent=75`) for activation. This is because environments have certain capacity limits, as described in this chapter's "Infrastructure and Resource Constraints" section. In addition, undefined scaling can result in substantial cost or insufficient fault tolerance if too many instances are added or removed. It is important to note that auto-scalers are reactive and may not be sufficient for massive traffic spikes in short time frames. As a result, capacity planning and proper monitoring are essential.

Be careful when using auto-scalers with stateless clusters that pull data, as it may result in duplicated or out-of-order data collection, which can impact observability. For example, the `hostmetricsreceiver` and `prometheusreceiver` components in the OTel Collector covered in Chapter 5, "Managing the OpenTelemetry Collector," pull data from endpoints. Typically, when using these receivers, the Collector runs in agent mode or as a single instance per application or host. Sometimes, a Collector may be configured to collect data from a large number of endpoints, such as within a K8s namespace. In this scenario, splitting the data collection responsibilities may be necessary. This would require service discovery capabilities that could dynamically configure the Collector configuration, such as the `TargetAllocator` available as part of the OTel Operator (`https://opentelemetry.io/docs/collector/scaling/#scaling-the-scrapers`). As such, leveraging auto-scaling for this scenario would require additional thought and configuration.

For stateful services, auto-scaling can be more challenging. For example, adding or removing instances from a stateful cluster may take hours or days to complete depending on the amount of data that needs to be indexed or rebalanced. Until the operation completes, certain other operations may be unavailable, impacting your ability to maintain availability or performance of the cluster. In addition to the amount of time it can take to scale stateful services, there are additional considerations. For example, the read versus write ratio should be considered when scaling databases. Scaling databases may only require one type of replica, such as a read replica. In addition, sharding[12] and partitioning[13] may require scaling by a specific ratio of instances to avoid hot spots.[14] For back end services that are queried, such as databases, beyond scaling, implementing data caching strategies, such as Redis or Memcached, can also reduce the load and should be considered in addition to or instead of scaling out.

Be careful when using auto-scalers with stateful clusters that must process data before being persisted. For example, when using the `tailsamplingprocessor` in the Collector, all spans for a given `traceID` must be processed by the same Collector instance. Luckily, the Collector offers a `loadbalancingexporter` which is demonstrated next, that can used in agent mode to route data based on aspects, including the `traceID` (`https://opentelemetry.io/docs/collector/scaling/#scaling-stateful-collectors`). This means agents in front of a gateway cluster configured with the `tailsamplingprocessor` can be configured with a pipeline configuration like the one shown next. The use of auto-scalers for stateful OTel Collector clusters using the `tailsamplingprocessor`, is *not recommended*. This is because if the cluster size for a `tailsamplingprocessor` cluster is changed, a temporary loss of `traceID` stickiness would occur resulting in the possibility of disconnected or inadvertently dropped traces.

```
receivers:
  otlp:
    protocols:
      grpc:
        endpoint: 0.0.0.0:4317

processors:

exporters:
  loadbalancing:
    protocol:
      otlp:
    resolver:
      dns:
        hostname: otelcol.observability.svc.cluster.local

service:
  pipelines:
    traces:
      receivers:
        - otlp
      processors: []
      exporters:
        - loadbalancing
```

Speaking of load balancing, proper load balancing is critical for both stateless and stateful services. While a simple round robin policy can work in many scenarios, some environments require other policies or advanced configurations.

- **Load balancing policies:** A round robin policy is great when all nodes in the pool have similar capacity and the processing load required by each request does not vary significantly. A round robin policy may result in hot spots if a single node goes down, at least initially, if load is not considered. Alternatively, a least connections policy can more quickly balance connections across the pool but may not factor in the processing load of the node.
- **Advanced configuration**: Keepalive[15] settings may be required, including time-out for the client side and connection age for the server side. For example, if connections are not reestablished, then the round robin load balancing policy may not result in an equal connection balance across nodes in the pool.

Leverage Cloud Native Technologies

Implementing scalable solutions for modern observability requires leveraging cloud native technologies, including:

- **Containerization:** A container is a self-sufficient software package that includes everything needed to run an application, including the code, runtime, libraries, and dependencies. In short, a container separates the operating system's responsibilities from the application. The benefits of containerization include portability, scalability, resource efficiency compared to bare metal and virtual machines (VMs), enhanced security including isolation and immutability,[16] and the ability to support rapid deployment and updates. Docker is an example of a popular container technology.

- **Orchestration:** An orchestration engine is a system that automates containerized applications' deployment, management, scaling, and networking. In short, orchestration engines provide lifecycle management capabilities of an application, reducing operational management tasks. The benefits of orchestration include automated deployment and scaling, self-healing capabilities, service discovery[17] and networking including load balancing, declarative and policy-driven configuration, enhanced security including role-based access control (RBAC)[18] and secrets management, and seamless rollout and roll-back capabilities. K8s is an example of a popular orchestration engine technology.

By encapsulating observability components in cloud native technologies, organizations can achieve greater flexibility, scalability, and efficiency in managing observability infrastructure. For example, Docker and K8s help offload responsibilities that would otherwise need to be handled by the application or the underlying infrastructure. Additionally, for workloads running in the cloud, cloud providers offer capabilities, such as object storage[19] and managed databases, which can also help reduce complexity. For example, observability platforms leveraging cloud provider capabilities can efficiently store and retrieve large volumes of telemetry data with less operational complexity. Another benefit of cloud provider capabilities includes built-in support for auto-scaling, allowing organizations to adjust resource allocation based on demand automatically. Alternatively, open source software can be used to provide these capabilities. When deployed via container and orchestration technologies, open source software (OSS) can have the same qualities that cloud infrastructure platform services provide.

Unsurprisingly, OTel provides rich support for cloud native technologies in addition to other environment types, including bare metal and virtual machines (VMs). For example, the OTel Collector has specific receivers and processors to collect telemetry data from Docker and K8s. In addition, Collector packaging for these technologies, including a Docker container as well as a Helm chart and operator, exist. To understand some of the complexity that needs to be managed even in a cloud native environment, assume your applications are partially running in K8s on a cloud provider and leverage serverless and non-K8s compute. Focusing on just the Collector, this environment may include:

- Agents per K8s node and non-K8s compute host
- A gateway cluster to support tail-based sampling or metric transformations as well as possibly receive serverless telemetry
- A gateway cluster instance to collect K8s cluster metrics and events

As you can see, managing the Collector at scale can also be a challenge. In addition to properly leveraging auto-scaling for the Collector, leveraging configuration management tools, such as Ansible or Puppet, is also essential. To help with this, OTel provides the Open Agent Management Protocol (OpAMP), which can be used to configure and manage Collector instances. OpAMP was covered in Chapter 5.

Filter, Sample, and Aggregate

Data filtering, sampling, and aggregation allow organizations to manage the volume and velocity of telemetry data more effectively. Organizations can reduce storage and processing overhead by selectively collecting and aggregating telemetry data while still capturing relevant information. Implementing these strategies requires careful consideration of factors such as sampling rate, aggregation intervals, and data retention policies to ensure that valuable insights are not lost. Data filtering and sampling are similar concepts that can occur in various places within the lifecycle of telemetry data, including:

- **Pre-collection:** Instrumentation can be configured to not generate telemetry data under specific scenarios. Examples include head-based sampling configured with ratio-based sampling as well as instrumentation that filters for and exports specific attributes or drops specific instruments. Performing operations at the source reduces the overhead of generating, processing, and sending data that will eventually be discarded.
- **Collection:** The OTel Collector features a rich set of processors that can be used to reduce or drop telemetry data. Examples include tail-based sampling as well as capabilities to create, remove, update, and delete (CRUD) metadata operations or drop specific signals. Of course, multiple operations can be performed prior to ingestion and the order may matter. For example, you may wish to filter out data before sampling it or may wish to sample it before removing specific pieces of metadata. Performing operations at the collection step allows for more sophisticated mechanisms to be used and helps centralize configuration. Many observability platforms also offer ingestion-based processing, which behaves similarly to the functions the Collector provides, just closer to the persistence layer. The downsides to configuring processing capabilities here include network egress costs and proprietary configuration leading to vendor lock-in.
- **Query time:** Observability platforms may offer features that allow for control of what data is returned for a given query. Examples include role-based access control (RBAC) and normalization of data returned, such as the name or metadata. Performing operations at query time allows flexible and quick redactions or transformations without the need to reprocess data. With that said, given the adhoc nature, expensive transformations are not a good candidate for this approach and vendor lock-in remains a concern.

Saving Costs by Dropping Diagnostic Data

One example where data filtering and sampling may be necessary is with traces and diagnostic data like health checks. Traces generate spans for all transactions by default. For many applications, health checks are a common way to determine the status of an application. Examples of health checks include K8s liveness and readiness probes or load balancer health checks. Given a health check is a transaction, it would result in a trace being generated. Typically, health check traces are not valuable. Reasons for this include health checks being lightweight and when they are not working properly, they already result in an alert or some action.

To prevent health check traces from being generated, you have a few options. Ideally, a head-based sampling policy could be created to prevent the trace from being sampled in the first place. While head-based sampling policies exist in OTel instrumentation, the included policies are often limited and include *always on* (collect everything or always sample), *always off* (drop everything or never sample), and *ratio-based* (collect some percentage of transactions or sample some percentage). This means a custom head-based sampling policy would need to be created to prevent health check traces from being generated. Using the OTel Java instrumentation as an example, a sampler extension could be defined to perform this operation (`https://github.com/open-telemetry/opentelemetry-java-instrumentation/tree/main/examples/extension`). Of course, creating and maintaining custom samplers per language requires extra effort and introduces its own complexity.

Alternatively, the Collector can be used to drop health check spans. In this scenario, the telemetry data is still generated but dropped by the Collector before being sent to an observability platform. The Collector supports multiple mechanisms to drop trace data, including the `filterprocessor`, `probabilisticsamplerprocessor`, and `tailsamplingprocessor`. The `filterprocessor` is a stateless processor and allows for rules to be defined which would drop a specific span (not trace). While this could be used to remove a health check span, if a health check trace consists of more than one span then the other spans would remain. As a result, unless you attempt to drop single span traces, using the `filterprocessor` to drop spans, whether health check or otherwise, is *not recommended* as it would result in a disconnected trace. The `probabilisticsamplerprocessor` behaves like a head-based sampler using criteria such as a proportion to make sampling decisions. Since this processor is an all-or-nothing approach, by itself it would not be that useful to exclude diagnostic data. Instead, the `tailsamplingprocessor`, which is a stateful processor, should be used when attempting to drop traces that contain more than one span (which is most traces). The `tailsamplingprocessor` requires that all spans for a given trace be sent to the same Collector instance. The `loadbalancerexporter` can be used in agent mode in front of a gateway cluster running the `tailsamplingprocessor` to achieve this configuration. The `tailsamplingprocessor` supports rich logic to determine which data to keep versus drop. Given that the `tailsamplingprocessor` is stateful, care must be taken to ensure the Collector is properly sized and monitored.

As you can see, dropping traces containing diagnostic data can be challenging. In the worst case, if diagnostic traces are sent to an observability platform, they could either be configured to be dropped, persisted in a lower-cost storage tier, or be filtered out at query time. In short, there are many ways to filter and sample data depending on your needs. In general, it is recommended that these operations be performed as close to the source as possible. With that said, configuration complexity needs to considered as well.

Data aggregation involves collecting and summarizing telemetry data to provide meaningful insights. In observability, aggregation helps condense large volumes of raw telemetry data into something more manageable and insightful. It is commonly used for metrics and can involve operations such as summing, averaging, min/max calculations, and creating histograms. Data aggregation is also applicable to other signal types, such as building service maps with trace data or performing summarization of logs via machine learning (ML). Data aggregation provides multiple benefits, including:

- **Efficiency:** Aggregating data reduces the volume of telemetry data that needs to be stored, processed, and transmitted, leading to more efficient resource utilization.
- **Clarity:** Aggregated data provides a more explicit, high-level view of system performance, making it easier to identify trends, anomalies, and patterns.

- **Scalability:** Effective aggregation strategies are essential for scaling observability systems to handle data from large, complex infrastructures.

While data aggregation is powerful, it does come with some challenges, including:

- **Granularity:** Deciding on the level of granularity for aggregation is crucial. Too coarse aggregation can obscure important details, impacting observability, while too fine can lead to overwhelming data volumes.
- **Latency:** Aggregating data in real time versus near real-time can impact system performance. Real-time aggregation provides immediate insights but may introduce processing overhead. In addition, care must be taken for observability platforms that are sensitive to out of order data.
- **Accuracy:** Ensuring that aggregation policies do not introduce significant inaccuracies or lose important context is vital. This requires careful design and validation of aggregation logic.

For telemetry generation and collection, OTel provides several features and components to facilitate data aggregation, including:

- **Metric instruments and export interval:** OTel instrumentation offers various metric instruments such as counters, gauges, and histograms that inherently support aggregation, as covered in Chapter 4, "Understanding the OpenTelemetry Specification." For example, aggregating the response times of a web service into histograms helps in understanding the distribution of response times, identifying slow requests, and calculating percentiles for service level agreements (SLAs). In addition, the metric export interval is configurable, allowing you to choose the amount of aggregation.
- **Processors and connectors:** The OTel Collector can use processors to aggregate data before exporting it to an observability platform. In addition, the Collector supports batching, which groups telemetry data for more efficient processing and exporting. The connector component in the Collector can also be used for aggregation purposes, including the service graph connector, which can build a map from trace data.

Observability platforms also provide features to facilitate data aggregation, including:

- **Stream processing:**[20] Allows for real-time analysis and aggregation of data as it flows through the system. Windowed aggregations are also supported with stream-based processing.
- **Rollups and data summarization:** Rollups are a technique used to aggregate fine-grained data points into coarser intervals, reducing storage requirements and speeding up queries. Rollup mechanisms include periodic aggregation, which automatically summarizes data over fixed intervals to retain long-term trends while discarding high-resolution data, and hierarchical storage, which stores data at varying levels of granularity, for instance, high-resolution data for recent time frames and lower resolution for older data.
- **Query languages:** Observability platforms often support sophisticated query languages tailored for timeseries data. For example, the Prometheus Query Language (PromQL) has built-in aggregation functions like `sum()`, `avg()`, `min()`, and `max()`, allowing users to aggregate metrics over specified intervals. SQL-like query languages are also common,

providing familiar structured query language (SQL) syntax to perform complex queries and aggregations. Many query languages also support window functions, which enable calculations over a sliding window of time, such as moving averages, which are helpful for trend analysis.

- **Data federation:** Allows for aggregating and querying data across multiple sources and systems. Examples include performing queries that aggregate data from multiple clusters or data stores, providing a unified view across different environments, and unified access, enabling seamless access and aggregation of data from various sources, such as metrics, logs, and traces.

Real World Scenario

ADJUSTING METRIC AGGREGATION AT JUPITERIAN

Almost a year into Jupiterian's observability journey, Riley had successfully onboarded 90% of the company to Watchwhale. While some teams chose to keep their existing instrumentation, others opted to enhance or replace their instrumentation with OTel. Beyond measuring Watchwhale and OTel adoption, Riley was also interested in measuring and improving operations, including mean time to detection (MTTD) and mean time to recovery (MTTR). To facilitate this, she began investing in synthetic tests to validate system behavior and performance while hopefully uncovering undetected issues. In addition, she regularly attended incident postmortems to understand where problems were occurring and what could be done to improve observability. Recently, her synthetic tests caught an interesting issue.

One of the services for which Riley had added synthetic tests was the checkout service. A couple weeks after being implemented, the tests indicated that the checkout service sometimes experienced high latency and a small percentage of checkout operation tests returned an error. Initially, the team responsible for the service could not reproduce the issue. They indicated that their tests were passing, and their alerts and dashboards looked healthy. The checkout service team had decided to keep their existing instrumentation as part of the move to Watchwhale. As a result, they were relying on Prometheus to scrape metrics from their service and for that data to be forwarded to Watchwhale via the OTel Collector. Given the intermittent nature of the failures, Riley wondered whether a metric aggregation issue could be the reason for the blind spot.

Upon reviewing configurations, Riley noticed that the metric scrape interval for the checkout service was set to 60 seconds. Since the synthetic tests only seemed to fail for around 15 seconds, Riley suspected that the Prometheus metrics aggregated at the scrape interval were too coarse to catch the issues reported by the synthetic tests. To prove her theory, she changed the scrape interval to 10 seconds, and sure enough, the next time the synthetic test failed, the checkout service team's alerts also caught the issue. During the postmortem, the checkout team stated they had changed the scrape interval when they cleaned up the unused and costly custom metrics Riley had reported previously. They thought less frequent data collection would also help save costs and thus made the change. While it did, it also led to a blind spot in observability.

The checkout service team was also responsible for a couple of other services in the environment. They wondered if they should consistently set the scrape interval across all services. Their hesitation included the potential performance overhead of more frequent scrapes and the costs the additional data collection might incur. Riley advised setting the scrape interval between 10 and 15 seconds as she believed this would provide the best observability with the least impact. Riley also knew she had some options to reduce costs in the Collector, such as the interval processor, that could be configured if needed.

Anomaly Detection and Predictive Analytics

As systems scale, the volume of telemetry data grows exponentially. As such, automatic mechanisms to detect and predict issues are becoming more essential. In addition to the traditional strategies for scaling observability, there are also advanced techniques. The two most common are anomaly detection[21] and predictive analytics.[22] These techniques can supplement or replace manual observability.

Automated anomaly detection helps to pinpoint potential issues. It is a technique used to identify observations that deviate significantly from the expected pattern within a dataset. These deviations can indicate unusual or potentially problematic behavior, such as system failures, security breaches, or performance bottlenecks. Anomaly detection techniques include:

- Z-score (or standard score),[23] moving averages,[24] and percentile-based methods to establish what constitutes normal behavior and flag deviations.
- ML models, such as clustering,[25] neural networks,[26] and support vector machines,[27] can learn from historical data to identify anomalies.
- Timeseries Analysis[28] analyzes sequences of data points to detect unusual patterns over time.

Of course, anomaly detection is not without its challenges, which include:

- **False positives and false negatives:**[29] Incorrectly flagged anomalies can lead to alert fatigue and wasted resources (false positives) or missed issues (false negatives).

- **Data quality:** Poor-quality data can undermine the effectiveness of anomaly detection models.
- **Complexity:** Configuring and tuning anomaly detection systems to suit specific environments can be challenging.

Another advanced approach is to implement predictive analytics. Predictive analytics leverages historical data to forecast future events, enabling organizations to anticipate and mitigate potential issues before they occur. Predictive analytics techniques include:

- **Regression analysis:**[30] Predicts continuous outcomes based on one or more predictor variables.
- **Timeseries forecasting:**[31] Models like autoregressive integrated moving average (ARIMA),[32] exponential smoothing,[33] and Prophet[34] forecast future data points based on historical trends.
- **ML:** Algorithms such as decision trees,[35] random forests,[36] and deep learning[37] models can predict future events by learning from past data.

Like anomaly detection, predictive analytics is not without its challenges, which include:

- **Data quality:** Accurate predictions rely on high-quality, comprehensive historical data.
- **Model accuracy:** Predictive models must be continuously tuned and validated to ensure reliability.
- **Dynamic environments:** The constantly changing nature of modern systems can complicate prediction efforts.

Integrating anomaly detection and predictive analytics into your observability strategy is recommended for comprehensive observability at scale. In fact, it is something you should look for when evaluating an observability platform. This integration allows organizations to shift from reactive to proactive management, ensuring issues are identified and addressed before they impact system performance or UX. By leveraging anomaly detection and predictive analytics, organizations can ensure robust observability at scale, enhancing their ability to monitor, troubleshoot, and optimize their systems effectively. This proactive approach is key to maintaining high performance, reliability, and user satisfaction in large-scale, complex environments.

Emerging Technologies and Methodologies

Systems will continue to become more complex and data volumes will continue to grow. Even with all the previously discussed strategies for scaling observability, you may still have challenges reaching the scale necessary to achieve observability. There are multiple emerging technologies and methodologies that could help. Two worth discussing are *serverless architectures* and *edge computing*.

Serverless computing is gaining traction due to its automatic scaling, cost efficiency, simplified management, and improved reliability. Many cloud providers and open source projects are beginning to support deployment on serverless architectures. Depending on requirements, this architecture can be used to scale observability tooling and platforms. Technologies, including Cassandra, Kafka, and OpenSearch, support deployment on serverless architectures. In addition, many vendors support managed deployments. One cloud provider example is Amazon managed streaming for Kafka (MSK).[38]

Another emerging trend is edge computing,[39] which brings computation and data storage closer to the data source, reducing latency and bandwidth use. Use cases for edge computing in observability include:

- **Edge-native monitoring:** Solutions specifically designed to monitor and manage edge infrastructure, including sensors, gateways, and edge servers.
- **Federated learning and analytics:** Techniques that allow ML models to be trained across decentralized data sources while preserving data privacy.
- **Reduced data transmission:** Processing and filtering telemetry data locally to minimize the amount of data sent to central servers. The net result is cost savings on network egress and observability platform processing and storage.

Best Practices for Managing Scale

Scaling observability is not just about handling more data; it involves refining processes and technologies to ensure the observability platform remains agile, responsive, reliable, and cost-effective. From prioritizing data quality and efficient collection methods to implementing advanced storage solutions and retention policies, each step plays a crucial role in sustaining observability as your systems scale. Even at query time, scalable performance is essential to provide timely and actionable insights without overwhelming teams with noise. Beyond the platform, automation and orchestration tools are pivotal in managing the complexities of large-scale observability. They streamline operations, reduce manual overhead, and ensure consistency across diverse environments. Of course, security and compliance considerations must also be integral to your observability strategy, safeguarding sensitive information and meeting regulatory requirements even as data volumes grow.

General Recommendations

There are some general best practices that should be adopted across all observability components, including:

- **Automation and orchestration:** These tools are essential for managing the complexity and scale of observability systems. Automate routine tasks and use orchestration to manage dependencies and workflows. Examples include implementing auto-scaling policies for stateless observability infrastructure to handle varying loads, using configuration management tools to automate setup and maintenance tasks, and leveraging orchestration tools, like K8s, to manage containerized observability components.
- **Cost management:** Organizations must balance the need for comprehensive data collection and analysis with cost constraints to ensure that observability initiatives remain cost-effective. Implementing data lifecycle management policies, such as tiered storage and data archiving, can help organizations reduce storage costs by moving less frequently accessed data to lower-cost storage tiers. Additionally, monitoring and optimizing resource utilization, such as CPU, memory, and network bandwidth, can help organizations minimize infrastructure costs while maximizing observability capabilities. Regularly reviewing and optimizing observability tooling and platform configurations can help organizations identify and eliminate unnecessary costs.

- **Security and compliance:** Maintaining security and compliance at scale is critical to protecting sensitive data and adhering to regulatory requirements. Implement robust security practices and ensure compliance with industry standards. Examples include encrypting data both in transit and at rest to protect against unauthorized access, implementing fine-grained access controls to restrict data access based on user roles and responsibilities, and regularly auditing and monitoring your observability platform to ensure compliance with relevant regulations and standards.
- **Continuous improvement:** Observability systems at scale require continuous improvement to adapt to changing needs and technologies. Regularly review and refine your observability practices to maintain effectiveness and efficiency. Examples include establishing feedback loops to gather input from users and stakeholders on observability performance and usability, conducting periodic performance reviews to identify bottlenecks and areas for improvement, and staying up-to-date with the latest advancements in observability tools and technologies and integrating them into your platform when beneficial.

Instrumentation and Data Collection

At the instrumentation and data collection layer, it is critical to prioritize data quality. Ensuring high-quality data is paramount for effective observability. By prioritizing data quality, you enhance the accuracy of insights derived from your observability platform. Steps to ensure data quality include prioritizing:

- **Accurate instrumentation:** Ensure that all critical parts of your application are instrumented correctly to capture relevant telemetry data.
- **Data validation:** Implement regular checks to validate the integrity and accuracy of collected data.
- **Noise reduction:** Use filtering and sampling strategies to reduce noise and focus on meaningful data.

You also need to implement efficient data collection. Efficient data collection mechanisms are vital to handle the high volume and velocity of telemetry data in large-scale systems. Optimize your data collection processes to minimize performance overhead and ensure timely data availability based on business requirements. This would include:

- **Batching and compression:** Always use batching and compression techniques to reduce data transmission overhead.
- **Edge processing:** Perform initial data processing at the edge to aggregate, filter, and/or enrich data while reducing the load on central systems.
- **Asynchronous collection:** Implement asynchronous data collection methods, when possible, to minimize impact on application performance.

Observability Platform

Optimizing data storage and retention policies is essential on the observability platform side. Scalable data storage solutions and effective retention policies are crucial for managing large datasets over time. These practices help balance storage costs and data availability. Examples of capabilities to configure include:

- **Tiered storage:** Use a tiered storage approach, storing recent, frequently accessed data on high-performance storage and older data on cost-efficient storage.
- **Retention policies:** Define and enforce data retention policies to automatically archive or delete old data based on its relevance and usage.
- **Data deduplication:**[40] Implement deduplication strategies to avoid storing redundant data.

In addition, scalable query performance is also important. As your data grows, ensuring scalable query performance becomes essential for maintaining fast and reliable access to insights. Optimize query execution to handle large datasets efficiently. This includes appropriately configuring:

- **Indexing:** Use appropriate indexing strategies to speed up query execution. Remember that more indexing means more cost, so only index what is necessary to achieve observability.
- **Partitioning:** Partition your data to distribute query load and improve access times.
- **Caching:** Implement caching mechanisms to reduce the load on services and improve query response times.

The Bottom Line

Identify observability scalability challenges. Scaling any system is challenging and scaling a system that touches every part of your environment and is critical to the availability and performance of your environment is essential. Recognizing challenges early allows organizations to address data management, system performance, and resource allocation issues, ensuring that observability efforts remain effective and scalable.

Master It Identifying observability scalability challenges is crucial for maintaining effective monitoring and insights as systems grow. What are some things that make scaling observability difficult?

Implement strategies to overcome observability scalability challenges. Once you understand observability scalability challenges, you must have strategies to overcome them.

Master It Implementing strategies to overcome observability scalability challenges involves adopting advanced tools and methodologies designed to handle high volumes of telemetry data and complex system architectures. What are some strategies you can implement to overcome observability scalability challenges?

Describe best practices to scale observability at every step. Always remember that scaling observability is not just about handling more data; it involves refining processes and technologies to ensure the observability platform remains agile, responsive, reliable, and cost-effective.

Master It Scaling observability effectively requires following best practices at every step of the implementation process. What are some best practices to scale observability?

Notes

1 https://en.wikipedia.org/wiki/Data_orientation
2 https://en.wikipedia.org/wiki/Data_lake
3 https://en.wikipedia.org/wiki/CAP_theorem
4 https://en.wikipedia.org/wiki/Eventual_consistency
5 https://en.wikipedia.org/wiki/Distributed_transaction
6 https://en.wikipedia.org/wiki/State_(computer_science)
7 https://www.freecodecamp.org/news/design-patterns-for-distributed-systems/#heading-common-challenges-in-distributed-systems
8 https://www.finops.org/introduction/what-is-finops
9 https://en.wikipedia.org/wiki/Elasticity_(system_resource)
10 https://en.wikipedia.org/wiki/Seasonality
11 https://aws.amazon.com/autoscaling
12 https://en.wikipedia.org/wiki/Shard_(database_architecture)
13 https://en.wikipedia.org/wiki/Partition_(database)
14 https://en.wikipedia.org/wiki/Hot_spot_(computer_programming)
15 https://en.wikipedia.org/wiki/Keepalive
16 https://en.wikipedia.org/wiki/Immutable_object
17 https://en.wikipedia.org/wiki/Service_discovery
18 https://en.wikipedia.org/wiki/Role-based_access_control
19 https://en.wikipedia.org/wiki/Object_storage
20 https://en.wikipedia.org/wiki/Stream_processing
21 https://en.wikipedia.org/wiki/Anomaly_detection
22 https://en.wikipedia.org/wiki/Predictive_analytics
23 https://en.wikipedia.org/wiki/Standard_score
24 https://en.wikipedia.org/wiki/Moving_average
25 https://en.wikipedia.org/wiki/Cluster_analysis
26 https://en.wikipedia.org/wiki/Neural_network_(machine_learning)
27 https://en.wikipedia.org/wiki/Support_vector_machine
28 https://en.wikipedia.org/wiki/Change_detection
29 https://en.wikipedia.org/wiki/False_positives_and_false_negatives
30 https://en.wikipedia.org/wiki/Regression_analysis
31 https://en.wikipedia.org/wiki/Time_series
32 https://en.wikipedia.org/wiki/Autoregressive_integrated_moving_average
33 https://en.wikipedia.org/wiki/Exponential_smoothing
34 https://facebook.github.io/prophet
35 https://en.wikipedia.org/wiki/Decision_tree_learning
36 https://en.wikipedia.org/wiki/Random_forest
37 https://en.wikipedia.org/wiki/Deep_learning
38 https://docs.aws.amazon.com/msk/latest/developerguide/serverless.html
39 https://en.wikipedia.org/wiki/Edge_computing
40 https://en.wikipedia.org/wiki/Data_deduplication

Chapter 12

The Future of Observability

As technology continues to evolve at an unprecedented pace, the future of observability stands at the intersection of innovation and necessity. Observability in complex systems presents unique challenges that require careful consideration and strategic planning. As systems grow in size and complexity, the volume and velocity of telemetry data increase exponentially, making it challenging to capture, store, and analyze relevant information effectively. Moreover, the growing complexity of modern architectures, driven by trends such as microservices, serverless computing, edge computing, and artificial intelligence, demands increasingly sophisticated observability solutions. These advancements are not just about keeping up with the pace of change but about harnessing new capabilities to drive insights, enhance performance, and ensure reliability in dynamic environments.

In this chapter, you will explore the emerging trends, technologies, and methodologies that will shape the future of observability. From the integration of machine learning and artificial intelligence to the rise of observability in edge and serverless contexts, you will examine how these developments will transform how organizations monitor, manage, and optimize their systems. You will also consider the challenges and opportunities that lie ahead, preparing you to stay ahead of the curve in the ever-evolving landscape of observability.

IN THIS CHAPTER, YOU WILL LEARN TO:

- Approach observability cost management
- Leverage artificial intelligence in observability
- Future-proof observability practices

Challenges and Opportunities

The increasing complexity of modern environments, characterized by distributed systems, microservices, and multi-cloud architectures, presents significant obstacles to achieving observability. Organizations must navigate cost, complexity, and compliance issues while integrating observability seamlessly into their continuous integration and continuous delivery (CI/CD) pipelines. However, these challenges also bring opportunities for innovation. Balancing these challenges and opportunities will be crucial for organizations aiming to stay ahead in the dynamic landscape of observability.

Cost

Vendor-agnostic telemetry generation and processing was arguably the most crucial issue in observability, but it is now becoming a solved problem thanks to open standards like

OpenTelemetry (OTel). As a result, ever-increasing costs are emerging as the most significant concern for organizations striving to maintain comprehensive visibility into their systems. As applications and infrastructure scale, the volume of telemetry data grows exponentially. This surge in data requires substantial storage and powerful processing capabilities to analyze and interpret the information effectively. Additionally, the integration of advanced observability tools, pricing structures, and the overhead introduced by monitoring agents and sidecar proxies further contribute to the financial burden. In summary, cost challenges include:

- Infrastructure costs
  - **Scalability:** As the volume of telemetry data grows, so do the costs associated with storing and processing this data. Scaling observability infrastructure to handle large datasets can be expensive, particularly in cloud environments where storage and compute resources are billed based on usage.
  - **Resource utilization:** Running observability tools requires additional central processing unit (CPU) and memory resources. In addition, network egress costs are usually significant, given cloud provider pricing structures.
- Licensing and tooling costs
  - **Commercial solutions:** Many advanced observability platforms and tools come with licensing fees. Evaluating the cost-benefit ratio as well as usage reporting capabilities to manage costs is critical.
  - **Integration and customization:** Costs can also arise from the need to integrate various observability tools and customize them to meet specific requirements, necessitating an investment in skilled personnel and development time. This is true for both self-managed and vendor-managed observability platforms.

Balancing the need for detailed insights with budget constraints necessitates strategic approaches for observability to remain effective and economically sustainable. There are multiple opportunities to address the challenge of cost, including:

- **Cost optimization:** Leveraging cost-effective storage solutions and efficient data retention policies, as discussed in Chapter 9, "Choosing an Observability Platform," and optimizing data filtering and sampling, as discussed in Chapter 10, "Observability Antipatterns and Pitfalls," can help manage and reduce observability costs. Cost optimization is not a one-time effort but a continuous process as a company grows.
- **Edge processing:** Utilizing tools between telemetry generation and observability platform ingestion is the likely next frontier of cost optimization, as introduced in Chapter 11, "Observability at Scale." This approach can empower users and, if open source, could help minimize vendor lock-in.

BALANCING OBSERVABILITY AND COST EFFICIENCY

Managing cost is one of the most significant challenges in observability, particularly as organizations scale their infrastructures and increase the volume of telemetry data they collect and analyze. Reducing costs requires understanding what data is being collected and how it is used. Once done, strategies can be implemented, including data retention policies to store only essential data for the necessary duration, data filtering techniques to reduce the volume of collected telemetry or drop unimportant data, and leveraging cost-effective observability tools. Additionally, it is crucial to continuously evaluate and fine-tune observability configurations to ensure that they provide actionable insights without excessive resource consumption. Balancing the need for comprehensive visibility with cost-efficient practices is critical for organizations to maintain effective observability without compromising budgets. It should be prioritized before it becomes a real problem. In addition, care should be taken to ensure that steps are taken to reduce costs and do not impact the ability to achieve observability.

Complexity

Complexity also poses a formidable challenge as modern environments become increasingly intricate. The shift towards microservices, containerization, and multi-cloud deployments introduces numerous interdependencies and dynamic components, making maintaining a coherent and comprehensive observability strategy challenging. Integrating various observability tools to collect, process, and analyze telemetry data from diverse sources requires significant expertise and coordination. The sheer volume and variety of data can overwhelm teams, complicating the task of filtering and correlating relevant information to generate actionable insights. Moreover, ensuring consistent observability practices across different environments and services adds another layer of complexity. In summary, complexity challenges include:

- Integration challenges
  - Heterogeneous environments: Modern infrastructures often consist of a mix of on-premises, cloud, and hybrid environments. Integrating observability across these heterogeneous systems can be complex and requires robust, flexible tools. In addition, the dynamic nature of microservices and container orchestration platforms like Kubernetes (K8s) adds layers of complexity to monitoring and managing service interactions and dependencies.
  - Multiple observability tools: The use of multiple observability tools can lead to a fragmented view of the system, making it challenging to correlate data across different sources. This increases operational complexity, as teams must juggle different interfaces, data formats, and alerting mechanisms, which can hinder effective troubleshooting and slow down incident response.
- Data overload
  - Telemetry data management: Collecting and processing large volumes of telemetry data, if not managed effectively, can overwhelm teams. Filtering relevant data and correlating it across multiple sources is a significant challenge and, if done incorrectly, can significantly impact observability.
  - Visualization and analysis: Making sense of vast amounts of data requires advanced visualization tools and analytical capabilities. Ensuring that observability dashboards and alerts are useful and actionable is vital to managing complexity.

Addressing these issues demands robust tooling, standardized practices, and effective automation to manage the observability landscape without sacrificing clarity and effectiveness. There are multiple opportunities to address these challenges, including:

- Standardization: Adopting standards like OTel can simplify instrumentation and integration across different systems and tools while reducing the number of managed agents.
- Automation: Automating observability tasks, such as instrumentation and alerting, can reduce complexity and free up teams to focus on higher-level analysis and problem-solving.

THIRD-PARTY OBSERVABILITY

Regarding complexity, holding third-party dependencies, including cloud providers, accountable through observability is highly desirable by end users. As modern systems increasingly rely on third-party and vendor-provided services, the performance and reliability of these external components directly impact the overall system health. However, managing and monitoring these dependencies is challenging and introduces additional layers of complexity. Ensuring that these services meet their service-level agreements (SLAs) becomes critical, and observability plays a key role in achieving this accountability. What end users need is transparent monitoring through unified observability. By leveraging observability data, organizations can use data-driven accountability to ensure proactive SLA management of vendors. As the observability landscape continues to evolve, embracing these practices and technologies will be key to navigating the challenges and opportunities ahead.

Compliance

In observability, security and compliance are becoming more and more critical. As regulatory requirements, such as the General Data Protection Regulation (GDPR),[1] Health Insurance Portability and Accountability Act (HIPAA),[2] and Federal Risk and Authorization Management Program (FedRAMP),[3] become increasingly stringent, ensuring that observability practices align with these regulations is crucial. Telemetry data may contain sensitive and personally identifiable information (PII), which must be protected to avoid compliance violations and potential fines. Implementing robust security measures, such as encryption, access controls, and regular audits, is essential to safeguard this data. Additionally, maintaining detailed logs and records to support compliance audits can be complex and resource intensive. Organizations must ensure that their observability tools and processes do not inadvertently expose vulnerabilities or compromise data integrity. In summary, compliance challenges include:

- Data privacy and protection
  - Sensitive data: Telemetry data can contain sensitive information. Ensuring that data collection and storage comply with data protection regulations is a significant challenge.
  - Access controls: Implementing strict access controls to observability data is essential to prevent unauthorized access and ensure data integrity.

- Regulatory compliance
  - Auditability: Maintaining detailed logs and records of observability practices is necessary for compliance audits. Ensuring that observability tools and processes are audit-ready can be complex and time-consuming.
  - Compliance monitoring: Continuously monitoring systems for compliance with industry regulations and internal policies requires robust observability frameworks.

Balancing the need for comprehensive visibility with stringent compliance and security requirements demands meticulous planning, advanced security protocols, and continuous monitoring to navigate this complex landscape effectively. Opportunities include:

- Security integration: Integrating security monitoring with observability can provide comprehensive insights into system health and security, enabling proactive threat detection and response.
- Automated compliance: Leveraging observability tools to automate compliance checks and generate reports can streamline regulatory adherence and reduce manual effort.

Code

Integrating observability into the software development lifecycle (SDLC), particularly within unit and integration testing as well as CI/CD pipelines, is the next frontier and presents a unique set of challenges. Ensuring that observability is embedded at every stage of development and deployment requires seamless integration with existing tooling and workflows. This integration must be automated to consistently apply observability configurations across all environments, such as instrumentation, logging, and monitoring settings. However, the dynamic nature of testing frameworks and CI/CD processes, with frequent code changes and rapid deployments, can lead to observability gaps if not meticulously managed. Additionally, the need to balance detailed telemetry collection with performance and resource utilization constraints complicates this task. In summary, software development challenges include:

- Integration with unit and integration testing
  - Enhanced test observability: By integrating observability practices directly into unit and integration tests, developers can gain deeper insights into the behavior of their code during the testing phase. Instrumenting tests with telemetry can help capture signals to provide a clearer picture of how code changes impact the system's performance and reliability.
  - Automated testing and observability integration: Automation frameworks can be enhanced with observability tools to continuously monitor and validate the system's health and performance during automated test runs. This continuous integration of testing and observability can lead to more robust CI/CD pipelines, where every code change is automatically tested and monitored for potential issues.
- Integration with CI/CD
  - Continuous monitoring: Ensuring that every deployment is continuously monitored for performance and reliability issues is critical. Integrating observability into CI/CD

pipelines can be complex and requires seamless coordination between development and operations teams.

- Automated testing: Observability should be part of automated testing to catch issues early in the development process. Setting up automated tests that include observability checks can be challenging.

Effective integration demands close collaboration between development, operations, and security teams to align on observability standards and practices. Furthermore, ensuring that observability data is actionable and provides real-time insights into the CI/CD process is critical for identifying and resolving issues promptly, thereby maintaining the reliability and performance of the software delivery pipeline. Opportunities include:

- Shift-left observability: Embedding observability practices early in the development cycle (shift-left) ensures that performance and reliability are considered from the start. This can lead to higher-quality releases and faster issue resolution.
- Observability as Code (OaC): Treating observability configurations as code allows teams to version, review, and automate observability setups, integrating them seamlessly into CI/CD pipelines.

See the Appendix for OTel solutions that can be leveraged to integrate into CI/CD pipelines.

Emerging Trends and Innovations

To discuss the future of observability, you must first understand the direction of the software industry. Over the last decade, there have been multiple shifts, including:

- On-premises to cloud
- Monolith to microservices
- Separate development and operations to DevOps

As a result of these shifts, new technologies and architectures have emerged with the potential to impact observability. For example, Chapter 11 talked about using edge computing to bring computation and decision-making closer to the source and serverless technology to help address scale issues of observability platforms. In addition, Chapter 5, "Managing the OpenTelemetry Collector," talked about the Open Agent Management Protocol (OpAMP), which can be used to manage any agent. As the landscape of technology and infrastructure continues to evolve, so will the field of observability. Some emerging trends can already be seen and are discussed in the following sections.

Emerging Trend: Edge Computing

It seems feasible that edge computing will be a significant part of future architectures. Several open source and commercial edge-based solutions already exist for the observability space. Observability at the edge allows for immediate monitoring and analytics, providing faster detection and response to anomalies and issues, which is critical for applications that demand real-time performance. Additionally, edge computing enhances security and privacy by keeping sensitive data localized, reducing the risk of data breaches during transmission, and ensuring compliance with data privacy regulations. As edge computing continues to grow, it will drive the evolution of observability practices, making them more context-aware, resilient, and efficient. Moreover, edge computing can effectively control observability platform costs and can even be enriched with artificial intelligence.

Artificial Intelligence

While machine learning (ML) has been integrated into observability platforms for a while, artificial intelligence (AI) is emerging as a way to help achieve observability even faster. While ML and AI sound similar, they do have some important differences. ML is a subset of AI and is generally trained on historical data to help understand when anomalies occur. It does this through pattern recognition and forecasting. AI can chain multiple pieces of information or actions together, offering comprehensive decision-making while bridging the gap between humans and machines.

One emerging use of AI in observability is generative AI,[4] which takes natural language processing (NLP),[5] translates human requests into observability query languages via large language models (LLMs),[6] and returns humanly understandable results. The idea is simple: instead of learning proprietary and often complex query languages, you can write questions in natural language and get answers back in natural language. Taking Prometheus Query Language (PromQL) as an example, say you wanted to know how many pods were running in a specific K8s namespace. With an AI assistant, also called a co-pilot, on top of PromQL, you could ask: *How many pods are running in the test namespace?* Notice this question does not even mention K8s. The PromQL required to answer this question is: `kube_pod_status_phase{namespace="test", phase="Running"}`. The user asking the question does not care which observability platform they are using or about the query required to get the answer. What they care about is the answer. An AI assistant makes it easy to go from a human question (such as *How many pods are running in the test namespace?*) to a human answer (5).

Prior to AI assistants, autocompletion was the only other assistance available outside product documentation to construct a query. For example, if you type `kube` in the Prometheus search bar, a list of metric names starting with `kube` will be shown. The limitations of this approach are that you need to know what the name is, for example, `kube` versus `k8s`, and for common names, such as those that start with `kube`. Sometimes not all results were shown, meaning additional manual completion, such as *kube_pod*, may be required to see the name you needed.

Instead of constructing a query yourself, you could also rely on a query built by someone else. For example, built-in or custom dashboards are constructed using queries, and a runbook, which on-call engineers use during an incident, may link to specific dashboards to answer particular questions. Users of these dashboards would not need to understand the underlying query language but may be forced to trust the results if they were unfamiliar with the query language used to construct them.

Determining the number of pods in a K8s namespace is a simple query. AI assistants can also make multiple queries and use results to understand behaviors. For example, a powerful AI assistant would support asking questions like: *Why is the checkout service slow?* This generic question may require issuing multiple queries to check request, error, and duration (RED) metrics. In addition, it would require understanding normal versus abnormal results and metadata analysis to distinguish between the service running in different environments or differences in metadata between slow checkout instances. In short, AI assistants make it easier and quicker to ask any question about your telemetry data, improving your ability to achieve observability while reducing mean time to recovery (MTTR).

Generative AI is only the beginning when it comes to what is possible with AI in observability. Over time, it is reasonable to assume it will be capable of even more capabilities, including being able to:

- Determine important versus unimportant data, helping configure filtering and sampling policies and thus saving money

- Adaptively alert with dynamic thresholds based on historical data and real-time insights, reducing noise and ensuring that alerts are actionable and relevant to the current system state
- Perform root cause analysis (RCA) instead of just problem isolation with data to prove the result
- Automatically remediate issues, including making policy changes to mitigate security problems or rolling back deployments

Even LLMs need observability. A few open source projects have emerged to generate and collect telemetry from LLMs. Some even support OpenTelemetry (OTel), as listed next. In addition, initial OTel semantic conventions for LLMs have been defined (`https://opentelemetry.io/docs/specs/semconv/attributes-registry/gen-ai`).

- OpenLIT (`https://github.com/openlit/openlit`)
- OpenLLMetry (`https://github.com/traceloop/openllmetry`)

Observability as Code

While AI is new and not widely adopted in the observability space, OaC is incredibly common and is a practice that applies the principles of Infrastructure as Code (IaC) to observability. It involves defining and managing observability configurations, such as dashboards and alerts as well as instrumentation and Collector configuration, using declarative code. This approach ensures that observability configurations are versioned, consistent, and repeatable, facilitating collaboration and automation in monitoring and maintaining complex systems. Examples of OaC include:

- Defining metrics and dashboards
  - Metrics: Use configuration files to define what metrics to collect, how to aggregate them, and how to visualize them.
  - Dashboards: Create and manage dashboards as code, specifying layout, panels, and data sources.
- Configuring alerts and notifications
  - Alert rules: Define alerting rules and conditions in code, specifying thresholds and actions.
  - Notification channels: Configure notifications as part of the observability codebase.
- Instrumentation and Collector configuration
  - Instrumentation: Use libraries and agents to instrument code for tracing, ensuring consistent application across all services.
  - Processor configuration: Specify processor settings in configuration files, such as sampling rates and metric aggregation rules.

- CI/CD integration
  - Pipelines: Integrate observability configurations into CI/CD pipelines to automate deployment and updates.
  - Validation: Implement validation steps in the pipeline to check observability configurations for correctness before applying them.

Examples of OaC in practice include:

- OTel Transformation Language (OTTL):[7] As described in Chapter 5, a language for transforming OTel data based on the OTel Collector processing exploration[8]
- OTel Operator:[9] Manages Collectors and provides automatic instrumentation of workloads using OTel instrumentation
- Prometheus Operator:[10] Facilitates managing Prometheus monitoring stack components as Kubernetes resources
- Grafana: Supports defining dashboards as code using JSON[11] or the Grafana Terraform provider[12]
- Terraform:[13] Allows managing observability infrastructure and configurations using IaC principles
- Kubernetes (K8s) custom resource definitions (CRDs):[14] Enable defining custom observability resources in Kubernetes
- Ansible, Chef, and Puppet: Configuration management tools that can be used to automate observability setups

Service Mesh

The rise of microservices architecture has led to the proliferation of distributed and often polyglot systems. One of the biggest challenges in this architecture is security, including:

- AAA, or authentication (to prove identity), authorization (to give permission), and accounting (to create an audit trail)[15]
- Encryption, especially via mutual authentication[16]
- Service identity[17] and access control[18]
- Policy enforcement, including network policies and resource quotas

One way to address this challenge is with a service mesh. A service mesh is a dedicated infrastructure layer designed to manage and control service-to-service communication within a microservices architecture.[19] In short, it sits between services and can inspect and modify network traffic. Popular service mesh technologies include Istio,[20] which uses Envoy,[21] and Linkerd[22]—all of which support emitting telemetry data to the OTel Collector.

Service mesh technology can also provide other capabilities, including reliability, resiliency, service discovery, traffic management, and observability. One significant benefit of a service mesh architecture is that it can standardize the way multiple capabilities are provided within an environment. On the flip side, many of these capabilities could also be provided outside of a service mesh architecture. In addition, deploying and managing a service mesh introduces significant complexity, cost, operational challenges, and security considerations to an environment. For high-compliance environments like FedRAMP, leveraging a service mesh is common.

Specifically for observability, leveraging a service mesh provides an opportunity to enhance visibility and control over microservices communication. By integrating observability into a service mesh, organizations can gain comprehensive insights into the performance, health, and behavior of their services. A service mesh allows for automatically collecting telemetry data from the sidecar proxies that manage service-to-service communication. Furthermore, if a service mesh is already configured within an environment, it enables an easy way to trace requests, offering end-to-end visibility of the entire transaction flow. As mentioned throughout this book, properly enabling tracing is typically nontrivial. A service mesh can more easily solve problem isolation at network boundaries, assuming context propagation can pass between services.

A service mesh also facilitates the implementation of consistent observability practices across all services, ensuring that every microservice adheres to the same monitoring, logging, and tracing standards. Additionally, a service mesh can dynamically adjust observability configurations in response to changing traffic patterns and workloads. For instance, it can enable more detailed tracing during periods of high error rates or disable specific telemetry collection to reduce overhead during peak loads. By providing these capabilities, a service mesh improves the depth and accuracy of observability and enhances the overall resilience and reliability of microservices architectures.

eBPF

eBPF, which stands for extended Berkeley Packet Filter, is a technology that can run user-defined code in the operating system (OS) kernel and respond to kernel events.[23] Like service mesh technology, eBPF can inspect and modify traffic dynamically and efficiently just via kernel instead of network inspection. While eBPF can be used for security purposes, like a service mesh, the focus is on network, runtime, and container security, including deep packet inspection (DPI),[24] firewall rules, and distributed denial-of-service (DDoS)[25] attacks. In addition, eBPF can provide traffic management and observability capabilities. While eBPF is a promising technology, it is not without its challenges. For example, eBPF has kernel version dependencies, has a steep learning curve, and introduces significant safety concerns, given that it often runs in a privileged context.[26]

Specifically for observability, eBPF provides an opportunity to gain visibility into system behavior with minimal performance overhead. eBPF allows for the dynamic instrumentation of running systems without the need for code changes or restarts, making it possible to collect granular telemetry data in real time. This capability is particularly valuable for performance monitoring, security auditing, and troubleshooting, as eBPF programs can capture detailed metrics, logs, and traces directly from the kernel level. eBPF's flexibility enables the creation of custom monitoring tools that can tap into a wide array of kernel events, such as network packets, filesystem operations, and system calls. Since eBPF is extremely resource efficient, it is suitable for high-performance and latency-sensitive environments where traditional instrumentation and data collection solutions might fall short.

eBPF technology is used in multiple ways within the OTel project today, including:

- Go automatic instrumentation (in development): `https://opentelemetry.io/docs/zero-code/go`
- Network Collector (not under active development): `https://github.com/open-telemetry/opentelemetry-network`

- As part of the profiling agent donated by Elastic (in development): `https://opentelemetry.io/blog/2024/elastic-contributes-continuous-profiling-agent`

The Future of OpenTelemetry

The OTel project plays a pivotal role in driving observability standardization efforts. It has made significant progress in addressing the generation, collection, processing, and exporting of the three pillars of observability. As a result, it is well set up to reach graduation status in the Cloud Native Computing Foundation (CNCF). With that said, its work is far from complete, as observability extends beyond the three pillars of observability. While the short- to mid-term roadmap was discussed in Chapter 2, "Introducing OpenTelemetry!" the future of OTel is even bigger. The following sections explore what the future may hold for OTel.

Real World Scenario

OBSERVABILITY AT JUPITERIAN

During the peak holiday traffic, Jupiterian broke its previous checkout record and reported record profits. It did so while achieving 100 percent uptime of its service. As a result, Jupiterian shares rose by over 10 percent. While the engineering team was paged on a few occasions, they quickly identified the issue and implemented mitigation strategies to ensure reliability. All of this was possible thanks to Riley's efforts in implementing OTel and helping establish observability governance practices. As a result of her efforts, Riley was promoted, and a budget was allocated to bring on two more SREs.

Riley was pleased with the process she made over the last year and the improved observability at Jupiterian. Looking ahead, she knew there was more work to be done to improve the availability and performance of the Jupiterian service. Over the next year, Riley was interested in implementing Observability as Code (OaC) at Jupiterian and becoming an OTel contributor.

Stabilization and Expansion

Beyond new major areas of investment, OTel will continue to invest in its existing capabilities, including:

- **Expanded semantic conventions:** The continued maturity of semantic conventions across all signals will take time, but it is arguably one of the most essential things for OTel to complete. It will allow automatic instrumentation to become stable and ensure data portability, thus eliminating another vendor lock-in possibility.
- **Ecosystem expansion and standardization:** The continued growth of the OTel ecosystem with more integrations, plug-ins, and community-driven enhancements, along with efforts to standardize observability practices across different platforms and technologies will always be a focus area for the project.
- **Advanced agent management:** Enhanced capabilities for managing and deploying the Collector will streamline the configuring, updating, and monitoring of agents across complex and distributed environments, ensuring consistent observability coverage and reducing operational overhead.
- **Improved user experience (UX) and tooling:** Enhanced documentation, tooling, and user interfaces will make it easier for developers and operations teams to configure, monitor, and analyze telemetry data, improving accessibility and usability of observability data.
- **Enhanced security features:** OTel will continue to integrate advanced security features to ensure the integrity and confidentiality of telemetry data, including encryption, secure transmission protocols, and access control mechanisms to protect sensitive information and comply with regulatory requirements.

Expanded Signal Support

The three pillars of observability (traces, metrics, and logs) are stable in OTel, but that is not to say that they are complete and done. As discussed in Chapter 2, the metrics and logs signals are in mixed status, with newer components being matured. In addition, some languages are not yet stable for all pillars. Over time, additional stability will be announced, and new components may be introduced to respond to industrial changes. In addition, the profiling signal has been introduced and will mature over the next couple of years. While the existing signals may be sufficient to support future use cases, the future likely holds additional signal types. Examples may include:

- Events, which are treated as a specific type of log record in OTel, useful in determining what actions occurred within an environment.
- Session replay data, typically in binary format, is required to support Real User Monitoring (RUM) or Digital Experience Monitoring (DEM) use cases.
- Crash analytics, another binary-formatted payload, is also required to support RUM and DEM use cases.
- Synthetic data, which is artificially generated data used to simulate user interactions, transactions, or system behavior, to ensure systems are behaving as intended.

- Security use cases and data, useful in auditing and identifying security issues.
- Network traffic analysis, including packet capture (PCAP) or flow data, such as NetFlow, sample flow (sFlow), and Internet Protocol (IP) Flow Information Export (IPFIX), required to gather telemetry data at the network layer.

When people think about OTel, they often think about either telemetry data or instrumentation and data collection. While these are critical parts of the project, what matters is what you can do with the information collected. In addition to telemetry data, there may be a need for other signal types. A great example of the power of standardized telemetry data is the ability to provide context and correlation, as discussed in Chapter 8, "The Power of Context and Correlation," which is powered in part by the baggage signal. Baggage is different from the three pillars of observability in that it is metadata that can enrich other signals.

It is likely that other nontraditional signals are needed—for example, to define and send entity information. An *entity* can be defined as an object of interest associated with produced telemetry data. Examples of entities may include a service, process, or host. You could say that entities are a subset of OTel's notion of a resource, but it seems likely an entity signal will be introduced in OTel. Entities will provide explicit correlation, and this correlation can be used by observability platforms to provide intuitive navigation, including:

- Entity-based dashboards
  - **Contextual views:** Create dashboards centered around specific entities, providing a contextual view of signals relevant to that entity. For example, a dashboard for a microservice might show its performance metrics, error rates, and dependency maps.
  - **Quick access:** Users can quickly switch between different entity dashboards, facilitating rapid navigation and focused analysis.
- Entity hierarchies and relationships
  - **Hierarchical navigation:** Organize entities hierarchically to reflect the structure of the system. For instance, an application might contain multiple microservices, which in turn run on specific hosts.
  - **Dependency maps:** Visualize relationships between entities, such as service dependencies or network topology, allowing users to understand and navigate the interactions and dependencies within the system.
- Search and discovery
  - **Entity search:** Implement a search function that allows users to find entities based on names, tags, or attributes. This provides a quick way to locate and navigate to specific entities.
  - **Auto-suggestions:** Provide auto-suggestions and entity recommendations based on user queries and context.

- Entity aggregation and grouping
  - **Group views:** Allow users to group entities based on specific criteria, such as all services in a particular region, and view aggregated metrics and health status.
  - **Comparative analysis:** Enables side-by-side comparison of multiple entities to identify performance differences and anomalies.
- Entity health and status indicators
  - **Health monitoring:** Display health and status indicators for each entity, allowing users to identify and navigate to entities experiencing issues quickly.
  - **Status dashboards:** Create dashboards that summarize the health status of all entities, providing an overview and easy navigation to problematic areas.

As you can see, entities are powerful, and making them vendor agnostic would help to mitigate vendor lock-in concerns. While it is early for entities in OTel, the concept has the potential to improve the ability to achieve observability significantly. A special interest group (SIG) in OTel is focused explicitly on entities and contains the latest information.[27]

Unified Query Language

As already seen with OTTL, standardizing the language used is powerful. With Collector processors adopting OTTL, it is clear that OTTL will continue to evolve. While not currently in the OTel project's scope, it is possible that one day, in addition to a configuration language, it may offer a query language. Once the telemetry data is standardized, standardizing how it is queried would help provide even more data portability. As mentioned throughout this book, while OTel helps prevent vendor lock-in if used to generate, collect, process, and export telemetry data, it cannot prevent how the data is used within observability platforms. Thus, vendor lock-in can still occur. Typically, the biggest vendor lock-in opportunity outside of telemetry data is the query language, as converting queries between platforms is nontrivial. As an example, it is common for companies to start out using Prometheus and Grafana to handle metric collection, dashboarding, and alerting. PromQL is used to generate the dashboards and alerts. Over time, companies may have reasons to move from Prometheus to another observability platform. When this occurs, they often ask whether the other observability platform has PromQL support, as this would help ease migration. In most cases, the answer is no. The reasons for this are severalfold, including the history and supported capabilities of the observability platform and vendor lock-in. Given the growth and adoption of OTel, if OTel provided a query language, it is possible that companies could force vendors to support it, eliminating another vendor lock-in segment.

Community-driven Innovation

OTel's success is not just rooted in the code or the architecture that underpins it—its true strength lies in the diverse, vibrant community that drives it forward. The open source nature of the project has attracted contributors from a wide variety of backgrounds, experiences, and industries. This diversity fosters innovation, with each contributor bringing unique perspectives to the challenges of observability. Community-driven development enables OTel to evolve at a pace that meets real-world needs, driven by those who are passionate about solving modern problems in distributed systems. While many of these contributions result in enhancements directly to the project, many also happen outside of the project. This is true of both end-users and vendors. As a result, the future of observability will be created by people like you! Whether opening an issue, submitting a pull request, improving the documentation, or releasing a new project, you can and should impact the future of observability. Here are some OTel examples of individual, community-driven innovations that have been released:

- OTel desktop viewer (https://github.com/CtrlSpice/otel-desktop-viewer)
- OTel terminal viewer (https://github.com/ymtdzzz/otel-tui)

The Bottom Line

Approach observability cost management. Effectively managing the costs associated with observability is essential for ensuring sustainable and scalable monitoring practices. Balancing the need for detailed insights with budget constraints enables organizations to achieve robust observability without financial strain.

Master It What are some ways to reduce observability costs?

Leverage artificial intelligence in observability. Integrating AI into observability practices holds immense potential for transforming how organizations monitor and manage their systems. AI-driven analytics can enhance anomaly detection, automate RCA, and provide predictive insights, enabling proactive issue resolution and optimization of system performance. By leveraging AI, organizations can move from reactive monitoring to a more predictive and automated approach, improving overall system reliability and efficiency.

Master It What are some ways to leverage AI in observability?

Future-proof observability practices. To ensure long-term success and resilience, organizations must future-proof their observability practices. By implementing forward-thinking strategies, organizations can build observability systems that are effective today and adaptable to future technological advancements and evolving business needs.

Master It What are some ways organizations can future-proof their observability practices?

Notes

1 https://gdpr-info.eu
2 https://www.hhs.gov/hipaa/index.html
3 https://www.fedramp.gov/program-basics
4 https://en.wikipedia.org/wiki/Generative_artificial_intelligence
5 https://en.wikipedia.org/wiki/Natural_language_processing
6 https://en.wikipedia.org/wiki/Large_language_model
7 https://github.com/open-telemetry/opentelemetry-collector-contrib/blob/main/pkg/ottl/README.md

8 https://github.com/open-telemetry/opentelemetry-collector/blob/main/docs/rfcs/processing.md
9 https://opentelemetry.io/docs/kubernetes/operator
10 https://prometheus-operator.dev
11 https://github.com/grafana/grafonnet
12 https://registry.terraform.io/providers/grafana/grafana/latest/docs
13 https://registry.terraform.io
14 https://kubernetes.io/docs/concepts/extend-kubernetes/api-extension/custom-resources
15 https://en.wikipedia.org/wiki/AAA_(computer_security)
16 https://en.wikipedia.org/wiki/Mutual_authentication
17 https://en.wikipedia.org/wiki/Identity_management
18 https://en.wikipedia.org/wiki/Access_control
19 https://en.wikipedia.org/wiki/Service_mesh
20 https://istio.io
21 https://www.envoyproxy.io
22 https://linkerd.io
23 https://en.wikipedia.org/wiki/EBPF
24 https://en.wikipedia.org/wiki/Deep_packet_inspection
25 https://en.wikipedia.org/wiki/Denial-of-service_attack
26 https://en.wikipedia.org/wiki/Privilege_(computing)
27 https://github.com/open-telemetry/community?tab=readme-ov-file#special-interest-groups

Appendix A

The Bottom Line

Each of The Bottom Line sections in the chapters suggest exercises to deepen skills and understanding. Sometimes there is only one possible solution, but often you are encouraged to use your skills and creativity to create something that builds on what you know and lets you explore one of many possible solutions.

Chapter 1: What Is Observability?

Differentiate between monitoring and observability. Monitoring and observability, while often used interchangeably, serve distinct purposes in the realm of system management. Monitoring involves the regular collection and analysis of predefined metrics and logs to ensure that systems are operating within expected parameters. It is a reactive approach, focusing on known issues and performance thresholds. Observability, on the other hand, is a proactive and comprehensive practice that goes beyond monitoring. It involves instrumenting systems to provide deep insights into their internal states, enabling teams to uncover and diagnose previously unknown issues and anomalies. While monitoring tells you when something is wrong, observability helps you understand why.

Master It What is the difference between a "known known" and an "unknown unknown"?

Solution A "known known" is an issue that you are aware of and understand. Monitoring tools allow you to configure alerts and visualizations of telemetry data to handle these reactive situations. An "unknown unknown" is an issue that you are unaware of and do not understand. Observability tools allow you to ask questions about your telemetry data to help proactively understand what is going on, where, and why in these situations.

Explain the importance of metadata. Raw telemetry data is not sufficient to achieve observability; it must be enriched. Metadata is a crucial piece of enrichment because it provides context to the raw telemetry data collected from various systems. Metadata can include information about the environment, version, location, and other attributes that help in identifying and contextualizing the data points. This enriched context allows for more accurate analysis, correlation, and troubleshooting, making it easier to pinpoint the root causes of issues and understand the behavior of the system under different conditions.

Master It What are the differences between dimensionality, cardinality, and semantic conventions?

Solution Dimensionality refers to the number of unique keys or names in a set. Dimensions increase the width of events and may be indexed by an observability platform to allow for quicker data analysis and insights. Dimensions help with problem isolation by context. Cardinality refers to the number of unique values in a set. High cardinality data may negatively impact an observability platform's performance. Cardinality helps provide problem isolation. Semantic conventions refer to the standardized naming of dimensions. Semantic conventions make it possible to rely on names in dashboards and alerts while ensuring consistency across services and environments.

Identify the differences between telemetry signals. Telemetry signals, the data components that power observability, typically include at least metrics, logs, and traces. Metrics are measured data, most commonly numerical representations, collected over intervals, such as CPU usage or request latency, providing a quantifiable view of system performance. Logs are timestamped records of discrete events that have occurred within the system, offering a detailed and chronological narrative of actions and states. Traces represent the flow of requests through various services in a distributed system, helping to visualize and understand the interactions and dependencies between components. Each signal type provides a unique perspective, and together, they offer a holistic view of the system's health and performance.

Master It Why are there at least three separate ways to collect telemetry data from applications?

Solution Metrics provide small payload, high frequency data that helps measure the health and performance of an application. They help answer the *what* question. Logs provide larger payloads necessary to determine how an application is configured and behaving. They help answer *why* an application is behaving the way it is and *who* made a change. Traces also provide larger payloads with rich transactional information. They help answer the question of *where* availability and performance issues are occurring.

Distinguish between instrumentation and data collection. Instrumentation and data collection are foundational activities in achieving observability. Instrumentation involves integrating code within applications to generate telemetry data, including metrics, logs, and traces, that reflect the internal state and activities of the system. This can be done through manual coding or using libraries and frameworks like OpenTelemetry. On the other hand, data collection involves gathering this telemetry data from various sources, processing it, and transporting it to observability platforms for storage, analysis, and visualization. Effective instrumentation ensures that the correct data is generated, while robust data collection ensures that this data is reliably transmitted and available for analysis.

Master It Given instrumentation, why is data collection necessary?

Solution Instrumentation may not be possible on all applications, such as third-party or managed applications. In addition, data collection can be used to offload processing from the application, including filtering and aggregation as well as buffering and retry logic. Separating concerns between telemetry generation and processing may be beneficial depending on business requirements. Of course, instrumentation can be deployed without data collection and data collection can be deployed without instrumentation.

Analyze the requirements for choosing an observability platform. Selecting the right observability platform requires careful consideration of several factors. Scalability is crucial to handle the growing volume and velocity of telemetry data in modern systems. Integration capabilities are important to ensure the platform can seamlessly work with existing tools and technologies. The platform should support comprehensive data ingestion and processing capabilities for metrics, logs, and traces. It should offer advanced analytics and visualization tools to make sense of the data. Security and compliance features are also essential to protect sensitive data and meet regulatory requirements. Cost-effectiveness and ease of use are also critical factors, ensuring that the platform delivers value without excessive complexity or expense. By carefully evaluating these requirements, organizations can choose an observability platform that effectively supports their operational needs and strategic goals.

Master It How are observability platforms different from APM?

Solution While both crucial for ensuring system health and performance, observability platforms and APM solutions differ in their approach and scope. Observability platforms provide a comprehensive view of entire systems, including infrastructure, applications, and services, by focusing on metrics, logs, and traces to explore unknown unknowns and offer dynamic querying for real-time troubleshooting. A true observability platform will offer APM capabilities. Alternatively, APM solutions rely on the trace signal only and are optimized for predefined metrics such as response times and error rates. While trace data can contain metric and log data, most environments are not sufficiently instrumented to take advantage of this capability. In short, observability platforms offer broader capabilities than most APM solutions.

Chapter 2: Introducing OpenTelemetry!

Recognize observability problems and the need for open standards. Understanding the nuances of observability is essential for maintaining the health and performance of modern distributed systems. One of the primary challenges in achieving effective observability is recognizing the problems associated with disparate monitoring tools and proprietary solutions. These fragmented approaches can lead to inconsistent data, lack of interoperability, and significant gaps in visibility. The need for open standards becomes evident as organizations strive for comprehensive, coherent, and scalable observability solutions. Open standards facilitate the seamless integration of telemetry data across various systems and platforms, ensuring that teams can obtain a unified view of their operational environments.

Master It What is an open standard and why does it matter?

Solution An open standard is a publicly available set of guidelines or specifications created through a collaborative process and intended for widespread adoption. Governed by neutral organizations and free from proprietary restrictions, open standards ensure interoperability, flexibility, and vendor neutrality, allowing diverse systems to work together harmoniously. They enable significant cost savings, foster innovation, and provide a reliable framework for the integration and evolution of technologies. By promoting a competitive market and supporting community collaboration, open standards help organizations achieve greater efficiency and future-proof their investments in an ever-evolving technological landscape.

Explain the history and goals of the OpenTelemetry project. The OTel project represents the convergence of two significant open source projects, OpenTracing and OpenCensus, with the goal of creating a single, unified framework for generating, collecting, and analyzing telemetry data. OTel's primary objectives include providing a vendor-neutral, open standard for observability, enhancing interoperability, and simplifying the implementation of observability practices. By standardizing telemetry data, OTel allows organizations to achieve better insights into their systems, regardless of the underlying technologies or vendors they use.

Master It What does the OTel project provide, and what does it intentionally not provide?

Solution OTel provides an extensible open standard, in the form of a specification, for creating, processing, and exporting telemetry data. From this specification, it offers reference implementations in the form of language-specific instrumentation and a Collector. OTel does not provide an observability platform or back end but instead supports a wide range of open source and commercial platforms, including concurrently sending data to multiple different back ends.

Identify the OpenTelemetry components and project status. At its core, OTel comprises several key components: APIs, SDKs, and the Collector. The APIs and SDKs provide the means for instrumenting applications, enabling the collection of traces, metrics, and logs. The Collector serves as a pipeline that can receive, process, and export telemetry data to various observability platforms, providing flexibility and scalability. The OTel project is actively developed and widely adopted, with support for numerous programming languages and integrations with major observability platforms. Its robust community and continuous development ensure that it remains at the forefront of observability solutions, evolving to meet the demands of increasingly complex system architectures.

Master It Is OTel generally available (GA) and production-ready?

Solution In general, OTel does not use the GA status and instead refers to production-ready components as stable. As of 2024, the three pillar signals are stable: traces, metrics, and logs. Some aspects of the project are in development, including many of the semantic conventions and the Collector. OTel is used in production environments at a significant scale by a wide range of adopters (`https://opentelemetry.io/ecosystem/adopters`).

Chapter 3: Getting Started with the Astronomy Shop

Get started with the Astronomy Shop. The Astronomy Shop provides a hands-on introduction to integrating OpenTelemetry into a real-world application with open source observability platforms. This fictional e-commerce platform serves as an excellent sandbox for experimenting with telemetry collection and instrumentation. Through the prescriptive guidance in this chapter, you learned the foundational steps of implementing OpenTelemetry, including adding instrumentation to track critical metrics, logs, and traces.

Master It Which components of the OTel project does the demo application showcase?

Solution The Astronomy Shop showcases the stable functionality of the project, including signal support for instrumentation and data collection. In addition to OTel, it also showcases open source observability platforms.

Customize the Astronomy Shop. The Astronomy Shop is batteries-included, meaning it showcases all the stable functionality OTel has to offer out of the box. Customizing the Astronomy Shop allows you to tailor the observability setup to meet your specific needs and requirements. By modifying the default configurations and adding custom instrumentation, you can learn about OTel and observability platforms while focusing on the most relevant aspects of the application for your use case. Customization ensures that you can derive maximum value from the telemetry data collected, making your observability efforts more meaningful and actionable.

Master It In order to send telemetry data to a different observability platform, which OTel component would you change and how would you change it?

Solution The OTel Collector extra YAML configuration would need to be changed by adding one or more exporters and overriding the service pipeline configuration. Once done, either the Collector service or the demo application must be restarted.

Walk through troubleshooting scenarios. The Astronomy Shop supports enabling troubleshooting scenarios to highlight the power of OTel and observability solutions. Walking through troubleshooting scenarios with the Astronomy Shop demonstrates the practical utility of OTel and observability platforms in diagnosing and resolving issues. Through real-world examples, you learned how to utilize the collected telemetry data to identify performance bottlenecks and trace errors, and to understand system behavior under various conditions. These scenarios highlight the importance of comprehensive observability in maintaining application reliability and performance.

Master It How do you enable troubleshooting scenarios in the Astronomy Shop?

Solution With the Astronomy Shop either started or stopped, edit the JSON configuration file located at src/flagd/demo.flagd.json and for the scenario desired, change the default variant to "on". Save the changes. You can also increase the load from the load generator UI at `http://localhost:8080` loadgen. Select Edit in the upper-right header section, increase the number of users, and then select Start Swarming.

Chapter 4: Understanding the OpenTelemetry Specification

Distinguish between OpenTelemetry versioning and stability, including support guarantees. Understanding the OTel specification is helpful for effectively implementing and leveraging its capabilities in your observability practices. A key aspect of this is distinguishing between OTel versioning and stability. OTel follows a clear versioning strategy where different components, such as APIs, SDKs, and protocols, are versioned independently. This allows for gradual and nondisruptive upgrades. Stability guarantees are provided for versions 1.0 and greater, ensuring that once a version is marked stable, it will be supported and maintained with backward compatibility. This stability is essential for building reliable and predictable observability solutions.

Master It What are the long-term support guarantees for OTel?

Solution Once stable, the API guarantees backward compatibility for at least three years after the next major release, while the SDK and contrib are guaranteed for at least one year.

Understand the OpenTelemetry data model, including protocol support and OTLP. OTel defines a data model, which standardizes how signals, including metrics, logs, and traces, are structured and transmitted. The OTel Protocol (OTLP) is a significant part of this model, providing a unified and efficient way to export telemetry data to various backends. Understanding the data model and protocol support helps to ensure that your telemetry data is consistent, interoperable, and can be effectively processed and analyzed across different systems and platforms.

Master It How is OTLP leveraged in OTel, and what value does it provide?

Solution OTLP is the default data format and protocol method for OTel. All data generated or processed by OTel components, such as instrumentation and data collection mechanisms, is done in OTLP format. Communication between OTel components as well as from OTel components to observability platforms is optimized for the OTLP protocol. OTLP allows the OTel project to be extensible and vendor-agnostic. It provides a superset of capabilities to support open standards and commercial requirements. It enables the project to receive data in one format but export it in another.

Differentiate between the OpenTelemetry API and SDK. The OTel API and SDK are intentionally separated given the concerns they address are different. The OTel API defines the standard interfaces and abstractions for generating telemetry data, ensuring a consistent way to instrument applications. The SDK implements these interfaces, including functionalities like data processing, exporting, and resource management.

Master It Who or what typically implements the OTel API and SDK?

Solution Since the API provides interfaces necessary to generate, but not emit, telemetry data, it is typically implemented by automatic instrumentation or manually by software development teams. The SDK includes the API and provides interfaces necessary to configure, process, and export telemetry data. It can also be implemented by automatic instrumentation and software development teams. In addition, it can be implemented by DevOps teams and SREs through environment variables and runtime parameters.

Chapter 5: Managing the OpenTelemetry Collector

Distinguish between agent and gateway mode. The Collector comes in various packaging and can be deployed in two primary modes: agent and gateway. Each mode provides capabilities that may be beneficial when processing telemetry data. While using the Collector is not required, deploying at least the agent to separate telemetry generation from processing and exporting is highly recommended.

Master It What is the difference between agent and gateway mode?

Solution In agent mode, the Collector runs as a local agent on the same host as the instrumented applications, collecting telemetry data directly from these applications. This setup is ideal for environments where you must gather data from multiple sources with minimal latency. On the other hand, gateway mode involves deploying the Collector as a centralized service, which aggregates telemetry data from multiple agents or directly from applications across the network. This mode is particularly useful for centralized processing, transformation, and export of telemetry data to various backends, offering scalability and centralized management.

Identify Collector components. The Collector is composed of several key components that work together to facilitate the collection, processing, and export of telemetry data. These components include receivers, processors, exporters, connectors, and extensions. Receivers are responsible for ingesting telemetry data from various sources, such as applications and other telemetry producers. Processors provide the capability to modify, filter, and enrich the data as it flows through the Collector. Exporters are used to send the processed data to different observability backends. Connectors are both receivers and exporters and are used to process or reprocess data after the completion of a pipeline. Extensions add functionality to the Collector, such as health checks and authentication mechanisms.

Master It When getting started, what are the most essential components to configure?

Solution Receivers and exporters. With these components, you can get data flowing through the Collector. If OTel instrumentation is leveraged and an observability platform that supports receiving data in OTLP is used, then the OTLP receiver and exporter may be sufficient to get started. Depending on your environment and services, you may want to configure additional receivers, such as the host metric or Docker stats receiver. Over time, and as you move to production, you will likely need one or more processors to aggregate, filter, or modify the data. In addition, one or more extensions, such as the health check extension, may be needed.

Configure and run the Collector. Configuring and running the Collector involves defining the appropriate settings for its components and ensuring that it operates efficiently within your environment. Configuration is typically done through YAML files. You define and configure receivers, processors, exporters, connectors, and extensions settings in each file. To run the Collector, you must ensure that it is properly installed and the configuration file is correctly set up. Depending on your infrastructure, you can run the Collector in various form factors, including a stand-alone application, Docker container, or K8s pod. By carefully configuring the Collector, you can ensure that it collects, processes, and exports telemetry data effectively, providing valuable insights into your system's performance and behavior.

Master It How are Collector components configured?

Solution The Collector is primarily configured via YAML files. Collector component configuration is a two-step process. First, receivers, processors, exporters, connectors, and extensions need to be defined. While all components come with default settings, you may be required to specify certain settings and may want to change some default settings. All of this is done when defining the component. Defining and configuring the component does not enable it. Next, you need to enable components. All components except extensions are enabled as part of one or more service pipelines. Service pipelines are signal specific. Extensions are enabled in the top-level service section (outside of pipelines).

Size, secure, observe, and troubleshoot the Collector. Proper sizing, securing, observing, and troubleshooting of the OTel Collector are critical to maintaining its performance and reliability. Sizing involves allocating sufficient resources, such as CPU and memory, to handle the expected volume of telemetry data without bottlenecks. Securing the Collector includes implementing authentication and encryption to protect telemetry data in transit and at rest. Observing the Collector entails monitoring its performance metrics, such as throughput and latency, to ensure that it operates within acceptable parameters. Troubleshooting involves diagnosing and resolving issues, such as misconfigurations or resource constraints, that may impact the Collector's functionality. You can maintain a robust and secure observability infrastructure that meets your organization's needs by addressing these aspects.

Master It Which components can be used to observe and troubleshoot the Collector?

Solution Prometheus telemetry metrics (OTel metrics coming soon), the debug exporter, and zPages extensions can and should all be configured and enabled to ensure proper observability and troubleshooting of the Collector.

Chapter 6: Leveraging OpenTelemetry Instrumentation

Instrument an application in various ways. Successfully instrumenting an application involves understanding and utilizing the different methods available to collect telemetry data. OTel offers versatile options for instrumentation, including automatic, manual, programmatic, and mixed approaches. You can choose the approach that best fits your application's architecture and observability needs, ensuring comprehensive data collection with minimal overhead.

Master It What is the difference between the automatic, manual, programmatic, and mixed methods of instrumentation?

Solution

- Automatic instrumentation leverages prebuilt integrations that are injected at runtime to automatically capture telemetry data without code changes, reducing the effort required to get started. While it is the easiest way to add instrumentation, it is limited in what it can instrument and how it can be configured. It may also introduce more overhead compared to manual instrumentation.
- Manual instrumentation involves directly adding OpenTelemetry API calls to your application code, providing fine-grained control over the data collected. While this is the hardest way to add instrumentation, it is also the most flexible way.
- Programmatic instrumentation is added directly to the code and ensures that commonly used frameworks and libraries seamlessly integrate with OpenTelemetry, further simplifying the process. It abstracts many concepts, making it easier to add while still being quite flexible. Programmatic instrumentation is library-or framework-specific and thus limited in the amount of code it supports.
- Mixed instrumentation is a combination of automatic and manual instrumentation. It can provide the best of both worlds, easing initial instrumentation and providing full flexibility to extend instrumentation in code.

Add production-ready instrumentation. Transitioning from initial instrumentation, like what can be found in the OTel getting started guides, to a production-ready state requires a focus on robustness, scalability, and minimal performance impact. Production-ready instrumentation involves ensuring that your telemetry setup can handle the load and complexity of real-world environments. This includes optimizing data collection to manage data volume, configuring error handling to ensure reliable data collection even under failure conditions, and validating that the instrumentation does not introduce significant latency or resource consumption. Implementing secure practices, such as encrypting telemetry data in transit and applying appropriate access controls is also essential. By rigorously testing and refining your instrumentation setup, you can achieve a balance between detailed observability and system performance, providing valuable insights while maintaining a seamless user experience.

Master It After the basics of generating telemetry data that is exported to the console, what are some additional capabilities you should add in preparation for production?

Solution

- Change the exporter to what will be used in production. For example, the OTLP exporter could be used when leveraging the Collector or sending data to a destination that supports OTLP.
- Enrich the telemetry data with metadata. For example, consider adding processors such as the resource detector processor to enrich telemetry data or leveraging Collector processors to provide this functionality.
- Consider adding signal-specific capabilities. For example, span errors and events for traces or views for metrics.
- Ensure security best practices are being followed, including adding authentication and encryption.

Enrich instrumentation with metadata. Enriching your instrumentation with metadata is crucial for providing context to the raw telemetry data collected, enabling more meaningful analysis and troubleshooting. Metadata can include information such as service names, environment tags, version numbers, and user-specific identifiers. Adding this contextual information allows you to filter, aggregate, and correlate data across different dimensions, making it easier to identify patterns, trends, and anomalies. OTel supports the inclusion of metadata through attributes and resources, which can be attached to signals. By systematically enriching your telemetry data with relevant metadata, you enhance its usability and effectiveness, empowering your team to gain deeper insights into system behavior and quickly pinpoint the root causes of issues.

Master It What are some ways you can enrich telemetry data with metadata?

Solution

- Add processors, such as the resource detector processor.
- Manually add attributes either at runtime, from the code, or from values available at telemetry generating time.
- Leverage signal-specific capabilities. For example, span errors and events for traces.

Chapter 7: Adopting OpenTelemetry

Prepare to adopt OpenTelemetry. Preparation is key to a successful adoption of OTel. Start by setting clear objectives for what you aim to achieve with enhanced observability, such as reducing MTTD and MTTR, improving performance monitoring, or gaining deeper insights into user behavior. Next, assess your current observability maturity and identify gaps that OTel can fill. In addition, stakeholders across development, operations, and business units should be engaged to secure buy-in and align on goals. Finally, develop a detailed implementation plan that includes timelines, resource allocation, and training requirements.

Master It Preparation will ensure that your OTel adoption is strategic, well-supported, and aligned with organizational goals. What are some reasons why you might want to adopt OTel?

Solution

- A desire to remove proprietary instrumentation or agents
- A desire to standardize observability tooling
- A desire to take advantage of OTel capabilities, including semantic conventions, resources, and processors

Approach adopting OpenTelemetry in brownfield deployments. Adopting OTel in brownfield deployments, or environments that already contain observability tools, requires careful planning to integrate new observability practices without disrupting current operations. Begin by conducting an inventory of your existing monitoring and observability solutions and identify how OTel can complement or replace these tools. Start with a pilot project, selecting a noncritical application to instrument and test the integration. Gradually expand the scope to more critical systems, ensuring that each step is thoroughly tested and that the team is comfortable with the new tools and processes. Focus on interoperability and backward compatibility to minimize disruptions and provide continuous training and support to help your team adapt to the new observability framework.

Master It What are the recommended steps to adopt OTel in a brownfield deployment?

Solution Replace proprietary agents and collectors with the OTel Collector. Replacing gateway clusters initially is recommended if applicable.

- If not handled in the previous bullet, consider deploying a Collector in either agent or gateway mode.
- Replace automatic instrumentation with OTel, if applicable. Remember that using more than one automatic instrumentation mechanism is never recommended. Otherwise, consider adding OTel automatic instrumentation at least for easier SDK configuration.
- Consider replacing proprietary manual instrumentation with OTel. Remember that having more than one manual instrumentation is usually acceptable during the transition state.

Approach adopting OpenTelemetry in greenfield deployments. Greenfield deployments, or environments without existing observability tools, offer a unique opportunity to build observability into your infrastructure from the ground up. In these deployments, you can leverage OTel's capabilities to design a robust observability strategy that is integrated into your development lifecycle. Instrument your applications from the start, incorporating telemetry data collection as a fundamental aspect of your system architecture. Start with a single signal and use OTel's components, including semantic conventions, to ensure consistent and comprehensive data collection across all services. Expand instrumentation and data collection over time and be careful not to over-instrument. If telemetry generation is implemented correctly, you will establish a strong observability foundation, enabling you to quickly identify and address issues, optimize performance, and maintain high system reliability as your applications evolve.

Master It What are the recommended steps to adopt OTel in a greenfield deployment?

Solution

- Consider deploying a Collector in either agent or gateway mode. Starting with agent mode at a minimum is recommended.
- Consider adding OTel automatic instrumentation to applications regardless of the signal you are adopting.
- Consider adding manual instrumentation to applications and be careful not to over-instrument.

Chapter 8: The Power of Context and Correlation

Differentiate between context and correlation. Context and correlation play a pivotal role in enhancing the effectiveness of observability in complex, distributed systems. They enable teams to gain deeper insights into system behavior by connecting various data points and providing a comprehensive view of operations across multiple services and components. This interconnected understanding allows for more precise identification of performance bottlenecks, quicker diagnosis of issues, and a clearer picture of how different parts of the system interact. By leveraging context and correlation, organizations can improve their ability to monitor and optimize their systems, ultimately leading to more reliable and efficient operations. This holistic approach to observability ensures that issues are detected and resolved faster, enhancing the overall stability and performance of the system.

Master It Understanding the distinction between context and correlation is fundamental to observing systems and leveraging OTel effectively. What is the difference between context and correlation?

Solution Context refers to the additional metadata and information that provide a more complete picture of each telemetry data. This can include details such as the environment, version, user IDs, or specific service identifiers. Conversely, correlation involves linking related data points across different telemetry signals to uncover relationships and dependencies within a system. While context enriches individual data sources, making them more meaningful, correlation connects them across a system, revealing the bigger picture and helping to identify the root causes of issues.

Identify the types of context and the value each provides. Several types of context can be added to telemetry data, each providing unique value. Temporal context includes timestamps and durations, allowing you to track when events occur and how long processes take. Environmental context encompasses details like the deployment environment, such as development or production, and infrastructure information, such as host or container, which helps you understand the operational conditions. User context includes identifiers and session data, enabling analysis of user behavior and experiences. Service context involves metadata such as service names, versions, and dependencies, which aids in mapping out service interactions and performance. Each type of context enhances the clarity and usefulness of telemetry data, making it easier to diagnose issues, understand user impacts, and optimize system performance.

Master It In OTel, context is available through concepts including attributes, resources, and baggage. What is the difference between these concepts?

Solution An attribute is a piece of metadata attached to a signal and commonly includes temporal, user, or service context. A resource is a specific type of attribute typically generated at application start time and containing infrastructure and application runtime data. Baggage is metadata that can be passed within or between services and signals and needs to be explicitly added to signals. Baggage is commonly used when metadata is generated by one part of a system but required by a different part of the system.

Explain the value proposition of correlation. The value proposition of correlation lies in its ability to provide a holistic view of system behavior and performance. By linking related telemetry data across different services and components, correlation helps to identify patterns and dependencies that are not immediately apparent when looking at isolated data points. This interconnected view is essential for diagnosing complex issues that span multiple services or layers of the stack. Correlation enables more effective root cause analysis by tracing the flow of requests through the system and highlighting where bottlenecks or failures occur. It also enhances the accuracy of anomaly detection by considering the broader context in which events happen.

Master It Correlation transforms disparate telemetry data into a coherent narrative, empowering teams to make informed decisions and maintain robust, high-performing systems. What are some examples of correlation?

Solution Various forms of correlation exist, including time and context. Time can easily be achieved by creating a dashboard with data from different signals and manually comparing based on the dimension of time. Context is usually more involved, but it is also more powerful. Examples of context-based correlation include span links, which associate separate requests with one another, and trace correlation, which allows linking between traces and other signals.

Chapter 9: Choosing an Observability Platform

Distinguish between observability platform capabilities. Understanding the varied capabilities of observability platforms is essential for making an informed choice. Observability platforms offer a range of features, including signal collection, real-time data processing, and advanced analytics and visualization tools. Evaluating these capabilities in relation to your organization's unique needs will help you determine which platform can best support your observability goals, ensuring that you have the right tools to gain deep insights into your systems.

Master It What are some of the primary differences among observability platforms?

Solution Some platforms excel in specific areas, such as robust alerting mechanisms, customizable dashboards, or AI-driven anomaly detection. In contrast, others may offer comprehensive integrations with a wide array of existing tools and services. Some differences to consider include:

- Sampling strategies
- Real-time processing capabilities
- Scalability and performance

- Price structure
- Homogeneous versus heterogeneous architecture
- Suite versus point solution

Decide which observability platform is right for you. Observability can be achieved in many ways depending on your requirements. Choosing the right observability platform requires a thorough assessment of your current and future requirements. By aligning the platform's strengths with your specific use cases and organizational goals, you can make a decision that will provide long-term value and effectiveness.

Master It What are some of the key considerations and decision factors that need to be decided to choose the right observability platform?

Solution Consider factors such as the scale of your operations, the complexity of your systems, and your team's expertise. Assess the ease of integration with your existing technology stack and the platform's support for open standards like OTel. Cost is another crucial factor, encompassing both the initial investment and ongoing operational expenses. Additionally, evaluate the quality of customer support and the platform's ability to scale with your growing needs. In summary:

- Price versus value
- Self- or vendor-managed solution
- Ability to correlate across signals
- OTel compatibility (assuming OTel is or will be adopted)

Get a quick return on your observability platform investment. Even after deciding on an observability platform, implementation and adoption takes time. Without proper planning and reporting, observability may not be achieved. Maximizing the ROI for your observability platform involves leveraging its features to achieve quick and tangible benefits. By demonstrating early successes and improvements, you can build momentum and support for further observability initiatives, ensuring that the platform delivers sustained value and drives continuous operational enhancements.

Master It How can you get a quick return on your observability platform investment?

Solution Start by focusing on high-impact areas such as improving system reliability and reducing downtime. Implement best practices for instrumenting critical parts of your applications to gain immediate insights into performance bottlenecks and error rates. Utilize the platform's analytics and alerting capabilities to proactively identify and resolve issues before they affect users. In summary:

- Start small and prove that value can be provided.
- Start in an area with previous observability challenges.
- If migrating, consider using the OTel Collector to send the existing signal data to the new observability platform.

Chapter 10: Observability Antipatterns and Pitfalls

Distinguish between observability antipatterns and pitfalls. Observability antipatterns and pitfalls are common mistakes or ineffective practices that hinder the successful implementation and utilization of observability in software systems. By distinguishing between these two concepts, organizations can better identify and address systemic issues and specific errors that hinder their observability objectives.

Master It Understanding the difference between observability antipatterns and pitfalls is crucial for building effective observability practices. What is the difference between an antipattern and a pitfall?

Solution Antipatterns refer to commonly adopted practices that seem beneficial but ultimately undermine observability efforts. These include over-monitoring, relying solely on automated instrumentation, and ignoring contextual metadata. Pitfalls, on the other hand, are more generalized mistakes or traps that teams may fall into, such as creating alert storms, neglecting historical data, and underestimating the need for resource allocation. In summary, antipatterns represent specific recurring patterns of behavior, while pitfalls are specific challenges or shortcomings.

Recognize and overcome common observability antipatterns and pitfalls. Observability antipatterns and pitfalls can happen at any step in the observability journey, be it telemetry generation and collection or telemetry querying and alerting. Remediation depends on the issue being experienced. To avoid over-monitoring and alert fatigue, teams should prioritize key metrics and implement strategic alerting thresholds. Addressing the pitfall of insufficient resource allocation involves ensuring that observability tools and infrastructure are adequately funded and maintained. Overcoming the challenge of inconsistent tagging and metadata application necessitates adopting standardization practices across the organization. Regularly reviewing and updating observability practices, fostering collaboration between development and operations teams, and investing in training can help mitigate these issues, leading to more robust and effective observability solutions.

Master It What is an observability antipattern that the OTel project is helping to mitigate?

Solution Vendor lock-in. The OTel project helps prevent the need to re-instrument an environment by providing an extensible solution that ensures data portability.

Describe the impacts of company culture on observability goals. Company culture has a profound impact on the success of observability initiatives. A culture that values transparency, continuous learning, and cross-functional collaboration will support the effective implementation of observability practices. In contrast, a siloed or reactive culture can hinder these efforts, leading to fragmented observability data and delayed problem resolution. Encouraging open communication and shared responsibility for system health can help integrate observability into the fabric of the organization. By fostering a proactive mindset and prioritizing observability as a critical aspect of operational excellence, companies can achieve their observability goals more effectively, ensuring system reliability and performance.

Master It How can you use company culture to help achieve your observability goals?

Solution Use the positive aspects of your company culture to accelerate your roadmap. For example, if your company prioritizes work or career advancement based on impact, spend the time to properly articulate and communicate the impact of your observability project.

Chapter 11: Observability at Scale

Identify observability scalability challenges. Scaling any system is challenging and scaling a system that touches every part of your environment and is critical to the availability and performance of your environment is essential. Recognizing challenges early allows organizations to address data management, system performance, and resource allocation issues, ensuring that observability efforts remain effective and scalable.

Master It Identifying observability scalability challenges is crucial for maintaining effective monitoring and insights as systems grow. What are some things that make scaling observability difficult?

Solution

- The volume and velocity of telemetry data and the impact it has on systems
- The nature of distributed systems and the complexity they introduce
- Infrastructure and resource limitations and how to overcome them

Implement strategies to overcome observability scalability challenges. Once you understand observability scalability challenges, you must have strategies to overcome them.

Master It Implementing strategies to overcome observability scalability challenges involves adopting advanced tools and methodologies designed to handle high volumes of telemetry data and complex system architectures. What are some strategies you can implement to overcome observability scalability challenges?

Solution

- Auto-scaling stateless services
- Leveraging containerization and orchestration technology
- Using data filtering, sampling, and aggregation techniques as close to the source as possible

Describe best practices to scale observability at every step. Always remember that scaling observability is not just about handling more data; it involves refining processes and technologies to ensure the observability platform remains agile, responsive, reliable, and cost-effective.

Master It Scaling observability effectively requires following best practices at every step of the implementation process. What are some best practices to scale observability?

Solution

- Ensure telemetry data is generated, accurate, and relevant.
- Leverage strategies to reduce telemetry overhead, including batching, compression, edge processing, and asynchronous instrumentation.
- Implement tier-storage and retention policies.
- Properly index, partition, and cache data.
- Prioritize automation and orchestration.
- Do not ignore cost management aspects.
- Strive for continuous improvement.

Chapter 12: The Future of Observability

Approach observability cost management. Effectively managing the costs associated with observability is essential for ensuring sustainable and scalable monitoring practices. Balancing the need for detailed insights with budget constraints enables organizations to achieve robust observability without financial strain.

Master It What are some ways to reduce observability costs?

Solution Organizations must adopt strategic approaches such as implementing data retention policies, utilizing intelligent filtering techniques, and leveraging cost-effective observability platforms. Companies can significantly reduce storage and processing expenses while maintaining comprehensive system visibility by optimizing the volume and granularity of collected telemetry data. Additionally, continuous evaluation and fine-tuning of observability configurations can help identify and eliminate unnecessary resource consumption.

Leverage artificial intelligence in observability. Integrating AI into observability practices holds immense potential for transforming how organizations monitor and manage their systems. AI-driven analytics can enhance anomaly detection, automate RCA, and provide predictive insights, enabling proactive issue resolution and optimization of system performance. By leveraging AI, organizations can move from reactive monitoring to a more predictive and automated approach, improving overall system reliability and efficiency.

Master It What are some ways to leverage AI in observability?

Solution Leveraging generative AI to assist with constructing queries and gaining insights is a great place to start. In addition, configuring alerts that use dynamic thresholds and anomaly detection can help reduce mean time to detection (MTTD). Intelligent alerts, or alerts that are aware of the state of the environment, can also minimize on-call noise. AIOps solutions can also be leveraged to provide automated remediation to known issues.

Future-proof observability practices. To ensure long-term success and resilience, organizations must future-proof their observability practices. By implementing forward-thinking strategies, organizations can build observability systems that are effective today and adaptable to future technological advancements and evolving business needs.

Master It What are some ways organizations can future-proof their observability practices?

Solution

- Adopting OaC to standardize and automate observability configurations
- Integrating observability deeply into CI/CD pipelines for continuous monitoring throughout the SDLC
- Staying abreast of emerging technologies and industry standards, such as OTel, to maintain a unified and scalable observability framework

Appendix B

Introduction

Issues filed while writing this book:

- https://github.com/open-telemetry/oteps/issues/245
- https://github.com/open-telemetry/oteps/issues/246
- https://github.com/open-telemetry/opentelemetry-demo/issues/1306
- https://github.com/open-telemetry/opentelemetry-demo/issues/1315
- https://github.com/open-telemetry/opentelemetry-demo/issues/1622
- https://github.com/open-telemetry/opentelemetry-demo/issues/1623
- https://github.com/open-telemetry/opentelemetry-demo/issues/1624
- https://github.com/open-telemetry/opentelemetry-demo/issues/1625
- https://github.com/open-telemetry/opentelemetry-demo/issues/1626
- https://github.com/open-telemetry/opentelemetry-demo/issues/1627
- https://github.com/open-telemetry/opentelemetry-demo/issues/1628
- https://github.com/open-telemetry/opentelemetry.io/issues/3717
- https://github.com/open-telemetry/opentelemetry.io/issues/4734
- https://github.com/open-telemetry/opentelemetry-python-contrib/issues/2109

PRs submitted while writing this book:

- https://github.com/open-telemetry/opentelemetry-collector/pull/9284
- https://github.com/open-telemetry/opentelemetry-demo/pull/1634
- https://github.com/open-telemetry/opentelemetry.io/pull/3646
- https://github.com/open-telemetry/opentelemetry.io/pull/3648

- https://github.com/open-telemetry/opentelemetry.io/pull/3667
- https://github.com/open-telemetry/opentelemetry.io/pull/3723
- https://github.com/open-telemetry/opentelemetry-python-contrib/pull/2108

Chapter 2: Introducing OpenTelemetry!

OpenTelemetry Concepts > Roadmap

In terms of reference implementations, both the instrumentation and the Collector will need to incorporate changes from the specification and ensure stability. For example, log support needs to be stabilized for all languages. In addition, the Collector also needs to reach stability, at least for the core distribution. Work for both aspects is underway.

In terms of the latest areas of investment in 2024, you will find:

- Work has begun to define the scope and implementation for profiling (a new signal type), including defining a data model OTEP.
- Work has begun to define the scope and implementation for entities (a new signal type), including defining a data model OTEP.
- Work continues on client-side instrumentation, such as web and mobile, which is necessary to support Real User Monitoring (RUM) use cases.
- The Open Agent Management Protocol (OpAMP) has been created, and several vendors are beginning to implement it. This will be discussed in Chapter 4 and Chapter 5.
- A domain-specific language (DSL) for collector configuration called the OpenTelemetry Transformation Language (OTTL) continues to evolve. This will be discussed in Chapter 5.

The OTel backlog includes leveraging eBPF more and adding capabilities related to security, to name a few.[1] Of course, all of this is scheduled to change over time.

Chapter 3: Getting Started with the Astronomy Shop

Background > Architecture

Astronomy Shop support and functionality.[2] Any column marked as "Yes" supports at least one of the capabilities of that signal but may not support all of them. Note that this information is likely to change rapidly, so check the OTel documentation for the latest information.

Language	Automatic Instrumentation	Instrumentation Libraries	Manual Instrumentation	Traces	Metrics	Logs
.NET		Cart Service	Cart Service	Yes	Yes	Yes
C++			Currency Service	Yes	Yes	No
Erlang/Elixir		Feature Flag Service	Feature Flag Service	Yes	No	No
Go		Accounting Service, Checkout Service, Product Catalog Service	Checkout Service, Product Catalog Service	Yes	Yes	No
Java	Ad Service		Ad Service	Yes	Yes	Yes
JavaScript		Frontend	Frontend, Payment Service	Yes	Yes	No
Kotlin		Fraud Detection Service		Yes	Yes	Yes
PHP		Quote Service	Quote Service	Yes	No	Yes
Python	Recommendation Service		Recommendation Service	Yes	Yes	Yes
Ruby		Email Service	Email Service	Yes	No	No

Chapter 5: Managing the OpenTelemetry Collector

Background

While the Collector handles traces, metrics, and logs, there may be other telemetry data you want to collect or processing you want to perform. OTel offers the following additional data collection integrations:

- **OTel eBPF Collector:** Provides kernel-level telemetry data. eBPF (`https://ebpf.io`) is a newer data source requiring kernel-level access to gather network data. Splunk (now Cisco), through its Flowmill acquisition, donated its kernel Collector and reducer technology written in C++ to the OpenTelemetry project (`https://github.com/open-telemetry/opentelemetry-network`). The reducer supports exposing Prometheus metrics or sending OTLP metric data to the Collector.
- **Apache Arrow integration:** A network protocol that uses Apache Arrow encoding. The Apache Arrow project (`https://arrow.apache.org`) offers an efficient columnar format that is vendor-agnostic and can be used to perform in-memory analytics. The project is housed independently within the OTel organization (`https://github.com/open-telemetry/otel-arrow`), though will likely be archived in the future. Integration with the Collector includes a native receiver (`https://github.com/open-telemetry/opentelemetry-collector-contrib/tree/main/receiver/otelarrowreceiver`) and exporter (`https://github.com/open-telemetry/opentelemetry-collector-contrib/tree/main/exporter/otelarrowexporter`) in the Collector contrib repository.
- **Stanza log agent:** For the sake of completeness, the Stanza log collector was donated to the OTel project by ObservIQ. Stanza has been merged with the Collector repository.

The Basics > Components

Available OTel Collector components, whether they support traces (T), metrics (M), or logs (L), and the server licensing model. Check `https://github.com/flands/mastering-otel-book` for the latest information.

Type	Name	T	M	L	Server Licensing
Receiver	(Microsoft) Active Directory		X		Commercial
Receiver	Aerospike		X		Commercial
Receiver	Apache (HTTP Server)		X		Open source
Receiver	Apache Spark		X		Open source
Receiver	AWS CloudWatch			X	Commercial
Receiver	AWS CloudWatch Metrics		X		Commercial

Type	Name	T	M	L	Server Licensing
Receiver	AWS Container Insights		X		Commercial
Receiver	AWS EC2 Container Metrics		X		Commercial
Receiver	AWS Firehose		X		Commercial
Receiver	AWS S3	X	X	X	Commercial
Receiver	AWS X-Ray	X			Commercial
Receiver	Azure Blob	X		X	Commercial
Receiver	Azure Event Hubs		X	X	Commercial
Receiver	Azure Monitor		X		Commercial
Receiver	F5 BIG-IP		X		Commercial
Receiver	Carbon		X		Open source
Receiver	Chrony		X		N/A
Receiver	Cloudflare			X	Commercial
Receiver	Cloud Foundry			X	Open source
Receiver	collectd		X		Open source
Receiver	(Apache) CouchDB		X		Open source
Receiver	Datadog		X		Commercial
Receiver	Docker Stats		X		Dual licensing
Receiver	Elasticsearch		X		Dual licensing
Receiver	(Go) expvar		X		N/A
Receiver	Filelog			X	N/A
Receiver	File Stats		X		N/A
Receiver	(Apache) Flink metrics		X		Open source
Receiver	Fluent Forward			X	Open source
Receiver	Git Provider		X		N/A
Receiver	Google Cloud Pub/Sub	X	X	X	Commercial
Receiver	Google Cloud Spanner		X		Commercial

Type	Name	T	M	L	Server Licensing
Receiver	HAProxy		X		Open source
Receiver	Host Metrics		X		N/A
Receiver	HTTP check		X		N/A
Receiver	(Microsoft) IIS		X		Commercial
Receiver	InfluxDB		X		Dual licensing
Receiver	Jaeger	X			Open source
Receiver	JMX		X		Dual licensing
Receiver	Journald			X	Open source
Receiver	K8s cluster			X	Open source
Receiver	K8s events			X	Open source
Receiver	K8s objects			X	Open source
Receiver	(Apache) Kafka	X	X	X	Open source
Receiver	(Apache) Kafka metrics		X		Open source
Receiver	(K8s) Kubelet Stats		X		Open source
Receiver	Loki			X	Dual licensing
Receiver	Memcached		X		Open source
Receiver	MongoDB		X		Dual licensing (SSPL)
Receiver	MongoDB Atlas		X	X	Commercial
Receiver	MySQL		X		Open source
Receiver	named pipe			X	N/A
Receiver	nginx		X		Dual licensing (SSPL)
Receiver	(VMware) NSX-T		X		Commercial
Receiver	OpenCensus	X	X		Open source
Receiver	Oracle DB		X		Commercial
Receiver	osquery			X	N/A

Type	Name	T	M	L	Server Licensing
Receiver	OTel (Apache) Arrow	X	X	X	Open source
Receiver	OTLP	X	X	X	N/A
Receiver	OTLP JSON file	X	X	X	N/A
Receiver	Podman		X		Open source
Receiver	PostgreSQL		X		Open source
Receiver	Prometheus		X		Open source
Receiver	(Apache) Pulsar	X	X	X	Open source
Receiver	Pure Storage FlashArray		X		Commercial
Receiver	Pure Storage FlashBlade		X		Commercial
Receiver	RabbitMQ		X		Open source
Receiver	Receiver Creator	X		X	N/A
Receiver	Riak		X		Dual licensing
Receiver	SAP HANA		X		Commercial
Receiver	(Cisco) SAPM	X			Commercial
Receiver	(Cisco) SignalFx		X	X	Commercial
Receiver	Simple Prometheus		X		Open source
Receiver	(Apache) SkyWalking		X		Open source
Receiver	SNMP		X		N/A
Receiver	Snowflake		X		Commercial
Receiver	Solace	X			Commercial
Receiver	(Cisco) Splunk Enterprise		X		Commercial
Receiver	(Cisco) Splunk HEC		X	X	Commercial
Receiver	(Microsoft) SQL query			X	N/A
Receiver	SQL server		X		Commercial
Receiver	SSH check		X		N/A
Receiver	Stats		X		N/A

TYPE	NAME	T	M	L	SERVER LICENSING
Receiver	Syslog			X	N/A
Receiver	TCP			X	N/A
Receiver	UDP			X	N/A
Receiver	(VMware) vCenter		X		Commercial
Receiver	(VMware) Wavefront		X		Commercial
Receiver	Webhook event			X	N/A
Receiver	(Microsoft) Windows event log			X	Commercial
Receiver	(Microsoft) Windows Perf Counters		X		Commercial
Receiver	Zipkin	X			Open source
Receiver	(Apache) ZooKeeper		X		Open source
Processor	Attributes	X	X	X	Open source
Processor	Cumulative to Delta		X		Open source
Processor	Delta to cumulative		X		N/A
Processor	Delta to rate		X		N/A
Processor	Filter	X	X	X	N/A
Processor	Geo IP	X	X	X	N/A
Processor	Group by attributes	X	X	X	N/A
Processor	Interval		X		N/A
Processor	K8s attributes	X	X	X	N/A
Processor	Logs Transform			X	N/A
Processor	Metrics generation		X		N/A
Processor	Metrics transform		X		N/A
Processor	Probabilistic sampler	X			N/A
Processor	Redaction	X			N/A
Processor	Remote tap	X	X	X	N/A
Processor	Resource	X	X	X	N/A

Type	Name	T	M	L	Server Licensing
Processor	Resource Detection	X	X	X	N/A
Processor	Routing	X	X	X	N/A
Processor	Schema	X	X	X	N/A
Processor	Span	X			N/A
Processor	Sumo Logic	X	X	X	Commercial
Processor	Tail sampling	X			N/A
Processor	Transform	X	X	X	N/A
Exporter	(Prometheus) Alertmanager	X			Open source
Exporter	Alibaba Cloud Log Service	X	X	X	Commercial
Exporter	AWS CloudWatch Logs			X	Commercial
Exporter	AWS EMF		X		Commercial
Exporter	AWS Kinesis	X	X	X	Commercial
Exporter	AWS S3	X	X	X	Commercial
Exporter	AWS X-Ray	X			Commercial
Exporter	Azure Data Explorer	X	X	X	Commercial
Exporter	Azure Monitor	X	X	X	Commercial
Exporter	Carbon		X		Open source
Exporter	(Apache) Cassandra	X		X	Open source
Exporter	ClickHouse	X	X		Dual licensing
Exporter	Coralogix	X	X	X	Commercial
Exporter	Datadog			X	Commercial
Exporter	Dataset	X		X	Commercial
Exporter	Elasticsearch		X		Dual licensing
Exporter	File	X	X	X	N/A
Exporter	Google Cloud	X	X	X	Commercial
Exporter	Google Cloud Pub/Sub	X	X	X	Commercial

TYPE	NAME	T	M	L	SERVER LICENSING
Exporter	Honeycomb Marker			X	Commercial
Exporter	InfluxDB	X	X	X	Dual licensing
Exporter	Instana	X			Commercial
Exporter	(Apache) Kafka	X	X	X	Open source
Exporter	Kinetic	X	X	X	Commercial
Exporter	Load balancing		X		N/A
Exporter	LogicMonitor	X		X	Commercial
Exporter	Logz.io	X		X	Commercial
Exporter	Loki			X	Dual licensing
Exporter	Mezmo			X	Commercial
Exporter	OpenCensus	X	X		Open source
Exporter	OpenSearch			X	Open source
Exporter	OTel Arrow	X	X	X	Open source
Exporter	OTLP	X	X	X	N/A
Exporter	OTLP HTTP	X	X	X	N/A
Exporter	Prometheus		X		Open source
Exporter	Prometheus Remote Write		X		Open source
Exporter	Pulsar	X	X	X	Open source
Exporter	RabbitMQ	X	X	X	Open source
Exporter	SAPM	X			Commercial
Exporter	Sentry	X			Commercial
Exporter	(Cisco) SignalFx	X	X	X	Commercial
Exporter	(Cisco) Splunk HEC	X	X	X	Commercial
Exporter	Sumo Logic	X	X	X	Commercial
Exporter	Syslog			X	N/A
Exporter	Tencent Cloud Log Service			X	Commercial

Type	Name	T	M	L	Server Licensing
Exporter	Zipkin	X			Open source
Connector	Count		X		N/A
Connector	Datadog	X	X		Commercial
Connector	Exception			X	N/A
Connector	Grafana Cloud		X		Commercial
Connector	Round robin	X	X	X	N/A
Connector	Routing	X	X	X	N/A
Connector	Service graph		X		N/A
Connector	Span metrics		X		N/A
Connector	Sum		X		N/A

Available OTel Collector extensions, which components they work with, server licensing model, and category. Sorted by category. Check `https://github.com/flands/mastering-otel-book` for the latest information.

Name	Works With	Server Licensing	Category
ASAP Auth	Exporters	Commercial	Authentication
Basic Auth	Receivers and Exporters	N/A	Authentication
Bearer Token Auth	Receivers and Exporters	N/A	Authentication
Google Client Auth	Exporters	Commercial	Authentication
Header Setter	Exporters	N/A	Authentication
OAuth 2 Client Auth	Exporters	N/A	Authentication
OIDC Auth	Receivers	N/A	Authentication
(AWS) SigV4 Auth	AWS Exporters	Commercial	Authentication
Sumo Logic	Sumo Logic Exporters	Commercial	Authentication
SolarWinds APM Setting	SolarWinds	Commercial	Configuration
(Apache) Avro encoding	Receivers (Logs)	Open source	Encoding
Jaeger encoding	Receivers (Traces)	Open source	Encoding

Name	Works With	Server Licensing	Category
JSON log encoding	Receivers (Logs)	N/A	Encoding
OTLP encoding	Receivers	Dual licensing	Encoding
Text Encoding	Receivers (Logs)	N/A	Encoding
Zipkin encoding	Receivers (Traces)	Open source	Encoding
OpAMP	Stand-alone	Dual licensing	Management
OpAMP Custom Messages	Stand-alone	Dual licensing	Management
Health Check	Stand-alone	N/A	Observability
Health Check v2	Stand-alone	N/A	Observability
pprof	Stand-alone	N/A	Observability
Remote Tap	Stand-alone	N/A	Observability
ACK	Receivers	N/A	Other
AWS Proxy	Stand-alone	Commercial	Proxy
HTTP Forwarder	Stand-alone	N/A	Proxy
Jaeger remote sampling	Stand-alone	Open source	Proxy
(AWS) ECS Observer	Receivers	Commercial	Service Discovery
(AWS) ECS task observer	Receivers	Commercial	Service Discovery
Docker Observer	Receivers	Dual licensing	Service Discovery
Host Observer	Receivers	N/A	Service Discovery
K8s observer	Receivers	Open source	Service Discovery
DB Storage	Receivers	N/A	Storage
File Storage	Receivers	N/A	Storage

Chapter 12: The Future of Observability

Challenges and Opportunities > Code

Some of the available ways to integrate CI/CD or test frameworks with OTel. Note that vendor-specific integrations also exist but may result in vendor lock-in. Check `https://github.com/flands/mastering-otel-book` for the latest information.

Description	Supported By	Notes
OTel Java Instrumentation Maven Plug-in[3]	OTel	
Filelog receiver for OTel Collector[4]	OTel	
Git provider receiver for OTel Collector[5]	OTel	
GitHub action receiver for OTel Collector[6]	OTel	In development
Ansible OTel notification callback[7]	Ansible	
Jenkins Observer with OTel[8]	Jenkins	
Tekton tracing with OTel[9]	Tekton	
Python tracing plug-in with OTel[10]	Third-party	
Command-line interface (CLI) tool for sending OTel traces[11]	Third-party	
OTel GitHub Trace Exporter Action[12]	Third-party	Not active
CircleCI OTel Webhook Processor[13]	Third-party	GPL 3; not active

Notes

1 https://opentelemetry.io/community/roadmap
2 https://opentelemetry.io/docs/demo
3 https://github.com/open-telemetry/opentelemetry-java-contrib/blob/main/maven-extension/README.md
4 https://github.com/open-telemetry/opentelemetry-collector-contrib/tree/main/receiver/filelogreceiver
5 https://github.com/open-telemetry/opentelemetry-collector-contrib/tree/main/receiver/gitproviderreceiver
6 https://github.com/open-telemetry/opentelemetry-collector-contrib/issues/27460
7 https://docs.ansible.com/ansible/latest/collections/community/general/opentelemetry_callback.html
8 https://plugins.jenkins.io/opentelemetry
9 https://github.com/tektoncd/community/blob/main/teps/0124-distributed-tracing-for-tasks-and-pipelines.md
10 https://pypi.org/project/pytest-otel
11 https://github.com/tobert/otel-cli
12 https://github.com/inception-health/otel-export-trace-action
13 https://github.com/DavidS/circleci-hook

Index

D

E

F

G

H

I

N

O

P

R

S

T

U

V

W

X

Y

Z